THE RISE AND FALL OF
ANNE BOLEYN

THE RISE AND FALL OF
ANNE BOLEYN

Family politics at the court of Henry VIII

RETHA M. WARNICKE

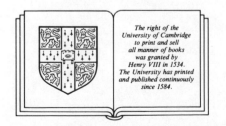

The right of the
University of Cambridge
to print and sell
all manner of books
was granted by
Henry VIII in 1534.
The University has printed
and published continuously
since 1584.

CAMBRIDGE UNIVERSITY PRESS

Cambridge
New York   Port Chester
Melbourne   Sydney

Published by the Press Syndicate of the University of Cambridge
The Pitt Building, Trumpington Street, Cambridge CB2 1RP
40 West 20th Street, New York, NY 10011, USA
10 Stamford Road, Oakleigh, Melbourne 3166, Australia

First published 1989
Reprinted 1990

Printed in Great Britain by the University Press, Cambridge

British Library cataloguing in publication data

Warnicke, Retha M. (Retha Marvine), 1939–
The rise and fall of Anne Boleyn.
1. England. Politics, 1520–1536
I. Title
320.942

Library of Congress cataloguing in publication data

Warnicke, Retha M.
The rise and fall of Anne Boleyn: family politics at the court of
Henry VIII/Retha M. Warnicke.
        p.   cm.
Bibliography.
Includes index.
ISBN 0 521 37000 0
1. Anne Boleyn, Queen, consort of Henry VIII, King of England,
1507–1536. 2. Great Britain – Politics and government – 1509–1547.
3. Great Britain – Queens – Biography. I. Title
DA333.B6W37   1989
942.05'2'0924–dc19   88-37708   CIP
[B]

ISBN 0 521 37000 0

CONTENTS

ILLUSTRATIONS

Illustrations 8, 12, 16, 20, 21, 22, 23, 25, and 27 are reproduced by gracious permission of Her Majesty The Queen. The frontispiece and illustrations 10, 11, 13, 24, 28, and 29 are reproduced by kind permission of the National Portrait Gallery, London.

PREFACE

While I was engaged in investigating the life and person of Anne Boleyn, Henry VIII's second queen, Professor E. W. Ives' monumental biography of her was published and its appearance would seem to call for a justification of this book. This study of Anne is not a biography but an analysis of the crucial phases of her life and more specifically of her role in the politics of her day, with particular emphasis on the rules and conventions of the society in which she played her part. Great attention has been given here for the first time to her vital place in the family network created by her father, Sir Thomas Boleyn, who was to become the earl of Wiltshire and Ormond, and by her Howard relatives, especially the second and third dukes of Norfolk. Consequently, I have come to conclusions quite different from those put forward by Professor Ives, whose biography builds upon the outlines established by Paul Friedmann in 1884 and asserts that for political reasons Cromwell joined with an Aragonese faction at court to effect the downfall of Anne and her five alleged lovers.

This study draws upon my five articles on Anne Boleyn each of which explored a specific controversial issue in her life. No one chapter is a reproduction of any of these articles although parts of Chapter 8 do follow closely "Sexual Heresy at the Court of Henry VIII," which appeared in the *Historical Journal* in 1987. That journal also published my first article on her childhood, which I wrote in 1983. I wish to thank the journal's editors for their early support of this research and the editors of *Albion*, *History*, and *Parergon* for publishing my other articles on her.

After I completed a rough draft of my first manuscript on Anne, I asked Sir Geoffrey Elton, Regius Professor of History at

Cambridge University, for a critical review of it. He kindly responded, reading not only that paper but all of my subsequent work on Anne. Indeed, it is due to his encouragement that I embarked upon this book-length study of her role in court politics. I am truly grateful for his many helpful suggestions and for the time he has generously and patiently given to my research efforts. I wish also to thank John Guy, Reader in Modern History in the History Department at Bristol University, for his criticism and help in the last stages of the final draft of this book.

In 1984 I traveled to the Huntington Library, San Marino, California, to become a charter member of the British History Seminar, which was launched under Professor Elton's direction. This seminar was chaired by David Cressy, Professor of History at California State University, Long Beach. I wish to thank all of its members, but particularly Joseph Block of California Polytechnic at Pomona, and Mary Robertson, Archivist at the Huntington, who are both Cromwellian scholars, for supporting and sometimes challenging my research conclusions. As a result of my participation in this seminar, I have had the opportunity to present papers on Queen Anne at sessions in the Pacific Coast Conference on British Studies (two of them), at the Pacific Coast Conference of the American Historical Association, at the North American Conference on British Studies, and at the Western Conference on British Studies. I also gave papers at the Sixteenth Century Studies Conference, at the Berkshire Conference on Women's History, and at the Rocky Mountain Conference on Medieval and Renaissance Studies.

This research was accomplished at a number of archives and libraries: in the United States at the Huntington and at the Hayden Library, Arizona State University, and in England at the Bodleian, the British Library, the Public Record Office, Lambeth Palace, the Institute of Historical Research, and the Royal College of Music in London. I am grateful for the assistance provided by the staffs of these institutions.

There are still other thanks that must be given. My trips to the Huntington and to England were in part funded by the College of Liberal Arts Grant Program and the University Research fund at Arizona State University. Linda Breedlove of my husband's law firm has been of tremendous and loyal assistance in printing out various versions of this manuscript for me. She has been an indispensable link in the chain of research related activities that resulted in this book.

My family, which includes my husband, Ronald, my son Robert, now a junior at Vanderbilt University, and my daughter Margaretha, an eighth grader at Clarendon Elementary school, have formed a powerful cheering section. They have applauded every step of the way in this research project, rejoicing with me when my essays were completed and accepted for publication and finally when this long manuscript was done.

While I was writing this book, my husband and I celebrated our twenty-seventh wedding anniversary. It is ironic that this milestone occurred when I was absorbed in detailing Anne's political struggles. Most modern studies have characterized her as an aggressive woman, who manipulated or bewitched Henry VIII into ending his union with Catherine of Aragon, a marriage that had endured some twenty-four years by the time it was officially dissolved. By linking politics to social customs, I have been able, I believe, to replace this view with a much more reasonable analysis of her role at the Tudor court. Undertaking and completing this work has been the scholarly adventure of my life, and I can do no less than dedicate it to Anne the Queen, whose unsuccessful attempts to raise the Boleyn family permanently into the Tudor dynasty made this research possible.

INTRODUCTION: QUEEN ANNE

On 19 May 1536, Anne the queen consort of Henry VIII, was beheaded on Tower Green in London in front of a small number of spectators. Four days earlier she had been tried and convicted of having committed adultery with five men, among them her brother, George, Lord Rochford. Commentators differed about the nature of her guilt, some offering reasons for her execution, such as her influence on foreign policy, that had nothing to do with the public charges. There was, as John Foxe, the martyrologist later contended, some impenetrable mystery behind the events that led to her death. Hailing her as a new Deborah, he maintained that God had proved her innocence by permitting Elizabeth, her only surviving child, to reign as queen of England.[1]

His "Book of Martyrs" was unquestionably one of the most frequently purchased volumes in Elizabethan England. After its first appearance in the English language, in the homes in which two books could be found, often one was the scriptures and the other his "Martyrs." Despite the enormous popularity of his work, his detailed accounts of Anne's activities as a religious and charitable queen did not long survive the reign of her daughter. Instead, the compelling and condemnatory statements of Eustace Chapuys, the Imperial ambassador assigned to Henry VIII's court, and of Nicholas Sander, a priest active in Catholic Reformation politics, prevailed over Foxe's laudatory statements.[2]

For almost seven years, from 1529 when he first arrived in England at the age of thirty until 1536 when Anne was beheaded, Chapuys, a native of Savoy and a graduate of the University of Turin, was her greatest critic. During these years he wrote countless letters to Charles V and other correspondents about

Henry's attempts to obtain a divorce from Catherine of Aragon so that he could take a second wife. Because the envoy never altered his view of Anne as a concubine who desecrated the marriage sacrament, he characterized her not simply as a representation of evil but as its very embodiment, a she-devil, an Agrippina.[3]

As evidence for her role at court in the 1530s, scholars have, since Paul Friedmann in 1884, cited Chapuys' dispatches eclectically, failing to analyze them within a critical framework or to apply the same rigorous test to them as has been applied to Foxe's anecdotes. This haphazard approach to the envoy's letters has perpetuated both minor and fundamental inaccuracies about Anne, for it ignores the extraordinary inconsistency of his remarks, even in reports forwarded to the emperor only weeks and sometimes days apart. Because Charles held the same prejudices and expectations as Chapuys, he may have overlooked these contradictions, but historians need to notice them and to be more cautious in their use of these documents.[4]

A close reading of the ambassador's correspondence between 1529 and 1536 readily indicates that his information should be divided into at least the following four categories: (1) repetition of ubiquitous rumors at court; (2) information deliberately leaked to him by royal servants; (3) original, and sometimes unsubstantiated, speculations of his own; (4) actual, first-hand information, such as interviews with the king and his ministers, announcements of arrivals and departures of envoys, and seasonal movements of the court. Often it is extremely difficult to decide into which of the first three categories the gossipy, second-hand news should fall, a difficulty that must alert scholars to the need for handling all of his letters with caution. This plea for caution is not based upon merely one or two episodes in which Chapuys' self-contradictions can be isolated. It is the mass of information, the innumerable facts that cannot be reconciled with each other, that lend credence to this warning about crediting his comments in the absence of corroborative evidence.

Efforts will be made in this study to deal with this envoy's information within the context of domestic and foreign events, determining whenever possible the accuracy of his accounts and their probable source. This approach is the first that recognizes both the enormity of his partisanship and the extent of his deception by the royal ministers. Not only did they have accurate insights into his weaknesses and strengths but so also did Catherine and her daughter Mary, who realized he was their most loyal and dutiful ally. When the news imparted by Chapuys has been given its proper interpretation, his single-minded view of Anne as a flirtatious, evil desecrator of the sacred sacrament of marriage must, as a matter of course, be rejected.

Although Chapuys characterized her as the other woman, who, he thought, used witchcraft to manipulate and control the king, it was left to a later scholar, Nicholas Sander, to describe her fully as a witch. Because he believed that she had been grossly libidinous, the seducer of numerous men, including Sir Thomas Wyatt, the great Tudor poet, Sander chose to give her the features of a witch, as he perceived such people. Anne had, he asserted in his posthumously published study of the divorce in 1585, a monstrous appearance, including a tumor on her neck and a sixth finger on her right hand.[5]

These assertions are absolutely false, but although Edward Lord Herbert, Gilbert Burnet, bishop of Salisbury, and other historians disputed them publicly, modern scholars have generally discarded Foxe's statements and adopted some modified form of Sander's and Chapuys' characterizations. For many historians Anne remains the lady with an extra fingernail who was too flirtatious, even if in a harmless courtly way, for her own safety and well being. The result of this interpretation is that the responsibility for her tragic death resides with her, the victim, rather than with the king and his ministers, the ones who orchestrated her execution.[6]

This study of her life takes seriously the claims of Sander, who probably never saw her, and of Chapuys, who refused even to have a personal conversation with her, that many of her contemporaries actually viewed her as a witch. Her life will be analyzed within the framework of sixteenth-century values and impulses, including the honors system, attitudes toward deathbed statements, fears about the birth of monstrous babies, and the association of incest and sodomy with witchcraft. In an attempt to understand her by the terms of her society, information from a wide range of sources will be used to support the argument that she miscarried a defective fetus in 1536. It was because Henry viewed this mishap as an evil omen, both for his lineage and his kingdom, that he had her accused of engaging in illicit sexual acts with five men and fostered rumors that she had afflicted him with impotence and had conspired to poison both his daughter Mary and his illegitimate son, Henry, duke of Richmond. All of these are activities his contemporaries associated with witchcraft.[7]

Since theologians and clergymen charged that god visited deformed babies upon parents who were guilty of gross sexual conduct, her husband's ministers began to search for Anne's lovers among his courtiers. The candidates chosen were those reputed to be libertines or more specifically those suspected of having committed illicit sexual acts, in at least two of the cases buggery, for sodomites, like witches, were characterized as devil worshippers. Not until the nineteenth century was the concept of a separate species of homosexuals developed, for, until then, individuals with enormous sexual appetites were expected to move in a progression from adultery and fornication to buggery and bestiality. No attempt will be made here to set forth the actual nature of sodomy and witchcraft in the sixteenth century; it was her contemporaries' fearful perception not their real knowledge of these phenomena that caused her death.[8]

To set the stage for her fall, this book begins with Anne's childhood, which was spent in royal nurseries in the Netherlands and France. Then it examines her love affair with Henry in 1527 and follows the unsuccessful efforts of Thomas, Cardinal Wolsey, to persuade Clement VII to invalidate the king's first marriage. Attention will then turn to the activities of Thomas Cranmer and Thomas Cromwell, and to the legislation that made it possible for Anne to marry Henry and for her daughter's place in the succession to be established. Special consideration will be given to the demands and goals of both Anne's immediate Boleyn and Howard relatives and her more distant kin. She was not an autonomous figure, but the daughter of an ambitious father and the niece of an arrogant uncle, Thomas, third duke of Norfolk, who had much to gain by her rise to the queenship.

Analyzing events from these perspectives makes it unnecessary to justify or to condemn by moral standards the actions of Catherine and Anne, who are usually viewed as competitors for the queenship, for they were both struggling to preserve and to advance their lineage. They became the involuntary victims of the king's drive and ambition for his own lineage, and of the rules of their Church and society that drastically limited divorces. The issue at stake was not which one of these noblewomen Henry loved more but which one of them, given the constraints of the human anatomy, would be more likely to present him with the desired male heir. It is a testimony to the success of the sixteenth-century socialization of women that several women believed that they were destined to resolve his succession crisis. Anne's story is one of five failures although ultimately her daughter contributed to the history of England one of its finest chapters.

When the details of Anne's life are viewed within the framework of these social and cultural values, the modern conception of her as a *femme fatale* must be discarded. Establishing a valid explanation of her role at court that takes into consideration the beliefs and fears of sixteenth-century Christendom and treats them with sensitivity is an useful undertaking, not only because historians owe it to the dead to depict them in a rational manner but also because the events of the Reformation will not be clearly understood until her crucial place in that revolution is sorted out.

1 ~ BOLEYN ORIGINS

In 1509 just before his eighteenth birthday, Henry VIII became king of England. Young and optimistic about his dynasty's future, he confirmed the Spanish alliance by marrying Catherine of Aragon, his brother's widow, and supporting the efforts of her father, Ferdinand, and Pope Julius II to limit French territorial expansion. Hoping to obtain Habsburg support for this alliance, called the Holy League, Henry sent three diplomats to the Netherlands in May 1512, to meet with its regent, Margaret, archduchess of Austria and daughter of Maximilian I, Holy Roman Emperor. One of those envoys was Sir Thomas Boleyn, whose daughter, Anne, would some twenty years later become Henry's second wife.

Determined to advance his lineage, Sir Thomas took advantage of his immediate family connections and of his skills in French, the personal and governmental language of the Habsburgs in the Netherlands, to win favor with its regent.[1] By 12 August 1512, he had developed such a friendly relationship with the archduchess that she asked him if he would be willing to wager that their negotiations would be concluded in ten days. Upon his agreement, they shook hands: if she won, he would present her with a hobby, and if he won, she would give him a courser of Spain. When she settled on these horses as suitable stakes, it is possible that she remembered the hackney that the king of England had only recently sent to her nephew.[2] Whether or not she actually gave Thomas a courser when she lost the wager is unknown, but technically, if he did not receive payment, she remained in his debt.

The dispatches of the envoys reveal that during the following months, Boleyn took the leading role in explaining matters to the

6

regent or in translating official documents into French for her. By April 1513, when the Holy League was signed, he had won from her an invitation for his daughter Anne to join the schoolroom of her four wards, the children of Philip le Beau, her deceased brother, and the grandchildren of Maximilian. Among them was Charles, prince of Castile, the future Holy Roman Emperor, who was then betrothed to Mary, the younger sister of Henry VIII. Charles' mother, Juana, too ill to supervise the care of her children, was the sister of the English queen.[3]

Sir Thomas surely did not dream of using the opportunity for Anne to reside with the regent's wards as a stepping stone for finding her a royal husband. Rather more within the realm of expectation was that her education would facilitate her appointment as a maid of honor at the English court where French was considered the language of the cultured. There was also the possibility that she might be able to remain in the Netherlands, first attending Mary, if the princess did wed Charles, and later marrying a foreign nobleman, as a few of Catherine of Aragon's Spanish ladies had recently done in England.

To win this prestigious educational advantage for Anne required more than Boleyn's skills in French and his clever, if not charming, treatment of the thirty-two-year-old regent, the widow of the duke of Savoy. A woman of intelligence with an "easy and natural manner" in social discourse, she was a capable ruler and in 1513 held an important political position in the Netherlands. She was reputed to have a long-standing respect and fondness for the English and a desire to promote closer diplomatic relations with their kingdom. Endowed with a shrewd understanding of human nature, she realized that visitors to her court, even a young English resident, could, when they returned home, become ambassadors of good will for the Habsburgs.[4]

The regent's desire to maintain friendly ties with England was in part based on memories of her beloved namesake, her step-grandmother, Margaret of York, sister to Richard III, a well-known promoter of rebellions against the Tudor dynasty and widow of Charles the Bold, the last great duke of Burgundy. Sir Thomas had close connections with the Yorkist family that surely made him more welcome to the regent than the ordinary envoy. His wife, Elizabeth Howard, was daughter to Thomas, earl of

Surrey, whose father, the first duke of Norfolk, had died fighting for Richard III at Bosworth Field. In 1508, furthermore, Surrey had been one of the ambassadors appointed to negotiate the marriage treaty between the regent's nephew and Henry VIII's sister.[5]

Both the Howards and the Boleyns were descendants of Edward I, but the latter's rise to noble status was quite remarkable since their ancestors can be traced back only to the thirteenth century when they were at best small tenant farmers in Salle, Norfolk. By 1457 Sir Geoffrey, a descendant of these humble folk, was serving as Lord Mayor of London, had married Anne, the eldest daughter and co-heiress of Thomas, Lord Hoo and Hastings, and had acquired Blickling Hall in Norfolk and Hever Castle in Kent.[6] Sir Geoffrey's second son and heir, William, who inherited manors in Hertfordshire and Bedfordshire from his maternal grandfather, became a knight of the bath at the coronation of Richard III and an Exchequer baron in the reign of Henry VII.[7]

Following his father's example, Sir William also married a noble co-heiress: Margaret, the younger daughter of Thomas Butler, seventh earl of Ormond. A direct descendant of Edward I, the earl was one of the richest men in the king's dominions when he died in 1515, leaving thirty-six manors in England to each of his two daughters, Margaret and Anne, and ultimately the disputed earldom and Irish estates to a male cousin. Ormond had sat in parliament as first baron of the kingdom and had occasionally acted as ambassador, serving in that capacity to the Netherlands in 1497. Testifying to his great family pride, he bequeathed to Thomas Boleyn, his eldest grandson, the following heirloom:

a white horn of ivory, garnished at both the ends with gold and corse thereunto of white silk barred with barres of gold and a tyret of gold thereupon, which ... was myn ancestors at first time they were called to honour, and hath sythen continually remained in the same blode; for which cause my father commanded me upon his blessing, that I should do my devoir to cause it to continue still in my blode ... to the honor of the same blode.[8]

In 1501 that grandson had married Elizabeth Howard and had fathered at least three surviving children by 1512 when he was assigned to the regent's court. The birthdate of his son, George, undoubtedly named after England's patron saint, is a matter of conjecture but came relatively early in the marriage, perhaps in 1503. Thereafter, despite Elizabeth's annual lyings-in, only two infants survived to adulthood: Anne and Mary, apparently born in 1507 and 1508 respectively, although no firm evidence of their birthdates has survived. The scholarly debate about their ages and sequence of birth, thought resolved by James Gairdner in 1893 and 1895, was reopened by Hugh Paget in 1981. Upon proving indisputably that it was Anne, not her sister Mary, who joined the regent as her maid of honor in 1513, Paget accepted the year 1501 rather than Gairdner's choice of 1507 as the date of her birth. At first glance this would seem to be an obvious selection since when girls received appointment as maids of honor they were usually older than the twelve years Paget claimed for Anne in 1513. Since the publication of Paget's findings, which were based on his careful analysis of a letter written by Anne from the Netherlands in 1514, a more convincing interpretation, which will be discussed later in this chapter, supports the 1507 birthdate. A reading of her letter in association with prevailing royal customs indicates that Anne actually lived in the schoolroom of the Habsburg children instead of at their aunt's court.[9]

Although there is no extant contemporary record of the sequence of the girls' births, as it was indisputably Anne who resided in the Netherlands, she had to have been the elder sister. By contemporary custom, the younger child would not have been favored with such a splendid opportunity to the detriment of her older sister unless the latter were, as Anne was not, already disqualified by marriage or some other impediment. The place of the children's birth similarly remained unrecorded. In the case of the sisters, tradition has claimed that Anne was born variously at Blickling, the residence of her widowed paternal grandmother from 1505 until 1539, Hever Castle, the headquarters of Sir Thomas during that same period of time, and a London home, and Mary at Hever; all of these were properties that had descended to their father at their grandfather William's death in 1505.[10]

Since several women in the family were named Anne, the elder Boleyn girl could have been the namesake of one of them, possibly

Ormond's elder co-heiress. But late in the reign of Henry VII, when Thomas' two daughters were born, his political position, particularly in Norfolk and at court, depended greatly upon his relationship to his wife's father. In 1495 Surrey had succeeded in winning Anne, sister to Queen Elizabeth of York, as the bride of his heir, Lord Howard. It would have been in keeping with Boleyn's ambitions for him to have selected his royal sister-in-law as godmother to his first-born daughter and to have encouraged her to name the child after herself. His other daughter could easily have been named after Mary Tudor, whose marriage to the prince of Castile her grandfather Surrey had been authorized to negotiate in 1508.[11]

As politically ambitious aristocrats often sought royal god-parents for their children, it is relevant to the conjecture about the name of Anne that her father was the client of Surrey, who was successfully overcoming the disgrace caused by his father's support of Richard III. In the 1490s when the earl allied his son with a daughter of Edward IV, he was rebuilding the family's status and finances; by 1500 his lands in East Anglia alone were worth £600 a year and by 1501 he had become Lord Treasurer of England. A patron of scholars and an accomplished military leader who won his greatest victory against the Scots at Flodden Field in 1513 when he was seventy years old, Surrey was able to earn the respect and favor of the Tudors through faithful and useful service to them. Even before his success at Flodden Field, his increasing influence had made it possible for him to obtain appointments and grants for his dependants, thereby developing a network of support in the countryside and at court.[12]

One of the kinsmen Surrey favored was his daughter Eliza-beth's husband. In 1503 when he escorted the young Margaret Tudor to Scotland for her marriage to its monarch, James IV, the earl obtained a place in her train for Thomas Boleyn. From 1506 Boleyn was occasionally associated in royal grants in Norfolk with Surrey and two of his sons, Lord Howard and Sir Edward Howard, and received in his own right estates and lands in several counties. In 1508 he obtained a minor customs position and in 1509 served as squire for the body at the funeral of Henry VII. Elevated to knight for the body at the succession of Henry VIII, Sir Thomas, along with his wife, Elizabeth, a member of the new queen's privy chamber, participated in the coronation ceremonies. The year before he joined the embassy to the Netherlands, he was present at the festivities honoring the birth of the king's son and the activities mourning his premature death.[13]

As Sir Thomas and his wife were both descendants of Edward I, the regent of the Netherlands may have incorrectly assumed that the Boleyns possessed extensive political power in England. In the spring of 1512, when he was sent as envoy to her court, a position that was often accompanied by membership on the king's council, all of the other offices he possessed were actually rather minor. Prior to his joint grant with Sir Henry Wyatt of the office of constable and keeper of the castle and gaol of Norwich that February, Thomas had held only the county positions of sheriff and of justice of the peace and keeperships: the exchange in the town of Calais and the foreign exchange in England and keepership of a park in Nottinghamshire.[14]

The first extant reference to his daughter's sojourn in the Netherlands is in a letter the regent sent to him, probably in the spring of 1513. She informed him that Claude Bouton, Captain of the Guard to the prince of Castile, had brought Anne to her and assured him that his daughter would soon be able to communicate in French. Although the date of Anne's arrival at her court is impossible to determine, it is surely relevant that in April 1513 the archduchess had sent a Burgundian servant to join the English household of Mary, her nephew's betrothed. It was likely Bouton, the *saige and adroit* equerry of the prince, who escorted this individual to the princess and who brought Anne back with him to the Netherlands, arriving after her father's departure for Calais on about 10 May.[15]

In her letter, Margaret had anticipated Sir Thomas' return to her court. Although he was not again to serve as envoy to the Netherlands, they both were aware that he would soon be back on the continent, for the recently signed Holy League had committed England to an offensive war against France. During the early autumn of that year, in fact, Henry and his advisers, among them Charles Brandon, viscount Lisle (the future duke of Suffolk), and Sir Thomas had several meetings with the regent at Lille and Tournai to celebrate their recent victories over the French.[16]

She brought with her young Charles and perhaps her other wards, although there is no evidence that the girls accompanied her on this progress. During these meetings, the regent and the widowed Lisle had some informal conversations in the course of which he took and kept a ring from her and she gave him one of her bracelets, causing rumors to reverberate through Christendom that the two might marry. The result of this encounter for the viscount, a virile and athletic man who was a personal friend of Henry, was that although the regent was disinclined to marry him, she was willing to invite his daughter, Anne Brandon, to reside at her court. Undoubtedly, the presence of Anne Boleyn in the Netherlands offered Lisle the opportunity to press for a similar opportunity for his child. The date of Anne Brandon's arrival at the regent's court remains uncertain, but William Sidney, who was in the service of the viscount, may have escorted her there in December 1513. If so, she was in Malines for well over a year before her father requested her return in May 1515.[17]

As far as Boleyn family history is concerned, the significance of Anne Brandon's residence in the Netherlands is that she had been born in 1506, just one year before the birthdate reported for Anne Boleyn by William Camden, the antiquary, who made the first extant specific remark about her age. The birthdate of 1507 has been challenged because of the unlikelihood that in 1513 a child of six could have won appointment as a maid of honor. But in addition to the age of Anne Brandon, all other extant documentation points to the youthfulness of Anne Boleyn. In her letter confirming the arrival of *la pettite Boulain*, the regent had said that she was so well spoken and so pleasant for her young age (*son josne eaige*) that she was beholden to Sir Thomas for sending his daughter to her. Other contemporary or near contemporary reports about her sojourn on the continent also referred to her tender years. Had she been twelve or thirteen and thus old enough to be a maid of honor, these reporters would not have regarded her age as noteworthy. In fact, canon law had long held that girls of twelve were legally capable of consummating a marriage.[18]

The reason that maids of honor needed to be about thirteen years old is that on ceremonial occasions they were expected to serve as "decorative foils" to their mistress. In preparation for these appointments, for which there was great competition as parents hoped their daughters would be able both to attract eligible husbands and to advance their family's social goals, the girls were instructed in how to dress fashionably, to behave properly in social relations, to play musical instruments at least competently, and to sing and to converse pleasantly. Using these skills, they entertained guests and performed other light tasks, such as escorting their mistress to church. As upon her arrival in the Netherlands Anne clearly knew little if any French, she was incapable of performing the chores of a maid of honor properly. Instead, she must have resided with the regent's wards, for monarchs and rulers customarily permitted young people of gentle birth to live with their children and to share in their schoolroom lessons.[19]

The Habsburgs, with whom the two English girls were for a short time educated, were three of the sisters of Charles: Eleanor, born in 1499 and the future queen of Portugal and France; Ysabeau, born in 1502 and the future queen of Denmark; and *la petite* Mary, born in 1505 and the future queen of Hungary. Although the archduchesses resided in a household separate from their brother's, it was situated in the same building as his: the Hotel de Bourgoyne on Keyserhof, which was located in Malines, a town with spacious streets and a large number of canals. Until her death in 1503, their step-great-grandmother, Margaret of York, had supervised their upbringing at this old ducal palace. In 1506, only three years later, when their father Philip died, his sister, the dowager duchess of Savoy, returned to the Netherlands at the behest of her father, the emperor, to become its regent and the guardian of his grandchildren. She also established her headquarters in Malines, moving into a small palace just across the street from her wards'. Although she frequently went on progresses, her nieces and nephews rarely left this town except for an annual summer holiday in Brussels.[20]

The servants, who directed the children's households with the same formal protocol as that which was in force at the regent's palace, were cosmopolitan in origin. Born into the Navarre royalty, Anna de Beaumont had been in charge of the girls' chamber since the birth of Eleanor in 1499. Except for Semmonet, her special French tutor, Anne probably had the same teachers as archduchess Mary who was only two years her senior. Among her instructors were Marguerite de Poitiers, the Spaniard Louis de Vaca, and the musician Hendrik Bredemers. It would be interesting to know whether Anne had any contact with Adrian of Utrecht, the future pope, who was appointed as the prince's tutor in 1512. Since the archduchesses learned to play the lute and clavichord, their English companion probably also received instruction in how to play these instruments. When Anne left Malines, she may even have carried with her a manuscript, only partially and crudely illuminated in the Flemish style. Now deposited at the Royal College of Music in London, it contains copies of compositions written before 1515 by eminent Franco-Flemish musicians.[21]

The splendid court at Malines was a "humanist centre, the capital of arts and letters in the north." Gathering around her poets, painters, sculptors, architects, and literary scholars, the regent kept in her palace works by Jan van Eyck, Jacopo de' Barbari and other renowned artists. She also collected a fine library with many books and illuminated manuscripts and was something of a poet, for she penned verses in French about the fickleness of human nature. During her regency, music reached greater heights than the other arts under her patronage. Besides Bredemers, the organist who was responsible for the musical education of her wards, Margaret kept in her employ a young man skilled on a variety of instruments to provide entertainment for her charges. Among the many musicians residing at Malines from 1513 to 1514 was Josquin des Prez, the greatest composer of the day.[22]

In addition to Margaret's acknowledgment of Anne's arrival, two other references to the girl's stay in the Netherlands are extant. The first is in a letter Sir Thomas sent to the regent from Greenwich on 14 August 1514, the day after Henry VIII's sister Mary had wed Louis XII of France by proxy, thereby confirming the repudiation of her betrothal to Prince Charles. In his letter Boleyn informed the regent that the new queen had asked to have with her in France his daughter *la pettite Boulain* who was then residing at Malines. Mary's brother Henry and his minister, Thomas Wolsey, had negotiated the French alliance in reaction to Maximilian's decision to delay the marriage of his grandson to her beyond the originally promised May 1514 deadline. That in this volte-face the English had adopted a pro-French policy came as shocking news to Margaret, who at first refused to believe that her beloved teenaged nephew had been jilted for an aged and visibly sick almost invalid king.[23]

The second extant reference is in an undated French letter from Anne to her father. Her message, probably written in response to his news about her invitation to live in France, was scrawled in extremely bad handwriting, like that of a child, and has many misspelled words, most of them penned phonetically. She apologized for her errors and penmanship, explaining that it was the first letter she had composed by herself, the others apparently having been copied from models that Semmonet had written out for her.[24] The reason for her note was to express the joy she felt upon learning that when she came to court, the queen would take the trouble to converse with her, a credible statement only if Anne were a child and not expecting to attend the queen personally as a maid of honor. This great privilege, Anne went on to predict, would encourage her to apply herself even more diligently to her French lessons. Almost certainly the queen to whom she referred was Henry's sister, who had been addressed by this title from 13 August when her proxy marriage was celebrated. As this ceremony had taken place on the day before Thomas wrote to the regent about Anne's removal to France, he must have sent a similar message to his daughter at the same time.[25]

In the formal phrasing often utilized by children addressing their parents in the sixteenth century, Anne also spoke of her love for her father, promising to be obedient to his wishes and to lead a holy life.[26] She ended her letter with the words, *scripte à Veure*. Before the remarkable translation by Hugh Paget in 1981, no scholar had been successful in interpreting the meaning of this phrase, but as he pointed out "Veure" was the French name for a 700-acre royal park with a palace and a hunting lodge near Brussels (Terveuren in its Flemish form) where the Habsburgs usually spent the summer months to escape the humidity of Malines. In 1514 the regent, accompanied by her wards, resided here from 1 June to 21 August; it was in this lovely wooded setting that she learned of Mary's proxy wedding and of the imminent departure of *la petite Boulain* for France.[27]

In his analysis Paget asserted that the Veure letter had been written earlier than August 1514, in which case, Anne could not have been discussing her trip to France and must have been referring to a future meeting with Catherine of Aragon. His major reason for supporting the earlier date is the speculation that Anne would not have bothered writing to her father in August since there was not enough time for her letter to reach him at Greenwich before she herself would. Surely she did not cross the Channel merely for the purpose of accompanying Sir Thomas and the new French queen back across the same body of water to Boulogne but instead went directly to France. At best travel in the sixteenth century was a difficult business and a crossing of the Channel even in the summertime was always a great challenge.[28] For Anne to reach Greenwich before Mary's expected September departure was barely, but theoretically, possible, although, given the grisly and unpredictable nature of travel, it was not likely that her father would have approved such a tight schedule for his child.

In mid-September the French queen and her retinue of well over 2,000 individuals, including Anne's father, her grandfather Surrey, recently elevated to the dukedom of Norfolk as a reward for his great victory over the Scots, his duchess, and several other Howards left Greenwich for Dover where for about two weeks they remained, waiting for a break in the stormy weather that would permit them to sail to France. On 2 October, once they had finally left the harbor, the weather turned nasty again. Mary spent the next twenty-four hours being buffeted about on the high seas, arriving at Boulogne on 3 October only after her ship had been grounded and she had been carried ashore, sick and exhausted. As the storm had scattered her flotilla, she had to wait for the remainder of her party to catch up with her before she could resume her journey.[29]

Since Anne's tender years would not permit her to join the queen's household or to attend her personally, it must have been her father's knowledge of the Valois family that encouraged him to seek a place for her in France. As the widower of Anne of

Brittany, Mary's new husband was the father of two children: Claude, born in 1499 and recently wed to her cousin, Francis the dauphin; and *la petite* Renée, born in 1510 and only four years old. Approval of the request for Anne to join the French nursery depended on the good nature of Louis and his reputed wish to please his eighteen-year-old consort, who, with her red-gold hair and slim figure, was described by all who saw her as a beauty. Louis' decision to permit Anne to live with his daughter may also have been prompted by Henry VIII's decision to place her grandfather Norfolk in charge of Mary's journey to France.[30]

Because of Anne's youthfulness, her father probably instructed her escort to take her directly to the French nursery rather than to the queen's entourage in transit to Paris. Any attempt to meet the English procession before it reached the French capital where Mary was to arrive in triumph on 6 November, after her marriage in person to Louis at Abbeville and her coronation at Saint-Denis, would have been fraught with scheduling difficulties. Not only was the queen tardy in sailing from England because of the weather but she was also forced to linger a week at Abbeville after the wedding on 9 October because of Louis' recurrent problems with the gout.[31]

During the delay at Abbeville, an event occurred that could have hastened Anne's departure for England. Concerned about the number of dependants his bride had brought with her and the expense of supporting them, Louis abruptly pared down their number and ordered those dismissed to return home. On the list of the attendants with permission to remain in France was the name of Mademoiselle Boleyn. Her whereabouts at the time of the controversy cannot be determined, but if she had been taken directly to the royal nursery, she was with Renée, who had arrived in Paris some time before 3 November.[32]

Since the new queen accused Anne's grandfather of acquiescing too readily in Louis' arbitrary treatment of her attendants, it is possible that, as has been suggested, the duke was indifferent to their plight because he had been given less control over their appointments than had Wolsey. But it is equally likely that Norfolk both sympathized with the king's action and hesitated to jeopardize his granddaughter's stay in France by protesting too vigorously. In any event Louis would not have viewed the

continued residence of the duke's young grandchild in his kingdom as repugnant, for his royal anger was directed toward Joan
Guildford, the somewhat domineering mistress of the queen's
household, who, from his point of view, had been interfering in his
relations with his bride. Despite her initial complaints, the queen
later confessed to one of the English envoys that even she
had begun to find mother Guildford's manner restrictive, an
admission that can be interpreted to mean that Mary had been
less concerned about the feelings of the dismissed attendants than
about the slight to her honor caused by her husband's interference in the running of her household.[33]

Although the dauphin and his wife, Claude, attended both the
wedding and the coronation, there is no evidence that Louis'
other daughter was present on either occasion. Since Anne's
relatives returned home after the wedding, in the event that she
had joined them in Abbeville, she was surely sent to reside with
Renée as soon as the wedding was over. As a new bride preparing
for her coronation in a foreign country, the queen could not have
been expected to be personally responsible for the young girl's
welfare. Although Anne and Renée may not have been witnesses
to either Mary's wedding or her coronation, they surely were
both permitted to view from a private window the queen's public
entry into Paris on 6 November. If Anne was present for this
grand spectacle, it was the kind of childhood experience that she
would remember for the rest of her life.[34]

Renaissance monarchs, as Roy Strong has noted, "transmuted
traditional forms of entertainment into a vehicle for dynastic
apotheoses." By the end of the fifteenth century ruling families
had turned simple ceremonial meetings arranged by urban
leaders to welcome their monarchs on their first visits to their
towns into grand spectacles for the purpose of dazzling both
foreign and domestic onlookers with their kingdom's wealth and
power. As part of the welcoming ceremony, scholars and artists
were commissioned to create pageants with actors dressed in
elaborate costumes, giving high-sounding speeches, reciting
poetry, and singing songs on stages and scaffolding decked with
magnificent decorations.[35]

Even within this grand tradition Mary's entry into Paris must
be considered truly splendid. All the streets on the route of her

procession from the Porte Saint-Denis to the Cathedral of Notre Dame were grandly decorated. At strategic places scaffolding was erected, displaying a mixture of Christian and classical representations of virtue, honor, truth, justice, and peace. There were seven pageants in all, three of them sponsored by the municipality and four by private concerns. The last one had a garden with lilies, called the garden of France, in which shepherds and shepherdesses extolled in song the peaceful relations that the union of Louis and Mary would bring to England and France. Some of the earlier pageants had prominently displayed the Tudor rose.[36]

In honor of the wedding, the dauphin held a tournament at the Parc des Tournelles in Paris on 13 November that dragged on for ten days because of intermittent rain. With an impressive display of courage and valor, the duke of Suffolk, who had just arrived as ambassador, led the English warriors to a great victory over the dauphin and his fellow knights. The grand finale of the festivities was a dinner at the Hôtel de Ville in Paris, during which the queen arranged for some dessert to be sent to Renée, her stepdaughter, who was lodged at Vincennes Palace just a few miles east of Paris. There is no extant record of Anne at Vincennes, but it is likely that she was there and able to share in this part of the celebration.[37]

On 27 November the court retreated to St. Germain-en-Laye for a respite from the festivities before returning to Paris for the Christmas holidays. Although Renée occasionally resided at that palace, which lay a few miles west of the capital, her household may have remained at Vincennes since her father and his consort planned to be gone for only three weeks. After his court returned to Paris in mid-December, Louis became extremely ill and died about a fortnight later on 1 January 1515, after only eighty-two days of wedded life with his new consort. The next few weeks were busy and eventful for all adult members of the royal family except the queen dowager who was required by custom to retire to a secluded, dark room for forty days while everyone waited to see if she would prove to be with child.[38]

Eager for political power, the dauphin assumed after conversations with Mary that she was not pregnant and in late January had himself crowned monarch, since the Salic law prevented the succession of his wife Claude, the elder daughter of Louis. The Paris entry of Francis, because the country was still in mourning and because it had been organized at relatively short notice, was not as brilliant as Mary's. It took place in early February, soon after she had emerged from her forty-day hibernation. She viewed the entry from a private window and then rode to a state dinner in a procession, which was preceded by Suffolk and twenty of his servants on horseback, all clad in gray damask. In her litter were both the new king's mother, Louise of Savoy, and his young sister-in-law, Madame Renée. Behind them was a second litter with two children, perhaps one of them Anne Boleyn, since she was a companion of Renée and technically a maid of honor to the former queen. Besides Renée there were at this time no other children in the immediate royal family. The king's sister, Margaret, wife to Charles, duke of Alençon, and another noble lady rode in a third litter; they were followed by fifty more litters each carrying two ladies.[39]

That Claude had assumed responsibility for Anne from her first arrival in France seems obvious from the queen dowager's subsequent actions. Widowed and without protection in a strange land, perhaps frightened and certainly determined to become Suffolk's wife, Mary persuaded the duke to marry her and risk her brother's displeasure. After Henry had finally forgiven them for their transgression and had sent permission for them to return to England, they departed for Dover on 2 May 1515, exactly seven months from the day that Mary had set sail from that harbor to join her royal spouse. During those months if she had ever felt any concern for Anne, whom she left behind in France, the queen dowager made no mention of it in her letters that are still extant. She was so engrossed by her own troubles that she seems never to have given a thought to Anne's welfare.[40]

After the death of Louis, Anne and Renée continued to reside together in the royal nursery although officially Louise of Savoy, the new king's mother, had become the guardian of Renée, as the child's mother, the late Queen Anne of Brittany, had wished. During the rest of her life, Louise served as one of her son's most important advisers, becoming the country's regent as early as 1515 when he led his army to press his territorial and dynastic claims in northern Italy. Even when she was not regent, Louise, whose life's passion had been to see her son succeed as monarch even to the point of rejoicing when Louis' children had been born female or died prematurely, was usually preoccupied with assisting her son in ruling his kingdom.[41]

Pregnant and unwell when her husband succeeded as monarch, Claude spent most of her tenure as queen before her death in 1524 in giving birth to her seven children. As she was often absorbed in childbearing duties, she was frequently in residence near Renée and most concerned, by her personal presence at least, with her sister's welfare and therefore with Anne's. Claude's young English ward surely shared Renée's schoolroom lessons, which were supervised by her governess, Françoise de Rohan, countess of Tonverre. The only extant statement by a Frenchman about Anne's education is in a poem written in 1536 by Lancelot de Carles, the future bishop of Riez. Confirming her close contact with the queen, he revealed that she had zealously watched and imitated Claude's maids of honor in order to learn how to conduct herself properly at court. As part of her training, Anne learned to play the lute and other instruments well, to dance pleasantly, to converse fluently in French, and to do needlework exquisitely. William Thomas was later to claim that she was "imbued with as many outward good qualities in playing on instruments, singing, and such other courtly graces, as few women were of her time."[42]

During their years together the girls apparently developed a cordial relationship, for in 1561 Renée, by now the dowager duchess of Ferrara, made a point of discussing this childhood friendship with Sir Nicholas Throckmorton, the English ambassador to France. Commanding him to attend her in her private quarters, she confessed in a nostalgic moment that she was especially fond of his monarch, Elizabeth, whose mother had been her acquaintance when she served as maid of honor to Queen Claude.[43]

Although Anne lived in the royal nursery, it is difficult to find any evidence about her or even to discover any information about the activities of the French princess, who has been described as a "pale star in the brilliant firmament of the Valois court."[44] The physical appearance of Renée, who, like her sister Claude, was short with a slight limp in her walk, cannot be blamed for the infrequent references to her. Early modern Europeans categorized people with physical handicaps as monsters and were both fascinated and repelled by disfigurements much more minor than hers. In 1527, after deciding to obtain a divorce, Henry VIII for a short time actually considered marrying Renée. During that summer he spoke with a Hungarian envoy who, upon seeing her, had rejected her as a bride for his monarch because he thought she would not be able to "bring forth frute, as it apperith by the liniacion of her body."[45]

The French royal nursery, which was a smaller version of the king's household, had grown to a membership of well over 200 by the early 1520s. Although it was peripatetic, it moved less often than the court, for Francis was and is still famous for his frequent changes of residence, dashing from town to town and from hunting lodge to hunting lodge. This huge amount of traveling was partly the result of the royal headquarters lying in the beautiful Loire valley rather than in a specific town. Although the children were housed in several palaces, such as St. Germain-en-Laye near Paris where the last four of Claude's infants were born and Plessis-sur-Vert in Brittany where her three-year-old Louise died in 1518, they could most frequently be found at Blois and Amboise.[46]

Blois, the birthplace of Claude, had belonged to Louis XII's branch of the family before he succeeded his cousin Charles VIII to the throne. Situated on the Loire about halfway between Amboise and Orléans, it was Claude's favorite residence, where she often arranged for her children to be housed.[47] In contrast, the château at Amboise where Francis had spent his childhood remained his favorite residence. With its elevated position and walled gardens, it offered a peaceful refuge for the family and served as the birthplace of the first three of the royal infants, including the dauphin in 1518. During the following year, in October 1519, when the plague brought great sickness to France, the Valois family retreated here, refusing admission to outsiders until the epidemic had abated.[48]

This flight from the plague was recorded by Anne's father, who had been serving as ambassador to France for about one year. He had first entered the kingdom in late 1518 for the purpose of obtaining the approval of Francis to a treaty of universal peace, called the Treaty of London, which was to be signed by most of the major powers. At that time he confirmed a second alliance with the French king that provided for the betrothal of Mary, the daughter of Henry VIII, to the dauphin, who was some two years younger than his future bride. As the English envoy, Boleyn was also called upon to act as proxy sponsor for his king at the christening of his namesake, the infant Henri, born to Claude in March 1519 at St. Germain-en-Laye. Finally, he discussed the preparations for the meeting called the Field of Cloth of Gold scheduled for the early summer of 1520.[49]

In his dispatches, Sir Thomas referred often to the recurrent illnesses Claude suffered while carrying Henri, the fourth child she had borne since 1515. During his conversations with her, he undoubtedly spoke about his daughter and probably arranged, before his return to England in March 1520, for her to leave the royal nursery some time after late May when she was due to celebrate her thirteenth birthday. Since Claude was seldom at court except on ceremonial occasions and was expecting another child in August 1520, she may have decided to ask her sister-in-law to take charge of her ward at that time. Although the date remains uncertain, Anne was transferred to the household of the duchess of Alençon sometime before the end of 1521 when she returned to England.[50] Her father would have wanted her to attend court regularly in the hope that she might be able to contract an advantageous marriage with a French nobleman.

It would be interesting to discover whether, as is likely since she was about thirteen years old, Anne was at the Field of Cloth of Gold, that magnificent summit meeting in which the courts of France and England entertained each other outside Calais for three weeks in June 1520. As many of her relatives, including her mother and father were there, she would have wanted to participate in the festivities. Perhaps Sir Thomas had been able to arrange for her presence, but if not, he was surely able to have her promoted out of the schoolroom by the end of 1520. If so, she spent her last year in France at its court, probably in attendance on the duchess of Alençon who was some twelve years her senior. During those months Anne must have developed a strong affection for this noblewoman, as a French envoy was to report in 1535 that she had revealed to him she had two wishes: to have a son and to see Margaret again.[51]

Although Francis has the reputation of a roué and rake, Anne's residence at his court, either under the care of his gentle queen, who spent her days doing needlework and reading her devotions, or under that of his religious and cultured sister would have served to protect her virtue, had it needed such protection. Despite the king's high jinks on the streets of Paris and his notorious love affairs, when in the presence of the ladies of the royal family he was normally well behaved and well mannered, treating them with the respect that the standards of his day demanded. The French court was not so cultured or so refined as Burgundy's, but it did have set patterns of behavior or of etiquette that on the prevailing hierarchical schedule served to satisfy the honor of the courtiers in attendance. Anne could have learned of the king's sensational activities only by rumor and gossip and not by being a witness to them. Little evidence has survived, for example, about Frances, countess of Châteaubriant, who became his mistress sometime between 1515 and 1517; for historians, she remains a "shadowy" figure. Most of the scandalous stories about the king's extra-marital liaisons had little basis in fact until after the death of Claude in 1524 and the marriage of his sister to Henri d'Albret, king of Navarre, in 1527.[52]

Francis was greatly concerned about his reputation as a king of Christendom. His goal was not only to defeat the Imperial armies and those of its allies, as he did at Marignano in 1515, but also to surpass their courts in magnificence and splendor. Most of the patronage of arts and letters for which he is now famous occurred in the second half of his reign after Anne had returned to England. Although he remodeled Blois between 1515 and 1524, he completed the splendid palaces at Fontainebleau and Chambord only after her departure. In 1516 he did play host to Leonardo da Vinci, who brought the *Mona Lisa* with him to France. Before the great master's death in 1519, Anne may well have met him, for he was housed at the manor of Cloux near Amboise. Among the other artists of Francis' patronage was Jean Clouet of Flanders, whose detailed work serves as a portrait history of the court.[53]

Anne must also have become acquainted with some of the royal scholars, surely Guillaume Budé, later the head of the king's library, and certainly Clément Marot, the premier French poet of the day, since he began his royal career in 1519 as a protégé of the duchess of Alençon. His scholarship had a greater impact on Protestantism than that of any other poet of the French Renaissance primarily because of the popularity of his translations of the Psalms, which, after they were first published in 1533, were to appear in another 500 editions by 1600. Experts on his scholarship have pointed out that his work changed significantly in the middle 1520s. When Anne was in France, neither his advanced reformist ideas nor his great poetic ability was fully developed or articulated.[54]

Marot's first royal patron, the duchess of Alençon, had two passions in life: supporting her brother as king of France and encouraging a religious reform that can essentially be characterized as non-doctrinal in nature. A restless, intelligent woman with considerable writing skill, she was the author of both religious and secular literature that contained mystical and Neo-Platonic themes. In 1531 the Sorbonne was to attack as heretical her mystical work, *Le Miroir de l'âme pecheresse* which had just appeared in print, but then retracted their charge when the identity of its author was discovered.[55]

The roots of her spiritual beliefs can in part be found in the movement called the *devotio moderna* begun in the Netherlands by the Brethren of the Common Life. The greatest of their devotional writings was the *Imitatio Christi*, a fifteenth-century mystical work by Thomas à Kempis. The long-term impact of this movement on religious reform can only with difficulty be overstated. Stressing an inner faith and seeking to imitate Christ in their daily lives, the Brethren spread their views through their charitable works and their educational activities. Two important individuals touched by their teachings were Pope Adrian VI and Erasmus, who had been trained by them as a youth.[56]

Like many reformers, Margaret's religion was Biblical in focus, but her personal, mystical beliefs were more reminiscent of those of Erasmus than of Martin Luther. In the early Reformation no obvious boundaries existed among those who championed reform of the church. Only slowly were individuals, such as Erasmus,

forced to define their beliefs, so as either to support or to deny
Luther's doctrines. Most of the humanists, such as Budé and
Jacques Lefèvre d'Etaples in France, were in principle opposed to
schism and chose to remain within the Church. Lefèvre, also a
protégé of the duchess of Alençon and a leader of the reforming
Meaux Group, wrote commentaries on the Psalms and on Paul's
Epistles in 1509 and 1512; he was to begin publishing his Bible
translations in 1523. Although Margaret's patronage of reform
and her authorship of the religious and secular writings for which
she is now famous manifested themselves principally after she had
moved to Navarre in 1527, she did favor Marot and Lefèvre when
Anne was in residence at the French court.[57]

When, late in 1521, Sir Thomas asked for his daughter's return,
her presence seems to have been required because of the possibility that she might become betrothed to the heir of the disputed
earl of Ormond. After the death of Anne's paternal great-
grandfather in 1515, her grandmother and her great aunt, his
heirs general, had been prevented from occupying their father's
Irish estates by their Irish cousin, Piers Butler, who styled himself
earl of Ormond. It was thought that the marriage of Butler's son
to Anne would resolve this family dispute and effect a public
truce in Irish politics. Her return may also have been related to
the rapidly deteriorating relations between England and France.
Despite the cordiality displayed between these two kingdoms at
the Field of Cloth and Gold, Henry and Wolsey had chosen to
ally with the Habsburg family, then headed by Charles, prince of
Castile, the new Holy Roman Emperor. Sir Thomas Boleyn was
acutely aware of this change in his country's policy, as he had
gone on an assignment to the emperor's court in September 1521.
By 19 November of that year, he was at Bruges on his way home;
it is likely that he arranged for Anne to meet him at Calais for the
difficult Channel crossing, but the only record of her departure
for England is the simple statement of Francis in January 1522
that she was no longer at his court. As the two kingdoms were on
the brink of war, Thomas could rightly have suspected that the
duchess would show little enthusiasm for finding a spouse among
the French nobility for his daughter. With that option no longer
available, he must have welcomed the Ormond alliance, for

Anne's formal training was complete and it was time for her marriage to be arranged.[58]

Four summarizing points can be made about her education and how it had prepared her for marriage and adulthood. The first and most obvious is that she had spent her formative years absorbing French culture. Not only was she fluent in French but she may also have spoken English with a slight accent. As only her countrymen knew their language in the early Tudor period, she could have had few opportunities to converse in her native tongue with visitors, even diplomats, from the time she journeyed to France until the last year or so of her residence in the kingdom when she had left the schoolroom. She seems also to have developed a taste for Franco-Flemish music and French fashion; the portrait of her now at the National Gallery in London bears witness to her adoption of French clothing styles.[59]

Secondly, she was introduced to a religious reform that centered on a personal spiritual experience bolstered by scripture reading. In 1521, when she left Margaret's household for England, there is no evidence that Anne had been in contact with more radical beliefs than those held by the duchess and her protégés who eschewed schism from the Roman Church.

A third point is that her opportunity to be educated with the most esteemed royal children of Christendom served to heighten her sense of her personal worth and to strengthen her determination to elevate her status and lineage. At seven years of age she promised her father that she would strive to please him and to lead a respectable life; during the next few years in preparation for her residence at court, she studied hard, carefully observing the queen's maids of honor to learn how to conduct herself properly and how to dress with style.

Finally, nowehere in Europe except in France and the Netherlands were such strong female role models available for the guidance of young gentlewomen. Margaret of Austria and Louise of Savoy were not only intelligent ladies with drive and ambition but they also served as regents, wielding considerable political power adroitly. The regent of the Netherlands and the duchess of Alençon provided examples of how patronage could be used to support the arts and scholarship and to promote religious reform.

All three ladies are noteworthy for their commitment to their family's future and for their deep, personal sacrifices to ensure the future of their Houses.

Imbued with a persevering and determined personality, Anne returned to England well equipped by education and by heritage to seek a noble marriage for the advancement of her family's lineage. Her great-grandfather, the wealthy London merchant, had inaugurated the Boleyns' rise to noble status by earning a knighthood and marrying the daughter of a baron; her grandfather had wed the daughter of an earl, and her father the daughter of a future duke. In 1521 the goal of her relatives was to match her with the heir of an earl, thereby offering her the chance to become a countess; but in 1527 she took advantage of an unexpected opportunity to capture a king's heart.

2 FAMILY ALLIANCES

By the end of 1521, when Anne Boleyn was on her way home, her grandfather, the duke of Norfolk, was nearing his eightieth birthday. Despite his advanced age, he had not yet retired from public life and in May had been called upon to carry out an unpleasant but necessary assignment. As Lord High Steward of England for the occasion, he had been required to head a commission to try for treason Edward Stafford, third duke of Buckingham, the father-in-law of Norfolk's son, the earl of Surrey since 1514. The marriage had been an important match for Surrey, whose first wife had died about 1512, as Buckingham's daughter Elizabeth was through her extremely wealthy father a descendant of Edward III.[1]

At the trial several witnesses were willing to corroborate the charge that Buckingham, who had been arrogant and boastful about his royal antecedents, had threatened the king's life. Observers said the old duke cried when it was time for him to read the verdict of guilty on his son's father-in-law; perhaps a principal reason for his distress was that the downfall of this nobleman, the premier of only three dukes in the kingdom, carried with it an implicit threat to the other two. Henry made Buckingham's death as palatable as he could for the Howards and others of the aristocracy by distributing to them many of the convicted nobleman's landed possessions. The Boleyns were among those who were so rewarded, Sir Thomas himself, along with other justices of *oyer et terminer*, having presided over three of the panels that had indicted the duke.[2] But Buckingham's death remained a chilling reminder that the uncertainty of the kingdom's succession caused by the lack of a male heir could lead to the destruction of even the greatest subject if he were perceived to be a threat to the continuation of the Tudor dynasty.

The major connection of the Boleyns to Buckingham had been through their kinship with the Howards who continued to act as their patrons. Clearly in East Anglia and at court Anne's father had relied greatly upon the influence of the second duke of Norfolk for advancement, but as the Boleyns were related to other noblemen, such as Ormond, they were never totally dependent upon Norfolk's favor and support. They had some contacts that were not based on kinship. In 1489, for example, Sir William Boleyn had served as one of the executors of the will of Henry Lovel, seventh Lord Morley, a responsibility that has special significance for the Boleyns because some thirty years later Sir Thomas was to contract a marriage for his son with a daughter of that same Lord Morley's nephew, Sir Henry Parker, who acquired his uncle's title in 1523. From his youth, Parker had served in the household of Lady Margaret, countess of Richmond, the mother of Henry VII and the guardian of Buckingham during his minority. The Howards also had a connection with the Parkers, as after Alice Lovel Parker, Henry's mother, was widowed, she married Sir Edward Howard, the Lord Admiral who was killed at Brest in 1513.[3]

To understand Anne's role in court politics and her place in the family's network of social relationships, the marriage alliances that Sir Thomas made and attempted to make for her and his other offspring between 1520 and 1527 need to be examined. The unions can on close scrutiny be found to support at least three goals: to return to the family the Irish title and estates of his grandfather Ormond, to bolster Boleyn kinship to the Tudor dynasty, and to develop a dependable, political network at court.

Before the events leading to Buckingham's death, Surrey, surely with his father Norfolk's support, had proposed a union between Anne Boleyn and James, the heir of Sir Piers Butler, the disputed earl of Ormond. The first extant evidence of this scheme can be found in two dispatches from the autumn of 1520, one written to Wolsey by Surrey, then the King's Lieutenant in Ireland, in association with the Irish council, and the other directed to Surrey by Henry VIII. The Lieutenant's letter to Wolsey, which was dated 6 October, alluded to discussions about this marriage that had been held the previous spring shortly before the earl's departure for Dublin.[4]

The noble relative, who thus proved willing to undertake this important matchmaking role for Anne, was by 1520 one of the king's major military advisers. He had not only been picked to succeed his deceased brother Sir Edward as Lord High Admiral but had also proved to be a fierce leader on the battlefield. Increasingly after 1513, the year of Flodden Field, he had gradually assumed the tasks that his aging father, the acclaimed victor of that battle, had previously performed. Surrey never became a great hero in the same sense as the second duke although in 1536 his command of crown forces against the Pilgrimage of Grace was considered essential to a royal victory. Later, in 1542, he missed winning the Tudors' second great battle with the Scots because he was raiding the Eastern Marches when their army invaded the Western ones.[5]

In May 1520, when he arrived in Ireland as the King's Lieutenant, a more prestigious title than Deputy Lieutenant, England's control of that island, never very secure, was slipping from royal hands. Traditionally, English monarchs had selected Anglo-Irish lords, most recently the earls of Kildare, as deputies to rule the Pale, the area around Dublin that was under the crown's direct control, and to keep order in the remainder of the island by a combination of force of arms and local political associations. From September 1519, Gerald Fitzgerald, ninth earl of Kildare, who had most recently served as deputy, was retained in England, while Surrey was sent to the island to pacify it. In one of his "spasmodic fits of reforming energy," Henry VIII had decided through the agency of his Lieutenant to reorganize the government, the church, and the bureaucracy of Ireland. After spending only a few months in Dublin, a frustrated Surrey, who was unable to pacify the island or to obtain needed legislation from its parliament, such as a salt monopoly for the king, became persuaded that the proposed reforms could be implemented only after a military conquest, a solution that was not a viable possibility because it would require the use of resources that were scarce and that the crown would prefer to apply to its continental enterprises.[6]

It was from his post in Ireland that Surrey wrote the letter of 6

October 1520 in which he revealed that the previous spring he had joined "divers" others in petitioning Wolsey for a marriage between Sir Thomas Boleyn's daughter and the earl of Ormond's heir, who resided in England under the protection of the Cardinal. Shortly after raising the issue with Wolsey, Surrey had left for Ireland while the Cardinal had directed his attention first to the events at the Field of Cloth of Gold and then to the diplomatic consequences of that celebrated summit meeting. During the summer of 1520, Wolsey seems to have had little time to spare for the Butler match or even for Irish affairs. By September a concerned Surrey was complaining that since his departure from England the previous May, he had received no communication from either Wolsey or Henry.[7]

In a now lost dispatch, probably dated in mid- to late September, Surrey must also have discussed with the king the advisability of a Butler/Boleyn match, for Henry responded with a promise to advance the matter with Boleyn. This marriage, as Surrey believed, had the potential for resolving two problems: it would establish greater English ties with an important Irish leader who might, as a consequence, look more favorably upon effecting "good order" in his homeland, and it would also respond to the needs of Boleyn's mother and aunt who had been futilely attempting to gain possession of their father's Irish honor and estates that by English law were to descend to the heirs general. Their difficulty was how to persuade Sir Piers to relinquish control of them without fomenting a rebellion in the process or without having to chance legal proceedings in Ireland that would inevitably treat the Butler claim with great sympathy. A union between the late earl's English great-granddaughter and the heir of his Irish cousin might lead to a peaceful end to that dispute.[8]

There is no evidence that Sir Thomas was among the "divers" who in the spring of 1520 requested Wolsey to arrange a marriage between his daughter and James Butler, but, given the social customs of the day, it is inconceivable that the petitioners should have failed to obtain his prior permission for the match, especially as the prospective bride was not quite thirteen years old. Sir Thomas surely would have encouraged and even welcomed discussions about a union between her and a future Irish earl that carried with it the promise that the family's dispute might finally be settled. Certainly in 1520, he and his relatives had little other reason to hope that they would be able to obtain a favorable resolution to the controversy. In 1529, of course, the king's love for Anne was to lead him to ennoble her father as Ormond; that Sir Thomas would never have obtained this honor without the influence of his daughter is a reasonable assumption when it is recalled that after her disgrace in 1536, Sir Piers regained this earldom.[9] In the spring of 1520, however, when questions about the Butler match were first raised officially, Boleyn would probably have been a tough negotiator concerning the details of his daughter's dowry and jointure. Since English and French diplomats were even then absorbed in arranging for the journey of their monarchs to the Field of Cloth of Gold, he must have believed that a splendid French marriage for Anne, as a maid of honor to Queen Claude and as an attendant of the duchess of Alençon, was still a good possibility.

The next and final extant reference to a match between Anne and James is dated near the end of 1521, some eleven months after Henry had promised Surrey he would support the marriage. Comments made to the king by Wolsey in a letter of mid- to late November 1521, and sent from Calais where he was negotiating an Anglo-Imperial détente, can be interpreted to mean that Sir Piers had been slow to approve an English marriage for his heir. When he wrote this report to Henry, Wolsey had just read some letters from Sir Piers, forwarded to him by the king, that had asked for the return of his son James, who was still a member of the Cardinal's household and was, of course, as yet unbetrothed to Anne. In his dispatch, Wolsey explicitly stated that he wished to use the Boleyn marriage as an excuse to keep James in England partly because he believed that Sir Piers would be a less dependable ally if he had his heir with him. Keeping him loyal was of the utmost importance, since at the end of 1521, when Surrey returned to England, Sir Piers acted as his deputy, becoming the official Deputy Lieutenant of Ireland in the spring of 1522. Here are Wolsey's complete comments about the problem:

Finally, Sir, I have considred the request and desire made unto Your Grace by Sir Piers Butler, conteigned in his letters, whiche I thinke veray reasonable; and surely Sir, the towardnes of his sonne considred, who is right active, discrete and wise, I suppose he, being with his fader in that lande, shulde do unto Your Grace right acceptable service. Howe be it, Sir, goode shall it be to prove, how the said Sir Piers Butler shall acquite hym self in thauctoritie by Your Grace lately to hym committed, not doubting but his said sonne being within your reame, he woll doo ferre the better; trusting therby the rather to gett hym home. And I shall, at my retourne to your presence, divise with Your Grace, how the marriage betwixt hym and Sir Thomas Bolain is doughtier, may be brought to passe, whiche shalbe a reasonable cause to tracte the tyme for sending his said sonne over unto hym, for the perfecting of whiche mariage I shall indevour my selff, at my said retourne, with all effecte.[10]

To have committed himself so strongly to "perfecting" the match, Wolsey must have obtained either an oral or written approval from Anne's father. Probably the two had met together at Calais before this letter was composed and before the Cardinal sailed for England on 28 November, since nine days earlier, Sir Thomas, who was returning from an assignment to the emperor's court, had written to Wolsey from Bruges, apologizing for the illness that had delayed his arrival at Calais for the meeting they had previously scheduled. Wolsey was subsequently unable to arrange the Butler alliance, as he had hoped to do, but, unfortunately, the reasons for that failure, by May 1523, at the latest, remain unknown. It is likely that Butler's recalcitrance was more responsible than Boleyn's reluctance for the rejection of this plan, since in November 1521, when the Cardinal promised the king to perfect the marriage, Sir Thomas was favorably enough disposed toward it to arrange for Anne to return home, undoubtedly believing that she was to become the wife of a future earl.[11]

Over a year before she left for England, expecting to wed James Butler, her younger sister Mary was married. On 4 February 1520, she became the wife of William Carey, an alliance that would seem to offer strong evidence for identifying Mary as the elder sister, since English families often sought to wed their daughters in order of seniority. Two special circumstances indicate that in Anne's case her family had deliberately chosen to ignore this custom. First, in early 1520 she was still on the continent, reaping the benefits of a royal education and probably hoping to wed a foreign nobleman, a much more esteemed union than that of her younger sister to a mere English commoner. Although it cannot be known precisely what their father's original goals were in sending Anne to the Netherlands and then to France, he may have been expecting her to remain abroad for the rest of her life, relying on her guardians there to find her a suitable husband. Indeed, when Suffolk recalled his daughter from Malines in 1515, he acknowledged in his letter to the regent that he had originally planned for her to stay in the Netherlands permanently. Secondly, at just about the time William and Mary were wed, Surrey and "divers" others were petitioning Wolsey for an alliance between his ward James Butler and Anne Boleyn, thus beginning the process that, if it succeeded, would see her one day elevated to the nobility as the wife of an earl.[12]

In the late winter and early spring of 1520, at the time these events occurred, Anne was not yet thirteen years old and her sister not quite twelve. Although the average marriage age of sixteenth-century ladies was about twenty, some ambitious noblemen and gentry did begin seeking spouses for their offspring when they were still children. The consummation of the Carey marriage, like that of other unions in which one of the two newlyweds was quite young, was undoubtedly delayed for some time, although their first child Catherine must have been born about 1524.[13]

Because Mary was the younger Boleyn daughter, her marriage to twenty-four-year-old William Carey can be viewed as an important achievement for her family, for he was a gentleman of the royal privy chamber with direct and daily contact with Henry. The political significance of membership in this chamber, which had only recently been reorganized on the French model, had been demonstrated by the decision in 1519 to purge it of four young men reputed to be a bad influence on the king. The importance of their positions arose in part from the habits of monarchs like Henry, who turned to the men with whom they spent their leisure hours to carry out governmental assignments. Even if Carey was never able to use his office to promote his father-in-law's career in a direct way, he could still give him up-to-date information about royal policies and plans, provide his new wife Mary with lodgings at court, and offer her the opportunity to participate in court revels and to attend grand events such as the Field of Cloth of Gold.[14]

As a descendant of Edward III, William had a more immediate royal heritage than the Boleyns. He was a younger son of Thomas Carey of Wiltshire and Margaret Spencer, a daughter of Lady Eleanor Beaufort, who was herself a child of Edmund, third earl of Somerset, and thus a relative of Henry VIII and his grandmother, Margaret Beaufort, countess of Richmond. The Careys also provided the Boleyns with a link to the Percies, for Catherine Spencer, a sister of William's mother, had married Henry, fifth earl of Northumberland.[15] Both politically and socially Mary's marriage served to bolster her family's ambitions at court.

That Mary's wedding was celebrated on 4 February 1520, a few weeks before her father's return home, lends support to the suggestion that he had at least tentatively approved of William as her future husband before he had departed on his diplomatic assignment to France. Because the Church forbade the celebration of marriages during certain holy times, such as Lent, Sir Thomas, who was not due home until after the beginning of that somber season, had obviously agreed to have the marriage take place while he was still abroad. The precise date of the wedding is known because the king provided the newlyweds with a present of 6s. 8d. As a younger son, Mary's husband lacked a personal power base in the county of Wiltshire, but between 1520 and his early demise in 1528, he obtained two keeperships, a stewardship, an annuity, and manors in two counties.[16] Had he lived to witness his sister-in-law's royal marriage, he might have reaped even greater rewards.

The extent to which Mary's union with William enhanced her father's position at court cannot be ascertained. Sir Thomas had already served as a diplomat to Malines and Paris, and along with his wife had played a prominent role in important royal ceremonies. In 1516 he had been one of four gentlemen to carry the canopy at the christening of the Princess Mary and the next year his wife Lady Elizabeth had acted as deputy sponsor for Queen Catherine at the christening of Frances, the infant of her sister-in-law, the former French queen. Although he had obtained a claim to the office of comptroller of the king's household, the first major position he seems to have held was treasurer of the household, an appointment he gained in 1522, only two years after his daughter had become William's wife.[17]

Having the Careys in a position to solicit favors for him in private conversations with the king would have been desirable from his point of view even though his diplomatic usefulness to the crown had been more than sufficient to earn him the treasurership. Indeed, it is likely that both Wolsey and Henry had been pleased with his French mission, for Francis had written that Sir Thomas had with honor performed the proxy sponsorship at the christening of Prince Henri in 1519. That he had earned a reputation as a successful diplomat there is no doubt: in 1521 and 1523 he was sent on two embassies to the emperor and by 1525 was one of ten Englishmen receiving a pension from Charles V.[18]

After crossing the Channel in late 1521, possibly with her father who was returning from his first Imperial mission, Anne must have immediately traveled to London, for a record has survived of her presence there on Shrove Tuesday 1522. She and her sister Mary were two of eight ladies who participated in revels arranged by Wolsey at York Place for the benefit of visiting Imperial ambassadors. After supper the Cardinal and these envoys entered a great decorated chamber in which stood a large construction called the *Château Vert*, which had three towers all bedecked with banners. Clothed in white satin with bejeweled headdresses of gold, the ladies, who were placed in these towers, were all given pleasant and virtuous names, with Anne playing Perseverance, her sister, Kindness, her future sister-in-law Jane Parker, Constancy, and the former French queen, Beauty. Eight choristers of the royal chapel dressed as Indian women with unpleasant names, such as Disdain and Unkindness, prepared to defend the Château and its inhabitants from assault. After the attackers, whose spokesman Ardent Desire, probably played by William Cornish, pled unsuccessfully for the castle's surrender, the king, accompanied by the roar of cannon, led the gentlemen in releasing a barrage of dates, oranges, and other fruits at the defenders. Although the Indian women fought gallantly, returning rose water and comfits for the fruit, they were finally, as all had expected, forced to surrender the Château. Dancing and a great banquet followed these grand festivities. There is no reason to believe that the king paid the youthful Anne, or even her sister, who was to become his mistress by 1525, any particular notice that evening. He was already acquainted with most if not all of the ladies, some of whom seem to have been his consort's maidens, although naturally his sister and Mary Carey, who were both married, did not serve Catherine in that capacity. As all the other female revelers had regular lodgings at court, the question of Anne's status there needs to be addressed.[19]

George Cavendish, Wolsey's gentleman usher, said in his now famous study of his master, written in the 1550s, that when Anne was betrothed to Lord Henry Percy, the heir of Northumberland, she was a maid of honor to Queen Catherine. Since Cavendish also claimed that in a pique of jealousy the king had refused to permit the two young people to marry, seventeenth-century writers, who were aware that Anne did not become one of the queen's maidens until about 1527, believed that the Percy liaison had taken place in 1529. As evidence in Surrey's letters, which was unknown to those authors, indicates that by the end of 1523 the young nobleman was formally betrothed to Lady Mary Talbot, daughter of George, fourth earl of Shrewsbury, a more reasonable time to date Anne's romance with Lord Henry is the spring of that year. Their private and unapproved understanding may, in fact, have been directly responsible for the finalizing of the plans for his betrothal to Lady Mary Talbot. It is also relevant to the dating of Anne's liaison with Lord Henry that by May 1523, at the latest, the negotiations for her alliance with the heir of Ormond had been broken off.[20]

Since she was not one of Catherine's maidens in 1522 or 1523, Anne's right to lodgings at court had to derive from some other source. It is entirely possible that she was visiting her mother, Lady Boleyn, whom she had not seen since 1513 or perhaps 1520 at the Field of Cloth of Gold, but it is more likely that she was one of the attendants of Mary, the former French queen, who resided in Catherine's household when she was at court. Early in 1522, as noted above, Anne could be found at York Place in the company of the French queen. Evidence of other Boleyn contacts with her household are extant. In 1517 Lady Boleyn had, of course, acted as a proxy sponsor for Catherine at the christening of Mary's daughter, Lady Frances. By 1530, when Anne had become the king's lady, one of her closest companions was Bridget, widow of the diplomat Sir Richard Wingfield. As the numerous members of the Wingfield family were relatives and clients of the duke of Suffolk, the French queen's husband, it is possible that Anne became acquainted with Bridget through their mutual service to his wife. It would seem appropriate in 1522, eight years after following her to Paris, that Anne would once again become an attendant of the French queen, who must have been eager to learn about French politics and fashion from someone who had so recently returned from that kingdom. Mary's royal honor required her to be attended by several ladies, and at least one of them, Anne Jerningham, who had been with her at the French court, continued to serve her in England; evidence from the year 1527 indicates, moreover, that the dowager French queen had in her household seven gentlewomen, two knights, one esquire and forty men, a number that did not include her domestic staff.[21]

Since there is indisputable evidence of Anne's presence at York Place in 1522, she may have first attracted the attention of Lord Henry on that festive occasion. Cavendish was positive, however, that the young people actually conducted their secret courtship during the opportunities offered when Percy, as Wolsey's page, accompanied his master to court. Although there is no extant evidence that either Anne or Lord Henry was at court in the spring of 1523, other events of that year, including his later betrothal to the daughter of Shrewsbury, seem to point to the blossoming of their romance at that time. A discussion of those events and a brief suvey of the political and diplomatic developments of 1523 will be instructive.[22]

In their November 1521 agreement with Charles V the English had promised him substantial military aid against the French. Wolsey had subsequently been reluctant to comply with this commitment, partly because in response to the renewed Anglo-Imperial friendship, Francis had ratified a suspended treaty with Scotland and had sent John Stuart, duke of Albany, to stir up trouble on the Anglo-Scottish border. Fearing a northern invasion similar to that of 1513 and concerned about finances, Wolsey had decided by late 1522 that instead of launching the promised full-scale attack against the French, he would dispatch Surrey on a raid to Brittany and then station him on the Scottish border to carry out forays in cooperation with the northern lords.[23]

In 1523 Wolsey was forced to seek funds from parliament to pay for these expeditions as well as to finance an invasion of France, for during the summer of that year the original treaty promises to Charles V were revived in order to support an opportune rebellion against Francis by Charles, duc de Bourbon, Constable of France.[24] Following customary procedures, Wolsey also called into session the two convocations of the Church. With these meetings in progress, the Cardinal was very busy, and he probably had to confer longer and more frequently with the king than was usual. There were many other pressing matters to discuss with Henry, including preparations for the state visit in June of Christian II, king of Denmark, and his consort, Ysabeau, sister to Charles V.[25]

Distracted by this business, Wolsey seems to have lost track of his page, who whiled away his leisure hours entertaining Anne Boleyn. That her sister Mary was the wife of his maternal first cousin would have been all the excuse Lord Henry needed to win an introduction to Anne, if the two had not previously met. Members of the aristocracy habitually had a firm knowledge of their kinsfolk and not only because they might need to find a willing patron or client. They looked for lucrative inheritances from their relatives, and they had to be aware of where their potential spouses fell on their respective family trees to ensure the legality of their marriages. The canon law strictly regulated which alliances were acceptable and required that dispensations be sought for those that were not.[26]

If Anne was an attendant of the former French queen in 1522 and 1523, she would have been lodged on Catherine's side of the court where Cavendish said that Lord Henry found her. Soon the clandestine meetings of the young couple seemed to have led to an exchange of *de futuro* marriage vows, which the Church considered binding only if they were followed by sexual intercourse. Over and above her other personal characteristics, Lord Henry must have been greatly impressed by Anne's fluency in French and her intimate knowledge of the European royal families, among them the Danish queen who was shortly to visit England and with whom Anne had resided at Malines in 1513–14. When

Wolsey discovered their secret love affair, he called his page before him in his palace at Westminster and scolded him in front of his servants. The Cardinal explained that Percy must not forget his position as the heir to one of the "worthiest earldoms of the realm" and that he must obtain permission from his father and the king before selecting his bride.[27]

Perhaps Wolsey's reference to the king caused Cavendish mistakenly to believe that the romance had been broken up as a result of Henry's jealousy. In 1516, in fact, Wolsey had already prevented, perhaps with royal blessings, the betrothal of Lord Henry and Lady Mary Talbot. Having pursued a policy of allying his children with the offspring of northern nobles, Shrewsbury had been completing the arrangements with Northumberland when Wolsey interfered to suggest that Lady Mary ought to marry instead the son of Buckingham, whose major concentration of estates was in Wales. As noble alliances could greatly affect the well-being of a local community and of the entire kingdom, the crown expected to be consulted about them. Power politics not royal jealousy was the issue involved in the considerations concerning Lord Henry's marriage in 1516 and in 1523.[28]

The distressed young nobleman responded to Wolsey that since he was of "good years" (almost twenty-one, in fact) he believed it was convenient for him to chose a wife whom he fancied. Defending Anne's lineage as "equivalent" to his, for she was a descendant of Ormond and Norfolk, he admitted that it would be difficult for him to retract his vows, since he had committed himself in front of witnesses. In short, his personal honor as a gentleman was at stake.[29]

After finally obtaining Percy's agreement to submit to his father's and the king's wishes, the Cardinal then wrote to Northumberland, requiring his immediate presence in London. On 5 June 1523, the earl grumbled in a letter to a friend that although he had just attended parliament at great expense to himself, he was now obliged to return to London.[30] He did not explain the reason for his recall, and it could have been about an entirely different matter, but during his return to London, he would have been informed about his heir's romance.

When he arrived at York Place, Northumberland reportedly did not spare his son further humiliation, also reprimanding him in front of Wolsey's servants. In a prophetic statement, perhaps entirely created by Cavendish who had the advantage of hindsight, the earl warned his son that royal "displeasure and indignation were sufficient to cast [him] and all [his] posterity into utter subversion and desolation." He then revealed that the king and the Cardinal had "devised an order to be taken" for him. In letters written that September by Surrey, who was stationed at Newcastle, the details of that "order" for Percy were made clear. He was to marry Shrewsbury's daughter, the very union that Wolsey had earlier found so undesirable. Shortly after these letters were written, Percy arrived in the north of England to lead the forays against the Scots.[31]

When she had chosen to become betrothed to Lord Henry, Anne had agreed to marry into an extremely important and wealthy noble family. Her prospective father-in-law, a patron of scholarship and music, had an establishment of 166 persons that was modeled on that of the king. After his son inherited this wealth as the sixth earl in 1527, his life can only be described as unfortunate and tragic. His unhappy marriage to Lady Mary Talbot remained childless and at his death in 1537 he bequeathed his estates to the crown, leaving her with a greatly reduced income. In his ten years as earl he had wasted his inheritance, spending lavishly on his friends and transferring his estates to private individuals.[32]

What Anne's reaction was to the loss of the future earl as her husband and what her relatives thought about the incident were left unrecorded. Cavendish later charged that as she believed it was Wolsey rather than the king who had broken up her romance, she waited patiently for the day she would be able to punish the Cardinal for his interference. Cavendish must have overstated the single-mindedness of her hostility, for surely Wolsey did not personally scold her. Not having as yet returned from his second mission to the emperor, her father, who was made a knight of the garter *in absentia* that spring, must have been as surprised as Wolsey to learn of the unauthorized pre-contract. Surrey, who in September proved to be so knowledgeable about the marriage plans of Lord Henry, probably found out about the private betrothal during a quick one-week trip to London at the end of June to confer about the Scottish problem.[33]

Assuming that Anne had returned to the dowager French queen's household, Mary's role in her sixteen-year-old attendant's betrothal must remain a mystery. There is intriguing evidence that the French queen did not always maintain a firm control over the actions of her servants, for in 1517 her attendant Anne Jerningham had privately arranged a betrothal between Anne Grey, one of her mistress's ladies, and John, heir to Sir Maurice Berkeley. That episode had forced Suffolk to send a letter of apology to Wolsey, protesting that he would rather have lost £1,000 than to have had this event take place in his household. Clearly in 1523 someone, either the former French queen or Lady Boleyn, had been remiss in providing the close supervision considered essential for young ladies with good marriage prospects.[34]

One lesson Anne must have learned from this courtship was that in contemplating marriage to a nobleman, satisfying personal and family needs was not enough. Community and royal interests also required consideration. For over seven years Shrewsbury had been trying to arrange a union between his daughter and Northumberland's heir as part of a deliberate scheme of building up a network of friendly relationships that would bind northern families together during crises such as an attack by a French-dominated Scotland. Surrey alluded to this community aspect of the Percy/Talbot marriage when he wrote about it in his September letters.[35] In other words the Talbot union would benefit the kingdom more than the Boleyn one.

After Anne's rustication because of the Percy liaison, the next dated reference to her at court is in May 1527. During those intervening years some momentous changes had occurred in her family as well as in the king's. In May 1524, her grandfather Norfolk, who had retired from all public life in the second half of 1523, died and in June was buried at Thetford, Norfolk. His eldest son Surrey, who had been Lord Treasurer of England since 1522, succeeded his father in the dukedom and in his estates, which were worth well over £4,000 a year. At the age of fifty her uncle had become head of the family and one of the wealthiest men in the kingdom.[36]

Less than a year after her grandfather Norfolk's death, the king lost Charles V as a potential son-in-law. Since 1521 England had been allied with the Holy Roman Emperor, to whose court Anne's father had been sent on two friendly assignments by 1523. Two years later, in 1525, Charles V's forces succeeded in defeating the French army at Pavia, capturing Francis and holding him for ransom. This triumph was achieved without any substantial assistance from the English whose full-scale invasion of France, which had been revived under the leadership of the duke of Suffolk in the summer of 1523, had proved to be unsuccessful. The conqueror of western Europe at the age of twenty-five, Charles decided it was time to marry and set up his nursery.[37]

When he made this decision, the emperor was betrothed to Henry VIII's nine-year-old daughter, Mary, who in 1521 had exchanged the French dauphin for Charles as her prospective bridegroom. Viewing Europe as though it were a "large estate map," the emperor decided that the best bride for him was to be found not in England but in Portugal – a valid judgment, for his union with wealthy Isabella of Portugal ultimately led to Habsburg control of that kingdom. Since Charles had already been engaged or half-engaged some ten times, that he should decide to break off his most recent betrothal was an all too familiar process. Characteristically, he made excessive demands to which Henry would not or could not agree, such as requiring that his betrothed be sent immediately to his court for her education. And the engagement with Mary was broken off.[38]

In a sense the emperor's decision was a great turning point in Henry's reign, for it embittered him toward the Habsburgs and their relative, his consort, who had not been able to conceive since 1518 when she had been delivered of a stillborn child. For the second time in little more than a decade Charles had refused to marry one of Henry's closest relatives. On 18 June 1525 at Bridewell Palace, the king had several individuals raised to the English peerage, including his illegitimate son, Henry Fitzroy, born in 1519 to Elizabeth Blount. In addition to his new titles, the dukedoms of Richmond and Somerset and the earldom of Nottingham, Fitzroy was appointed Lord High Admiral of England, Lieutenant North of the Trent, and Warden General of all the Marches toward Scotland. Among the others ennobled on that day were Sir Thomas Boleyn as viscount Rochford and the French queen's son, Lord Henry Brandon, as earl of Lincoln.[39]

Since the king immediately began to seek brides for Fitzroy among foreign noble and royal families, the reason for the boy's elevation was probably to bolster the monarchy with sympathetic relatives who would be committed to the continuation of the Tudor line. Perhaps a pleasing but secondary result of Fitzroy's elevation was the insult to Catherine's honor that she and her Habsburg nephew, the emperor, took it to be, but it was not meant to be a challenge to her daughter's position in the succession. Mary continued to be addressed as princess, the first female member of the royal family to hold that title in her own right, and was sent in 1525 to Wales, the customary home of the heir to the throne. Although Fitzroy's dukedoms were associated with the Tudors, they were not those normally bestowed upon members of the royal family who held a high position in the line of succession. As the second son, for example, Henry VIII's title had been that of duke of York. In fact, it was not until 1529 that Charles V became unduly alarmed about Fitzroy's honors. In that year when the duke became Lieutenant of Ireland, the emperor expressed the fear that the office might eventually enable Richmond to carve the island out of Mary's inheritance.[40]

Of more immediate interest to this study of Anne than the honors of the young boy, her future stepson, was the relationship that had probably developed between Henry and her sister. Circumstantial evidence supports the conclusion that for at least a short time Mary was the king's mistress. In 1527, after he had decided to marry Anne, Henry sought and obtained a papal dispensation that permitted him to wed the sister of someone with whom he had engaged in illicit intercourse. Later, Reginald Pole, who was in London between 1527 and 1529, made that charge in correspondence with Henry, and Sir George Throckmorton, an irate member of the Reformation Parliament, challenged the king's morals to his face, claiming that he had meddled both with Anne's mother and her sister. Somewhat startled and caught off guard, Henry responded, "never with the mother," leaving a quick-witted Thomas Cromwell to add, "nor never with the sister either." In 1532 Francis was surely aware of the rumors about Mary's morals when he met her in the company of her sister Anne during their visit to Calais with Henry, since four years later the

French king was quoted as saying that he had known Mary *per una grandissima ribalda et infame sopre tutte*.[41]

Although the beginning of Mary's liaison with Henry cannot be dated, it must have come to an end shortly after June 1525, when the ennoblement ceremony for his natural son and her father took place, for about that time she became pregnant. On 4 March 1526, she gave birth to a boy, named Henry who, rumors were to claim, was begotten by the king. That the son, raised to the peerage as Lord Hunsdon in the reign of Queen Elizabeth, apparently resembled his royal namesake lends support to these charges. There were, in fact, contemporary questions about his paternity. In 1535 John Hale, vicar of Isleworth said that a Bridgettine had shown him "young master Carey," saying he was the king's son. Finally, it may only be a coincidence but the first manors and estates, as opposed to minor keeperships and stewardships, that Mary's husband possessed, were granted to him by the crown in June 1524 and Feburary 1526.[42]

By 1526, the year of her son's birth, her brother, George Boleyn, born about 1503 and recently appointed to the royal privy chamber, had also married. The first extant reference to George occurs in a 1522 joint grant to him and his father of various offices at Tunbridge that had belonged to Buckingham. The wife of George was Jane Parker, a daughter of Henry, Lord Morley, and Alice St. John of Bledsoe, herself a maternal half-niece of Henry VIII's grandmother, the countess of Richmond. Whether or not the Howards were involved in the negotiations that led to this marriage and indeed, the previous ones that had resulted in the union of Mary Boleyn with a Beaufort connection, cannot be determined. Although Morley's mother Alice, who had been married to Sir Edward Howard, had died in 1518, the Boleyns' well-known association with the Howards might have been all the credit that was necessary to bring about both the Parker and the Carey alliances. If by drawing upon others in their network of friends and relatives, the Boleyns had been able to reinforce the opportunity the Howard patronage offered them to win Jane Parker for George, they were doubly victorious, for Morley's elder daughter, Margaret Parker, became the wife of Sir John Shelton the younger, a son of Sir Thomas Boleyn's sister Anne and her husband Sir John Shelton the elder.[43]

By 1526 the marriages of everyone in Anne's immediate family except hers had been finalized. These unions had resulted in new contacts at court for her father and a closer kinship with the royal family. All of these advantages had been won while Anne, who had been educated for a noble alliance, remained single despite futile efforts of herself and her family. On every side circumstances beyond their control had thwarted them. Although her kinsfolk and the king had approved of Ormond's heir as her spouse, it was probably Irish politics that had prevented that marriage. Shortly thereafter, her betrothed, Lord Henry Percy, who was not permitted to place private feelings above community needs, was forced to break his personal vows to her. The Percy episode provides evidence that in her search for a husband Anne was willing to ignore, as the French queen had earlier ignored, the accepted procedures for contracting an aristocratic marriage. The issue was not one of sexual improprieties but of improper actions that circumvented the normal channels for arranging a betrothal. By those standards, it was not Anne's choice that was at fault but the process by which he was chosen.

In selecting a spouse, she was far too independent to suit the tastes of her family. That she must have been acting without their knowledge in 1523 is indicated by the disappearance of her and not her Boleyn relatives from the official documents for more than three years. But when she reappeared in the records in 1527, the evidence makes it clear that she was once again marking an independent course in her drive to marry well for her family and her lineage. It was a course that would ultimately bring her to the throne and would bring great power and influence to her relatives.

3 ~ HENRY'S CHALLENGE

Shortly after he had succeeded to the throne in 1509, the king married Catherine of Aragon and shared the triumph of his coronation day with her, but within two years of these festivities, the royal couple's initial optimism about their ability to have surviving children had begun to wane. In February 1511, their second child and first son died when he was only a few weeks old. Several more deliveries, including two boys, were to follow before the queen gave birth to a surviving child, a girl in February 1516. At the birth of this daughter, the namesake of her paternal aunt, Mary, the French queen, Henry told the Venetian ambassador that he and his consort were both still young and that "if it was a daughter this time, by the grace of God the sons will follow."[1]

About two years later, in the summer of 1518, Henry left further evidence of how much he needed and desired a male heir. Straying from his usual practice of avoiding the chore of handwriting, he sent a letter in an excited but cautious vein to Wolsey, telling him of Catherine's just-confirmed pregnancy. The king anxiously awaited the outcome of this lying-in, an expectation that took on more than usual significance that year, if that was possible, since in October, as part of the universal peace negotiated by Wolsey, Henry agreed to betroth his two-year-old Mary to the dauphin. Without a male heir, this marriage of the princess, had it taken place, could have led to French annexation of England, a fear talked about and alluded to in the Venetian ambassador's remark that had Catherine's delivery of a stillborn girl in November 1518 occurred earlier, "the conclusion of the betrothal . . . might not have come to pass."[2]

Crucial to any treatment of the succession issue is the recognition that early modern Christians did not regard childbirth

48

purely from a natural or biological point of view. Most people believed that God interfered with nature to pass the sins of parents onto their children or to punish would-be parents by closing up women's wombs altogether. Christians of all stripes accepted this view of human generation, for even Martin Luther claimed that the birth of deformed children was a divine omen, a prediction of momentous political events. In a world that possessed only primitive ideas about science and medicine, God was thought to inflict disease and natural disasters upon individuals and society as punishments for their transgressions, although it was sometimes believed that he was usurped in this causal structure by Satan, whose clergy, the witches, were reputed to be able both to cure and to injure their patients and victims.[3]

Henry's assertion that "by the grace of God, the sons will follow," ought to be interpreted in a literal sense. The king did not invent the connection between divine favor and successful childbirth; it was a pervasive view among literal-minded Christians and non-Christians in his society, and without evidence to the contrary, it must be assumed that he seriously shared those beliefs. From early in his reign, he sought to appease God in part to ensure the birth of surviving sons and the future of his lineage. Although he spent many hours in the chase and in revelry, he was careful to allot an appropriate amount of time to God. On days when he was in the saddle from dawn to dusk, wearing out eight or ten horses, he heard mass three times, on other days five times. Every evening he joined his consort for vespers and compline; the two of them also went on pilgrimages.[4]

There is evidence that his close attention to religious matters was related to the succession crisis. In a letter to Pope Leo X of August 1519, for example, when Henry offered to go on a crusade he promised: "If our longed-for heir shall have been granted before the expedition sets out to do battle with the Infidel, we will lead our force in person." This offer, made again in December, may have fortified Wolsey's attempt to win Leo's approval for an extension of his authority as legate a latere, but it is also an example of how Henry associated the quality of his Christian leadership with the birth of a surviving male heir. A compelling anecdote about him, though apocryphal, is consistent with this view of his personality. It tells of a heavily built man in a penitent's smock who at dusk was making his way on his knees to a shrine, praying for the survival of his infant son.[5]

An acceptance of Henry's genuine religious belief, although it was often expressed in the rote and conventional method of the medieval Church, is essential to an understanding of the events that carried England into the Reformation.[6] The king's deep religious commitment and theological interests explain and underline his attitudes toward papal power and toward the Holy Roman Empire that can be discovered even in documents written out or corrected by his own hand.[7] His unremitting determination to free himself from his first wife, despite the lack of support he found in both Vienna and Rome, must be examined in association with his attitudes toward the Church and its teachings on marriage and childbirth. Only by viewing the king's passion for Anne against the backdrop of his deeply felt religious and social impulses can the story of his love for her be fully understood.

It surely was not a coincidence that in 1518, when Catherine became pregnant with what seems to have been her last conception, her husband began to write a response to Martin Luther's attack on indulgences that had appeared the previous year. By June he had finished the manuscript and was pleased enough with it to share it with Wolsey. Three years later, shortly after Catherine and he had gone on separate retreats during Lent to fulfill a vow, Henry began to respond to Luther's recent work, *De Captivitate Babylonica*.[8] The king seems to have "rescued" from "oblivion" his earlier manuscript and to have used it as the first two chapters to this new work, published that summer under the title of *Assertio Septem Sacramentorum*. Despite its defects, the book, according to J. J. Scarisbrick, "was one of the most successful pieces of Catholic polemics produced by the first generation of anti-Protestant writers." Skillfully written, it revealed that Henry's views verged on heresy, for he had a "semi- or crypto" Pelagian view of faith, placing an inordinate amount of emphasis on human merit in salvation. Two significant facts about his book in terms of the later attempts to divorce Catherine are these: it demonstrated "a telling use of the Old Testament" and it became a "best-seller," establishing the king, whatever were the opinions of the pope and his clergy, as a published expert on theology and the Roman primacy. In fact, it went through some twenty editions in the sixteenth century, and as early as 1522 had appeared in two different German translations.[9]

The motives behind the writing of the *Assertio* have not been fully established. Henry, himself, was to credit Wolsey with suggesting the project; perhaps the Cardinal had anticipated, and rightly as it turned out, that if the king were to write in defence of the papacy, Leo would be moved to bestow upon him the Christian title that Henry had been seeking for some time. In October 1521, the reluctant pope did please the king greatly by naming him Defender of the Faith.[10]

The book served to highlight Henry's support for the Universal Church at a time when he had been searching for the answer to the question of why God had not permitted his infant sons to live. The king surely viewed his winning of the papal title as yet another piece of evidence in the case he was building to prove in his own mind at least that God had not visited the royal nursery with dead male children as a punishment for his sins. A "crypto" Pelagian, he may also have been struggling to achieve a favored position with God in order to merit a divine blessing in the form of the birth of a surviving son.[11]

Although in 1521, when his book appeared and when he went on a retreat, Catherine and he were still hoping for a son, Henry must have begun to view a new treaty Wolsey negotiated that year, which arranged for the princess to marry the emperor rather than the dauphin, as offering an alternative method for settling the succession. Henry was personally acquainted with the regent of one of the many semi-autonomous states that made up the empire of Charles V. On at least two separate occasions he met with Margaret, ruler of the Netherlands, whose successful leadership must have persuaded him that a woman could perform well in a high governmental position under the general authority of the emperor.[12] In England there was no similar, viable precedent for a female ruler, a fact that Henry knew only too well, as his capable grandmother, the countess of Richmond, whose claim to the throne had made it possible for her son to become the first Tudor monarch, had lived to witness her grandson's coronation. Perhaps if Mary became the wife of Charles, she would be able to rule England under his authority with powers similar to those of a regent. This circumstance would not only serve to preserve a measure of control for her and semi-independence for England but would also be accompanied by the appealing possibility that her child would some day be elected emperor. It was an office to which Henry had unsuccessfully aspired in 1519 after the death of Maximilian, and as late as 1531 he was still thinking about that campaign and musing about what might have been.[13]

Despite the somewhat strained relationship between England and the Empire after 1521, partly because of Wolsey's inability to send substantial military aid to Charles, Henry was jubilant when he heard of the Imperial victory at Pavia and the capture of the Valois king in February 1525. Giving vent to the anti-French feelings that were "deeply embedded" in him, he immediately proposed the dismemberment of France. Setting aside the old duchy of Burgundy and some other areas for the Empire, Henry hoped to rule the rest of France as its king. He promised Charles that both France and England would be inherited at Henry's death by his daughter Mary, the emperor's betrothed, paving the way by their marriage for a renewal of the political unity of Christendom. In this statement Henry thus acknowledged that he no longer believed Catherine was capable of childbirth.[14]

The hopes of 1525 were completely dashed. Not only did Charles have no interest in dismembering France for the benefit of Henry but also the emperor no longer had any desire to wed the English princess. Soon he was betrothed to Isabella of Portugal, leaving Henry little option but to explore peace negotiations with the French.[15] In the meantime, the king ennobled his natural son as duke of Richmond and dispatched his daughter to Wales as its princess.

In August 1525 the Treaty of the More (the Hertfordshire home of Wolsey), establishing peaceful relations between England and France, was signed. Subsequent discussions centred on bolstering the treaty with a union between Mary and the recently widowed French king or his second son, the duke of Orléans. That Wolsey might actually succeed in arranging such a marriage began to seem likely after the release of Francis from the Imperial prison in January 1526 and, indeed, the betrothal was to be accomplished in the spring of 1527. Henry's feelings must have strained against making the future of his lineage so dependent upon the Valois House, particularly since the custom of that dynasty was to seek to annex its acquisitions rather than to permit a continuing semblance of autonomy. To prevent a similar absorption of England by Francis, who was to be either Mary's husband or her father-in-law, was a heavy burden for Henry to ask his ten-year-old daughter to bear.[16]

Although she resided in her own separate household, normally Mary was at court during the Christmas and Easter festivities, but in the winter and spring of 1525–6 she had been in residence in Wales. As her father planned his itinerary for the hunting season in 1526, he decided to have her visit with him for several days. Evidence of those plans survives primarily because of the anger he expressed when he learned that an outbreak of the plague was threatening to prevent the rendezvous. Determined to see Mary, he first changed his itinerary and then refused Wolsey's request that the court travel to manors more accessible to London. In early September, despite the plague, the princess did meet with her father for a few days, although whether her mother was also present cannot be established. According to the Venetian ambassador a few months later, the daughter Henry saw was "so thin, spare and small" that it would be impossible for her to be married for the next three years.[17]

Although speculative, the following account of how Henry arrived at his decision to obtain a divorce from Catherine seems reasonable considering what is known about his beliefs and those of his society. By late 1526 he had been recognizing publicly for over a year that Mary was his heir, thus conceding that Catherine and he would have no more children. He had also been struggling with the difficult question of what would happen to Mary and his lineage after his death, since the husband he had chosen for her was no longer available. Suspicious of French goals, he cannot have expected them to treat his child or his kingdom fairly, and he must have felt great concern about Mary's welfare when in September he saw how "thin, spare and small" she still was.[18]

Over the years and more seriously in 1525–6 he had repeatedly asked himself why God had prevented him from having a male heir. That one of the places he would search for the answer to this question was in the Old Testament should not be considered extraordinary since he had studied it carefully when he wrote the *Assertio*. By the time he returned to Greenwich in December 1526, after having visited with Mary the previous September, he had surely made up his mind to have his marriage invalidated and was considering which of several Old Testament verses were applicable, ultimately focusing on the warning in Leviticus 20:21 that a man should not take his brother's wife for they would be childless. This chronology seems likely since Wolsey would have needed time to prepare for the divorce hearings that could not be held until after the departure of the French ambassadors, who were scheduled to arrive in February 1527 to negotiate the marriage treaty between Mary and Francis or his son Orléans.[19]

That the divorce was Henry's own idea and that it was truly a matter of conscience would carry him through many a bad session but it also meant that he was prevented from putting forth his best case. Subsequently, the Cardinal, who, according to Cavendish, got down on his knees to beg the king to reconsider, could and did find better reasons than Henry's for ending his marriage, but his arguments (and those of other scholars) can all be characterized as legal technicalities that are by their nature subject to retroactive dispensation. In contrast, Henry's reasoning was quite straightforward: the pope could not dispense from Biblical law and more specifically from the Levitical commandment that a man must not marry his brother's widow. Henry held to this interpretation even though other scholarly opinion said that it was a decree against seducing the wife of a living brother and that for it to apply to his marriage he would have to prove that the union of Catherine to Arthur had been consummated.[20]

As the Defender of the Faith, as a published expert on theology, and as a believer in the indissolubility of marriage, Henry was unwilling to argue that God had permitted his sons to die because of a human error, a legal technicality. He wanted to solve his succession problem but not at the risk of losing his credibility as a supporter of the Church and of the sacrament of marriage. This confidence in his personal theological expertise was to continue even after England's schism from Rome. He later cross-examined heretics and made copious corrections of the ecclesiastical statements that defined England's faith.[21]

That his status as a published expert on religious matters was central to his self-identification cannot be doubted. In late 1526, as he was preparing for the arrival of the French ambassadors, it was announced that he had been reconciled to Francis for the sake of his faith. During the visit of those same French envoys to his court in March 1527, his *Assertio* was reportedly one of the topics that was discussed. Later that same month George, duke of Saxony, wrote to Henry that he had thought so well of this book that he had ordered a German translation of it to be published, a version that Luther had considered worthy enough to attack.[22]

Having decided that he would resolve both the problem of his conscience and of his succession by divorcing Catherine, Henry must have felt a sense of relief, perhaps even of euphoria, for he was at last in a position to act, to devise strategies with his clergy for establishing that his present marriage was invalid and the cause of the tragic death of his infant sons. There is no reason to believe that as he was coming to grips with this momentous decision he had as yet seriously considered the obvious next step in ending the crisis in the Tudor nursery: the selection of a new wife.

Maintaining secrecy about their plans, Henry and Wolsey met with the French envoys to arrange the marriage alliance between their two countries. During the course of several sessions in London and at Greenwich, the diplomats insisted, under instructions from Francis, on the inclusion of a disclaimer clause that would void some of the commitments in the treaty in the event that Mary or her children, as her parents were still young enough to have sons, did not succeed to the English throne. Later, both the king and the Cardinal were to provide a disingenuous interpretation of this demand, suggesting that by the mere questioning of Mary's status in the succession the Frenchmen had actually meant to challenge the legality of her parents' marriage.[23] This purposeful twisting of the envoys' remarks was nothing less than a cover-up, a conspiracy to conceal that on his own initiative the king had ordered an investigation into the legality of his union with Catherine.

Sir Thomas Boleyn was present at many of the meetings with these envoys, probably because he was a seasoned diplomat with a fluent command of their language and first-hand knowledge of their country. Sometime in the winter or early spring of 1527, he had at last succeeded in obtaining for Anne a position as maid of honor to the queen. It is possible that the more than £3 he paid for a bill of Anne in December 1526 was associated with her return to court. When she had been rusticated in 1523 because of the Percy affair, it is likely that the French queen, in whose charge she had formerly been placed, had also expelled her from her household, leaving the young lady as the only member of the Boleyn family without the right to regular lodgings at court. As Catherine normally was attended by only six maidens, these highly competitive positions were extremely difficult to secure, especially for someone who had disgraced herself in the eyes of the Cardinal as well as those of her family.[24]

The anticipated arrival of the French ambassadors in 1527 may have been the key to her father's success in obtaining this appointment for her. The envoys would have been interested in conversing with a noblewoman who had lived in their kingdom for about seven years and who was personally acquainted with Renée and other members of the French royalty. Evidence of Anne's presence during the entertainments at Greenwich for these diplomats has, in fact, survived only in a French manuscript, an indication that the ambassadors spoke with her and were impressed by her knowledge of their country and its language. In this manuscript it was noted that when Henry led them into the queen's chamber on 5 May to visit the princess, one of them, Francis, viscount Turènne, danced with Mary while the king danced with Anne Boleyn.[25]

This version of how she entered Henry's life in a serious way is partially corroborated by evidence from a work by William Forrest, a supporter of Catherine who was present in England during the divorce controversy. In 1558 he presented verses in manuscript to Queen Mary that were sympathetic to her mother Catherine. After explaining that Henry had first decided on a divorce and had then instructed Wolsey to obtain it, Forrest introduced a young, energetic Anne:

> At tyme of canvasinge this mateir so,
> In the Courte (newe entred) theare dyd frequent
> A fresche younge damoysell, that cowld trippe and go,
> To synge and to daunce passinge excellent,
> No tatches shee lacked of loves allurement;

She cowlde speake Frenche ornately and playne,
Famed in the Cowrte (by name) Anne Bullayne ...[26]

The encounter on 5 May was not, of course, Henry's first
introduction to Anne, but it may have been the first time that he
had ever danced with her. Having concluded to his satisfaction
that his union with Catherine was invalid, he surely had begun to
observe the ladies around him in a new light, that is, from the
perspective of an unmarried man. His singling out of Anne from
the other ladies on 5 May can be interpreted to mean he had been
looking forward with some enthusiasm to becoming better
acquainted with Catherine's newest attendant. That the envoys
showed an interest in her may have piqued the royal curiosity, for
despite his deep antipathy to their country as a European power
he greatly admired their fashions and language.[27] Although a
long, painful soul-searching period may accompany the making
of any decision so serious as entering or ending a marriage, love,
the kind of passion the king was to feel for Anne, often comes in
the flash of an instant. At the age of thirty-six he fell deeply in love
with a young lady some sixteen years his junior, perhaps while
dancing with her in his wife's chamber, and, as he was soon to
discover, his feelings were reciprocated.

Unfortunately, it is difficult to penetrate all the contemporary
and modern verbiage to find the historical person that Henry's
new love was. Most reporters have let their attitudes toward the
Reformation color their descriptions of her appearance and her
sexuality. Later Protestant writers regarding her as the mother of
Queen Elizabeth approved of her actions, but Catholic writers
who viewed her as the destroyer of the sacrament of marriage
disparaged her and her relationship with the king. The work of
modern scholars has further compounded the problem, for while
they have at the same time tried to accept and to reconcile both
the positive and the negative remarks about her, they have failed
to analyze them within a valid social framework. In histories that
treat men as three-dimensional and complex personalities, the
women shine forth in universal stereotypes: the shrew, the whore,
the tease, the shy virgin, or the blessed mother. Continuing to
view Anne in the same condemnatory manner in which she was
portrayed by hostile contemporaries, a few writers have more

than merely hinted that if she had acted properly, she would have turned her back on his love, and perhaps by doing so would have been instrumental in saving his marriage.[28] Thus the burden of moral guilt is neatly transferred from the king's shoulders to hers alone. By placing the events of 1527–36 within an appropriate historical context, as will be done in this and the remaining chapters of this book, it will be possible to refrain from imposing these moral judgments that have prevented a credible analysis of her role in court politics and to see that the actions and motivations of all three individuals, Anne, Henry, and Catherine, who were caught up in this lover's triangle, were rational and fell within the bounds of the social expectations of their culture.

The most complete extant description of Anne's appearance that has survived from her lifetime is in a hostile report of a Venetian ambassador, who described her when she was on a visit to Calais in 1532. Sympathetic to Catherine of Aragon, he said disparagingly about the king's Love: "Madame Anne is not one of the handsomest women in the world; she is of middling stature, swarthy complexion, long neck, wide mouth, bosom not much raised, and in fact has nothing but the English king's great appetite and her eyes, which are black and beautiful."[29] In contrast, Nicholas Sander, who probably never saw Anne, claimed in his Latin history, which was published almost fifty years after her death, that she was very tall and physically disfigured. An enemy of her daughter, Queen Elizabeth, Sander attempted to ridicule the English Reformation by clothing Anne with the outer appearance that he thought best reflected her inner nature, as he perceived it. Believing that by her enchanting and sensuous ways she had manipulated a king besotted with passion for her into destroying both his marriage and the English Church, Sander gave her the invented monstrous features of a witch. A contemporary literary convention that followed the Neo-Platonic tradition, which he adopted, was the signaling of the innate evil of villainous characters by giving them ugly, outward physical manifestations, for "the sins of the flesh were regarded as actual physical diseases, as poisonous growths."[30]

Some biographers have tried to reconcile the scurrilous remarks of Sander, the first writer to portray Anne publicly as deformed, with the earlier detailed, contemporary account of the

Venetian diplomat, thus incredibly giving equal evidential weight to both documents. One of these descriptions must be completely discarded, for the two cannot logically be reconciled to each other. Had there been even a hint of a deformity in Anne's appearance, the Venetian, as well as the Imperial ambassadors, some of whom knew her father quite well because of his diplomatic experience, would have eagerly revealed this intriguing fact to their respective governments. Like their contemporaries, these envoys believed that as part of the divine plan for humanity, God punished the sexual sins of parents by afflicting their children with deformities.[31]

Despite the claims of Sander and even of the Venetian ambassador whose somewhat negative description of her must be generally accepted as valid, some of Anne's contemporaries were rather more enthusiastic about her appearance. In 1528 another Italian, who may not have seen her personally, reported from Paris that she was "very beautiful." Offsetting this comment is the statement in 1532 of her father's chaplain who asserted that Anne was only *competement belle* and that Elizabeth Blount, the mother of Henry's natural son, was better looking. A summary of these views would indicate that Anne was attractive, but by contemporary standards not a classic beauty in the style of Mary, the former French queen. Anne's charm arose primarily from the deep-seated confidence with which she was able to handle herself in courtly surroundings. She was the perfect woman courtier, for she had learned her lessons in France well: her carriage was graceful and her French clothes were pleasing and stylish; she danced with ease, had a pleasant singing voice, played the lute and several other musical instruments well, and spoke French fluently. She is also reputed to have written a masque and to have composed music. A remarkable, intelligent, quick-witted, young noblewoman with a personal knowledge of many of the players in European politics, she surely had a repertoire of anecdotes about the Habsburg and Valois courts that first drew people into conversation with her and then amused and entertained them. In short, her energy and vitality made her the center of attention in any social gathering.[32]

While the king was delighted with her, she could not help but be captivated by him. Of several rather detailed and flattering reports of his appearance, the one dated early in 1529, about two years after the beginning of their love affair, is the basis for the following description. It was in a report also written by a Venetian ambassador, who said quite simply that in the king, who was then almost thirty-eight years old, nature had chosen to create "a perfect model of manly beauty." He was fair, tall (well over 6 feet in height), agile, graceful in his movements, and perfectly proportioned. Other accounts reveal that he was learned, very religious, a composer of music, a fine musician, a splendid jouster and huntsman, an elegant dancer, and a skilled tennis player; "the prettiest thing in the world to see him play," another Venetian diplomat had exuded enthusiastically in 1519. He was also reputed to know the French, Latin, and Spanish languages.[33]

On 6 May, the day after Henry had danced with Anne in his wife's presence, he held a grand feast and spectacle in honor of the envoys who were planning to depart for France. Two great chambers, the walls of which were decorated with rich and expensive tapestry, had been prepared. After a sumptuous banquet in the first hall, the royal guests went into the second chamber, the floor of which was covered with cloth of silk embroidered with golden lilies. It had been furnished with cloths of estate under which the king and queen sat and three tiers of seats for the spectators. To amuse their audience, performers sang, took part in combat, gave learned orations, and danced. Unfortunately, the accounts of these events name only two damsels of a group of eight: the princess and Gertrude, marchioness of Exeter. It is likely that either the remaining six girls or a second group of six dancing ladies, dressed in cloth of gold and cloth of silver, were the queen's maidens, among whom was their newest member, Anne Boleyn. When this part of the program was over, the king, the ambassadors, and the other noblemen having departed, reentered the hall in masks and black velvet slippers. As Henry had to wear a soft slipper on a foot which he had recently injured during a tennis match, he had persuaded the others to wear identical footwear to prevent his being distinguished from them. He thus revealed a genuine desire to dispense with social etiquette and to operate for a time as an equal among the courtiers. These gentlemen all then chose ladies as dancing partners before condescending to unmask and reveal their identities. After further entertainment, the revelers departed for the first chamber to drink wine and partake of a light supper. As it was daybreak before the festivities were ended, the weary ambassadors decided to rest two days before beginning their journey home.[34]

Less than two weeks later at York Place, Thomas Wolsey, William Warham, archbishop of Canterbury, Stephen Gardiner, the Cardinal's secretary, and other dignitaries, convened the first of four secret hearings, the last being held on 31 May, to inquire into the nature of the king's marriage. These sessions in which Henry was cited for having lived in an incestuous union with his wife for eighteen years, were halted before a verdict could be reached, perhaps because on 1 June news of the recent Sack of Rome had finally reached London. Christendom was shocked to learn that mutinous Imperial forces had raided the holy city and that Clement VII, who had fled from his capital, was imprisoned in his Castel Sant' Angelo. As a consequence, Wolsey, who was already scheduled to visit France for talks with its king, adopted a new strategy for obtaining the divorce. Once on the continent, he would assemble at Avignon a group of independent cardinals to take charge of the Church during the papal imprisonment. Planning to dominate this governing body, Wolsey would ask it to decide whether or not the royal marriage was valid.[35]

In the meantime, he had hoped to keep the news about Henry's intentions secret. On 22 June at Windsor, however, the king decided not to delay his confrontation with Catherine any longer, surely because he had learned that rumors about the York Place sessions had been leaked to her but also because he had begun seriously to consider marrying Anne. By the time he felt it was necessary to reveal his scruples personally to his consort, she must already have been informed about the issues involved, for before she understandably broke down in uncontrollable tears during this extremely painful conversation, she vowed that her marriage to Arthur had never been consummated. Surely she had sought legal assistance, probably from her confessor, John Fisher, bishop of Rochester, for she would have needed to be advised that the

Levitical verse did not apply to a *de praesenti* union, which was otherwise binding in law, unless it had been sealed by sexual intercourse.[36]

She may also have been concerned about Henry's increasing interest in her newest maid of honor. Caught up in the passion of the moment, lovers often assume that they have been so discreet in their attentions to each other that no one else will notice. On the contrary, it is likely that all of Henry's and Anne's associates, especially the members of the royal privy chambers, were aware of their mutual attraction. The Cardinal's friends at court must have informed him about the deepening nature of the affair before he had set sail for France on 22 July, for three days later, on 25 July, in a letter to Wolsey written at Beaulieu, a royal manor in Essex, Richard Sampson reported the following: "The great matter is in very good train; good countenance, much better than was in mine opinion; less suspicion or little; the merry visage is returned not less than was wont; The other party, as your grace knoweth, lacketh no wit, and so sheweth highly in this matter." Considering that the king was attempting to end his marriage, Sampson also commented on an event that seemed extraordinary. When on 23 July, Henry had been ready to leave Hunsdon in Hertfordshire for Beaulieu, although it had meant a lengthy delay in his departure, he had "tarried" for Catherine so that their households could ride forth together. What Sampson did not have to reveal to Wolsey was that as usual the queen's maids of honor accompanied her.[37]

After developing a passion for a young unmarried noble-woman, early modern monarchs customarily found her a husband either before or after taking her as an official royal mistress. Henry may have momentarily considered this solution to the problem of his love for Anne; the stickler was that he had never elevated any of his temporary loves to such a semi-permanent position and may have had personal, religious scruples that prevented him from establishing an illicit relationship on such an official basis. Deeply in love with Anne, he surely was also reluctant to consider having to marry her off to someone else, but had he made such an offer to her in 1527, she might well have accepted it, for a noble liaison that provided social and political advantages for her lineage had long been the goal of her and her family.[38] An arrangement that, given Anne's background, her personality, her maiden status, and her family's political and social goals, was not possible in 1527, was for her to become merely another of a series of temporary royal lovers. The Boleyns had earlier looked with complacency if not satisfaction upon a liaison of this nature for their daughter Mary, partly because she was already married and partly because her father had not yet been elevated to the peerage. In 1527 the honor of Anne and of her family demanded something more tangible from the king.

It may not have been until after he had departed for Windsor in early June that Henry began seriously to consider resolving both the problem of his succession and his love for Anne by marrying her when his divorce from Catherine was approved. The journey to England a month later of Jerome à Lasco, a Hungarian ambassador who had just been at the French court, may have had the effect of sealing that decision. On his way to Dover where he was scheduled to board a ship for France, Wolsey met with this envoy near Faversham. In his letter to Henry of 5 July, describing this encounter, the Cardinal repeated the ambassador's statements about the appearance of Francis's sister-in-law, Madame Renée, information that was of some interest to the king, since she was at the head of Wolsey's list of potential royal brides for him. Lasco had also been considering her as a wife for his monarch, but upon seeing her he had rejected her candidacy on the basis that the "liniacion" of her body was not suitable for the bearing of children. Both Renée and Claude had inherited from their mother, Anne, duchess of Brittany, a physical defect that caused them to limp slightly when they walked. Two French kings (Charles VIII and Louis XII) had chosen to marry Anne anyway, and Francis had made a similar decision about her heiress, Claude, because possession of the duchy of Brittany had been at stake.[39]

On 15 July Henry met with the Hungarian ambassador to hear from him in person what he had already learned from Wolsey's letter. Neither the king's nor England's honor, which Henry never thought of as separate concepts, would permit him to wed Renée. A perfect manly specimen himself, he wanted a son in his own image, one who would excel at sports not one who suffered from even a minor physical handicap. In 1530 the French ambassador made an indirect reference to this bias of Henry's in his report to the French government that the duke of Richmond was a fine boy for his age (then about eleven) and was beloved by his father on account of his "figure (*forma*), discretion and good manners." The Venetian ambassador later noted that Richmond greatly resembled his father in looks.[40] Finally, the king's honor surely would have prevented him from taking a lady as his bride whom the Hungarian envoy had judged unworthy of his monarch. Since his father, Henry VII, and his grandfather, Edward IV, had both wed Englishwomen and since he himself had developed a great passion for Anne, a descendant of Edward I, Norfolk and Ormond, the king concluded that she would be more than satisfactory as a consort. Together they would fill the royal nursery with perfect sons.

By 23 July when his court had reached Beaulieu, which ironically was a manor the Boleyns had sold to the king, his decision to marry Anne was virtually irrevocable. Seven days later Wolsey's correspondent pointedly revealed to him that contrary to his usual frugal summer habits, the king was keeping a great and expensive house at Beaulieu. He was playing host to an extraordinary number of nobles and their wives, including the dukes of Norfolk and Suffolk, the marquess of Exeter, the earls of Oxford, Essex, and Rutland, and the viscounts Fitzwalter and Rochford. Every evening the king supped with Norfolk, Suffolk, Exeter, and Rochford, the noblemen who were either his most trusted companions or Anne's closest relatives. It is noteworthy that although her father had been part of a large embassy that had traveled to France in late May, he had left that kingdom on 17 June, well in advance of his colleagues, perhaps needed by a family concerned about the king's increasing interest in his daughter. By the time Rochford arrived in England, Henry was surely already searching for ways to speed up the divorce process to make possible a more immediate marriage to Anne. The news of these schemes must have quickly spread out of the privy chamber, for by the middle of August even the Imperial envoy was aware that the king had chosen for his next bride Rochford's daughter, to whom he had recently presented an emerald ring.[41]

Given this chain of events that spring and summer, the assertion that Anne had a love affair with Thomas Wyatt, the great Tudor poet, sometime between May 1527, when he returned to England from a visit to Italy and August 1527, when it had become general knowledge that the king was planning to marry her, is somewhat incredible. Indeed, no record linking Anne's name to Wyatt's has survived prior to the date of his imprisonment in 1536 when five other men were executed for committing adultery and incest with her. Early in May 1536, Wyatt, along with Sir Richard Page, a gentleman of the privy chamber, was also incarcerated in the Tower but was released after only a few weeks of confinement. While Page retired from the privy chamber, Wyatt went on to serve the crown as a diplomat, to write his famous verses, and to be accused posthumously of having had a sexual liaison with Anne.[42]

The claims about Wyatt can be found both in nearly contemporary and modern sources, but for entirely different reasons. Believing that Anne was guilty of the charges for which she was executed and not realizing that Page, as well as Wyatt, was released from the Tower, two Catholic writers in the 1550s were only too ready to claim in manuscripts, which were not published until the nineteenth century, that the poet and Anne had been lovers. They resolved their sticky problem of how to account for the crown's release of the guilty Wyatt with the fantastic explanation that he had with amazing foresight confessed to Henry about the illicit relationship with Anne before the king took her as his consort! In Nicholas Sander's book, which was published in 1585, furthermore, she was not only clothed with deformities but also accused of having had sexual relations with Wyatt. Sander either copied from the earlier manuscripts or merely repeated the ubiquitous gossip about Anne and Wyatt that had arisen from the mere fact of the poet's arrest in 1536. These Catholic authors did not hesitate to credit the rumors because they were convinced that the queen had committed adultery and incest with the five men who were executed for those crimes, charges that modern scholars now discount entirely.[43]

Some recent scholars wanting to believe, as Hugh Richmond has suggested, that Anne must surely have been attracted to the greatest poet of the early Tudor period, have also speculated that she was Wyatt's lover although they have doubted that she was guilty of the crimes for which she was executed. To prove their case they have mined the State Papers, identifying Wyatt as an anonymous man whom Eustace Chapuys, the hostile Imperial envoy, associated with Anne. In a dispatch of May 1530 to the emperor, Chapuys reported the rumor that she had recently caused an unnamed gentleman, who had previously been dismissed from court because of a "criminal" connection with her, to be rusticated a second time. He also claimed that the king had interceded for the man's return.[44]

The courts of Europe were seedbeds of rumors, for observers regularly spread erroneous statements about the deaths of rulers and even of the pope, momentous events which were far easier to verify than the fact of whether Anne ever had a secret love affair. A good example of the ridiculous comments circulating about her and her family can be found in a letter of June 1530, written only one month after the above dispatch of Chapuys. In it the Imperial envoy at Rome, apologizing to Charles for forwarding the third version of a story he had heard about the marriage of Norfolk's son (the poet Surrey), said he fervently hoped that he had finally gotten the facts right. He had not: Surrey did not marry Anne Boleyn, as the envoy predicted, but the earl of Oxford's daughter. From 1527 through 1533, moreover, a favorite game of Christendom was speculating, usually in the affirmative, about whether Anne was carrying the king's child. Unless the information about her sexual experiences and political motivations, which abound in diplomatic dispatches, especially those of Chapuys who almost certainly did not speak English and who was devoted to Catherine, can be corroborated by other evidence, it must be accepted for what it surely was: self-interested, second-hand gossip rather than facts. In October 1529, in response to a complaint of Cardinal Lorenzo Campeggio about some gossip that was circulating about him, Henry VIII responded with the remarkably good advice that wise men will ignore ordinary rumors.[45]

Many of her contemporaries, especially the Imperial envoy, eagerly looked for evidence to prove that Anne had known several men sexually, for they wanted to believe that Henry was so besotted by his passion for her that he was willing to elevate a woman of questionable morals to the queenship. But the speculations that the king, who began the divorce process because of a matter of conscience and who needed a son to settle the succession, had so lost his self-control that he would marry a woman, who was by his standards either disfigured or despoiled, do not mesh with the known facts about him. In 1536 and in 1542 he signed the death warrants of Anne Boleyn and Katherine Howard respectively when presented with evidence convincing to him that these consorts, with whom he had been in love, had committed adultery. Zealously protective of his and England's honor, he was far less manipulated by his passion for his wives than the misguided rumors that can be found in the letters of court observers would suggest. Seeing him so devoted to Anne, it was difficult for many of his contemporaries to believe that the divorce action did have its origins in a matter of conscience; the vision of Anne at court got in the way of their understanding. For some historians, it still does.[46]

Any attempt to establish a close relationship between Wyatt and Anne must rely on a speculative reading of the evidence. It is possible that Wyatt neither wrote poetry in her honor nor harbored any special feeling for her, but the tradition, furthered by his grandson's testimony, is strong that he was one of her admirers. Certainly, by showering his favors on Anne that spring, the king made her one of the most popular and most sought-after ladies at court; it became fashionable for poets and musicians to pursue her, to feign their love for her within the conventions of the day. It is possible that Wyatt joined other courtiers, including her cousin Sir Francis Bryan and her brother George, in creating verses and songs to amuse her and other woman courtiers, but, even so, there is no reason to apply the scattered evidence of this courtly love in a selective way to create a close, personal relationship between Wyatt and Anne. It is doubtful that a gentleman like Wyatt, whose own livelihood and whose father's livelihood depended on royal largess, would ever have seriously considered himself a competitor of Henry for the love of any maiden. It is even more unlikely that the king of England would have recognized one of his subjects and a mere commoner at that as such a competitor no matter how splendid his poetry.[47]

Among Wyatt's extant verses, in fact, only one may be accepted as a piece that might have been composed with her in mind. If it was written in her honor, it must have been penned in

August when rumors were circulating that she was going to marry the king. In it the poet described his sorrow and pain:

> Who so list to hounte I know where is an hynde;
>> But as for me, helas, I may no more:
>> The vayne travaill hath weried me so sore,
>> I ame of theim that farthest cometh behinde;
> Yet may I by no meanes my weried mynde
>> Drawe from the Diere: but as she fleeth afore
>> Faynting I folowe; I leve of therefore,
>> Sithens in a nett I seke to hold the wynde.
> Who list her hount I put him owte of dowbte,
>> As well as I may spend his tyme in vain:
>> And graven with Diamondes in letters plain
> There is written her faier neck rounde abowte:
>> "Noli me tangere for Caesars I ame,
>> And wylde for to hold though I seme tame".[48]

Although Wyatt lamented that he was "of theim that farthest cometh behinde," from May 1527 no one except the king had ever truly been in the running.

Since in the late summer and early fall Henry usually spent only a few days at a series of different manors, that he remained at Beaulieu for over a month, from 23 July to 27 August, must be considered highly unusual. Here with a full court reminiscent of the high holidays, he concocted a plan that would permit the two lovers to cohabit immediately as husband and wife. It required sending William Knight, his secretary, on a mission early in September to Clement, who was still imprisoned in Castel Sant' Angelo, for the purpose of obtaining a bull that would permit the king to commit bigamy. The plan was to be kept a secret from Wolsey, who, although still in France, did succeed in discovering the nature of the secretary's errand. When the Cardinal had left England in July, he had assumed that Renée would remain the prime candidate as Henry's bride, but after Wolsey learned about this secret scheme he must have fully realized, if he had not known already, that a serious question existed about whom the king would marry, since neither Renée nor any other royal lady would have agreed to a bigamous alliance with the husband of a disapproving and hostile Catherine of Aragon. Henry's request to the pope was not quite so bizarre as it might immediately appear, for as he expected ultimately to be divorced from his consort through Wolsey's efforts, he wished only to begin his union with Anne before the completion of that slow, legal process.[49]

When he learned that Wolsey had discovered the details of the mission, the king discarded this first plan, thus relieving the imprisoned Clement of the unpleasant task of grappling with the bigamy issue at that time, although later in desperation he would himself propose this solution to the marital tangle. About three months after his secretary had reached the papal curia, Henry dispatched William Barlow to him with a request that Knight seek a concession from Clement that would make possible the king's marriage to Anne when he was divorced from Catherine. This communication was also kept secret from Wolsey, although he had been in England since late September and had been made aware of the intensity of Henry's passion for her. By the end of December, the pope, who had recently escaped to Orvieto, had reluctantly issued a bull permitting the king to marry the sister of someone with whom he had engaged in illicit intercourse and "even one with whom he himself had had intercourse already." Once Henry could reasonably expect the issuance of the divorce decree, he would be free to cohabit with Anne without worry that their illicit liaison would invalidate their subsequent marriage. This procedure was to be the one adopted in 1532, for begetting another illegitimate son was not one of his goals.[50]

When the court left Beaulieu on 27 August, it traveled to a number of places, finally arriving near the end of September at Richmond where Wolsey met with Henry personally for the first time since late May or early June. The only contemporary report of this session survives in a dispatch of Inigo de Mendoza, the Imperial ambassador, and reflects its author's hostility to Anne. According to him, she had assumed control of the royal appointments and had decided to prevent the Cardinal from having a private audience with the king. A reader with an understanding of court etiquette and procedure would immediately be alerted to the absurdity of this claim, for kings often used the hierarchical relationships at court to make social and political statements. A comment about Wolsey's attitude toward the divorce is necessary before his interview with the king can be judged by those proceedings.[51]

When he had decided to marry Anne, Henry had known that the Cardinal, who had originally disapproved of the divorce action, would be unhappy with his selection and might, if given the opportunity, once again fall on his knees to beg his monarch to change his mind. Indeed, after his initial negative reaction to Henry's plan for settling the succession, Wolsey seems to have been somewhat defensive about that subject in later communications with the king. In an attempt to rectify this mild misunderstanding, he had taken the time on 1 July, a few weeks before he sailed for France, to reassure Henry in writing that there was nothing his minister wanted more than to advance the divorce. Then in September, when he had discovered the nature of Knight's mission to the pope, the Cardinal must have realized that the rumors he had heard about Henry's love for Anne and the goings-on at Beaulieu were true. After his return home later that month, as he did not regularly reside at court, he had to make special arrangements to see the king, who otherwise might have been indisposed or out hunting upon the Cardinal's arrival at court.[52]

On 30 September, in his scheduled appointment with Wolsey, if the envoy's story has any basis in fact, Henry confirmed the rumors about Anne without having to offer an oral explanation or to suffer through another private and painful audience with his minister about the divorce. Instead of taking the Cardinal by the hand or arm and leading him to a window to talk, thus leaving Anne alone and free to depart, the king neither moved nor dismissed her. Unaccustomed as he was to this behavior, Wolsey must have hesitated at first, anticipating that Henry would draw him aside, but finally realizing that he was expected to report to them both about his efforts to obtain the divorce. He then discussed the failure of his scheme for convening the cardinals at Avignon and suggested that the best strategy would be that of requesting the pope to authorize his legate (Wolsey) to hold hearings in England on the validity of the king's marriage. By not conversing privately with his minister on these issues, Henry was able to accomplish two things: Wolsey had received confirmation that Anne was to be the king's next wife and was to be so treated; and she had learned at first hand the most up-to-date news about the progress of the divorce.[53]

The incident with Wolsey offers tangible evidence of the deep feelings the king had for Anne and his desire to reassure her that his ministers were doing all they could to make it possible for the two of them to be married. In the following years, he made similar efforts to keep her informed, asking his agents to address letters to her concerning their negotiations or to speak with her personally. In May 1528, for example, before he had talked with Edward Fox, his almoner, who had just returned from Orvieto, the king asked him to go to Anne's apartments to report on his mission's success. Later, when Henry reached the chamber, Anne departed at his signal to permit him to speak privately with his envoy.[54]

In the autumn of 1527, in the meantime, besides the divorce, Wolsey had many other domestic and diplomatic matters to settle, including the signing of some new agreements with the French ambassadors, who had recently arrived in England for that purpose. In their honor and to celebrate the proclamation of a perpetual peace with their kingdom, Henry held a grand banquet at Greenwich in early November, the same month that, incidentally, it was learned that Madame Renée was to marry the heir of the duke of Ferrara. It took about a month for the laborers to prepare the banquet hall for the festivities even though they were able to utilize some of the garments and props left over from the spring revels. At the end of the hall, which was dominated by a huge fountain, stood a hawthorne tree, displaying the arms of England and of the French chivalric Order of St. Michael, to which Henry had just been elected, and a mulberry tree, displaying the arms of France and of the English Order of the Garter, to which Francis had similarly been elected. The entertainment that followed the banquet included a play that lamented the imprisonment of the pope and showed St. Peter granting to Wolsey, as Cardinal, the authority to free Clement from captivity. Finally, the king, the ambassadors, and other gentlemen entered the hall in masks and danced with the ladies.[55]

During the winter of 1527–8, Henry remained at Greenwich to celebrate the Christmas and New Year holidays.[56] As this year ended, although she was still one of the queen's maidens, Anne could look back upon it with some satisfaction. She had won the king's love and respect, and he had sent for a papal dispensation that would make their marriage possible. At last it seemed that the noble alliance for which she and her family had been seeking was to become a reality. All that remained was for Wolsey to persuade Clement to issue a bull, authorizing his legate to hold a hearing in England to consider the validity of the king's union with Catherine. At this point in the process Henry, whose reputation as a learned man had surely helped him to persuade Anne, her relatives, and some of his ministers that his marriage was truly invalid, was optimistic, but the divorce proved to be beyond the powers of the Cardinal to obtain and would be the cause of his downfall.

4 PAPAL RESPONSE

In 1524 Clement VII extended Wolsey's appointment as legate *a latere* for life, thus making permanent the Cardinal's position as the pope's deputy for the whole English Church, a position which his automatic title of *legatus natus* did not create. As *legatus a latere*, however, he stood above all other ecclesiastical authority and, for instance, above his brother of Canterbury, normally regarded as the primate of all England. Greatly valuing his double papal agency, Wolsey always traveled in procession with two crosses borne before him in its honor and recognition. Furthermore, in 1521 at a special service at St. Paul's, as he dismounted from his mule in front of the cathedral, the canopy, to the amazement of the Venetian ambassador, was brought to him, "not as usual for a mere legate, but as if the Pope in person had arrived." These offices had become so central to his self-identification that in 1529 when he lost them because he had been unable to respond positively to the king's challenge for a divorce, Wolsey lamented to the duke of Norfolk that his "authority and dignity legatine is gone, wherein consisted all [his] honor."[1]

As legate *a latere*, he had wielded wide powers in England but, as he was to discover, he enjoyed much less influence at Rome. His requests there were treated with no more favor than those of many other churchmen, for Clement had agreed to Wolsey's appointment for political reasons rather than as a positive sign of confidence. At home the manner in which the legate customarily displayed his powers served to raise the expectations of many that he would be able to do the impossible, even to persuade the pope of the validity of the king's Levitical arguments.[2]

In February 1528, Wolsey, having assumed control of the divorce negotiations, sent Stephen Gardiner, his secretary, and

Edward Fox, the king's almoner, to Orvieto to obtain a decretal commission from Clement that would authorize hearings in England on the validity of the marriage and would ensure in advance papal approval of the legate's decision on that issue. In April, after many frustrating sessions with the pope, the two envoys believed that they had been able to secure the required authority. While Gardiner journeyed on to Rome to meet Cardinal Lorenzo Campeggio, Fox hurried to England, arriving at Greenwich on 3 May to inform a jubilant Henry and Anne personally of the details of the papal grant. Fox found Anne living in the gallery of the tiltyard away from the queen and her other maidens who had contracted smallpox; at least, that was their doctors' diagnosis, but it cannot have been a virulent form of the disease, for it caused the king far less concern than the sweating sickness that was shortly to descend upon his court.[3]

Soon the jubilation turned to disappointment as Wolsey was forced to conclude that the commission Fox had brought with him was inadequate. Gardiner was ordered back to Orvieto to resume the wearisome talks with Clement who finally conceded the proper commission and dispatched Campeggio as his legate *a latere* to assist Wolsey with the hearings. This news once again raised the king's expectations, but the long-drawn-out process that was to end in failure in the summer of 1529 had just begun. Campeggio's recurrent bouts with the gout made it necessary for him to take a painfully long time covering the distance between Rome and London. He did not reach Paris until 14 September and London until 9 October, where he remained in seclusion for several days too ill even to have an audience with the king.[4]

Far from displaying any overt hostility to Wolsey during the early months of 1528 while she was waiting for reports on the Fox/Gardiner mission, Anne sought to reassure him that she would consider him or anyone else who made it possible for her to marry the king as a friend. On 3 March, when the court was at Windsor, she required Thomas Heneage of the privy chamber to send a message to the Cardinal for her. In his letter, Heneage, who had just supped with Anne on a dish that Henry had sent down to her from his quarters, told Wolsey that she was concerned about the legate's apparent neglect of her and had expressed a desire for him to send as tokens of their friendship some presents of food, such as shrimp and carp. Heneage added: "I beseche your Grace pardon me that I ame so boulde to write unto your Grace herof, yt ys the conceyte and mynde of a wooman," but write thereof he did.[5] Wolsey responded to her plea, since on 16 March, Heneage forwarded to him another of her messages, expressing thanks for his writing and requesting favor for Sir Thomas Cheyney, a kinsman of hers in the privy chamber who had apparently displeased the legate.[6]

Her attempts to establish a working relationship with Wolsey continued, for on 6 June, when the court was at Greenwich, Heneage informed him that Anne, who had recovered from some unspecified illness, sent her commendations and said that she thought it had been a long time since they had spoken. It was probably later that month, once again to emphasize that she would be grateful for his help, that she personally wrote to Wolsey, confessing that she would never be able to compensate him for all his efforts except "alonely in loving [him], next unto the king's grace above all creatures living." Henry added a postscript to the letter, which he claimed Anne had repeatedly requested, expressing his concern at the great delay in Campeggio's arrival. This message was a reminder that both the king and his love were anxious to have the hearings begin.[7]

Shortly thereafter, an epidemic of the sweating sickness forced the lovers to undergo a separation. Although Henry interpreted the spread of the disease as a sign of divine displeasure, he was not a fatalist. As a "crypto" Pelagian, he believed that he could act to bring God's favor upon himself or at least to delay His vengeance. Whenever Henry learned of anyone becoming ill with the sweat, he would immediately isolate himself from that person and all his associates and commit himself to a rigorous, albeit conventional, religious routine, confessing regularly and hearing an increased number of masses at each of which he was careful to partake of the host.[8]

On 16 June, he had already been scheduled to leave Greenwich for Waltham, his estate in Essex some 12 miles distant, when he learned that Anne's attendant had the sweat. In great haste, he deserted his love with her infected servant and proceeded on his journey in the company of Catherine and the princess, whose household in Wales had recently been broken up. Under normal circumstances Anne would have joined them on this progress, as she was still officially one of the queen's maidens. For his beloved one of the most maddening of Henry's qualities must have been that the same deep religious conscience that compelled him to obtain a divorce, which would free him to marry her, also prevented him from dishonoring the marriage sacrament by separating from his consort before the legates had invalidated the union. Until the divorce was granted, or so the king was to maintain until the summer of 1531, it was his duty to treat Catherine publicly as though she were still his honored wife.[9]

That he loved Anne there is absolutely no doubt and that he exerted himself on occasion to reassure her of his affection there is also no question, for in 1528, beginning with this forced separation, he wrote to her at least seventeen love letters. That this number is still extant may indicate that there were others, a fact that in itself is an amazing piece of evidence, for he normally avoided writing with his own hand. The letters still stand as a tribute to how deep his passion for her ran. They are now preserved in the papal archives, probably because they were stolen from Anne's cabinet, either at Hever Castle or at her London lodgings, and were smuggled out of the country by someone opposed to the divorce.[10] Why they were seized, and when, cannot be determined, but the following speculation seems to make sense.

From May 1527 until June 1528, when she, as well as her attendant, was to fall prey to the sweating sickness, Anne and Henry had not been apart long enough for him to write to her; he must have penned those letters that are now at Rome sometime between June 1528 and the end of that year. They were sent to her at two different times: in June and July when she was absent from court because of the epidemic, and between early September and early December when she was in residence at her Kentish home, awaiting Campeggio's arrival. Surely, the documents were stolen all at once and not in two or more incidents, for one theft would have alerted her to the need to be more cautious in handling them. This theft was almost certainly a separate incident from their interception, which the French ambassador mentioned and to which Henry himself referred in one of the manuscripts now at Rome.[11] News culled from one or two of them and spread abroad would have provided the evidence of their existence to her enemies, who then could have schemed to obtain them either through bribery of her servants or through theft, probably the latter, for once they had acquired the documents the new possessors would have needed to maintain an absolute secrecy about their whereabouts.

The seizure of the letters may have been related to the arrival in England of Campeggio, who had been commissioned to begin the hearings on the validity of the royal marriage. Catherine and her friends would have felt a heightened need to undermine Henry's Levitical arguments and to raise doubts in the minds of the pope and Campeggio about the genuineness of the king's appeal to his conscience. Earlier that year in response to an inquiry of Clement's as to whether or not Anne was pregnant, Wolsey had already been forced to defend her morality and to deny that Henry's love for her was the real reason for the divorce. The Cardinal had sent word to Clement of her noble lineage and blood, her good education, and apparent ability to have children.[12] Catherine's best counterargument to these and other claims about Henry's motives and his beloved's modesty was to ask an ally to present to the pope a few of the king's love letters to Anne as proof that it was his lust for her that had initiated the divorce action or at least that had kept it alive.

Any explanation of how the purloined epistles reached Rome must also remain speculative, but it is interesting that when in the winter of 1528/9 Catherine sent her priest, Thomas Abel, to the emperor with a secret document, detailing six items, an explanation of one of them, No. 5, was omitted. Item No. 5 might very well have represented an oral message that had been entrusted to Abel or another courier and that referred to a special packet of letters. At any stage of the long divorce controversy, Catherine's cause could have been helped if these documents were presented to Clement, but especially in early 1529 when he was still vacillating on the issue of whether he would, despite having conceded the authority to his legates *a latere*, actually permit them to respond definitively in England about the royal marriage.[13]

The letters cannot be accurately dated, and no method of determining the order in which they were written now exists. An attempt will, nevertheless, be made to make some sense out of them. Six have a tone that allows them to be separated from the others and placed in a category that may be called royal supplication. The editors of the *Letters and Papers of Henry VIII* thought that these six must have been written in 1527 at the beginning of the romance. The problem with this suggestion is that in one of them the king said explicitly that he had been in love with Anne for over a year. Since there is no evidence that his passion for her predated 1527, that letter, and the others written in this suppliant tone, must have been composed in 1528.[14]

Instead of signaling the beginning of their relationship, when the king was at her side and aware of the depth of her affection, the letters represent evidence of a slight disagreement, a tiff between the two. It is likely that he wrote them between 16 June, when he left Greenwich for Waltham without her, and 20 June, the day he departed for Hunsdon.[15] That he felt it was necessary to write so frequently in such a short period of time, even though one of the messages was very brief, indicates not just a lover's frustration at being separated from his beloved but rather a gnawing fear that he was losing her affection. The result of the little tiff was a draw: neither side won the debate but each gained clearer insights into the other's personal weaknesses. In short, they discovered that the intensity of his fear of illness was equalled by her need for constant reassurance of his love.

Anne must have been greatly distressed when, on 16 June, he left Greenwich without her. This departure meant that she had to return to Hever, some 28 miles from Greenwich, with a sick attendant, while he traveled with his wife and daughter, who would, Anne must have feared, and they must have hoped, be able to take advantage of his love's absence to persuade him to change his mind about the divorce. Both Anne's fears and their hopes were unfounded. For Henry the divorce was, indeed, a matter of conscience and he would never be persuaded that his Levitical arguments did not apply to his marriage. He was also genuinely in love with Anne and was soon to prove it not only by the mere fact of writing to her but by what he brought himself to concede. An analysis of the first six letters will, therefore, be useful, as they are a key to understanding the nature of their love in 1528.

The suppliant letters, all of which were composed in French, played on the question of whether she was his mistress or his servant. He addressed her as his mistress in the first one, as though their relationship were not under a strain caused by the separation, but then inquired whether what he had been told was true, namely that she had vowed she would never again attend his court. He continued with caution: "and, if you love me with as much affection as I hope you do, I am sure, the distance of our two persons would be a little uneasy to you: though this does not belong so much to the mistress as the servant ... Written by the hand of your intire servant." In the second letter, he again called her his mistress and chastised her for not responding to his previous note. He also signed off as her servant, wishing her with him instead of her brother.[16]

When he penned the third letter, he was in "great agony," for he had received a response to his first message that had greatly upset him. Even though he had loved her for more than a year, he lamented, he remained uncertain of her true feelings and believed that he could no longer call her his mistress, since her love for him seemed to be no more than "ordinary affection." Now that his fear of losing her had become stronger than his fear of the sweating sickness, he went on to concede what was for him the ultimate personal sacrifice: "I beg you to give an entire answer to this my rude letter, that I may know on what and how far I may depend. But, if it does not please you to answer by writing; let me know some place, where I may have it by word of mouth, and I will go thither with all my heart."[17]

He was still unwilling to approach where the plague had been or to visit Hever, but he would see her in a neutral zone, even though there was a risk (and this was unsaid) that she might be a carrier of the infection. Their letters had begun to cross, for she had not yet responded to his conciliatory message when he wrote to her his fourth, brief note, in which he commented only that if she found it more agreeable to be his servant than his mistress, he was willing for her to hold that position. But his previous concession had served him well, for she did not demand the meeting but instead sent him a present: "a costly diamond, and a ship in which a solitary damsel was tossed about," obviously a representation of her lonely self. He thanked her graciously for the gift in his fifth letter, and in the sixth, completely reconciled, called her his mistress and his friend, sent her a picture of himself "set in bracelets," as he was unable to see her in person, and signed himself her servant and friend.[18]

The next group includes five of the remaining love letters, four of which have references to the members of the royal household who succumbed to the sweating sickness. The messages, some of which were in French, were written between 21 June, when he arrived at Hunsdon, and late July when he was at Ampthill, Bedfordshire. In the first of these five, he informed her that several members of his household, including her brother, who had fallen ill at Waltham, had all recovered from the sweat. Concerned about her health, he attempted to console her with the information that women seemed to be more immune from the disease than men. He also reaffirmed his love, for, as he vowed, wherever he was, he belonged to her.[19]

Shortly thereafter, she contracted the sweat, news which in his eighth letter, as counted here, he described as the "most afflicting" possible. It doubly upset him, he wrote, that he not only must now suffer her absence even longer but that he also could not send to her his favorite physician, who was away from court. Instead, he dispatched another doctor (William Butts, who had earlier treated her uncle Norfolk) and recommended that she follow his orders carefully so that she would soon be restored to health. On 23 June, upon learning with delight that she was past all danger, he forwarded to her copies of some documents he had just received from his French ambassador.[20]

The disease she had contracted, according to her step-grandmother, Agnes, dowager duchess of Norfolk, had a variety of symptoms. Some patients suffered from copious sweating while others sweated little while running a burning fever. Most patients also had problems with swooning and upset stomachs, for which she recommended "treacle and water imperial" and "setwell" respectively. The best remedies of all, she added in her letter to Wolsey, who was spared the sickness, were to fast for sixteen hours and to remain bedridden for twenty-four, since the ailment incapacitated its victims for only a short time, after which, for those that recovered, a quarantine period of about one week was suggested.[21]

During her convalescence Anne wrote a still extant letter to

Wolsey, who had inquired about her health. Thanking him for the rich present he had sent her, she thanked God that both the king and he had escaped the sweat. Once again she encouraged him to believe that she would be grateful for his help, promising to reward him for all his great pains on her behalf.[22] Another undated letter to him may also belong to this period. In it she promised he would have her undying gratitude when he brought the matter to a satisfactory conclusion.[23]

The next two love letters of Henry, which were composed in late June or early July referred to the death of Anne's brother-in-law William Carey and to matters concerning his elder sister Eleanor and his wife Mary. Until he contracted the sweat on 23 June, William had been seeking the position of abbess of St. Edith's Nunnery at Wilton for Eleanor, who was a member of that house. In April, shortly after the abbess had died, Wolsey had learned that most of the nuns favored their prioress, Isabella Jordan, as her successor but that an effort would be made on behalf of Eleanor. Naturally, William had turned for help to Anne, who appealed to Henry to obtain the appointment for her relative by marriage.[24] In what is here identified as his ninth extant love letter, Henry informed Anne that an inquiry into the morals of Eleanor had revealed that she was the mother of at least two children. He would not, he said, have it on their conscience for him to approve a woman of such dissolute habits as abbess. To mollify his love, he promised that some candidate other than Jordan, whose morals had been unjustly criticized, would be given that office.[25]

Although Henry then requested Wolsey by letter to find a third candidate, the legate chose to confirm Jordan tentatively as abbess, an action that on 14 July brought down the wrath of the king upon his minister. Henry was especially irate because Wolsey had responded to an inquiry about Jordan's election with the statement that he had not known of the king's wishes. For Henry this resort to ignorance only compounded the problem, since, and this was unsaid, even if he had never received the letter in which the royal requirements were stated, he should have made it a point to discover what his monarch's opinion was concerning a dispute in which he had taken a personal interest. As the legate was still a churchman on whom the king was accustomed to depend, he was able to end his letter of outrage by promising forgiveness to Wolsey if he would only make an abject submission. The Cardinal made the necessary apology, and if he had ever had any doubts about the depths of the king's love for Anne or the heights to which the royal anger could rise in the face of a direct violation of his orders, no question was left in Wolsey's mind after receiving that chastisement.[26]

Following William Carey's death on 23 June, the king granted to Anne the wardship of Henry Carey, her two-year-old nephew. In her messages, which are no longer extant, she had undoubtedly discussed this and other family matters with the king, for in his love letter, placed in tenth place here, he referred to the "extreame necessity" of William's widow and said he hoped "Eve shall not have the power to deceave Adam," but "whatsoever is said," her father owed it to his honor to aid his daughter. The gossip that the king mentioned was surely a reference to the reputation of Anne's sister as a woman of easy virtue, a reputation that Henry had helped to create. As was customary when a newly widowed woman was young enough to bear children, questions were raised as to whether she (Eve) would prove to be pregnant. Apparently, rumors were circulating that Mary was carrying a child whose father might not be her late husband (Adam), but as it turned out, she was either not pregnant or suffered a miscarriage. At the end of that year, the king extended to her an annuity of £100 that had belonged to William.[27]

Henry's final letter in this group (the eleventh) referred to Anne's scheduled return to court and his wish that her arrival might be hastened by at least two days. They were not reunited until sometime after 21 July, when she was accompanied by her mother rather than her father as expected, since he was still recovering from his bout with the sweat. By August, Rochford was well enough to seek from Wolsey the parsonage of Sonridge for William Barlow, his chaplain and the courier who had the previous December carried to Knight the king's request for a papal dispensation that would permit him to marry Anne. To underscore her willingness to see personally that individuals who assisted her in this cause would be rewarded, Anne also discussed this appointment with Wolsey. In the same letter she asked him to remember the parson of Honey Lane, who, because he had been convicted of reading heretical books, had been suspended from saying mass and preaching.[28]

Once she had returned to court in late July, Anne remained for only a few weeks, for she had departed by 8 September after learning that Campeggio was in France en route to Paris. She retreated to Hever Castle in the hope that when the legate arrived in England, he would be all the more willing to believe that the king's conscience and not his passion for her was the cause of the inquiry into the validity of his marriage. The remaining extant love letters were written to her during this second absence from court and will be briefly examined later.[29]

After Campeggio reached London, his actions indicated that he hoped to prevent a formal hearing on the royal marriage. As soon as he had recovered enough from the gout to speak individually to the king and queen, he attempted to find a political resolution to the dispute. When he had been convinced that it would be impossible to persuade Henry that the Levitical verse did not apply to his marriage and that, in fact, for him the issue was a genuine matter of conscience, Campeggio made a proposal to Catherine that, as a matter of conscience, she had to reject. He had hoped that he could talk her into retiring to a nunnery, since it was obvious that she had no chance of restoring a personal relationship with the king.[30]

From her point of view the concession Campeggio asked was unreasonable. Deeply religious, she was less interested in a restored spousal relationship than in the integrity of her honor and the future of her lineage. Had she agreed to his proposal, she would have been admitting, according to her standards at least, that she had lived in sin with Henry for over twenty years. She would also have been jeopardizing her daughter's inheritance, for Catherine feared, and correctly as it initially turned out, that the king would prefer the female offspring of his second marriage to the daughter of his first union. Catherine must also have been concerned about twelve-year-old Mary's legal status, since the English common law did not follow the canon law ruling that the children of an invalid marriage, if the parents had entered the union believing that it was valid, would be regarded as legitimate. Catherine would fight to her last breath to save her child from that disgrace.[31]

Only some of the English were with her in this dispute, for even Nicholas Harpsfield, one of her defenders, would later write that when people became aware of the king's intentions, they gave the divorce a mixed response: "Then was there nothing so common and frequent and so tossed in every man's mouth, in all talks and at all tables, in all taverns, alehouses, and barbers' shops, yea, and in pulpits too, as was this matter, some well liking and allowing the divorce, some others highly detesting the same." As Catherine had neither secured the succession nor disassociated herself from her Habsburg relatives, she had failed to win the confidence of her husband's subjects. Henry probably assumed that once Anne, as his queen, had given birth to the long-hoped-for male child, his countrymen would learn to love her as he did. In the meantime, those who opposed the divorce were usually more vociferous than those who did not; observers noted that the women, who feared that the sacrament of marriage was under attack, were especially distressed that the king would discard his first consort and for his "owne pleasure have another wife."[32]

During the three months or so between September and December when Anne was in residence at Hever Castle, Henry sent her at least six more letters. In them he kept her up to date on the journey of the legate, indicating Campeggio's arrival at Paris in September (the twelfth letter) and reporting to her at the beginning of October (thirteenth letter) that, as his court was on its way to Greenwich, he was at long last "comeing towards" her. It was in this letter that he also made the often quoted comment that he trusted shortly to kiss her "pritty duckys." That this is the only extremely intimate remark in the seventeen extant letters is as noteworthy as that he actually wrote it. In the fourteenth epistle he praised her reasonable behavior, for this separation had left her far less anxious than the first:

To informe you what joye it is to me to understand of your comformable-ness with reasone, and of the suppressing of your inutile and vain thoughts and fantasies with the bridle of reasone, I assure you all the good of this world could not counterpoise for my satisfaction the knowledge and certainty thereof: wherefore, good sweetheart, continue the same not only

·MARIA·REGINA·
·1520·   ·Anno Etatis·14·

1   Mary, archduchess of Austria, queen of Hungary, and regent of the
Netherlands, aged fifteen. Anne Boleyn had been in the schoolroom with
her and her sisters at Malines, 1513–14. Hans Maler. Society of
Antiquaries, London.

2 The first extant letter of Anne. It was written in 1514, when she was about seven years old, to her father from Veure, a palace and gardens outside Brussels. Corpus Christi College, Cambridge.

3   Claude, queen of France, surrounded by her daughters and daughters-in-law. From a miniature in Catherine de Medici's book of hours. Bibliothèque Nationale, Paris.

4   Francis I, king of France. Musée Condé, Chantilly.

5   Marguerite D'Angoulême, queen of Navarre. Musée Condé, Chantilly.

6   Renée of France, duchess of Ferrara. Anne Boleyn was in the French
royal nursery with her from 1514 to about 1520. Musée de Versailles.

7   Mary Tudor, dowager queen of France, with her second husband, Charles Brandon, duke of Suffolk. The marquis of Tavistock and the trustees of the Bedford Estates.

8 James Butler, earl of Ormond, formerly identified as Anne Boleyn's father, earl of Wiltshire and Ormonde. Hans Holbein the Younger. Royal Collection.

9 A choirbook that may have belonged to Anne Boleyn and in which, probably incorrectly, the figure of the person with a turban has been identified as Catherine of Aragon, queen of England, and the figure of the person with long hair as Anne Boleyn at her coronation. Royal College of Music, London, MS 1070, fos. 28–9.

10   Catherine of Aragon, queen of England. National Portrait Gallery.

11   Mary Tudor, daughter of Catherine of Aragon and Henry VIII. Hans
Eworth. National Portrait Gallery.

12   Henry VIII. Attributed to Joos van Cleve. Royal Collection.

13   Thomas, Cardinal Wolsey. National Portrait Gallery.

Labels on the image: Burly house, York house, Durham house, Ivy lane, Bedford house, Savoy, Somerset house, Whit Hall Stairs

14   Whitehall (Wolsey's York Place) in 1616. It includes a sketch of
Durham House where Anne Boleyn may have lived for a short time in
1528. Visscher's view of London, British Museum.

15   Henry Percy, sixth earl of Northumberland, who was a page of
Cardinal Wolsey in 1523 when he proposed to Anne Boleyn. Medallion in
the possession of the duke of Northumberland.

16   Sir Thomas Wyatt, the great poet admirer of Anne Boleyn. Hans
Holbein the Younger. Royal Collection.

in this, but in all your doings hereafter for thereby shall come, both to you and me, the greatest quietnesse that may be in this world.[33]

By the end of November 1528, Henry himself had become anxious about their separation and the refusal of Campeggio, the senior legate, to move more swiftly in scheduling the divorce hearings. Finally, the king visited a manor some 5 miles from Hever Castle to meet with his love and to make plans for her return to court. His last three brief love letters referred to her pending journey to London and to arrangements for her housing there. By 9 December, Anne had returned to London, although she no longer resided in the queen's household but lived in separate lodgings, perhaps at Durham House, which Wolsey had obtained for her. For the Christmas holidays she joined the court at Greenwich where she was provided with her own establishment apart from Catherine's. Thereafter, Henry and Anne would occasionally travel together on his progresses while the queen and her household would journey apart from them to the same destination. The king, his wife, and his lady would continue to live in this awkward arrangement until the summer of 1531, when Catherine was rusticated.[34]

At the beginning of 1529, three months after the legate's arrival, Henry appointed Sir Francis Bryan and Stephen Gardiner to head an embassy to Rome for the purpose of persuading the pope to speed up the divorce process. Following his usual habit, the king asked the diplomats to address letters to Anne, so that she might have personal reports of their progress. Although Bryan at first resisted writing because, as he said he had no good news to offer, the equally pessimistic Gardiner did send her a letter in March. On 4 April, she thanked him for his message and said that she hoped his difficult beginning would give way to a good ending. She also forwarded to him some cramp rings, which had been blessed by the king on Good Friday and which were thought to be protective against the cramp and fits. Later that same month, Bryan sent her a short note, saying only that Henry would make her privy to the news, for none of it was promising.[35]

In May, when an impatient king would wait no longer, Campeggio set the process in motion that led to the convening of the legatine court at Blackfriars. On 21 June, only a few days after it had opened, Catherine informed the court that she was appealing the case to the papal curia and refused any further participation in it. Finally, on 13 July, in response to her letters and the continuing Imperial pressure, Clement ordered Campeggio to halt the proceedings, but on 31 July, before he had received that news, the senior legate had already recessed the court in accordance with the Roman legal calendar. It was not to meet again.[36]

The king claimed that his wife had appealed to Rome because she trusted Imperial assistance more than the justice of her cause. Denying that he could obtain a fair hearing outside England, he accused Clement in September 1529 of indiscriminately relaxing divine law. Despite this setback, Henry, who believed that he was fighting for the future of his kingdom and his dynasty, remained persuaded that his arguments were valid. Earlier that year he had informed Clement that the divorce he sought ought to be granted to any good Christian, for the future of his lineage, peace in the kingdom, and the salvation of his own soul depended upon his obtaining it.[37]

When, after the adjournment of the legatine court, Henry began his summer progress, no plan of action was in place, for everything had depended on the results of this inquiry. Most of the royal anger must have been directed at Campeggio and Clement, but some of it also fell heavily upon Wolsey. Indeed, before he left England that year, Mendoza, the Imperial envoy, reported that the queen, who knew well the king's passion and frustration, believed that this minister would be the "victim" of his rage. In August, Henry and his advisers decided to have parliament meet in November, the first one to be convened since 1523, for the purpose of pressuring the pope on this issue.[38]

Hostile commentators then and now have interpreted Wolsey's fall as the culmination of a conspiracy that was rooted in Anne's deep hatred for him. Regarding her as the scheming other woman, they have charged that she effected the legate's ruin by manipulating a king besotted by his passion for her and by building a faction composed of Norfolk, Suffolk, and other allies. Both the Imperial and Venetian envoys, who favored Catherine's cause, and even the French diplomats, who were not yet friendly to Anne, wrote that she was the author of Wolsey's ruin. These claims are unreasonable for several reasons. First, these diplomats were all repeating the same rumors that circulated at court without any corroborative evidence. They assumed that if Anne could only be separated from Henry, who was "by nature kind and generously inclined," he would become once again a dutiful husband to Catherine. Having blamed the problem on Anne from this general, macrocosmic perspective, they proceeded to a specific microcosmic view, identifying her as the cause of every unpleasantness at court whether it had anything to do with the divorce or not. Second, this theory ascribes too much political power to Anne and ignores her major goal, which was to marry the king. Third, it gives to factions of this magnitude a greater stability than they had in the early 1530s and supposes a well-thought-out plan of action rather than the impulsive, self-interested reaction of individuals, who were otherwise political competitors but who were willing to cooperate to bring down a powerful minister when it became obvious he had lost the king's favor. One of this theory's obvious weaknesses is that it ignores Henry altogether, for this king "purposely" kept his court divided, not permitting any faction ever to gain this kind of dominance. George Wyatt later believed that "so great factions at home and abroad [were] set loose by the distorned favour of the king."[39]

Opposing the opinions of prejudiced observers about Anne's intentions toward Wolsey are her letters to the Cardinal, one composed as late as August 1528, in which she promised to reward him if he would help her marry Henry. Neither Anne nor any faction would have been able to remove him from his position of power had the legatine hearing ended with a decree ordering the king to separate from Catherine. More to the point, Anne would have had no reason to dislodge him, for she would have expected the chief royal minister, whoever he might be, to treat seriously her needs as the new queen. Although she sought favors for her friends and relatives, that search was secondary to her goal of furthering her lineage through the royal marriage. There is no evidence that at Wolsey's fall she won any of the spoils of victory. The king obtained York Place; Thomas More became Lord Chancellor; the two dukes assumed control of the council; and many others received rewards. The shrewdest court observer in

1530 was the Milanese envoy who in a disinterested way viewed the ubiquitous rumors that Wolsey's fall was the result of the "envy and fear of his rivals," as the "trivial opinion of the vulgar."[40]

One reason that many contemporaries blamed her for the legate's disgrace was that her relatives and other friends mendaciously informed the resident diplomats in England that she was responsible for his plight. The practice of deceiving each other about their true feelings was a well-used convention of royal ministers and ambassadors. An Imperial agent abroad was later to confess, for example, that he was amazed by the behavior of Thomas Cranmer, by then archbishop of Canterbury, because when he had served as envoy to the emperor's court he had greatly criticized the "matter of the divorce." Similarly, Sir John Russell of the privy chamber, who had a disagreement with Anne over the wardship of his stepdaughter but who also wished to ingratiate himself with Eustace Chapuys, the new Imperial ambassador, condemned her behavior. Russell alleged to Chapuys that her uncle Norfolk had confessed to him that she was angry because the duke had not used his "utmost influence" against Wolsey. Russell also reportedly recalled that when he had speculated positively to Norfolk about the chances for the Cardinal's return to power, the duke had growled that he would "eat him alive" first. To facilitate his negotiations with the envoys, Norfolk customarily told them whatever he thought they wanted to hear to the extent that he had actually persuaded Mendoza, before his departure from England in 1529, that he was secretly working against his niece. Suffolk must also have been hiding his true opinions, for at this time only the French envoy consistently associated him with Anne's interests. Both the Imperial and Venetian diplomats believed that he and his wife, the French queen, were personally repelled by the king's decision to marry Anne.[41]

When Henry withdrew his support from the Cardinal, the faction that opposed him materialized in reaction to that event and not before it happened. Noblemen such as Norfolk and Suffolk had for years been irritated and frustrated by the proud way in which Wolsey had flaunted his possessions and power: the processions with two crosses borne before him, the wealthy palaces, the expensive banquets, and the practice that probably galled them most of all, the assertion of his right as legate to take precedence over them in court rituals. Edward Hall and George Cavendish recorded two memorable events that seem contrived to reveal the hostility of the dukes toward Wolsey's position as an agent of the pope: Suffolk's declaration after Campeggio's recess of the legatine court in the summer of 1529, that "by the Masse, now I see that the olde sayd saw is true, that there was never Legate nor Cardynall, that dyd good in Eng-lande"; and Wolsey's painful meeting with Norfolk in which the duke insisted that the ex-legate taken an unmerited social prece-dence over him in a hand-washing ritual. This anecdote proves that Norfolk, like his king, was quite capable of manipulating social etiquette to humiliate Wolsey.[42]

As these two haughty dukes were suspicious of the motives of each other, they could not cooperate for long in any conspiracy. To Norfolk's disgust, Henry had rewarded Suffolk, the King's brother-in-law, with extensive estates in East Anglia, all but squeezing Norfolk out of the southern county of Suffolk and forcing him to focus his attentions on the northern county whose name he bore. By April 1532, the dukes' two households were on the verge of all-out war after Norfolk's servants had assaulted and killed one of Suffolk's retainers in Westminster sanctuary. According to the Venetian envoy, who claimed that the whole court was in an uproar, the affray was widely thought to be the result of a private quarrel, but he maliciously chose to speculate that "perhaps" it was the result of "opprobrious language" uttered against Anne by Suffolk's wife.[43]

In contrast to Cavendish's recollection of the confrontational anger of Norfolk toward the legate, the only incident this servant of Wolsey could cite to prove that Anne had been conspiring to effect his master's fall was her alleged attempt in September 1529 to prevent him from meeting with the king. According to Cavendish, she had so solidified her control of the royal household that she was able to reserve chambers at court for Campeggio, while neglecting Wolsey's needs, when the two legates arrived together for an audience with the king on 19 September. After preliminary meetings with Henry on that day, Cavendish further claimed, Wolsey had been forced, as Anne had planned, to retire to a private home for the evening. Upon his return to court the next morning, he allegedly discovered that Henry was too busy to see him because she had insisted on the king's going on a picnic with her that day.[44]

There are other accounts that do not bear out Cavendish's version of this last session between the king and the legates. Henry had, according to Stephen Gardiner, Wolsey's former secretary, been reluctant to permit the Cardinal an interview. On 12 September, Gardiner had informed him that the king was troubled by his request for a meeting and wished to know in writing the issues he planned to raise. In a dispatch he forwarded to the emperor that same month, Chapuys stated his belief that the king had agreed to Campeggio's and Wolsey's attendance at court only on the condition that they would arrive without pomp or ceremony and without their crosses preceding them.[45]

On 19 September, the two legates met with the king at Grafton, Northamptonshire. According to the account of Thomas Alvard, which can be found in a letter to Cromwell dated 23 September, Henry had upon Wolsey's arrival at court led him away from the others for a discussion before going to dinner. Afterwards, the king had called him into his privy chamber for a conversation that had lasted two hours. Both the legates were forced to retire to a private home (Sir Richard Empson's old house at Easton Neston which was 3 miles away) for the evening, because, as Chapuys, who had recently been at Grafton, revealed, accommodation was very limited, half the royal servants in ordinary having to be put up elsewhere. This envoy also believed that Suffolk was responsible for the failure to provide lodgings at court for the legates. On the morning of the 20th, according to Alvard, Wolsey had returned alone for another private session with the king and then had that afternoon accompanied Campeggio, who, before his departure for Rome, quite properly wished to take leave of the king. After the cardinals had paid their respects to Henry, he went hunting while Campeggio returned to the private home and Wolsey met with Suffolk, Rochford, and the other royal advisers then present at court.[46]

Alvard's account, which made no reference to Anne, must be taken more seriously than Cavendish's "partisan" memory. If she had scheduled a picnic for the morning of the 20th specifically to prevent Wolsey from seeing the king again privately, her strategy had failed miserably. Since Chapuys' account of his own recent visit to the court at Grafton seems to indicate that the king regularly "opene[d] the chase" with Anne, Henry probably had promised to go hunting with her that day as usual after he had completed his business with the legates. Even given this explanation, it is true that Wolsey and Campeggio had been "meanely received" at court, for they had been forced to make the journey without their usual pomp and had not been grandly entertained, as was the royal custom at the departure of eminent foreign agents such as Campeggio. Unlike Cavendish, the Imperial envoy, who usually faulted Anne for all unpleasant occurrences at court, did not blame her for the king's behavior at Grafton. In hindsight Wolsey himself may have become persuaded that she was responsible for his cool reception, for in October 1529 the French envoy, who had just visited with the legate, reported that she had made the king promise to give Wolsey no more hearings.[47]

On 17 October the dukes of Suffolk and Norfolk personally commanded Wolsey, as Lord Chancellor, to hand over the great seal. After he had surrendered it and had begun his trip to Esher, his home in Surrey where he had been ordered to remove, Henry Norris, of the privy chamber, brought him a ring from the king. Despite his joy at receiving this token, it was not a sign of his impending return to favor, for he was charged in the Court of King's Bench for violating the Statutes of *Praemunire* when he accepted the legatine commissions. He pleaded guilty to the charges in hopes of winning back royal favor, but the king only partially pardoned him, permitting him his freedom but confiscating his property and goods, including York Place, the archbishop's London home, which Henry visited with Anne and her mother on 24 October. Shortly thereafter, he sent a second ring to Wolsey and some furnishings for his empty Esher home; and when the legate fell ill at Christmas, Henry dispatched four physicians to him, along with a third ring and Anne's "tablet of gold hanging at her girdle." At Candlemas, after receiving more furnishings from the king, Wolsey was first permitted to move to Richmond and then required to travel to York to take up his duties as its archbishop. A few months later, when it was learned that he had been in contact with the agents of foreign governments, he was arrested and died on 29 November 1530, en route to London to be tried for treason.[48]

By sending these gifts to Wolsey, the king may have had two goals in mind other than the obvious and cruel one of raising his hopes only to dash them again. First, he may have meant them to be a signal that if Wolsey could even then find a way to have the royal marriage invalidated he would be restored to his offices. In the face of political disgrace, the hope of reinstatement might motivate Wolsey to find an answer to the marital crisis, if he had previously been preventing a favorable papal decision on the question, as the dukes and others had been claiming. Secondly, Henry may also have been expecting Clement to view the tokens as a sign that he could still save his disgraced legate from ruin if he would only relent enough to offer some way for the king to be released from his wedding vows.[49]

In the meantime all of Catherine's friends blamed Anne for Wolsey's plight. A statement in February 1530 of Chapuys is typical of the way in which the lady's every action was interpreted in the worst possible way. In a letter to the emperor, the ambassador confessed that a cousin of the Cardinal's physician had informed him that Anne had sent someone to visit Wolsey during his sickness in January 1530 to suggest that he might still be returned to favor. Finding this information almost impossible to credit, Chapuys wrote, "She must have thought he was dying, or shown her dissimulation and love of intrigue, of which she is an accomplished mistress."[50] Like Henry, Anne was willing to offer hope to Wolsey of a revival of his power if he would only assist her in becoming queen of England. Surely, her greatest anger was reserved for Campeggio and Clement.

Given her alleged extreme hostility to Wolsey, it is noteworthy that he made an effort to contact her through two of his secretaries, Thomas Cromwell and Richard Page. Cromwell reported that in response to the Cardinal's plea, Anne had spoken kind words but would not promise to speak to the king. Although she was certainly disappointed at Wolsey's failure to obtain the divorce, it is significant that she later had no difficulty in developing a working relationship with Cromwell, who, by all accounts, remained the most devoted of the Cardinal's servants.

In 1534, remembering her kind response to Wolsey's earlier pleas for assistance, Cromwell even advised Thomas Winter, the Cardinal's natural son, to seek aid from Anne as well as from Henry. It may also have been true, as Russell alleged to Chapuys, that in 1530 some individuals were afraid to speak to the king on behalf of the Cardinal for fear of her displeasure. Nevertheless, a few intrepid individuals, such as Gardiner and some visiting German dignitaries, did intervene on his behalf, but without success. As Catherine had earlier predicted, Henry's rage did fall heavily on Wolsey.[51]

If Anne had been so politically astute that she could organize and lead a faction with two quarrelsome and arrogant dukes, both of them military leaders, it follows that she must also have had enough power to win great favors for her family and friends. In that regard, it is true that even before the Cardinal's disgrace plans were underway to ennoble her father as earl of Ormond, for in February 1528 Sir Piers Butler had finally agreed to exchange this title for that of Ossory. On 8 December 1529, at York Place, viscount Rochford was elevated to two earldoms: Wiltshire (the honor formerly held by the brother of Buckingham) and Ormond. The next month, Wiltshire was made keeper of the privy seal and sent as envoy to the emperor and pope, who were meeting together at Bologna. One of the king's most experienced envoys, the new earl hoped to persuade Clement and Charles to support the divorce. After his predictable failure, since he was Anne's father, he journeyed to France for negotiations that kept him in that kingdom until August. From his advancement to the earldoms, his children took Rochford as their last name and used as their badge the black lion rampant, as previous offspring of the earls of Ormond had done. Until October 1532, when she became the lady marquess of Pembroke, Anne was styled Lady Anne Rochford and so signed her name. Her brother, who was addressed as Lord George Rochford, undertook his first diplomatic assignment, leaving for France in December 1529.[52]

Despite the rewards that came to her and her family as a result of her love affair, the evidence that between May 1527 and the end of 1530 Anne was in an unassailable position with the king that made it possible for her to obtain favors for her alleged political allies is extremely small. Outside her nuclear family, she seems to have sought assistance for only four individuals: William Barlow, for whom her father had already made a plea to Wolsey for a position, Eleanor Carey, whom she could not help, the parson of Honey Lane, London, who may have died before she could assist him and whose story will be briefly discussed in Chapter 5 as part of an examination of her religious beliefs, and Sir Thomas Cheyney, a kinsman of hers in the privy chamber. In March 1528, as noted earlier, Heneage had sent a message from Anne to Wolsey, asking him to restore Cheyney to favor. Three months later, in his attempt to obtain the wardship of the stepdaughter of Sir John Russell, Cheyney again sought her assistance. Russell, responding to his wife's desire to maintain control of her child, made his appeal to Wolsey, who by royal grant had the right to bestow the wardship. Neither of these two men won the long-drawn-out contest, for a compromise seems ultimately to have been effected; on 20 November 1529, shortly after the Cardinal's disgrace, the king granted the wardship to the dowager duchess of Norfolk, who had first written to Wolsey about the matter in late 1528. Later, Cheyney arranged to marry the elder sister of this young lady.[53] By his decision Henry indicated that he was quite capable of differentiating between Anne's requests for presents for herself and her immediate family and for politically sensitive rewards to her more distant kin.

These events form the background to the French diplomat's remark in January 1529, eleven months before the wardship dispute was settled, that Wolsey was in great difficulty because when a few days previously he had expelled Cheyney from court Anne had put her kinsman back in again, using very rude words of the legate. Whether Cheyney was actually rusticated is not known, but since Henry had characterized his attempts to obtain the wardship the previous July as rude and aggressive, if he was expelled it was more likely to have been at the king's command than Wolsey's. It is possible that Cheyney had simply left the court for personal reasons that had nothing to do with politics or the wardship dispute. In 1531, for example, rumors had spread that Norfolk had retreated home after an altercation with his niece, but, in fact, he seems to have planned the trip in order to take care of some pressing private concerns. What remains indisputable is that Anne's major goal early in 1529 was to encourage the legate to obtain the divorce so that she could marry Henry. It is unreasonable to believe that Cheyney's suit was so important to her that she would risk jeopardizing her relationship with Wolsey, who she still believed could get Henry's marriage invalidated, especially since after the Cardinal's ruin, she still did not have enough influence with the king to win the disputed wardship for her kinsman, even supposing that she was pushing the issue at that time.[54]

Following the legate's downfall, procedures to effect the divorce had no clear direction. In 1529, Thomas Cranmer, the future archbishop of Canterbury, suggested to Fox and Gardiner when he first became acquainted with them, some time between 2 and 10 August at Waltham, where the court was in residence, that an appeal to the universities of Christendom would be useful. As the king had a personal and well-known interest in scholarship, this suggestion must have immediately piqued his interest. Early the next year, Cranmer traveled to the continent and set in motion his plan for polling the opinion of theologians at the universities. Eight of these faculties, including Paris and Bologna, actually gave judgments in the king's favor, but no procedure had been developed to use these favorable verdicts in a constructive manner. At the end of 1530, Henry was still hoping that his success in marshaling the learned opinion of Christendom, both ancient and contemporary, in support of his Levitical arguments would have the effect of persuading the pope to invalidate his marriage.[55]

With these events as a backdrop, Anne's personal activities from late 1529 to the beginning of 1531 may be examined. Despite the king's determination to end his union with his consort, he still dined with her regularly. In early December 1529, Chapuys reported that someone had overheard an argument between Anne and Henry about this solicitude for Catherine. Apparently fearful that her lover would return to his wife, Anne was said to have worried aloud that her time and youth would all be spent for nothing. Although she naturally would have preferred that the king refuse ever again to see the queen, the comments as reported to Chapuys were surely apocryphal. At that exact moment Henry was planning to bestow upon her father two earldoms and the keepership of the privy seal. The day after the ennoblement, the king honored her and her family with a grand fete, at which according to this same envoy, Mary, the former French queen, and the dowager and young duchesses of Norfolk had been greatly offended because Anne had sat beside Henry. During the banquet itself, the arrangement of which followed a rigid hierarchical seating schedule, Anne cannot have been elevated above these noblewomen, for the disdain to their honor would have far exceeded any advantage to her own. It was surely during the later, more informal, entertainment that the king had sat next to her and had spent much time, as the ambassador interpreted, "dancing and carousing." Although the duchess and the French queen may have expressed hostility to Anne, there is no reason to believe that the dowager duchess was unhappy about the king's marital plans. At the divorce hearings, she was later to testify that Catherine's marriage to Arthur had been consummated.[56]

During the Christmas festivities in 1529, Henry and Catherine were once more together, presiding over a full court at Greenwich and, as observers noted, Anne did not make an appearance. As soon as the holidays were over, the queen departed for Richmond while the king remained at Greenwich with Anne, but by March he was once again with Catherine at Windsor in time to celebrate Easter and Whitsuntide. Perhaps in part to make up for the public attention to his consort, Henry had been presenting Anne with many gifts. His privy purse accounts, which have survived for the years 1529-32, indicate that he was spending large sums of money on her clothing and other "stuff." She received material worth £200 on 23 November 1529, and the sum of £100 on 31 December 1529. He was not the only one who wished to please her, for to show the increasing French support for the divorce that kingdom's ambassador gave her several pieces of jewelry and, in recognition of her expertise in the French language, Loys de Brun presented her with a treatise in French on the art of letter writing.[57]

Throughout 1530 Henry continued to purchase gifts for her, often for her amusement, as, for example, a shaft, bows, arrows, and a shooting glove in May. Archery was a sport she seems to have especially enjoyed, since additional bows were later obtained for her. She had also been receiving items to make her horseback riding more pleasureable. Among a huge inventory of such presents were elaborately decorated saddles in the French fashion, harnesses, reins, footstools, and pillions in black velvet. It may have been her use of one of these gifts that so shocked Chapuys, for he indignantly informed the emperor that she had ridden behind the king on a pillion, "a most unusual procedure," he sniffed. In this same letter he repeated the gossip, which modern scholars have erroneously related to Wyatt, that she had just expelled from court a man with whom she had previously had a "criminal" connection. If such an individual ever existed, he cannot now be identified; at best the rumor was an enlargement of the old Percy affair, for later the envoy was to refer to the earl's "intimacy and credit" with her.[58]

Throughout 1530 Chapuys continued to report rumors about Anne, which, as they cannot be corroborated, must be treated as untrue. In June he made a comment that indicates how severely he had lost touch with reality. He speculated that the queen might still regain her influence because he had heard that the king had asked her to make some shirts for him! Given Henry's angry reaction to Catherine's appeal of the divorce case to Rome, it is impossible to believe that he would beg his wife for this intimate and domestic favor or that even had he done so it could serve as a prelude to their reconciliation. Chapuys' charge that Anne was attempting to control all access to Catherine's apartments is just as ridiculous, for it is unreasonable to believe that the king, who had carefully indicated his public respect for the sacrament of marriage by refusing to separate permanently from his consort, would permit his lady, even if she had entertained such a desire, to interfere with the queen's household. If anyone was concerned about whom Catherine was seeing, it was her husband, who wanted to prevent her from sending any more letters to her friends abroad in the Imperial ambassadorial pouch.[59]

In November 1530, Chapuys witnessed an event which confirmed him in his opinion that all of the rumors about Anne's aggressiveness were true. The envoy reported to the emperor that during a royal audience, Chapuys had noted that she had stood at a window overlooking the gallery, listening to their discussion in which Henry repeatedly asked him about the divorce, questions that Chapuys had pointedly refused to answer. Later, the king moved him toward the middle of the room away from the window.[60]

Anne could only have known to be in that particular spot through prearrangement with Henry, who would have expected the envoy to notice her presence. By this little trick the king apparently intended not only to insult the emperor through his ambassador, but also Chapuys himself whom he knew to be a special friend of Catherine. Henry had only recently learned that the Imperial ambassador among others had been in secret communication with Wolsey who was even then on his way to London to be tried for treason. In 1532 the French ambassador, John du Bellay, bishop of Bayonne, later indicated a good understanding of the way in which Henry treated diplomats to express his feelings about them and their monarchs. In a letter to his king, the bishop first listed some hunting gifts, including a greyhound, that Anne had presented to him, and then explained that he had detailed these items because he viewed them as signs of Henry's friendship for Francis. This ambassador went on to reveal that "all that the Lady does is by the king's order." In 1529 both Bryan and Wiltshire were to interpret their treatment by a cardinal in Rome and the king of France, respectively, as signs of favor for their monarch.[61]

By the close of 1530, the records reveal that Anne had feted the French ambassadors, whose king was increasingly supportive of the divorce, and that she had received more expensive gifts from Henry, including some linen, other clothing, and rich furs. He was also providing her with spending money and with fine jewelry: rubies, diamonds, and emeralds mounted in necklaces, brooches, tiaras, and in decorations for her dresses. In November he even gave her £20 to redeem a jewel, perhaps a gambling debt, from her sister. There is no evidence to corroborate Chapuys' claim that at the beginning of 1531 both Anne and Henry were having restless nights, although the king dined publicly with her only once during that spring while he continued his habit of presiding with the queen over the full court during the religious holidays. These appearances of the royal couple moved the astonished Milanese ambassador to report that between the two "so much reciprocal courtesy [was] being displayed in public that anyone acquainted with the controversy cannot but consider their conduct more than human."[62]

By early 1531 to the satisfaction of the two dukes at least, Wolsey was no longer a political threat, but his death had moved Henry and Anne no closer to their wedding day than they had been three years earlier. Beyond sending empty threats to the pope, the king had been left with no strategy except for his attempts to marshal the learned opinion of Christendom on his side. Had he ever believed the charge that the Cardinal had stalled on the divorce issue, he had learned not only that this interpretation of Wolsey's actions had been inaccurate but also that no one else who had attempted to utilize traditional diplomatic channels to persuade the pope to invalidate the royal marriage had been as successful as the Cardinal. Deciding it was time to adopt a different approach, Henry was soon to authorize one of his new ministers, Thomas Cromwell, to implement procedures that would permit Anne at long last to have her turn as queen.

5 ~ ANNE'S TURN

In June 1531, the king left his consort behind and took Anne with him on his summer progress. As he moved from place to place hunting in his parks during the next few weeks, he finalized his plans for changing his domestic arrangements. Until that summer, when Catherine did not accompany him as usual, Henry had taken care to treat her on official occasions as his honored wife. This strategy, adopted largely to provide evidence that the divorce arose from a matter of conscience and not of lust, had long been a source of encouragement to Catherine and her friends who had clung to the futile hope that if only Anne would disappear from his life, Henry would once again become a dutiful husband. By August 1531, all pretense was over, for he had banished Catherine to the More, Wolsey's old home, never again to see her.[1] Her rustication was surely both a result of royal victories in the "*praemunire* manouevres" of the winter and late spring of 1531 and a response to papal letters forbidding the king to remarry.[2]

Throughout the six-year controversy, Anne's status at court represented on a personal level the major developments in the painstakingly long dispute with the pope. The first step occurred in 1528 when Campeggio's arrival had raised expectations of a favorable decree in the legatine hearings. Within three months of his arrival, Anne had been moved out of the queen's household into separate apartments of her own. The second step came in the summer of 1531, following the submissions of the convocations to the king as their supreme head in "so far as the law of Christ allows."[3] The third stage was to occur in 1532, when the death of William Warham, the aged archbishop of Canterbury, gave Henry the opportunity to seek a more amenable churchman as

Warham's replacement, thus ensuring in advance a favorable decision in the divorce hearing when and if it were to be held in England. At that time, in the physical sense, Anne seems to have become Henry's mistress.[4]

The recess of the legatine hearing by Campeggio in 1529 had forced Henry to look for new methods to resolve his marital dilemma, if only for the purpose of threatening the pope with their use. Later that summer, he had adopted Thomas Cranmer's suggestion to marshal the opinions of the universities of Christendom and had also delegated to him and other scholars, including Edward Fox, the task of discovering whether the provincial church could legally settle the marital crisis. Using a variety of ancient sources, many of them British and English, these researchers compiled a manuscript, called *Collectanea satis copiosa*, which established the principles that "secular *imperium*" and "spiritual supremacy" belonged to the king over a church which was to enjoy "provincial self-determination." Papal authority was thus identified as a late and illegal intrusion into the kingdom. These principles were to form the theoretical basis for the Statute of Appeals that in 1533 made it possible for the final decision in marital cases to be made in England.[5]

By the summer of 1530 Henry was studying the *Collectanea* closely. That he found its arguments somewhat compelling can be verified by his willingness to utilize some of its principles in the "*praemunire* manocuvres" of 1530–1. As seems clear from a note written by Cromwell in October 1530, the decision was made by then, apparently for the purpose of raising a tax, to charge the entire clergy of England with the illegal use of their spiritual jurisdiction rather than, as had been intended, to indict only a few of them with specific violations of *praemunire*. During subsequent "manouevres" in the southern convocation, convened in January 1531, it was determined to require as a part of their price for a royal pardon that they accept the king as their supreme head. Thus the crown's first official challenge to papal authority occurred in early 1531 when Cromwell appeared in the Canterbury convocation to pressure the clergy to pay £100,000 for a general pardon and to accept Henry as their "sole protector and supreme head."[6]

That these political machinations resulted in a lesser statement than was requested – "as far as the law of Christ allows" having been added by the clergy to the submission – may not have been interpreted by the king personally as the deep defeat modern scholars have supposed. Indeed, in May, Henry thought enough of the somewhat qualified phrase to have Cromwell require the northern province to make a similar concession. He had long held himself to be as great an expert (if not greater) on Christ's law as anyone in England. Long before he had met Cranmer, for example, he had been basing his case for a divorce on his own personal interpretation of Biblical commandments. From hindsight, and especially when they are compared to the strong assertions in the Appeals Statute, it has been customary to argue that the "*praemunire* manoeuvres" resulted in little if any royal achievement, but as John Guy has also pointed out, "Henry's offer to confirm ecclesiastical immunity in terms of his regal power and the statutes of the realm was fully demonstrative of the *Collectanea*'s intended purpose and the needs of the divorce crisis."[7]

The novel result of the "manoeuvres" may have been only a small beginning in the process that was to lead to the Act of Appeals, but the king seems to have regarded his victory as significant or, at least, to have wished it to appear in some quarters as though he did. In the spring of 1531, Chapuys was informed that Henry had not only ordered the release of a man who had been imprisoned for denying the papal supremacy but had also interrupted a preacher who had claimed that Constantine had refused to judge a dispute between two bishops. In June the king had *praemunire* charges levied against some of his consort's clerical supporters and in August she was rusticated. To the frustration of individuals like Cromwell, Christopher St. German, and others, Henry, who continued to seek a diplomatic victory, seems to have thought or hoped that he had challenged papal jurisdiction sufficiently to win his divorce. As late as 1532, in fact, he indicated a willingness to have the matter resolved in a neutral place, such as Venice. That the English clergy were forced to accept him as their supreme head in 1531 must, in fact, have been directly related to intensified papal pressure on behalf of Catherine, for, early in January 1531, Clement had raised the stakes in this game of nerves by warning that if the king did remarry, all of his issue would be illegitimate. Later that month, the king was forced to reply to a papal citation to appear at Rome about his divorce proceedings.[8]

Although Chapuys must not be viewed as an authority on the attitudes of the Boleyn family or of Henry and his ministers, the envoy did have good insights into Catherine's feelings. He personally believed that the clerical concessions were momentous and claimed that the queen called the crown's demands "monstrous." Like Cromwell, Anne's brother was also involved in these negotiations, but Chapuys' charge that she and her father were the principal promoters is obviously simplistic. That the decisions of the convocations gave her immediate "great joy," as the envoy also suggested, is problematic, for they brought her no closer to marrying Henry than she had been in 1527.[9]

The most significant step in 1531 from Anne's point of view, was, of course, Catherine's banishment, a move that surely gave her much satisfaction, and if it was the result of Cromwell's successful persuasion of the convocations to submit to the king as their supreme head, albeit with a disclaimer clause, then that event did give her "great joy." It is unreasonable to assume that the queen's rustication was the direct result, as some have claimed, of Anne's forceful and repeated scolding of Henry. First, this timing was all wrong. The period from December through May was when Anne would have most wanted Catherine to be absent from court, for the summer hunting season actually brought with it a respite of several months from high holidays when the king presided in state with his consort. The remainder of the year he spent his leisure moments with Anne, who had a separate household and who never came into contact with the queen or her personal servants. Secondly, the assumption that after four years the king finally caved in to his love's persistent complaints about Catherine's presence at court perpetuates the notion, expounded pointedly by Paul Friedmann in 1884 and reaffirmed by E. W. Ives in 1986, that as the dominant partner in their emotional relationship, Anne was able to egg on a long-suffering Henry to placate her by mistreating Catherine. This opinion of the royal courtship seems to carry with it another equally misguided view: that if Anne had suddenly died of the plague or some other disease, the king would have quietly recalled Catherine to court. But those who hold these assumptions cannot adequately answer the question of why Anne did not succeed in having the queen rusticated earlier, in 1529 or 1530, for example. A reasonable response is that it was only in 1531 that the clergy were forced to submit to the royal supremacy, almost surely as a reaction to increased papal pressure for Henry to take Catherine back. The king's insistence on this clerical concession did set a dangerous precedent, however, for he had, surely more easily than he had anticipated, obtained qualified clerical support for the very theory that would ultimately justify his obtaining the divorce in England; in the meantime, he seems to have been hoping for a diplomatic settlement.[10]

Henry's concerted but unsuccessful efforts to dissuade Clement from scheduling a hearing on the divorce in Rome, including a personal plea to him in December 1531, formed the backdrop to the next major move against the clergy. Early in 1532 Cromwell introduced into the Commons the "Supplication against the Ordinaries," a petition which harshly criticized the legislative independence of the Church. By May, after both convocations had agreed to surrender their legislative autonomy to the king, the councillors who had challenged this strategy found that they had been outmaneuvered. While Sir Thomas More resigned as Lord Chancellor, Gardiner, only recently promoted to the bishopric of Winchester, fell into momentary royal disfavor. Building on this victory over the clergy and on the political events of 1532 that left him increasingly in charge of the government, Cromwell was subsequently able to bring completely and unquestionably under the authority of statutory law the ancient and proud canon law, whose existence predated the common law.[11]

Anne's role in these public events was surely minor. Although there is no doubt that she was to develop a satisfactory working relationship with Cromwell, he was never her close ally in the sense that he has sometimes been described. The experience of having to restart his career after Wolsey's disgrace had taught Cromwell a valuable political lesson. After he became the king's man, he was well aware that to further his career he had thereafter only to please Henry directly. It suited him to support Anne as the king's wife because that was what Henry demanded and because he understood that it was the Cardinal's failure to effect this policy that had led to his downfall. Anne was to rely on Cromwell for assistance, as she had indicated in her letters to Wolsey she would have relied on him had he remained in power.[12]

Until 1533 when she became queen, there is in fact little evidence of cooperation between her and Cromwell. When he was on Wolsey's staff, she had asked him for a credence for a servant and later she may have had a conversation with him about the fate of the then disgraced Cardinal. Two different incidents of 1531 support the conclusion that she had not been his ally. Evidence for the first survives in a note written in August by Thomas Wharton. In an effort to gain Cromwell's support, Wharton forwarded to him copies of letters from both the king and Anne that favored his suit, which, according to Wharton, Cromwell had hitherto been doing his best to hinder. The second incident involved a competition in 1531 between Anne's uncles, Sir Edward and Sir James Boleyn, and Robert Hogan, the king's cook, for control of the wardship and marriage of the son of the deceased Roger Appleyard. Cromwell had been assisting Hogan in his suit for this grant.[13]

In 1532 the number of contacts between Anne and Cromwell increased, primarily because he was gaining the confidence of the king at the expense of the other councillors. Although early in that year Cromwell had written a reminder to himself on a copy of a message he had sent to Winchester to remember Anne's letters, the next extant evidence of his concern about her affairs does not occur until that autumn. A note of Stephen Vaughan to Cromwell in September may be a record of the earliest attempt of Anne to develop a working arrangement with Cromwell and his circle. Vaughan claimed that she had inquired of him whether he had brought anything for her from Thomas Alvard, another of Cromwell's close associates. Anne's request of him is reminiscent of the message asking for presents of food that Heneage had forwarded for her to Wolsey in 1528.[14]

In October, having accompanied the king and Anne on a state visit to Calais, Cromwell was the channel by which two individuals communicated with her. Christopher Hales, with whom Henry and Anne had stayed at Canterbury on their way to Calais, wrote to Cromwell asking him to deliver some letters to her from his brother. In response to Cromwell's official request of Sir Thomas Audley, the Lord Keeper of the Great Seal, to forward a patent to Anne at Calais, Audley asked his friend to request a favor of her. When she had been ennobled as the lady marquess of Pembroke on 1 September, the king had granted to her, among other property, two Essex manors. As possession of a copyhold belonging to one of them – Filolls Manor – was then under litigation in the Court of Chancery, it occurred to Audley to ask Cromwell whether Anne would appoint him the keeper of its park. That Cromwell was the steward responsible for overseeing the transfer to Anne of this and other property associated with her peerage is made clear by a warrant to him from the king about her creation that was dated 1 September and by references concerning the value of the estates in his "Remembrances," calendared early in 1533 by the editors of the State Papers. In a similar list of reminders, dated in late 1532, Cromwell also noted that he had sent a cupboard from the Tower of London to her.[15]

The only extant documentation before 1533 that might be viewed as evidence of Cromwell and Anne cooperating in an alliance survives in some letters of Richard Lyst, a lay brother of the Observant Friars of Greenwich, who communicated with them in late 1532 when it was widely known that they were both entrenched in royal favor. In his correspondence Lyst discussed an on-going dispute among the friars over the king's decision to divorce Catherine. Apparently, several of the queen's allies in the house were persecuting Lyst and those who supported the king's cause. In his letter to Cromwell, Lyst revealed that he had already written to the lady marquess, who, he supposed, had informed the king and his minister about his message. Lyst also asserted that he and his mother were both bound to Anne for her gifts. Although Lyst sent at least two other notes to her, only the one dated in February 1533, in which he complained about his treatment by the friars and asked for alms for his mother, is extant. After he entered Clare College, Cambridge, that spring, he continued to seek assistance from Cromwell and to ask him to contact Anne on his behalf, since apparently she did not respond to his pleas. In his last extant letter to Cromwell, dated March 1534, Lyst, still at Cambridge, referred only to the efforts the minister was making to help him financially. Ultimately, he became a priest and won the patronage of John Stokesley, bishop of London and a harsh enforcer of the heresy laws.[16]

That Anne was not a political ally of Cromwell's in the years 1531–3, and that she was not personally consulted about the legislative process that led to the English Reformation, emerges from a close reading of the evidence. First, her only experience of parliament prior to 1529 had occurred in 1523 when she was distracted by Lord Henry Percy's courtship. There is no reason to believe that down to 1533, when the statute that banned divorce appeals to Rome was passed, she had ever been attentive to parliamentary business. Why should she have? Henry himself does not seem to have been very knowledgeable about the potential of this institution until after Cromwell had joined his government. The king did learn quickly, for by 1532 Norfolk was spreading the word that the Commons had forced Henry to accept the Annates Bill.[17]

Secondly, there is no reason to believe that her support for schism predated that of Henry. Later Protestants have asserted that she was a promoter of their beliefs: John Foxe, the martyrologist, reported claims that she was a Lutheran and that she was the first individual to bring Simon Fish's anti-clerical book to the king's attention. John Louthe also stated in a document he sent to Foxe that she had given to Henry a copy of William Tyndale's anti-papal work entitled, *Obedience of a Christian Man*. Before turning to a discussion of her relationship to these reformers, it will be helpful to ascertain as precisely as possible just what her religious beliefs were.[18]

In March 1531, Chapuys had anticipated Foxe when he charged that Anne and her father, who he thought had been the "principal instruments" of a heretic's release from prison, were more "Lutheran than Luther himself." The diplomat also conceded that the king had a "natural inclination" for those who were critical of the pope. What Chapuys meant by Lutheran cannot now be determined, but was probably using the term to encompass a wide range of reformers, for often supporters of Erasmus were labeled Lutherans. There was at the time hardly any English subject who held all of the German reformer's views, for even Tyndale rejected his version of the sacrament of the Lord's Supper.[19]

As Cranmer was later to deny that he had ever accepted Luther's view of the Eucharist, it is reasonable to assume that Anne, who died before the archbishop was converted to an even more radical stance than the German reformer's, adhered to the doctrine of transubstantiation. During her imprisonment in 1536 when she was awaiting her trial for adultery and incest, Anne asked that the sacrament be placed "in the closet by hyr chamber that she myght pray for mercy." Catholics at this time believed that the sight of the sacrament or having it nearby was spiritually efficacious.[20]

The major issue separating Catholics, even some known as reformers, from heretics was the concept of justification by faith. When Erasmus was pressured into issuing a statement that differentiated his beliefs from those of Luther, he focused on this issue. In contrast to his explicit comments, the remarks of lay people concerning this doctrine are often impossible to interpret. The concept of justification by faith that included charity and obedience was a typical "medieval Catholic" formulation not easily distinguishable in lay accounts from references to Luther's justification by faith that was followed by obedience to God and the performance of good works. The medieval version seems to have been the one outlined in a volume presented to Anne in late 1532 when she was the lady marquess. In the introduction of the manuscript, which has the epistles and gospels for the fifty-two Sundays of the year in French and the expositions in English, the author, possibly Henry, Lord Morley, referred to good works as an essential part of the salvation process. Anne's prediction some four years later, in 1536, that she would go to heaven, for she had "done mony gud dedys," places her on the Catholic side of this controversy.[21]

There is also scattered evidence that she cherished many of the ceremonies of the medieval Church. In 1528 she forwarded to the English envoys at Rome some cramp rings; in June of that same year when Henry learned she had recovered from the sweat, he sent her a document, which he anticipated she would read with approval, that detailed how Francis I had defended the blessed images from their abusers; as queen she celebrated Maundy Thursday and had in her possession a traditional Catholic book of hours with a calendar containing the Franco-Flemish saints in addition to the English ones.[22]

Despite these conventional views, Anne believed that the scriptures ought to be read in the vernacular. Henry's attack on papal authority provided the opportunity for groups, which agreed on this issue but held views that were as diverse as those of Erasmians and other evangelicals, of Lollards and other anti-clerical protesters, of Lutherans, Swiss sacramentarians, and other heretics, to support him in his challenge to the Roman primacy.[23]

That Anne read the Bible in French there is no doubt. This habit can undoubtedly be traced back to her childhood, for during her stay at the court of Francis, she had surely been introduced to evangelicalism and must have become acquainted with the works of Lefèvre, one of its greatest leaders. When in 1530, Loys de Brun referred to her reading of the Epistles of St. Paul and other translations of the holy scriptures, he may have revealed that she possessed Lefèvre's commentary on St. Paul, first published in 1512. Earlier, in 1509, Lefèvre's *Fivefold Psalter* was printed. There is evidence that as queen she continued to ask travelers to bring her French religious books and manuscripts.[24]

It is not surprising to learn that she was interested in religious writings. In addition to her specific education, she was born into a culture just becoming accustomed to the advantages of having material available in print. For a long time religious works dominated those that were issued by William Caxton, Wynkyn de Worde, and other early English printers. Among the best sellers on the continent were works critical of the Church by Erasmus and Luther, but in England the authorized primers, psalters, books of hours, and saints' legends continued to pour forth from the press in great numbers. As noted, Anne owned in manuscript form a traditional book of hours.[25]

Besides her personal inclination and the impulse of her culture, there was another reason for her desire to read divine works. From her childhood she had studied how to achieve success for her family and lineage. While at Malines, she had promised her father, when offered an opportunity to go to Paris, that she would work very hard on her French. Later, as a childhood attendant of

Queen Claude, she had watched and imitated the maids of honor to learn how best to perform their tasks. When in 1527 the king had decided to marry her, he may at first have been attracted by her good looks, her musical and dancing abilities, and her charming, light-hearted conversation. These attributes may have served to win his love, but during the next six years, for him to insist tenaciously that he wanted to marry her, a deeper affection had to have grown out of that initial passion.[26]

Far from teasing him or flirting with other men, such as Wyatt, as she has been accused, Anne must have studied to please her intended bridegroom and to prove to him that she would be a suitable queen. An intelligent, quick-witted lady who was already interested in religious topics, she would have made every effort to become knowledgeable about new books and religious commentaries in order to discuss them with the king. After all, she had fallen in love with a man who believed himself to be and who was reputed to be a theological expert. According to her chaplain, William Latimer, as queen she "debated the scriptures" with the king when they took their "repaste abrode." To please Henry in 1532, she informed Nicholas Hawkins, archdeacon of Ely, who was going abroad on a diplomatic assignment, that the king was interested in obtaining works about the power of the papacy.[27]

Henry himself was not personally opposed to vernacular versions of the scriptures. In 1524 he had indicated that he did not deny the Bible ought to be read in all languages, but that he did not believe Luther's version was a proper one. In 1528 he invited to his court Erasmus, whose desire to have the Bible widely translated was well known, and in 1530 Henry quizzed his divines about whether the Bible should be printed in English.[28]

Although the king was willing to explore the possibility of translating the scriptures into English, he was reluctant to permit his subjects, even university scholars, to read heretical books. Because of her views about Biblical translations, Anne may have been sympathetic to petitioners who had been persecuted for possessing outlawed books. Before she became queen, she may have responded positively to three petitioners. The first support she offered was to Dr. Thomas Forman, the rector of All Saints, Honey Lane, who in April 1528 had been suspended from celebrating mass or preaching for owning Lutheran works, which he claimed he had read in order to know better how to combat the heresy. In August of that year she asked Wolsey to restore him to favor, but there is no way of knowing whether her plea had led to his restoration before he died about two months later.[29]

It is tempting to believe that she was able to assist Forman, for in 1530 or 1531 Thomas Alway petitioned her for aid on the basis that she had already done good deeds for other possessors of heretical volumes. Because Alway had owned the English testament and other outlawed works, he had at first been imprisoned but had since been prohibited from traveling into certain areas, such as the city of London. If she did respond to his plea, there is no extant record of it. In 1532, when she was lady marquess of Pembroke, Thomas Patmore, the parson of Hadham, Hertfordshire, petitioned her for release from the Lollards' Tower, where he had been confined for two years. Partly because of her personal appeal to Henry, Patmore was ultimately set free. There is good reason to believe that she intervened for these individuals with the king's full knowledge and approval, for in 1528 he sent a letter to Wolsey on behalf of the prior of Reading, who had, along with Forman, been arrested for possessing Lutheran books. It was a tradition for the queen (or in Anne's case the king's love) to intercede on behalf of his imprisoned subjects. In 1517 Catherine of Aragon, for example, had petitioned him on behalf of the May Day rioters. Anne's experience in France had also taught her that it was proper for royal ladies to protect reformers even when their religious views were more radical than their own.[30]

Besides reading the scriptures in French and attempting to aid individuals who were arrested for owning heretical works, Anne may have had in her possession books by Simon Fish and William Tyndale. The question of how she could have obtained them needs to be addressed. It is possible that the authors or their friends forwarded them to her, as is alleged for Fish's work, but it is also possible that she borrowed them from the king's collection. His privy purse accounts indicate that numerous volumes were obtained for him and the diplomatic dispatches prove that heretical books were forwarded to him for his information. Indeed, in 1530, the bishop of Norwich complained to Norfolk that many in his diocese believed that the king actually favored heretical works. It is noteworthy that at York Place, by 1532 at least, Anne would have had ample opportunity to search his library, for she and her mother were lodged directly below it.[31]

According to Foxe, Fish fled overseas after ridiculing Wolsey in a play at Gray's Inn. While in exile, he wrote *A Supplication for the Beggars*, which is an extremely biased anti-clerical work. In it Fish had the poor of England complain that they were dying of hunger because the clergy, characterized as "ravenous wolves," had seized control of one third of the kingdom's resources. He also accused the churchmen of seducing women in the confessional with the result that "no man shulde knowe his owne childe." Because Fish's charges were outrageous, it is possible that either he or a friend dared to send Anne his book only after the abrupt recess of the legatine court in 1529. Foxe did not claim that she had sought a copy of the *Supplication*, which may have been circulating in London as early as the spring of 1529, merely that someone had sent it to her. When she had read it, Foxe also asserted, her brother suggested that she give it to the king. She did present the *Supplication* to Henry who, because he enjoyed it, reportedly favored its author until his untimely death in 1531.[32]

Found among Foxe's papers, but not incorporated in his 1583 edition of the "Book of Martyrs," was a 1579 memorandum of John Louthe, recounting a story about Wolsey's discovery that Anne had owned Tyndale's *Obedience of a Christian Man*. Although copies of this outlawed book were available in England early in 1529, it is likely that Anne only became interested in it some time after the recess of the legatine hearing that summer. If Louthe's claim were correct that when she obtained the work she was lady marquess of Pembroke, then the incident he detailed would have had to have occurred between late 1532 and early 1533. He thoroughly confused any attempt to date the episode with his further assertion that the Cardinal's interference only served to hasten his downfall, which took place, of course, in October 1529.[33]

According to Louthe, after Anne had read the *Obedience*, she loaned it to her attendant, Anne Gainsford, whose suitor, George Zouch "plucked" it from his sweetheart's hands. When Richard Sampson, dean of the king's chapel, discovered that Zouch was reading the book, he confiscated it and informed Wolsey, who subsequently learned that it had originally been in Anne's possession. Before he could discuss the incident with the king she had petitioned Henry for the volume's return and had requested that he read it. Apparently, he thoroughly enjoyed it, exclaiming: "thys booke ys for me and all kynges to rede." By bringing the *Obedience* to his attention, so Louthe thought, Anne had encouraged Henry to "delyver his subjects owt of the Egyptione derkenes" and papal bondage.[34]

While Tyndale's *Obedience* justified challenging papal power and enhancing the authority of the secular ruler, it failed to presage a settlement similar to that confirmed in England by the Reformation Parliament in 1533–4. The book did not preach the unlimited spiritual obedience to the secular ruler that was to prevail in the kingdom, for Henry's supremacy was to be far more "stringent than anything the Lutheran princes had won and was looked at askance by the Reformers." The best interpretation of Louthe's anecdote is that Anne first obtained and then presented the work to the king when, because of the adjournment of the legatine hearing, they were both unfavorably disposed toward Rome. Chapuys was shortly to charge that Anne and Henry would rejoice if anti-papal books were printed in England.[35]

In the almost six years between 1527 when Henry began to court Anne and 1533 when she became queen, the extant evidence indicates that she interceded with the king and Wolsey for two heretics and that she shared with Henry two outlawed books. It was also known that she read French religious material. This information is sufficient to prove that she was interested in religious topics and that she understood well the king's reading tastes, but it is not enough to prove that she was working independently of him in a conspiracy to restructure the Church.[36]

With these activities as a backdrop, it is possible to turn to the events at court between 1531 and 1533. Besides Henry's separation from his consort, the year 1531 is noteworthy for his favorable treatment of Anne and her family. In the spring he had dined with her publicly and during that year gave her a farm at Greenwich, some costly jewelry, including diamonds and rubies, rich clothing, and money. In October, Chapuys grumbled to the emperor that she had been purchasing expensive dresses and that

Catherine had been forced to surrender the royal jewels to her. Both Anne's father and brother also received some land, minor offices, and other privileges.[37]

The envoy continued his practice of forwarding to the emperor rumors about Anne, whom he described as "fiercer than a lioness." He claimed that during 1531 she was the cause of two unpleasant events. In June the envoy wrote that Anne had so insulted Sir Henry Guildford that, over his monarch's protests, he had resigned his office of comptroller. But Chapuys also admitted that Guildford might have retired from public life because of ill health. The comptroller's departure from court, if he did depart, surely had nothing whatever to do with Anne. Guildford, who died in the spring of 1532, did not resign his position in 1531, as Chapuys asserted, but continued in that office until his death. The best speculation is that he voluntarily took a leave of absence in 1531 because of the illness that less than a year later took his life. Following his death the king granted Anne some parcels of plate that had been in the comptroller's possession. Six months after Chapuys had made the charge about Guildford, the envoy informed the emperor of the death of Sir Rees ap Griffith, who had been executed for his alleged intrigue with the Scots. According to Chapuys, Anne had refused to have him pardoned because he and his wife, Katherine, a half-sister of Norfolk, had spoken "disparagingly" about her. Considering that Katherine, as the second wife of Henry, Lord Daubeney, later claimed in a letter to Cromwell that Anne was her only source of comfort, Chapuys' insinuation appears farfetched.[38]

By the end of 1531 the public had become increasingly aware of Catherine's banishment. Late that year a Derbyshire man was imprisoned for disputing the rumor that the king would forsake his gracious queen and marry another. The chronicler, Edward Hall, also noted that there was no "myrthe" at the Christmas celebration because of the absence of Catherine and her ladies. He further revealed that Anne had gained so much favor in the king's eyes that many thought that she was the reason for the queen's rustication. Others, including Chapuys, might be unhappy that Anne, who he noted "commands absolutely," was lodging in Catherine's former apartments but the king and his love were enjoying the festivities. According to this envoy, Anne presented Henry with some richly decorated darts "worked in the Biscayan fashion," while he gave her rich hangings for a room and a bed covered with gold and silver cloth.[39]

From this Christmas to the late spring of 1533, when she was crowned queen, Anne was to experience one triumph after another. A major victory for her was the king's decision to invite her to accompany him to Calais in October 1532 for a meeting with Francis. The French envoys, reflecting the opinion of their monarch, who that year had signed a peace treaty with England, had for some time enjoyed friendly relations with Anne, attending, for example, two banquets that she had held in the autumn and winter of 1531. During the next spring and summer, John du Bellay, bishop of Bayonne, had several contacts with her, including deer hunting expeditions, in which the Calais visit was discussed.[40]

In July the bishop wrote that he had heard from an undisclosed source that Henry wanted Margaret, queen of Navarre (the sister of Francis) rather than Eleanor, queen of France (the sister of Charles V) to accompany Francis to Calais. As the envoy failed to disclose his source, it is possible that Anne, who seems to have had fond memories of Margaret, had made these remarks to him, but it is noteworthy that in the same dispatch he also said that all Anne did was at the king's order. There was no question of Francis taking his sister rather than his wife to Calais, for the prevailing court etiquette would not have permitted so marked a substitution without a better reason than the whim of the English king. What the queen of Navarre, whose husband attended the Calais meeting, thought about Henry's divorce was left unrecorded, although in June 1532 she sent a picture to Henry and during the spring of 1533 she was to have some friendly discussions at Paris with both Norfolk and Rochford. After Anne's coronation, Norfolk wrote to Henry that Margaret had expressed great affection for him and his new consort.[41]

The decision to elevate Anne into the peerage was related to the Calais meeting. For her to head an assembly of ladies on the state visit required her to be a titled lady and not just a nobleman's daughter. Had Henry's sister or even the duchess of Norfolk been available, they might have been placed in charge of the women, but Mary, the French queen, who was to die a few months later, was too ill for a Channel crossing and the duchess was estranged from her husband. In addition, Lady Norfolk was sympathetic to Catherine and, if Chapuys can be believed, so were Suffolk and his wife. Ennobling Anne at this time may also have suited the king because he wished ultimately to marry a titled lady, although he did not similarly favor his other English wives. The granting of the marquisate to Anne, which took place only a few days after the death of William Warham on 23 August, must have been planned before this aged archbishop's demise, for a lead time of more than these few days was required to finalize plans for a ceremony that was "carefully stage-managed" by the heralds.[42]

A few months prior to her ennoblement Henry gave Anne the manors of Coldkenynton and Hanworth in Middlesex. Then on Sunday, 1 September, in the presence chamber at Windsor, when she was created lady marquess of Pembroke, he granted her additional lands, many of them in Wales, which were worth over £1,000 a year. The ceremony in which he bestowed upon her the title to descend to her male heirs was an elaborate affair, witnessed by the French ambassador, the archbishop of York, the bishops of Winchester and London, dukes of Norfolk and Suffolk, her father, and seven other noblemen. Lady Mary, the young daughter of Norfolk, carried on her left arm the robe of state made of crimson velvet furred with ermine and in her right hand the coronet of gold. Anne, with her hair worn loose, clothed in crimson velvet and, according to the Venetian ambassador, "completely covered with the most costly jewels," walked between Eleanor, countess of Rutland, and Mary, countess of Sussex. While she kneeled before the king, the bishop of Winchester read the patent of creation. Henry then invested her with the coronet and the robe of estate and presented to her the charters of creation and of the lands, which had been carried by the heralds. Among the bills for the creation was one of almost £83 for "silks, etc." In honor of the day, Robert Whittington wrote some verses entitled, *In laudem Heroinae dominae Annae marchionissae Penbrochiae*.[43]

A few days before they departed for Calais, the new lady marquess gave a banquet for the king and the French ambassador. Then they traveled to Dover, stopping on the way at Stone,

Kent, the home of Lady Bridget Wingfield, at Shurland, Kent, the home of Sir Thomas Cheyney, and at the Canterbury residence of Christopher Hales, before sailing from Dover on the *Swallow* at five a.m. on 11 October. They had a speedy voyage, for they arrived at Calais at ten o'clock that same morning and were met by the Lord Mayor and the Lord Deputy. Subsequently, according to the Venetian envoy, the king accompanied Anne to mass and everywhere as though she were queen. On 21 October, he traveled alone to Boulogne to visit Francis, the two kings returning to Calais on 25 October, where Francis remained until 29 October. The monarchs shared the expenses of the festivities, which included bull-baiting, bear-baiting, wrestling, and dancing. For Anne, who was attended by thirty ladies, including Lady Mary, her sister, and Lady Rochford, her sister-in-law, the highlight of the trip occurred on Sunday, 27 October. When the two kings had finished eating together privately in a chamber at Staple Hall, Anne and seven ladies entered in "Maskyng apparel, of straunge fashion, made of clothe of golde" and chose dancing partners, Anne selecting Francis, who had earlier given her a diamond in honor of her visit. After Henry had removed the visors of the ladies to show their beauty, the dancing continued for some time. At its end, before Henry accompanied Francis to his lodging, Anne and the French monarch had a short conversation, perhaps reminiscing about her youth in his country. As further tokens of his friendship, Francis had Norfolk and Suffolk elected to the order of St. Michael and invited the duke of Richmond and the earl of Surrey (Norfolk's son) to reside at his court. After the departure of Francis, bad weather prevented Henry and Anne from recrossing the Channel for two weeks, until 13 November. They spent a few days at Dover, stopped again at Stone on 20 November, and reached Eltham on 24 November.[44]

Anne's ennoblement was not an outcome of Warham's death, but his demise coinciding, as it did, with increased pressure from Clement, who had scheduled the divorce hearing to be held in Rome in November of that year, does seem to have set the king and Anne free to consummate their love and to have enabled Cromwell to begin drafting the Appeals Statute. This act, prohibiting the appeal of testamentary, matrimony and divorce cases to Rome, made it possible for the marital dispute to be settled in England. Some historians have argued against this sequence of events and have maintained that, on the contrary, it was Anne's pregnancy that led to this legislation. It has been suggested that during the two weeks' interlude in rainy Calais a bored Henry with extra time on his hands at last overcame Anne's resistance to his advances. When the weather permitted them to sail home, they then took their time returning from Dover to Eltham, providing themselves with an idyllic autumn of romance. As a result of her subsequent pregnancy, Cromwell hastily drafted the Appeals Statute and Cranmer was recalled to England from his diplomatic assignment abroad.[45]

This timetable makes little sense for many reasons. From dispatches written on 27 September and 1 October, it is clear that within five weeks of Warham's death, the crown had finalized plans for Hawkins to replace Cranmer as resident Imperial ambassador. To have so quickly selected a replacement for Cranmer, the chosen successor of Warham, was to have acted with extraordinary speed. Interestingly, the following evidence indicates that the government was associating the archbishop's demise with the question of the papal primacy: (1) a letter of Henry to the University of Oxford, in which the death of Warham was mentioned, requesting a discussion on the powers of Rome; (2) a message to Cromwell asking for the return of a borrowed book about the privileges of the province of Canterbury; (3) Anne's reminder to Hawkins, as he was going abroad, that the king was looking for books on papal authority. When he decided to recall Cranmer, Henry must have agreed to the drawing up of an appeals bill, for, although he could still look forward to some fruitful negotiations with Francis at Calais that might break the impasse with the pope, he could not have been overly optimistic about this result. In September Clement ordered him to send a proxy to Rome with power to act on his behalf at the divorce hearing, which had been prorogued until November. After the Calais meeting, while Henry and Anne were visiting Dover, the pope threatened both of them with excommunication if they did not separate within one month and forbade Henry to obtain a local divorce. Care had, of course, already been taken to ensure that Cranmer would be in England if and when he were needed to convene a provincial hearing. If the king was to resort to this radical step, he required an archbishop who was not only sympathetic to his cause but also one whom the kingdom's laws would permit to act as the final authority in marital cases. Since Henry seems to have been in disagreement with some of his councillors about the wording of a statute that would limit appeals to Rome, a compelling reason existed for Cromwell to begin a first draft well before Cranmer began making his way home, especially as Henry was then being threatened with excommunication.[46]

Secondly, why should a fortnight of rain in Calais affect the king differently from a fortnight of rain during the English hunting season, when he would have been thrown back on his own resources and those of the gentlemen of his privy chamber for entertainment? In fact, not only were these gentlemen with him at Calais but so were his son, Richmond, the dukes of Norfolk and Suffolk, Cromwell, and numerous other ministers. The evidence indicates that Henry took advantage of this idle time in Calais to complete a variety of official tasks, such as the knighting of several gentlemen. Thirdly, the somewhat lengthy time he and Anne spent in Dover was caused by his wish to view the construction of its new harbor. He seems actually to have planned to inspect this site on the way to Calais but had decided to advance the departure date from Dover, leaving no opportunity for this business in October, as he had hoped.[47]

During the weeks after their return from Calais, Anne was often in Henry's company. In December he took the French envoy and her to visit the treasure room at the Tower, where, according to a somewhat envious Chapuys, the Frenchman was granted a fine gold cup. The king also gave Anne a cupboard from the Tower and many other precious gifts, including gold plate and fine black satin apparel. In addition to these presents, she won money from him at least five times that autumn in a card game called Pope Julius. Earlier in the year, Henry had paid over £12 for money she had lost in playing at bowls, the only extant evidence of her participation in a sport that he greatly enjoyed.[48]

Among her triumphs and rewards, Anne may have lost the company of a close friend, who had been in attendance on her for at least two years. In 1530 Chapuys had noted that Bridget, wife to Sir Nicholas Harvey, then on a diplomatic assignment to the emperor, had recently arrived at court with Anne. The widow of Sir Richard Wingfield, who had died while serving as envoy to Spain, Bridget was the heiress of Sir John Wiltshire of Stone, Kent, who had served as comptroller of the town and marches of Calais. Sometime between December 1529 and August 1532, when she still signed herself Anne Rochford, she wrote a letter to the lady, referring to the latter's removal from court and to her "trouble". Possibly the "trouble" was the death of Sir Nicholas in August 1532, although it may also have been a problem Lady Bridget had encountered in childbirth earlier that year. On their way to and from Calais, Henry and Anne had visited her at Stone, Kent.[49]

That this letter is the only one from Anne to a woman friend that has survived is somewhat ironic. For although in it she affirmed that "next mine own mother, I know no woman alive that I love better," Bridget, who died shortly after wedding her third husband, Robert Tyrwhitt, left a deathbed statement, either in 1533 or 1534, which was highly critical of her friend's morals. Although the details of that statement are no longer extant, it is possible to speculate that they referred to Anne's having conceived a child (Elizabeth) out of wedlock. Apparently, the subsequent royal wedding failed to diminish the outrage Bridget felt when she learned, perhaps during Anne's visit to Stone during 1532, of her pre-marital relations with the king.[50]

On 25 January 1533, well before the passage of the Appeals Statute permitting the divorce to be settled in England and even before the confirmation of Cranmer as archbishop of Canterbury, Henry and Anne, who was a few weeks pregnant, were wed. Cranmer could not be chosen to marry them, thus making him a party to the divorce case, since he would later be called upon in his official capacity to judge the validity of both the king's marriages. Rowland Lee, the future bishop of Coventry and Lichfield, was chosen to officiate at the service which was held in the west turret at York Place in the presence of Henry Norris and Thomas Heneage of the privy chamber and Anne Savage, later the wife of Thomas, sixth Lord Berkeley. The date and place of the wedding were kept so secret that it has led to speculation that it occurred in November 1532, and to a tradition that it took place at Blickling Hall, Norfolk.[51]

In February 1533, signals were given of Anne's new status and secret marriage. The Imperial ambassador noted that on 23 February, she held a banquet for the king in her grandly decorated apartments and that she sat to his right while the dowager duchess of Norfolk sat lower to his left. The next day the king invited Anne and the French envoy to dine and, according to Chapuys, she sat where the queen had formerly sat. There was much speculation about their marriage in his dispatches. He reported that the king never "talked so much or so openly" about it and he had heard that both Anne and her father were spreading the word that the wedding would soon take place.[52] It was also noted that her brother crossed the Channel in March to meet with the king of France, who had presented the nobleman with a beautiful and expensive litter as a gift for Anne. Undoubtedly Rochford had been dispatched to inform Francis officially of the marriage.[53]

Henry had delayed the announcement of the union until after the end of the spring session of the Reformation Parliament, which, before it was prorogued on 7 April, had approved the Appeals Statute. Five days after the prorogation, all speculation about the king's new marriage ended. On 12 April, the morning of Easter Eve, Anne accompanied him to high mass "with all the pomp of a queen, clad in cloth of gold and loaded with the richest jewels." The Venetian envoy, who also claimed that she had a son several months old, noted that the train of her gorgeous outfit was carried by Mary, daughter of Norfolk. A few days later this politic diplomat dined at court with the duke, the earl of Wiltshire, and some other noblemen, and then went into the presence chamber where he talked to the king and saluted Anne as queen. At Dunstable early in May, Cranmer, the new archbishop of Canterbury, held a formal inquiry into the marriage of Catherine and Henry and declared on the 23rd that it was invalid. Five days later he pronounced the union of Anne and the king fully lawful.[54]

From 1527 when Henry first became attracted to her, hostile observers had speculated about whether she was pregnant. In

February 1533, Chapuys forwarded a ridiculous anecdote about her to the emperor that a few historians have credited completely. According to his second-hand or third-hand news, she told a favorite, but anonymous, courtier, sometimes identified as Wyatt the poet, that when she had recently had a violent desire to eat apples, the king had predicted it was a sign she was with child. Chapuys claimed that members of the court, who overheard this remark, were astonished, as they surely would have been, if she had actually made this statement. It is noteworthy that there was an old apple-throwing custom in some parts of England, perhaps dating back to the Tudor period, that at Easter, people, who had been married that year, had to throw three times as many apples as everyone else into the churchyard. If Anne told an apple story, it was surely a hint about the wedding that Chapuys misunderstood, perhaps intentionally. It is unlikely that she would have referred to her pregnancy before the announcement of her marriage.[55]

In April after the public had been informed of the wedding, Chapuys succeeded in provoking Henry into hinting that Anne was with child. When the diplomat warned the king that even though he had remarried, he might not have any offspring, Henry retorted, "Am I not a man like others?" and then added, "I need not give proofs of the contrary, or let you into my secrets."[56]

Once they were married, especially as Anne was pregnant, it was necessary to demand that Catherine relinquish her title, for there could not simultaneously be two queens of England. Even before the Easter Eve procession, a commission headed by Norfolk had waited on Catherine to entreat her to agree to be addressed as the dowager princess of Wales. Naturally, she refused, for a concession of this nature would have carried with it the implication that she was accepting the king's claim that their marriage was invalid. Later, William, Lord Mountjoy, her chamberlain, made the same request of her, but until her death, she was to resist with angry words the substitute title. To honor Catherine the Imperial envoy refused to recognize Anne as queen, often referring to her in his correspondence as the concubine. This attitude of Chapuys became the official policy of the

Church in July when the pope formally condemned her alliance with Henry.[57]

By the time Clement had reacted to the marriage, Anne had already been crowned queen of England. The festivities honoring her elevation took place on five successive days from 29 May to 2 June. In preparation for her coronation, scheduled for 1 June at Westminster Abbey, the ancient center for these ceremonies, she went to stay, as was the royal custom, in the Tower of London, which had recently been remodeled in anticipation of her visit. Since her coronation took place in association with her entry, as the queen, into London, Sir Steven Pecock, its Lord Mayor, and other civic leaders were made responsible for many of the secular festivities.[58]

On Thursday, 29 May, the Haberdashers' Company, to which the Lord Mayor belonged, assembled fifty barges that had been decorated with festive flags, streamers, and banners for their trip down the Thames to Greenwich where they were to meet and to escort the queen's barge to the Tower. Leading the way, immediately in front of the Lord Mayor's barge, was a foist with a great red dragon, wildmen, and monsters that cast "wyldfyres" and made other terrible noises. To the right of the mayor was the bachelor's barge equipped with trumpets and other melodious instruments and to his lordship's left a foist with a mount on which stood Anne's device, a white crowned falcon, sitting upon a root of gold with red and white roses, around which were virgins singing and playing sweetly. When their barges reached Greenwich, the Londoners anchored and waited for the queen, who appeared at three o'clock, dressed in rich cloth of gold and attended by many ladies. In addition to her barge, those of several noblemen, including the duke of Suffolk, Henry, marquess of Dorset, and her father, also rowed up the Thames to the Tower. As they passed the ships lining the shore, "divers peales of gunnes" rang out in their honor. On her arrival at the Tower, accompanied by a "mervailous shotte ... as ever been harde" there, the Lord Chamberlain and officer of arms took her to the king, who greeted her with a kiss. Before she accompanied him inside, she turned graciously and thanked the citizens for their kindness. This grand spectacle moved

Edward Hall, the chronicler to note, "he that sawe it not would not beleve it."[59]

As the barge of the new queen had formerly belonged to Catherine, Chapuys took it upon himself to protest its confiscation first to Cromwell, who responded, surely mendaciously, that the king would be displeased, and then to Norfolk, who as usual consoled the diplomat by agreeing that Anne was the cause of all the unpleasantness at court. The duke claimed that the king had been grieved to learn that Catherine's arms had been removed from the barge and had severely reprimanded Anne's chamberlain for appropriating the vessel. On 29 May Chapuys noted that despite the king's reported sorrow the lady had "unscrupulously" used the great barge with its twenty-four oars for her journey to the Tower. It must have been one of the finest in England, for in 1528 Campeggio had borrowed it for his voyage to Bridewell Palace.[60]

The day after her arrival in London Anne rested while Henry dined with the eighteen noblemen and gentlemen chosen to become knights of the bath. Later that night they were shriven and bathed according to ancient custom. They were to be given places of honor during the formal entry of the queen into the city and during the coronation ceremony itself, and to be entrusted with official functions at the banquet that followed.[61]

In the meantime, the civic authorities were completing their arrangements for the queen's entry into London. Because of the necessary delay in announcing his marriage and because of Anne's advancing pregnancy, the king was able to give the Londoners only a few weeks' warning. This limited lead time may be one reason why her entry celebrations, were, according to Sydney Anglo, when compared to those for Catherine of Aragon in 1501, "disappointing in their lack of a complex theme and imagery, and in their diffuseness."[62]

In the short time available, the city fathers, in association with scholars and workmen on the royal payroll, still were able to create an impressive spectacle. They had the streets on which Anne was to ride railed on one side, graveled to prevent the horses from slipping, and grandly decorated with tapestry, carpets, arras of tissue, gold, and velvet. Although they had arranged many and varied entertainments, the Imperial envoy, the only representative of a major power in England not to participate, wrote disparagingly: "The coronation pageant was all that could be desired, and went off very well, as to the number of the spectators, which was very considerable, but all looked so sad and dismal that the ceremony seemed to be a funeral rather than a pageant."[63]

Anne's procession was led by twelve attendants of the French ambassador, who were decked out in blue and yellow. They were followed by various gentlemen and knights, the judges, the knights of the bath dressed in violet, doctors, abbots, noblemen and bishops, the Lord Chancellor, the archbishop of York, the Venetian ambassador, the archbishop of Canterbury, the French envoy, two squires representing the king's claims to the duchies of Normandy and Aquitaine, Garter king of arms, the Mayor of London, Lord William Howard, acting as Earl Marshal for Norfolk who was in France, and Suffolk, the day's Lord High Constable. The spectators watching from the windows along the procession's route must have been overwhelmed by the panorama of color, for the lords were all clothed in crimson velvet and the queen's servants in scarlet.[64]

Immediately in front of Anne rode her chancellor, who was bareheaded. Sixteen knights carried her in a litter of white cloth of gold with a canopy of cloth of gold embellished by four gilt staves and four silver bells. It was led by two palfreys in white damask. Anne was dressed in a surcoat of white cloth of tissue and a mantle of the same furred with ermine, with her hair hanging down under a coif with a circlet of rich stones. Behind her were her chamberlain and her master of horse, who were followed by seven ladies riding on horseback. Between these ladies and seven more ladies on horeseback were two chariots, one of which carried the old duchess of Norfolk and the old marchioness of Dorset. After them came two more chariots, which were followed by thirty gentlewomen on horeseback, all dressed in velvet and silk, and by the guard in gold-embroidered coats.[65]

The procession passed by several places replenished with pageants and entertainment, starting with Fenchurch Street, where Anne was welcomed by children disguised as merchants who gave French and English speeches. At the corner of Grace-church Street was presented one of the most elaborate pageants, which had been sponsored by the merchants of the Steelyard. Designed by Hans Holbein, it had a replica of Mount Parnassus with the fountain of Helicon in marble from which shot wine up into air in four streams that met "in a litle cuppe above" before descending. On the mountaintop under an arch decorated with an eagle sat Apollo with Calliope nearby and on the sides of the mountain sat the muses playing instruments. At their feet epigrams and verses were written in golden letters in praise of the queen.[66]

Nicholas Udall and John Leland wrote many of the verses for the coronation pageants. Here Udall had Clio sing:

Beflower the way, citizens; offer your thank-offerings; burn your incense. Wreath your brows with laurel, and with roses. Sport ye in this day's honour. Go to meet your lady mistress, poor man and rich man. Anna comes, bright image of chastity, she whom Henry has chosen to his partner. Worthy husband, worthy wife! May heaven bless these nuptials, and make her a fruitful mother of men-children.[67]

Later Chapuys attempted to console the emperor with the news that Anne had complained bitterly about this pageant because the merchants had displayed the Imperial eagle above the arms of England and her own falcon. This is an absurd comment for several reasons. The extant design of Holbein, whose intention was to please the king, does not include either the arms of England or those of Anne, for neither one would have belonged in a scene representing pagan deities and personages. The eagle in this entertainment was a symbol of ancient antiquity and not the two-headed one of Charles' empire. Equally important is the recognition that, as the merchants, whose trade depended on royal concessions, were well aware, any insult to Anne on this day could only have been interpreted by the king of England as an insult to himself. Finally, Anne surely would not have been offended by seeing the eagle used in a pageant written to celebrate her status as queen on a day when her device was more greatly honored than the eagle or even the royal arms and when she shortly was to be anointed in the coronation ceremony with oil taken from a golden ampulla shaped in the likeness of an eagle.[68]

The pageant at Leadenhall featured a white falcon with a crown of gold. It also extolled the fruitfulness of Saint Anne. Two of the verses Udall wrote for this entertainment were:

Scarce had the Falcon found rest for the sole of its foot in the rosebed, when an Angel descending crowned the empire-worthy bird – a sure presage of Heaven's smiling on your marriage, O Anna. Therefore fear not to take your crown.

and

Fruitful Saint Anne bare three Maries; the off-spring of her body, by a strange conception, bare the first founders of our holy Faith. Of that daughter was born Christ our Redeemer, foster-father of a vast family. Not without thought therefore, Queen Anne, do the citizens form this pageant in your honour. By her example, may you give us a race to maintain the Faith and the Throne.[69]

Along the rest of the route, which passed the Cross and Conduits in the Cheap, the Standard, Paul's Gate, Paul's Churchyard, Ludgate, St. Martin's Churchyard, Fleetstreet, and Temple Bar were more flattering pageants, flowing wine, singing, and versifying. Near the Cross the recorder gave a speech and presented the queen with 1,000 marks in gold in a purse of gold, which she accepted with "many goodly wordes." Finally she reached and entered Westminster Hall, where she was assisted out of her litter and was led to the cloth of estate. After spice plates and cups of hippocras were offered to her and her ladies, she returned secretly to the barge and went to meet Henry at York Place.[70]

These festivities were extremely important to the crown. Not only did they offer the king the opportunity to introduce his new queen officially to his subjects and to the rest of Christendom but they also gave him and his subjects a chance to display publicly their wealth, their scholarship, and their gift for ceremonial extravaganza. Politically, the celebrations can also be seen as an attempt of the king to reconcile his subjects to the new order, for none of his last four queens was to be similarly honored. Even more significant were the religious rituals performed on the coronation day itself. To resolve the succession crisis in a satisfactory manner, it was necessary that the Church publicly approve Anne's elevation to the queenship. This marriage, unlike Henry's previous one, which he believed had been in violation of Biblical law, would be sealed with divine blessings. The services at Westminster Abbey would serve as a signal to Christendom that God himself had transformed Anne from a noble lady into a queen, a sign that she would be fruitful and would give birth to a son, the king's heir.[71]

On Sunday, 1 June, at seven in the morning, the Mayor, aldermen, and other participants went to Westminster Hall to await the queen's arrival. About one hour later, between eight and nine o'clock, dressed in a surcoat and robe of purple velvet trimmed with ermine and with her hair hanging down under her coif and circlet, Anne entered the hall and stood under the cloth of estate. Then the procession to Westminster Chapel was formed. First walked various gentlemen and knights, aldermen, judges, knights of the bath, noblemen, the Lord Chancellor, members of the king's chapel, monks, abbots, mitred bishops, sergeants and officers of arms, and the Mayor of London with his mace. Next came Dorset who bore the scepter of gold and the earl of Arundel who bore the rod of ivory with the dove. They were followed by the Lord Great Chamberlain (the earl of Oxford) who carried the crown, the Lord High Steward, the acting Earl Marshal, and knights of the garter. Then came Anne under a canopy borne by four men of the Cinque Ports. The ends of her robe were carried by the bishops of London and Winchester and her very long train by the old duchess of Norfolk. At the end of the procession walked numerous ladies, among them the queen's personal attendants.[72]

In the chapel she was led to a rich chair between the choir and the high altar where she first sat and rested. As the archbishop of Canterbury began the service, she descended and lay prostrate before the altar. When she arose, he anointed her on her head and breast from the ampulla and, after several orations, crowned her with the crown of Saint Edward and placed the scepter of gold in her right hand and the rod of ivory with the dove in the left. Following the singing of *Te Deum* by the choir, a lighter crown made especially for her was substituted for Saint Edward's. She returned to her chair for mass and at the appropriate time descended to take communion. At the end of the service she made an offering at Saint Edward's shrine and withdrew to the side of the choir. The procession returned in the same order to Westminster Hall, the queen assisted by her father on the right and by Lord Talbot, acting for the earl of Shrewsbury, on the left. The recessional was accompanied by the playing of trumpets.[73]

Once at Westminster Hall, she retired to her chamber until the preparations were completed for the banquet, a formal event staged for 800 people. When all was ready, Anne entered the hall, washed, and sat at the middle of the table. To her right stood the dowager countess of Oxford and to her left the countess of Worcester, who "divers tymes . . . did hold a fyne cloth before the queens face when she list to spet or do otherwyse at her pleasure." Throughout the meal the earl of Oxford with a white staff also stood near the queen and two gentlewomen sat at her feet. From their secret vantage point in a little closet in the cloister of Saint Stephen the king and several ambassadors observed the banqueters.[74]

When all were in their appointed places, Suffolk and Lord William Howard entered on horseback, the sergeant at arms preceding them. They were followed by the sewer (the earl of Sussex) and the knights of the bath who brought the first course, which was composed of twenty-eight dishes "beside subtilties and shippes made of waxe mervailous gorgious to beholde." This was the first of three courses that were offered to the queen and then to the others in order of rank. At the end of the third course wafers and hippocras were served. Throughout this feast, the festive playing of trumpets could be heard. When the queen had finished eating and had washed, she stood in the middle of the Hall to receive spice and comfits from the sewer and to drink from a cup of gold offered to her by the Lord Mayor. Finally, following ancient tradition, she gave the canopy to the barons of the Cinque Ports and departed, it being six in the evening. The next day, in celebration of her triumph, jousts were held at the tilt before the King's Gate. They were followed by balls and more banquets.[75]

Many writers and poets, besides Udall and Leland, lauded her coronation as queen. In her honor the king of France apparently sent her a volume with Clément Marot's poem, *Le Pasteur Evangélique*, and Edward Hall devoted many pages of his chronicle to the celebrations. Even Cranmer took the time to write a somewhat detailed account of them to Hawkins at the Imperial court.[76]

The high point of Anne's life occurred on 1 June, for on that day she reached the ultimate position in her social and political rise. With her coronation a leveling off of her career can be discerned. This change in direction was the prelude to her sharp and sudden descent in 1536 that was to end in her disgrace and death. One of her most noticeable features during her coronation was her pregnancy. Not only did Chapuys make reference to her condition in his dispatch but Cranmer also noted it in the above cited letter to Hawkins.[77] In June, Anne was still looking forward to the birth of this child, who, it was hoped, would be the long-desired male heir. In the meantime, she had a household to organize and a council to appoint, for she had become a great landowner and a wealthy lady of independent means.

6 QUEEN'S PATRONAGE

Anne's coronation in 1533 served both as the public recognition and religious confirmation of her elevation to the queenship. Since she had been the king's intended bride and then his mistress for almost six years, his palaces, manor houses, and hunting lodges were already familiar to her when she became his consort. As his queen she was to preside in these residences over her own court, controlling substantial sources of income and a large number of offices and sinecures. She had thus reached a position of great social and political importance, one for which she had been well prepared by her childhood education and by her apprenticeship at the English court.

Among the many royal palaces, Greenwich, Henry's birthplace and the birthplace of their daughter Elizabeth, was his favorite. It lies on the River Thames about 5 miles from the Tower of London, which was one of the five dwelling places he owned in London and Westminster. The others were Bridewell, Baynards' Castle, Westminster Palace, and the impressive York Place, confiscated at the time of Wolsey's fall. In the early 1530s Henry also had St. James' Palace built at Westminster. Outside London he owned four major structures: Eltham in Kent, Richmond in Surrey, Hampton Court, another former home of Wolsey's, and Windsor Castle, where he would choose to be buried with Jane Seymour, his third wife and the mother of his male heir. He possessed numerous smaller houses and lodges many of which he visited during the summer hunting season.[1]

These buildings were not as grand as the châteaux of Francis I, but after Wolsey's death no other English family was as well housed as the Tudors. As the queen consort Anne was allotted apartments in them that contained at least a private bedchamber with a withdrawing room. Whenever space allowed she had a much larger suite, as at Windsor where she controlled seven rooms. Unfortunately, specifics about the way her apartments were furnished have usually not survived, although it is known that the king possessed a bed that was 11 feet square. Some information about the way the rooms were painted and decorated is extant, for the ceiling in her privy chamber at Windsor was patterned with small mirrors and those in her presence chamber and bedroom at Greenwich with gilded bullions and birds in a lattice of white battens. The garden there was also stocked with peacocks, whose high-pitched screams so bothered her they had to be moved elsewhere.[2]

To support herself as queen, Anne could draw upon several sources of revenue. The major part of her income was derived from her estates, some of which were attached to the honor of Pembroke although the greater part of them was obtained after her marriage. In late 1533, before the transfer of the jointure lands from Catherine to her, the crown launched an inquiry into the farmers of this property to see if the commissioners had done good service in letting the leases. In early 1534, parliament granted the lands to Anne, the transfer being enrolled in a document garnished with silk and gold, which, according to Cromwell, then clerk of the hanaper, cost 18s. Later that year Henry added a manor in Hertfordshire to her possessions. When compared with anyone's but the king's, her estates were considerable, for they brought to her about £5,000 in income annually. Following royal custom, Henry also approved a statute that made Anne a *femme sole*, permitting her to conduct her business transactions without reference to him as her husband.[3]

Her council, composed of Thomas, Lord Burgh of Gainsborough, Lord Chamberlain, Edward Baynton, vice-chamberlain, Sir James Boleyn, her chancellor and her father's brother, John Uvedale, secretary, Sir William Coffin, master of the horse, and other officials, oversaw the work of George Taylor, her receiver general, and John Smith, her surveyor. The council's duties included protecting the rights and privileges attached to her lands, which were scattered in counties all over England and Wales. Reminders had to be sent out to sheriffs and other local officials that her property had been removed from their charge and that they must honor her claims and interests. When necessary her ministers could call upon the king's financial machinery for assistance in enforcing her rights.[4]

Many of her receivers had, like Sir Edmund Tame of Gloucestershire and Sir Richard Walden of Kent, also served her predecessor. That they remained in her service is evidence of an important continuity of service from Catherine to Anne in the membership of the queen's local machinery, for the gentlemen who functioned as receivers were individuals of stature, holding positions on a variety of county commissions, such as the commission of the peace. It is likely that Anne had to share control with the king over their appointments and perhaps over those of the members of her own household. In 1528, for example, after the death of Sir William Compton of his privy chamber, Henry formally granted his consort the right to dispose of all the offices that this minister had held of her.[5]

In addition to her rents Anne could claim the goods of certain felons and fugitives and had the customary right to the *aurum reginae* or queen's gold. This last source was one tenth the value of voluntary fines, such as licenses for the alienation of land or pardons for enclosures. The total amount of these fees cannot be determined although the *aurum*, which was a somewhat controversial right, probably added only a few pounds a year to her income. In 1466–7, for example, Queen Elizabeth had collected about £37, an amount that had dwindled in succeeding years to less than £7. The payment in 1534 of the queen's silver for the purchase of lands in Somersetshire seems to have been a reference to Anne's *aurum*.[6]

Besides significant income and prestigious housing, the lady who became queen gained access to enormous quantities of personal property, some of it purchased specifically for her and some of it transferred to her from her predecessor's wardrobe. These included silver cups with covers, one of them engraved by Hans Holbein, pots, beds, stools, and jewels. Anne's status as queen also required that she be clothed in precious material, cloth of gold and silver, satins, and velvets and that she ride or be transported by the finest horses. Within a few months of her coronation, she was ordering hobbies from Ireland and obtaining palfreys for her use. As queen she was to receive splendid New

Year's gifts, the value of which depended greatly on the status of the recipient, and in England only the king outranked her.[7]

A wide range of servants from ushers and pages to cooks and tailors saw to her personal needs and hauled her possessions from place to place during the royal progresses. Some of these dependents took advantage of their positions with her to acquire lands and offices from the king. Among them were Thomas Cokkes, her page for the mouth in her pantry, who was granted a messuage; Thomas Grey, a yeoman usher of her chamber, and Richard Bartlett, her physician, who won appointments as bailiffs; and Uvedale, who was presented to a Yorkshire hospital. Even some of her cooks who were caught up in a law suit pleaded for her aid.[8]

She had numerous female attendants, including ladies of the privy chamber and bedchamber and six maids of honor under the supervision of Mrs. Marshall. As customary, several of the queen's relatives joined her at court. Besides Mary her sister, Lady Rochford, her brother's wife, and Mary Howard, daughter to Norfolk, there were Elizabeth Boleyn, wife to Sir James, and Mary Shelton, daughter to Sir John and his wife, Anne Boleyn, the sister of the queen's father. Three other important ladies were Jane Seymour, the future consort of Henry, Elizabeth, countess of Worcester, and Margaret Douglas, the king's niece and daughter of the dowager queen of Scotland, who in a letter of 1534 saluted Anne as "our derrest cister." The next year Anne wrote to her sister-in-law and sent her some precious material: cloth of tissue, silver, and gold.[9]

Many of Anne's servants had transferred to her household from those of other noblemen. At least one, George Taylor, had served her father, and some, like Baynton, Coffin, and John Scott, her tailor, had been employed at her husband's court. A few seem to have come to her indirectly from Thomas Wolsey's service. John Smith, her auditor, had served both the Cardinal and Cromwell, and Bartlett, her physician, had attended Wolsey and Princess Mary. Uvedale, her secretary, continued to hold membership on the duke of Richmond's council.[10]

Although her household was separate from Henry's, there was a movement of personnel back and forth between them. Some servants held posts simultaneously in both households as, for example, John King who was a yeoman of the guard as well as a yeoman usher of her chamber. Still others were called upon by Henry for advice, her vice-chamberlain being one of her councillors most often consulted. In 1535 Thomas Starkey forwarded a message from Baynton, "to whom the king's pleasure is not unknown," to Reginald Pole, son of Margaret, countess of Salisbury, and a Yorkist claimant to the throne, reminding him of the king's many favors. As one of the crown's principal ministers, Cromwell was also concerned with administering her household, granting credences to her servants, delivering jewels to her, and depositing money with her receiver general.[11]

In addition to her staff and the members of the royal bureaucracy, others could be called upon for assistance, two of whom were associated with Cromwell. In 1532 his servant, William Brabazon, joined George Taylor and John Smith to survey her Pembroke lands, and in 1534 Anthony Denny, a servant at various times of Sir Francis Bryan and Cromwell and a relative of William Carey, the queen's deceased brother-in-law, completed an errand for her in London.[12]

The claim that Anne and Cromwell formed a political faction is a modern theory that is derived largely from evidence taken in an eclectic manner from the correspondence of Chapuys. His identification of opposing parties, one favoring Anne that included Cromwell, and the other supporting Catherine that included Norfolk, has usually been credited although his remarks about the cordiality of the partnership between the queen and the king's secretary were often inconsistent. As early as 1534, for example, he was claiming that Cromwell would give better treatment to Catherine and Mary if it were not "for fear of the king's mistress." Chapuys also believed that Anne's supporters were very few in number, but almost every English person of significance, not just Cromwell and some of her relatives, accepted as valid the statute of 1534 that placed the succession in her offspring and compelled allegiance to her as queen. An examination of the evidence about the battle at court for secular promotion and office before the winter of 1536 indicates that loosely structured groups focusing on family, household, and master–servant connections actually dominated political events. On most issues, as Mervyn James has pointed out, "the ties of blood were liable to assert themselves with a particular power."[13]

The evidence indicates that very few individuals believed Cromwell, so often appealed to for help as the king's secretary, to be the best means of access to office in Anne's household. Only two such cases can be found. In 1533 Cromwell's associate, Stephen Vaughan, noted that his wife, hoping to become a silkwoman to the queen, had "devysed certayne works" but had been unable to find anyone to show them to Anne. He asked Cromwell to inform her about the skills of his wife, who would serve her "better than any woman in the Realme." Cromwell must have intervened on behalf of Mrs. Vaughan, for she did become the queen's silkwoman. In 1534 David ap Powell petitioned the secretary, whether successfully or not is unknown, for the office of yeomen purveyor or yeoman of her chariot.[14]

Far more people acquainted with Cromwell used him to seek Anne's good opinion, a procedure that was commonplace and in no way identifies him as her follower or leader. Shortly after her coronation, Sir Gregory Casale, the king's envoy at Rome, implored Cromwell to inform the new queen, who he feared was hostile to him, that he had done all he could to further her cause. If she had personally been dissatisfied with Casale, who was concerned about some damaging reports circulating about his activities at Rome, Cromwell must have mollified her, for in his later dispatches the agent said nothing more about her displeasure. In 1534 Thomas Winter, Wolsey's illegitimate son, thanked Cromwell for a letter of introduction to Anne, who had promised to befriend him, and in 1535 Thomas Audley, the Lord Chancellor, was grateful to the secretary for making it possible for him to use one of the queen's houses. On at least three occasions members of the Boleyn family also sought Cromwell's assistance: in 1535 Anne about a wardship problem and her father about a legal dispute, and in 1534 her sister about her clandestine marriage to William Stafford.[15]

In contrast to this modest evidence of a working relationship between Cromwell and Anne, other information indicates that they often functioned independently of each other. In 1533 at least two individuals were able to obtain places in her household through the suit of ministers who have never been identified as his allies. First, according to later tradition, Sir Francis Bryan, who claimed the Seymours as his cousins in a 1531 letter to the king, won the appointment of maid of honor for Jane Seymour who had previously served Catherine in that office. Secondly, at Easter 1533, John Creke was granted a position as Anne's gentleman usher in response to Sir John Russell's petition to William, Lord Mountjoy, Nicholas Shaxton, the queen's almoner, and George Taylor, her receiver general. Despite his success, so Creke later informed Cromwell, the queen, who was preparing for her coronation, had decided to delay his and all other appointments "till such time as she may be more in quietness than now she is." Creke believed that if he would only be patient, he would be the first to be preferred, but necessity required him to look elsewhere, either to Cromwell or to Sir William Fitzwilliam, the treasurer of the household.[16] That Creke was unwilling to wait for the royal position is a clue to the extent to which his financial status had decayed. Servants, such as gentlemen ushers, earned a graduated scale of tips the amount of which was determined not only by the nature of the task they performed but also by the rank of their mistress or master. The only employment more lucrative than service for the queen was that for the king.

Evidence taken from the correspondence of Arthur, viscount Lisle, Lord Deputy of Calais, and of his wife, Honor, demonstrates how independently of the Master Secretary Anne's patronage network operated. While Lord Lisle, who moved to Calais with his wife in June 1533, often relied upon Cromwell for aid, Lady Lisle looked to Anne and her household for favors. The viscountess, who had accompanied the king and the lady marquess to Calais in 1532, was well known to Anne. As early as that summer, Lady Lisle had begun to send gifts to her, some peewits, for which she was grateful, and an archer's bow that was "somewhat too big." In exchange for these and other presents, Lady Lisle asked for assistance in obtaining an import/export license. Although Anne denied the suit "for certain causes", she promised thereafter to be of more help.[17]

Throughout Anne's tenure as queen, Lady Lisle continued to ply her with presents. In early 1534, Sir Francis Bryan wrote to her about the dog she had sent "which the Queen liked so well that she took it from him before it had been an hour in his hands." This was "little Purkoy" whose death from a fall a few months later no one but the king dared to reveal to her, an incident that seems to confirm a suspicion that Anne was unfortunate as a dog owner, for Urian, her greyhound, had earlier killed a cow. In the spring of 1534, the queen was pleased with Lady Lisle's gift of eighteen dotterels and a song bird. One agent wrote about her pleasure, informing the viscountess that Anne had promised to be "good lady" to her, and still another correspondent told his mistress that the queen had inquired about her health and whether she liked Calais. Even Rochford, who had actually presented to his sister the dotterels that had only recently been killed at Dover, referred to her gratitude. Lady Lisle continued to search for gifts to please Anne, one agent informing her in 1535 that the queen would not like a monkey, for she "loveth no such beasts nor can scant abide the sight of them."[18]

Despite this early show of friendship, Anne sometimes favored suitors whose interests ran directly counter to the viscount's. In 1535, John Husee, his lordship's agent, reported that the queen and Norfolk had won for Lord Edmund Howard, the impoverished brother of the duke then serving as comptroller of Calais, the king's part of some forfeited goods, which were worth about 200 marks. Husee also claimed that had Lisle only informed him earlier about the goods, Cromwell would have been able to obtain them for his lordship. At another time the Lord Deputy referred to competition from the queen's brother for some forfeited woolens at Calais.[19]

The Wheathill dispute is a good example of Anne's lack of concern for the interests of the deputy, even though he was known to be a client of Cromwell's. Despite the king's promise in 1531 that the next spear opening at Calais would go to Robert Wheathill, Lord Lisle gave that vacancy to Richard Wynebank instead, an appointment for which the viscount was able to win royal confirmation but only with Cromwell's backing. In the meantime, with Anne's assistance, Wheathill, who also had the support of Norfolk, Lord William Howard, and Baynton, obtained a patent for the room of the ailing John Highfield, who was not expected to live. After Highfield's recovery, Lisle was forced to confirm Wheathill's right to the next spear position but ultimately succeeded in retracting that promise. The seeking of a sick person's place before he had actually died may seen insensitive, but it was then a common practice, for the individual who first informed his influential friends about an opening was thought to have seized the advantage in obtaining it.[20]

The absence of organized faction also appears in the manner in which Anne could prove a further resort for suitors when Cromwell had failed to help them. In 1534 after Elizabeth Staynings had admitted to her aunt Lisle that her petitions to Norris and Cromwell on behalf of her imprisoned husband had been unsuccessful, she asked the viscountess to write to any gentlewoman at court familiar with the queen to obtain her aid.[21] This was a method frequently employed by petitioners seeking Anne's favor. Servants and attendants of hers whom the viscountess and others are known to have approached were Uvedale, Scott, Margaret Douglas, Elizabeth Boleyn, Mrs. Marshall, Jane Wilkinson, her silkwoman, Margery Horsman of the Wardrobe, and William Oxenbridge, whose office in her household is unknown.[22]

The queen's servants, whose domestic offices put them in a better position than most outsiders to obtain Anne's support, expected suitors to return their favors. After George Taylor presented to the queen a New Year's present and other gifts from Lady Lisle, he asked the viscountess to assist George Gainsford, his uncle, who had long possessed a spear's room at Calais. Taylor further sought and obtained from the queen a letter, which was addressed to Lord Lisle, requesting favorable treatment for this aged relative. Margery Horsman also sent a man with whom she was not personally acquainted to the viscountess for assistance. He was the friend of a Horsman associate.[23]

On occasion Anne favored individuals who belatedly informed Cromwell of that support. In 1534 John, earl of Oxford, first thanked the secretary for his friendship and then revealed that he had already made suit for his inheritance to both the king and the queen, who had put him in "much comfort." That same year George Greene asked Cromwell to expedite his license as agreed upon with the queen's chamberlain "in pursuance of the recompence granted to him by her grace." A year later, when Katherine, Lady Daubeney, a half-sister of Norfolk and of Anne's mother, was having marital problems, her ladyship wrote to Cromwell admitting not only that the queen had been her sole support but also that she had decided to contact Cromwell only because Thomas More of Dorset had told her of the secretary's goodness.[24]

Far from viewing Anne as a political ally of Cromwell, suitors believed that she was one of five or six influential individuals whose direct intervention on their behalf would ordinarily be quite useful, In 1534, Lady Anne Salvan's agent suggested that she write letters about her law suit either to Cromwell, Norfolk, Wiltshire, the king, or the queen. Ultimately, it was Cromwell who assisted this lady.[25]

When the issue at stake involved official decisions over which the suitor knew the queen had no immediate control, she might be asked to intercede with any number of people, not just Cromwell. Because the continued existence of her weir at Umberleigh was in jeopardy in 1535, Lady Lisle's agent recommended, for example, that she write to the queen to see if she would entreat the king, his secretary, or the Lord Chancellor to appoint an indifferent commission to resolve the dispute. Later it was learned that all such conflicts were regularly referred to Cromwell.[26]

The patronage race was so complex that occasionally even well-known enemies supported the same client. In 1533 the king asked that a lease in the possession of St. John's College, Cambridge, be granted to a sergeant of his pantry, on whose behalf the queen, Norfolk, Cromwell, and the bishop of Rochester had already written letters. The three individuals joining the royal couple in this suit were not then nor ever had been close allies or friends.[27]

If Cromwell and Anne had formed a powerful faction, in the natural course of events another one would have emerged in reaction to it, but before 1536 the king's honor would not have tolerated the activities at court of a party whose only reason for existence was the downfall of his new wife and the repeal of the Reformation statutes. It is noteworthy that the challenge to the royal supremacy that broke out into rebellion in 1536 occurred after Anne's death when issues other than the king's divorce were at stake. Until that time politicians had generally been unwilling to challenge the religious settlement that had made it possible for the king to continue his line through a second marriage. The intransigent supporters of Henry's first consort soon disappeared from court either through banishment or execution, and the few sympathetic courtiers who did remain kept a low profile, for once it became obvious to politicans that someone was losing power, as in the case of Catherine, it became a liability for them to associate too closely with her. It was also dangerous for them to be unduly discourteous to someone whose stock, like Anne's, was rising. For these reasons servants of a disgraced minister usually sought to sever their connection with him very quickly, a practice that makes the loyalty of Cromwell to Wolsey appear all the more remarkable.[28]

The dispatches of the Imperial envoy have been cited as evidence that many courtiers, even Anne's own father and uncle, belonged to a faction opposing her royal marriage. The views of this partisan of Catherine about the private thoughts and motivations of Anne's relatives must be rejected as erroneous in the absence of other contemporary evidence to corroborate his assertions. A cautious and skeptical treatment of his letters is thus justified when Anne's relationship to Russell, Henry, marquess of Exeter, Sir Nicholas Carew, Sir Edward Neville, Henry Pole, Lord Montague, Thomas, Lord Dacre, Sir William Paget, her uncle Norfolk, and her father is briefly examined.[29]

A review of the extant evidence concerning the above-listed men who were not her relatives indicates that before 1536 none of them had actively conspired against her although some of them may have had reasons to be displeased with her. In 1528 Anne had favored Cheyney's bid for the wardship of Russell's step-daughter, an acrimonious competition that was settled only after Wolsey's fall when the wardship was granted to the dowager duchess of Norfolk. At that time, Chapuys had forwarded to the emperor Russell's alleged statement that his continued support for Wolsey had deeply angered Anne. Despite these incidents, Russell did not follow the ambassador's example and treat Anne as a permanent enemy but sought to achieve a working relationship with her. In 1532 his wife sent a stag and a greyhound to her, and in 1533 he was able to obtain a place for John Creke in her household, an impressive achievement as the ability to win favors from the queen impacted upon Russell's standing among his friends at court.[30]

The marquess of Exeter, Carew, and Neville, who, like Russell, were members of the privy chamber, were executed in 1538 and

1539 for involvement in a conspiracy associated with the Yorkist claimant, Reginald Pole, and his family. Scholars have sometimes maintained that these three gentlemen were part of an Aragonese faction that had begun working for Anne's ruin even before she became queen and that had finally achieved its goal in 1536. Caution must be used in accepting this conclusion, for it is based largely on the assumption that these individuals must have banded together against the aggressive political unity of Anne and Cromwell. When the queen's activities and goals are separated from those of the secretary and associated with those of her family and household servants, it is clear that no such partnership between her and Cromwell existed and that other explanations for the later rise of political factions must be found. It is more reasonable to argue that after the spring of 1536, issues associated with the royal supremacy besides the mere fact of the king's divorce and second marriage surfaced to drive these men into treasonable activities.[31]

Little is actually known about the relationship of these three gentlemen to Anne except that they all held minor offices or keeperships on her estates. Most of the evidence that they were hostile to her survives in the correspondence of Chapuys. By 1531, for example, Catherine had informed this envoy that Exeter, a grandson of Edward IV through his mother Katherine of York, was a good friend of hers. Despite the official support the marquess gave for the royal divorce, even to signing a letter requesting Clement to favor the king's Levitical arguments, Chapuys remained confident of his sympathy for Catherine. A rumor the envoy forwarded to the emperor in 1531 indicates his belief that Exeter and Anne were implacable enemies. He reported that the marquess had been forbidden to appear at court because he had been accused of recruiting men in Cornwall but that Catherine believed Anne had initiated the charge against him because of his opposition to the divorce. The claim of Anne's involvement in the affair is preposterous, for Exeter's troubles arose from bickering in Cornwall and had absolutely nothing to do with her. Reginald Pole later recalled that, seemingly in a kind of paralyzed despair, the marquess had said to him about the divorce: "Being unable to find any other remedy for this, we pray God to find it himself."[32]

Although Exeter remained, however reluctantly, supportive of the king's cause, his wife, Gertrude, the daughter of Lord Mountjoy, acted in a "criminally naive" way in her communications with Chapuys. Her earliest known contact with the envoy occurred in November 1532, when she forwarded to him an official letter, probably written by her husband but sent without his consent. She later found herself in serious trouble for consulting with the Nun of Kent, who was executed for prophesying the ruin of the king in the event that he did marry Anne. The marchioness, who had acted as godmother to Elizabeth in her confirmation, was forced to made an abject submission to Henry, excusing herself on the basis that she was merely a woman, an argument that was apparently taken seriously. Except perhaps for the contents of the letter she sent to Chapuys in 1532, the marchioness seems never to have revealed any vital secrets to him but rather to have been used by the royal officials to feed him false information. In November 1534 she personally visited Chapuys in order to inform him that the ex-queen and princess were in grave danger. Apparently, Cromwell had hoped that if Chapuys could be convinced that their lives were in jeopardy, he would try to persuade them to submit to the recently passed Statute of Supremacy.[33]

Another gentleman who communicated with Chapuys was Carew on whose behalf in 1529 Catherine requested the envoy to write a letter of recommendation to the emperor. By the spring of 1530, Carew was paying marked attention to Chapuys, sending him venison and visiting his lodgings. Despite his reputed support for the Imperialists, Carew never revealed any vital secrets to Chapuys either and probably created compelling rumors for the envoy's benefit in an attempt to deceive him or to induce him inadvertently to disclose important diplomatic information. Although it is true that in late 1534, for example, Carew was prepared to discuss with Chapuys Anne's alleged quarrel with the king about his new mistress, the next spring, in fact, the knight was able to persuade a French envoy to lobby Henry VIII for his election to the Order of the Garter. Undoubtedly, Carew had recently performed some important services for the French government. Equally significant to a discussion of Carew's role at court is his letter to Cromwell in April 1535, thanking him for favoring his candidate for a priory and revealing the opposition of the countess of Salisbury to his suit. Although she was the mother of Reginald Pole, the countess seems to have been unaware of an Aragonese faction. Like Carew, Sir Edward Neville was later executed for his association with the Poles, but he cannot have acted in a resolutely hostile manner toward Anne, for in 1535 she agreed to grant him a keepership on one of her Kentish manors.[34]

At court the Pole family, for whom these gentlemen died in 1538 and 1539, was rather quiet during most of Anne's tenure in office. Of the three brothers, Reginald remained in exile; Geoffrey was unwelcome at court; and only Henry, Lord Montague, the eldest, was a member of the king's household. A court contact of Lord and Lady Lisle, Montague served as carver at Anne's coronation banquet and participated in the trial of Sir Thomas More. Until the winter of 1536, Montague seems to have communicated with Chapuys on only two occasions: in December 1534 and in February 1535. These communications, superficially at least, had very little to do with Anne personally, for Montague reportedly spoke only of a growing estrangement between Henry and Francis; these messages, in fact, merely confirmed information Cromwell wished Chapuys to believe. The secretary knew that the envoy would trust Montague because he was the son of Mary's old governess. Whether the nobleman was aware that he was being used to leak this information to the envoy is unclear, but it is noteworthy that in 1535 Montague wrote to the secretary that his father-in-law, George, Lord Bergavenny, who had just died, had "trusted Cromwell above all men." Bergavenny had also been the brother of Neville.[35]

Lord Dacre is the most intriguing of the individuals considered by Chapuys to be Anne's enemies, for very little is known about why he was indicted for treason in 1534. On 9 July of that year, Norfolk served as Lord High Steward for Dacre's trial that ended in his acquittal. Unaware of the reason for his lordship's arrest, Chapuys, as usual, blamed the whole unpleasant episode on the queen, but it would have been a curious action on her part, if true, since his lordship had subscribed to the letter sent to the pope in 1530 urging him to grant the royal divorce. As warden of the Western Marches toward Scotland, Dacre's problems arose from his private dealings with the Scots and not from any plots fomented by Anne. Tradition also suggests that Anne favored William Paget, whose activities during the reign of Mary were to move John Foxe to revile him as an apostate.[36]

In 1533 Chapuys informed the emperor that both Norfolk, whom Anne had reportedly accused of "too much familiarity and freedom of speech," and Wiltshire had opposed her marriage to the king. Undoubtedly the duke, who had given this information to the envoy, was deliberately being deceptive, for earlier Chapuys had reported that all the nobility except for Norfolk and two or three others supported the Imperialists. By pretending disapproval of his niece's actions, Norfolk surely hoped to ingratiate himself once again with this ally of the ex-queen. On every important issue concerning the divorce, the duke had officially supported the king, even testifying in his favor about the nature of Catherine's marriage to Arthur. At the end of 1533, Chapuys later conceded to the emperor that the duke had treated Princess Mary "roughly" because of her unwillingness to relinquish her title to Elizabeth, who was Norfolk's grandniece. By way of contrast to the language he used with the Imperial envoy, the duke allegedly told the French ambassador that although both the king and queen relied greatly upon him for advice, they distrusted him. This more realistic version of Norfolk's role is somewhat corroborated by a comment of Fitzwilliam's who told an unknown correspondent that the three individuals Henry relied upon the most for advice were Norfolk, Cromwell, and Fitzwilliam.[37]

By disassociating himself from the royal family and their policies, Norfolk could promise with some credibility to be the friend of these diplomats. Great benefits could result from the development of cordial relationships with the agents of foreign countries. After Henry's love affair with Anne had made it possible for the duke to be resurrected from political obscurity, the fall of Wolsey and the renewal of the French alliance had brought new rewards: election to the French equivalent of the Order of the Garter, a French pension, and an invitation for his heir, the earl of Surrey, to accompany Richmond for a stay at the French court. This visit had been so successful that in 1535 Norfolk even considered sending his younger son to Paris.[38]

In the meantime, his daughter Mary, who was born about

1519, had entered Anne's service, participating in the ceremony creating her lady marquess of Pembroke in 1532 and attending her in 1533 when she appeared as queen publicly for the first time. In the fall of 1533, at the age of fourteen, Mary and the king's illegitimate son, Henry Fitzroy, duke of Richmond, were married. Even Mary's mother, Elizabeth, duchess of Norfolk, was later to admit that Anne had promoted this prestigious match for her young Howard cousin with the kingdom's premier duke. Although the union had not been consummated in 1536 when Richmond died prematurely, Norfolk had been able for a short time to look forward to sharing a grandson with the king. That Anne's child might some day become ruler of England would seem also to have opened up splendid opportunities for the ambitious Howards.[39]

When Norfolk suffered reduced power and influence after 1531, it was less the result of a strained relationship with his niece than his own lack of talent and commitment, for he simply did not have the ideas, skill, or tenacity to help the king resolve the marriage tangle. As a peer of the realm, he also could not be expected to handle the tedious daily business of the secretariat, activities that could bring great political influence to ambitious commoners, like Cromwell. The duke, who had extensive estates to manage, sometimes resented being summoned to court for consultation. Even so, the king continued to call upon him for advice, and the queen often favored her Howard relatives. Her tenure as queen, in fact, "brought a swarm of Howard allies and relatives to court," all seeking favor and position. The major sour note was the growing estrangement of the duchess, whose antagonism had arisen partly from her support for Catherine but primarily from the duke's decision to place in their household his mistress, Elizabeth Holland, one of Anne's attendants.[40]

The charge that Wiltshire was opposed to his daughter's marriage is a preposterous statement that only someone as credulous as Chapuys could have believed. Other members of the diplomatic corps were more astute, for in 1530 when the Imperial agent at Rome believed incorrectly that the political tide was actually turning in Catherine's favor, he observed with pleasure that the earl had lost "much hope" of the alliance of his daughter with the king. In a letter of May 1533 to the emperor, Chapuys himself had to confess that Wiltshire had accused him of putting on "two faces," a statement which he took to mean, and which he not very convincingly denied, that he was trying to function both as the Imperial ambassador and as Catherine's proctor. By that time Anne's royal liaison had brought numerous rewards to her father and family. In 1529 Wiltshire had obtained the Butler earldom of Ormond and some of its Irish lands; shortly after, he had exchanged his office of treasurer of the household for the more prestigious keepership of the privy seal. That this success had depended upon Anne's queenship is easily proved, for at her fall he lost both the privy seal and his Irish property.[41]

Rebellion had, in the meantime, ravaged Ireland. In the island's confusing politics, Wiltshire and Norfolk had ranged themselves on the side of Gerald Fitzgerald, ninth earl of Kildare, only to see him replaced as Lord Deputy in 1532 by Sir William Skeffington, who along with Sir Piers Butler, earl of Ossory, was a client of Cromwell. In 1534 and 1535 Anne's father was forced to draw upon both judicial and parliamentary means to protect his interests against Ossory. He also found it necessary to deal with the poverty of his Irish tenants and to suffer the damage inflicted on his lands by the royal army, for in 1534 young Thomas, the future earl of Kildare, fomented a rebellion against the crown. In August 1535 Thomas surrendered to Lord Leonard Grey, marshal of the army, and was taken to England as a royal prisoner. That Anne was aware of and concerned about these events there is no doubt. As Grey, having delivered the rebel, was preparing for his return to Ireland, the king granted him land, money, and a ship, and the queen gave him a chain of gold from her waist worth 100 marks and a purse with 20 sovereigns. Three months later, after the death of the ailing Skeffington, his widow wrote letters to both the queen and Cromwell for financial assistance. Before Anne could respond to this plea, she had miscarried her child and the events leading to her execution had been set in motion.[42]

The queen's brother and sister likewise won favorable political and social positions. Rochford, whose viscountcy was only honorary, was made a baron in his own right, gained appointment as Lord Warden of the Cinque Ports, and served as one of the king's busiest diplomats, going to France on several missions between

1533 and 1535. He was also granted one of the Kentish manors of the late, martyred Thomas More. That Lady Mary Rochford did not receive greater rewards was the fault of her clandestine alliance with William Stafford, a soldier of the retinue of Calais. When her relatives discovered that she had married this commoner, they had her banished from court. Near the end of 1534 she not only pleaded with Cromwell to implore the king to speak to her sister on her behalf but also asked the secretary to intercede for her with her parents, brother, and Uncle Norfolk.[43]

In the meantime, her son, Henry Carey, benefited enormously from his position as ward of the queen, for Anne, a great admirer of French culture, made it possible for him to be tutored, along with Henry Norris (the younger) and Thomas or Edmund Harvey, by Nicholas Bourbon, an outstanding French poet. Early in 1534, after he had attacked the Roman Catholic "cult" of saints of his Church, Bourbon had been forced to flee into exile. Upon his arrival in England he had entered the household of William Butts, the king's physician, who contacted Anne about employing the refugee as schoolmaster to her ward. Like his patroness, Margaret, queen of Navarre, to whose daughter, Jeanne d'Albret, he was to be appointed tutor, Bourbon remained loyal to his Church and was free to return to his homeland after Anne's death. Two years later he published a volume of verses in honor of, among others, the king, the queen, Cromwell, Cranmer, Butts, and Hugh Latimer. According to her chaplain, William Latimer, Anne also befriended a Mrs. Mary, who fled to England from France, and tried to recruit John Sturmius, the future educator, when he was studying at Paris.[44]

With this impressive patronage at her disposal, Anne had reached the highest social rank available to her. Manifold responsibilities accompanied the advantages of her position, as the queenship restricted and mandated the actions of its holders who wished to be recognized for the proper use of their power. Lord Edmund Howard, her uncle, expressed the prevailing hierarchical notion best in a letter to Wolsey in 1527 about his decayed financial plight. Were he a poor man's son, he said, he "might dig and delve," but as a Howard he could not stoop to that level "without shame to his blood." How noble or royal persons conducted themselves reflected not only on the acceptance or rejection of their personal place in the social hierarchy but also on the standing and dignity of their lineage and family.[45]

In a letter to her daughter Elizabeth after her succession as queen, William Latimer later wrote that following Anne's coronation, she had charged her household "to take especiall regarde, and to omitt nothing that may seeme to apperteigne to [her] honor." She had forbidden all quarrels and had ordered her servants not to frequent "ynfamous" places or to keep company with lewd people. Foxe confirmed these reminiscences in his "Book of Martyrs." Quoting Anne's silkwoman, he wrote that Mrs. Wilkinson had claimed never to have seen "better order amongst the ladies and gentlewomen of the court than in Anne's day." Her maids were kept busy sewing for the poor to prevent idleness or "any leisure to follow such pastimes as daily are seen now-a-days to reign in princes courts." There were to be no "pampered pleasures" or "licentious libertie" among her attendants but "vertuous demeanor" and "godly conversation," at least in Anne's presence.[46]

In the conduct of her queenship she attempted to follow the examples of Claude of France, Margaret of Navarre, Catherine of England, and even of her husband's pious grandmother, the countess of Richmond. The statements of Latimer and Foxe about Anne's concern for the poor are virtually fungible with the nearly contemporary comments of William Forrest about Catherine and the earlier ones of the bishop of Rochester about the countess. The Maundy service in which poor women were rewarded with gifts links these three female relatives of the king together. While in 1535 Anne kept her Maundy, the king was willing to permit his ex-wife to "keep a Maundy" as his grandmother Richmond had done. In a manuscript, unpublished until modern times, which Forrest presented to Catherine's daughter Mary after her accession as queen, he recalled how her mother, who had loved to read the scriptures and had forbidden vain amusements in her household, had sent agents into the towns near where she stayed on her progresses to discover who the needy folk were so that she could assist them. She especially sought to aid childbearing women.[47]

In an echo of these sentiments, Foxe wrote about Anne:

and she ever gave three or four pound at a time to the poor people ... and
sent her subalmoner to the towns about where she lay that the parishioners
should make a bill of all the poor householders in their parish ... It hath
been reported unto us by divers credible persons who were about this queen
... how her grace carried ever about her a certain little purse, out of which
she was wont daily to scatter abroad some alms to the needy, thinking no
day well spent wherein some man had not fared the better by some benefit
at her hands.[48]

Confirming Foxe's comments, Latimer claimed that Anne gave
alms to householders "overcharged with children," providing
special alms for pregnant women, assisted one of her extremely ill
servants, and aided two poor folk whose need had been brought
to her attention by Hugh Latimer when she was at Baynton's
home, probably in August 1535.[49]

Later in that same year, William Marshall, a client of Cromwell's who had been favored by Anne, dedicated to her his
translation of a treatise on a poor relief scheme, entitled *The forme
and maner of subvention for pore people, devysed and practysed in the citie of
Hypres in flaunders* .... Probably influenced indirectly by the ideas
of Juan Luis Vives, this scheme condemned indiscriminate alms-
giving and called for distinguishing between the truly handi-
capped poor and able-bodied vagabonds. According to G. R.
Elton, it was published in 1535 to draw attention to the need for
the poor law legislation scheduled to be introduced into the next
parliament. Whether Anne approved of the Ypres plan is not
known, but it seems clear from Foxe and Latimer that there were
specific groups of the poor she especially hoped to assist. In his
dedication Marshall praised her goodness as the "floure of all
queens" and asked that she act as a mediator for him to the
king.[50]

Although both Henry's first wife and his grandmother had
provided stipends for poor students, the countess was more
celebrated for her bounty. Before her death in 1509, she had used
her great wealth as the heiress of the duke of Somerset to endow
two Cambridge colleges, St. John's and Christ's, and lectureships
at both universities. Following the examples of these ladies, her
grandson's second consort, Anne, who was praised by William
Latimer as a favorer of good letters and learning, attempted to

assist the universities. During her first year as queen she gave £40 to Cambridge and Oxford and thereafter £80 to each. Latimer claimed that she was subsequently able to obtain their release from paying their first fruits to the king, as mandated by parliament. In addition, she aided some poor students, for scholars were then and still are often reduced to begging and borrowing. Among them were John Becansaw, who went to Paris to continue his studies after earning his M.A. at Oxford; William Barker, whose education at Cambridge was financed by Norfolk after Anne's death; and William Bill, a fellow of Cambridge who was recommended to her by John Cheke and Matthew Parker. In addition, she admonished the abbot of St. Mary's, York, to send one of his monks, John Eldmer, bachelor of divinity, to Cambridge.[51]

Anne set not only a high moral and charitable standard but also a religious example, for she wanted her household to serve as a Christian "spectacle" to others. She required her attendants to hear divine service daily and reportedly presented each of them with a book of devotions that contained some prayers and a few English Psalms. There are two extant stories or legends about these books. A tradition that seems to have arisen in the eighteenth century claims that on the scaffold she gave a copy to Margaret Lee, the sister of Sir Thomas Wyatt, while an anecdote told by William Latimer recalled that Anne had chastised Mary Shelton, her young cousin who was also her maid of honor, for writing idle posies in hers.[52]

The story about Mary Shelton is interesting, for Anne herself has customarily been credited with composing romantic verses in a manuscript, now entitled the Devonshire Manuscript and deposited at the British Library. This manuscript, which has early versions of many of Wyatt's poems, does contain poetry written in the hand of several of Anne's attendants, including Margaret Douglas, Mary Howard, and Mary Shelton, but recent experts have been able to find no evidence that the manuscript was ever in the queen's possession.[53]

In keeping with their characterization of Anne as a love object, as the subject of Wyatt's love poetry, writers misunderstanding the crucial role of religion in early modern societies, have usually believed that she was insincere about her faith. Since these scholars were aware that she had been the king's lover before she became his wife and that she had died convicted of adultery with five men, they have viewed her as a flirtatious and immoral woman who could not have had any serious interest in religious matters.[54]

Anne's vice-chamberlain did write in a teasing way to Rochford in June 1533, shortly after his sister's coronation, that far from mourning the loss of the gentlemen who had departed from court the ladies of her household were having a grand time. They had reason to celebrate, for they had become the queen's servants with all the political and social advantages accompanying that high office, including expensive palfreys and saddles at the next New Year's festival. It is noteworthy that Baynton did not state that Anne was dancing and partying, an omission that probably reflected the true state of events since she was then almost six months' pregnant. Before 1536, the year she was executed, there cannot have been any gossip claiming that as queen she was sexually promiscuous or flirtatious. Had such rumors existed Chapuys almost certainly would have forwarded them to the emperor as confirmed truths.[55]

Even if her education and the cultural impulse of her society had not led her to treat religion seriously, her elevation to the queenship would have. A highly motivated and ambitious lady like Anne would have wanted, as Henry's consort, to have the reputation of a Christian woman. Since rulers then believed that they gained legitimacy through God's blessing and that the security and peace of their kingdoms depended on their support of the Church, she had political reasons for emphasizing her devotion to spiritual matters. In 1534, furthermore, a statute framed by Cromwell had recognized her husband as the supreme head of the Church in England, thus creating an additional reason for her to conduct herself as his consort in a Godly manner. Equally important for Anne's religious habits as this statute was Henry's conviction, which was shared by most of his contemporaries, that God would bless with male children the true believers who obeyed his laws. As Suffolk said in 1535 when Katherine, his new young duchess, gave birth to an infant: "It has pleased God to send me a son." Anne surely understood that as the crowned queen of England she must set an example that would help her deserve and receive a similar blessing.[56]

Unquestionably, her beliefs also had reformist overtones. On at least one issue besides the schism, she broke with English tradition, for she had long been reading the scriptures in French and continued to receive copies of divine books in this language after her marriage. Thus she asked William Locke, the king's mercer, when he went on his buying trips to the continent to obtain for her in French the gospels, epistles, and Psalms, perhaps Marot's recently published version. English scholars, some of them in exile, were aware of her commitment to vernacular translations. In 1533 when George Joye hoped, unsuccessfully as it turned out, to obtain the patronage of Henry and Anne for producing an English Bible, he sent to them two leaves of Genesis that he had printed.[57]

As the queen, Anne made accessible to her ladies an English translation of the Bible. This was probably Miles Coverdale's version of 1535, the first complete Bible printed in English, which the king, to whom it was dedicated, decided to license for publication in England. She was also presented with a deluxe copy of the 1534 edition of Tyndale's translation of the New Testament, which, minus its controversial introductory material, is now at the British Library. Her possession of this volume, which was bound in vellum and has *Anna Regina Angliae* in red on its gold edges, was not so radical an act as it might seem. At the end of 1534, convocation petitioned the king for a vernacular Bible, and this edition of Tyndale's scriptures, the best then available, was to form the core of all English Bibles that were legally printed in the kingdom during Henry's reign. Despite Tyndale's well-known heresies and his opposition to the divorce, Cromwell and Vaughan made some effort to recruit him into royal service.[58]

Because Anne was a schismatic and favored Biblical translations, later reformers chose to characterize her as a Protestant. From Elizabeth's succession on, many families began to claim that their ancestors had been Protestants, the members of the Bertie family, for example, placing the duke of Suffolk within that Christian faction. Caution should be used in attaching religious labels to Anne and her contemporaries. In the post-Reformation and Catholic Reformation age, Christendom was increasingly consolidated into two camps but in Henry's reign it was still fractured into several small parts. Many individuals challenging papal power and affirming the need for scriptural translations, among them the king, almost certainly his second consort, and others like Edmund Bonner, the Marian bishop of London, had many deep-seated impulses that can more easily be described as Catholic than as Protestant. In specific analyses of Anne's faith, it is also important to note that in 1536 she refused to accept Tristram Revell's version of Francis Lambert's *Farrago Rerum Theologicarum*, which approved of justification by faith and communion in both kinds. Revell had hoped for her acceptance of it, because, as he said in its dedication, she had done much to "promote, furder and sette forthe Goddes worde."[59]

The modern argument that Anne and Cromwell led a political faction is based in part on the premise that they both sought to assist reformers in obtaining places in the Church. Their religious patronage, as will be seen here, follows a path very similar to their secular patronage, for although in some cases they cooperated together, they often functioned independently of each other. It is also relevant to this discussion that Cromwell's reformist attitudes were more radical than Anne's. Before examining the evidence for these assertions about their attitudes toward these issues, some observations about early modern religion will be useful. First, in their approach to their faith, Henrician Christians had secular as well as spiritual goals, for no great division between the two was then perceived. In many respects theirs was a materialistic faith since they often attempted to promote themselves and their kin through displays of wealth and munificence on behalf of traditional religious causes. Secondly, in the dispensing of Church patronage, individuals frequently did not ask specific doctrinal questions of candidates under consideration. In the 1530s the clergy would have been expected to support the royal supremacy. Other qualities that might be required or considered necessary were good preaching skills, excellent scholarship, and special personal qualities, such as honesty, integrity, or family relationships.[60]

Although generally operating within this social and religious framework, Anne seems nevertheless to have singled out for special treatment individuals who agreed with her stand on Biblical translations. In 1534 she asked Cromwell to assist Richard Herman, an Antwerp merchant who had been expelled from his freedom and fellowship in the English House for setting forth the New Testament in English. Whether or not Herman was reinstated is unknown, but by the end of 1535 he was back at Antwerp working as a spy for Cromwell.[61]

Without reference to Cromwell, the queen appointed chaplains to her household who advocated making the scriptures available in the vernacular. One was William Betts who, along with Dr. Thomas Forman and others, had been arrested at Oxford in 1528 for reading forbidden works, but who had been able to obtain a surety to be released from prison since no outlawed books were found in his quarters. After Betts went on to earn his B.A. degree at Cambridge, the queen employed him as her chaplain. In 1535 he was replaced, with the support and encouragement of John Skip, her almoner, by Matthew Parker, also a Cambridge scholar and the future archbishop of Canterbury. Later that year, Anne obtained for Parker the deanery of Stoke-by-Clare College.[62]

William Barlow, whose family had long been associated with the Boleyns, was another favorer of scriptural translations. His brother John had switched to Anne's household from her father's and had obtained the deanship of Westbury-on-Trym College. For William, who had also served the crown as a diplomat, Anne was able to win the office of prior of the canons regular at Haverfordwest. In 1534 Cromwell secured his further appointment as suffragan to the bishop of St. David's, a position that brought Barlow into conflict with the bishop's officers partly because he possessed an English New Testament. A few months after this dispute, while Barlow was on a mission to Scotland, he was elected bishop of St. Asaph's and was shortly thereafter translated to St. David's.[63]

It is noteworthy that in a list William Latimer later compiled of Henrician bishops whom Anne had favored, he failed to include Barlow, although this churchman did not die until 1568. This omission may be evidence of Latimer's outrage at the "constant change of front" by Barlow during Mary's reign when he first resigned his episcopal office, then recanted his faith, and finally fled to Germany, displaying what has been described as "moral weakness." The five clerics Latimer named were: Thomas Cranmer of Canterbury, Hugh Latimer of Worcester, Nicholas Shaxton of Salisbury, Thomas Goodrich of Ely, and John Skip of Hereford. After lauding her support for reform, Foxe, a more honest reporter than William Latimer, revealed that she had also favored Nicholas Heath, the Marian archbishop of York, and Thomas Thirlby of Westminster. Although during Mary's reign Shaxton had abjured his beliefs and Goodrich had managed to keep his bishopric, the martryologist specifically lamented about Heath and Thirlby: "would to God they were now as great professors of the gospel of Christ" as they appeared in Henry's reign.[64]

To suggest that Anne alone had won for these men either the bishoprics or sufficiently advanced positions in the Church that made their subsequent episcopal election possible would be to exaggerate greatly her influence in religious matters. The king, his new archbishop of Canterbury, and Cromwell, vicegerent for spiritual matters and in charge of the inquiries concerning the monasteries, had personal agendas to fulfill and vital interests to protect in the selection of new bishops. All three in varying degrees supported the schism and held that the Bible ought to be made available in English.

Although Cranmer had been associated with the Boleyns since he joined Wiltshire's entourage on his journey to the continent in January 1530, the future archbishop had first been introduced to Henry by Edward Fox and Stephen Gardiner. As a co-compiler with Fox of the *Collectanea satis copiosa*, Cranmer, who agreed with Henry's interpretation of Leviticus 20:21, had established himself as a firm supporter of the right of the English Church with the king at its head to handle independently a variety of suits, including marital ones. This and other contributions to the royal cause must have been crucial factors in Henry's decision to promote him to Canterbury.[65]

The one issue that linked together six of the eight Henrician bishops favored by Anne was the polling of the universities about Leviticus. Cranmer, a Cambridge man who was lobbying continental scholars for their votes, would have been embarrassed and his career would surely have suffered had his own *alma mater* failed to decide for the king on this issue. In February 1530, after fierce political manoeuvering, Gardiner was able to report to Henry that at Cambridge the question had been referred to a committee, the members of which he listed. Beside the names of those who favored the royal arguments, Gardiner placed the letter "A." Among them were Shaxton, Hugh Latimer, Skip, Goodrich, and Heath. Although other future bishops, such as Thirlby and Barlow, enjoyed Anne's favor, many of the scholars who struggled to gain support for the king's divorce in 1530 were well rewarded.[66]

The outcome of this dispute partially explains Cranmer's patience with and promotion of Hugh Latimer, who was an extremely controversial preacher. It was not a foregone conclusion, as the example of the exiled Tyndale attests, that those who challenged papal power would also support the king's stand on Leviticus. Although traditionally Latimer has been associated with Butts, Cromwell, and Anne, it is significant that it was Cranmer who insisted that Richard Sampson, dean of the king's chapel, appoint both Latimer and Shaxton to preach at court during the Lenten season when the bishoprics of Worcester and Salisbury, then held by Jerome de Ghinucci and Cardinal Campeggio, were due to be vacated by parliament. That Cranmer had election to these offices in mind for his Cambridge friends seems evident from his letter to Latimer in which he advised him about his conduct. The archbishop suggested that he preach for no more than an hour or an hour and a half at most "for the King and Queen may perhaps wax so weary that they shall have small delight to continue throughout to the end."[67]

Although Sampson had no hesitation in scheduling Shaxton to preach, he agreed only with reluctance to include Latimer because of the controversy that usually surrounded his sermons. These arrangements seem to have pleased the king, for despite the charges of heresy that had been levied against Latimer, who had been forced to recant some views that were reminiscent of Lollardy, Henry enjoyed his sermons and appointed him as one of his chaplains. William Latimer also recalled that the king and Sir James Boleyn had debated scripture with Hugh Latimer and Shaxton, probably at the time they were being considered for the bishoprics. After their elections, the queen loaned them £200 for the payment of their first fruits.[68]

Another cleric Anne seems to have supported was Nicholas

Hawkins, the bishop-designate of Ely. A Cambridge man whose expertise was canon and civil law, Hawkins had attended convocation in 1529. Three years later, the king sent him as the English ambassador to Rome and to the emperor. While he was abroad, he obtained in response to Anne's reminder about Henry's wishes, some books about the power of the papacy and translated *A Glasse of Truthe* into Latin, endeavors that indicated he strongly agreed with the king's interpretation of Leviticus. Henry was so gratified that he designated Hawkins as bishop-elect of Ely, but he died in Aragon on his way home to accept this new office. Because of his support for the divorce, it is reasonable to suggest that both Anne and Henry were saddened by the death of this cleric, who was a friend of Cranmer. In February 1534, Chapuys claimed that he had heard from the French ambassador that the queen had wept bitterly at his loss.[69]

In addition to supporting Latimer and Barlow, Anne joined Cromwell in patronizing Robert Singleton and asked the vicegerent to provide monastic office for two individuals. Singleton was an Oxford M.A. who first served the queen as her chaplain and after her death became a client of Cromwell's. Known for his preaching, Singleton was the author of some sermons that were published as well as of the prologue of *The Court of Venus*. He died in 1544, as a martyr according to Foxe, but he was probably executed for committing treason rather than heresy. In 1535 Anne asked Cromwell to assist two men: an unnamed friend of Robert Power, who had joined Cromwell's household upon her recommendation, to be elected abbot of Vale Royal; and a poor man to become prior of Thetford.[70]

With these examples of her patronage as evidence, the argument that she and Cromwell formed a faction at court with the goal of increasing the number of reformist clergy in the Church must be described as misleading. First, that she favored Heath and Thirlby, two Marian Catholics, is an insurmountable drawback to this theory about her religious patronage, unless by reformer is meant anyone generally in favor of the royal supremacy, and, in that case, Edmund Bonner, another Marian bishop, who started as Cromwell's client, would have to be included in the reformist faction. Secondly, of the clergymen who became bishops that she favored, most were already her friends, for they had publicly supported the royal divorce before 1530, either at Cambridge or in diplomatic circles, the earliest possible year when she could have begun to build this alleged faction with Cromwell.

Another difficulty with this theory is that some evidence actually suggests a lack of cooperation on religious matters between Anne and Cromwell. Although the vicegerent was clearly the patron of John Hilsey, the prior of the Dominican house at Bristol who succeeded John Fisher at Rochester, there is no evidence that Anne ever assisted his career. In 1534, Hilsey, who had earlier complained about the religious views of Hugh Latimer, claimed that he was being threatened with the loss of the offices, which Cromwell had obtained for him, by a competitor who had won the support of a number of important individuals, including Mrs. Marshall, mistress of the queen's maidens.[71]

At least one churchman's strategy was to turn for relief from Cromwell to Anne. In 1535 after he had unsuccessfully petitioned Cromwell for a vicarage, John Smith a prebendary of St. Paul's asked Anne's vice-chamberlain to reveal to her the details of a conspiracy against him headed by John Incent, a fellow prebendary. According to Smith, Incent hoped to deprive him of his position in the Cathedral's deanery house, which for the payment of £40 he had originally gained with the help of Sampson, who also held a prebend there. Smith hoped she would aid him for the "diligent love and service" he had shown her at her coronation and at the birth of Elizabeth and for the assistance he had given to her chaplains. Nothing was said in his plea about his Christian views.[72]

Even more important to the argument that they did not form a faction with a well-developed religious policy is that Cromwell was a more radical reformer than Anne. Cromwell attempted to recruit heretics for royal service and to develop strong ties with German reformers, who, like Tyndale, happened to be opposed to the divorce. As late as February 1536, for example, Melanchthon was still repeating his belief that the law against a man marrying his brother's widow should be treated as dispensable. In 1535 an agent had earlier informed Cromwell of the duplicitous stand some members of the Hanseatic League were willing to take toward the queen. The Lubeckers were sending presents to her for which, according to this agent, she had no reason to be grateful because they had used "ungodly and spiteful words" about her. Apparently, they had also slandered Cromwell. Furthermore, the Protestant Schmalkaldic League, which was formed in the 1530s, attracted Cromwell's favorable attention, but it was not until 1538 that the first Lutheran embassy reached England. Factional politics based on ideology, which seem to have surfaced after Anne's death when the king's divorce from Catherine was no longer the major issue, were nurtured by Cromwell's support of the Germans.[73]

The vicegerent seems to have held a more extreme view about the monasteries than Anne, for the evidence suggests that she desired their reformation rather than their dissolution. According to William Latimer, she asked him in a sermon he was to give before the king "to dissuade the utter subversion of the said [£200 p.a.] houses and to induce the kinges grace to the mynde to converte them to some better uses." She also requested Henry directly to preserve Catesby Nunnery, which Cromwell's agents had found in perfect order. When some desperate monastic inhabitants appealed to her for help, Latimer recalled, she reportedly admonished them for departing from God's "true religion," for forsaking their obedience to their sovereign, for closing their gates to preachers of His word, and for refusing to help university students. Apparently, they had responded to her criticisms with a promise to reform their way of life. Latimer also claimed that she had personally presented an English prayer book to the nuns of Syon, whom she had found "prostrate and groveling" and that she had asked her chaplains, the "lanterns and lyght" of her court, to expose a false pilgrimage to the "bloudde of cryste" at Winchcombe, perhaps in 1535 when complaints were forwarded to Cromwell about its members who refused to support the Statute of Supremacy.[74]

There is evidence, moreover, that Anne accepted the advice of influential churchmen such as Cranmer. Often, as in the case of Hugh Latimer's appointment, the archbishop seems to have been a driving force, asking or threatening to ask a number of people, including Anne, the king, and Cromwell, to aid his clients. In a 1534 letter, for example, Cranmer explained that although he could obtain letters from the royal couple for a petitioner, he believed his correspondent ought to handle the matter without further suit. In another extant letter, dated in October 1535, which indicates that the archbishop was attempting to obtain better preachers for Calais, he wrote to Cromwell, asking for access to a benefice over which the secretary had influence and admitting that he had already written to Anne for the gift of two others situated there.[75]

David Hutton of Bristol was one of the many friends for whom the archbishop sought assistance. In 1534 Anne wrote to the corporation of Bristol, perhaps at Cranmer's urging, to grant the next advowson of the college or hospital of St. John the Baptist to Baynton, Shaxton, and David Hutton so that they could present to it a man "of learning, virtue and demeanor." Later, the archbishop not only became involved in an inheritance dispute on behalf of Hutton but also asked Cromwell to favor him.[76]

Dr. Edward Crome, who had served on the 1530 Cambridge committee that had responded favorably to the king's Levitical argument, was another friend of Cranmer. In 1534 Anne wrote to Crome that she was surprised to learn that after she had obtained for him the London parsonage of St. Mary Aldermary, which was then in the archbishop's gift, he had failed to take up residence there. As she said: "We minding nothing more than ye furtherance of vertue, truth & godly doctrine, which we trust shal be a little encreased & right much & better avaunced & established by ye . . . residence there."[77]

Apparently, her plea was successful, for at his death in 1562 he was buried in this parish. The queen may have decided to urge Crome, a pluralist, to move to St. Mary Aldermary, instead of appointing a curate to act for him, because his predecessor had been Henry Gold, an associate of the Nun of Kent who had predicted ruin for the king if he married Anne. Under these circumstances Anne would have wanted the parishioners to hear, as soon as reasonably possible, the preaching of someone who was favorably disposed toward her marriage to Henry. This is the only extant reference, and at best an indirect one, that links the queen to this Nun whose prophesies led to her execution for treason in 1534.[78]

Before her arrest, the Nun had communicated with the bishop of Rochester who was charged with misprision of treason in her conspiracy but actually executed for refusing to support the royal supremacy. There is no extant evidence of the queen's reaction to his death, although after a poisoning episode at Fisher's home in 1531 the Imperial envoy had, without any evidence, accused her of causing the tragedy that had killed two of the bishop's servants but had left him untouched. Despite Chapuys' earlier charge, he did not blame her for the bishop's execution, perhaps because the king's angry reaction to Fisher's elevation to the College of Cardinals had been so well publicized. The Imperial envoy also did not blame her for the death of Thomas More that same summer.[79]

Anne's association with Cromwell and Cranmer on religious issues operated in a fashion similar to that of her secular patronage. On some matters she did not contact either of them, but in other cases, because of their increasing importance in the Church and in the state, she surely would have had to communicate with at least one of them even had she not been so inclined. To use the extant evidence to argue that she formed a faction with Cromwell to recruit reformers into the Church can have at the most only limited meaning. The two reformist issues she is known to have favored, the royal supremacy and scriptural translations, were supported by individuals as different as Hugh Latimer, Cranmer, Bonner, and Heath, the first two churchmen becoming Marian martyrs and the latter two joining their persecutors.

In 1533 Anne assumed an important and influential role in the dispensing of religious and secular patronage. There is no doubt that as queen she sought to further the careers of many of her relatives. Others who supported the royal supremacy and favored scriptural translations also received her help, but it is clear that she favored some individuals for reasons that now must remain obscure. Statements about her household governance and of her charitable activities indicate that one of her major goals as queen was to meet the standards set by other respected noble and royal ladies. The evidence suggests that she would have succeeded in achieving that goal had she given birth to a surviving male child. The birth instead of a daughter brought cares as well as joy, for it was to plunge the royal family into a struggle that can best be described as harem politics and that left the succession in a troubled state.

The dispensing of her patronage and the governance of her household were backdrops to the more serious business of motherhood that Anne had agreed to undertake when she became queen of England. Her first and foremost duty was to give birth to the royal heir, for no consort was ever really secure in her position until she had accomplished that important task. It must never have been out of her thoughts for long that the opportunity to marry the king had arisen only because the male children of his previous wife had died shortly after birth. In this chapter the fate of Anne's pregnancies, which Henry closely monitored, will be examined from the perspective not only of succession politics but also of Anglo-French diplomacy between 1532 and 1536. During those years the Calais meeting between Henry and Francis stands as the high point of their kingdoms' relations that alternated between cordiality and mutual suspicion.

Since Anne was about five months pregnant on 1 June 1533, when she was crowned queen of England, the summer that followed her coronation proved to be a splendid season, a halcyon time, for her and her new husband as they departed on their annual summer progress marking the days until her lying-in. In July, Sir William Kingston wrote from Wanstead, Essex, that the royal couple and all the court were merry, and in August Sir John Russell noted at Sutton, Surrey, that he "never saw [his grace] merrier of a great while than he is now."[1]

In the meantime Anne's household staff had begun to prepare for the grand occasion. About a month before her delivery, the expectant mother customarily retired to a lying-in chamber, the roof, walls, and windows of which, except for one window to let in the light, were hung with arras. An altar was set up in the room; a cupboard was stocked with daily essentials, and a bed complete with curtains, coverlet, pillows, and cushions was installed. From her entry into the room in which she remained up to about forty days after the delivery, she was attended only by her gentle-women, some of whom assumed the tasks normally performed by men. In July, William, Lord Mountjoy, the ex-chamberlain of Catherine, sent to Cromwell some "remembrances" of things to be provided when the queen took to her chamber and asked that they be brought to the attention of Anne's chamberlain.[2]

The new queen, who was, according to Cromwell, in good health on 17 July, did not arrive at Greenwich where she was to take her chamber until about 26 August, for she was with the king at Westminster on 23 August and was not scheduled to arrive in Greenwich for three more days. As a consequence of this itiner-ary, she was confined in her chamber less than two weeks before the birth of Elizabeth, her only surviving child, between three and four o'clock in the afternoon on Sunday, 7 September. When she took to her chamber on 26 August, Anne signalled to the court, by way of this protocol, that she did not expect the delivery to take place before the end of September. It is possible that her husband, believing that she was actually due earlier in that month, took advantage of her good health to delay her arrival at Greenwich in order to create confusion about when the concep-tion had taken place. However, because he would necessarily have been concerned about following all the traditional guide-lines for the birth of a royal child, who he expected and hoped would be his male heir, and because the accuracy of due-date predictions was far less reliable in the pre-modern period than in the twentieth century, it is more likely that the royal couple genuinely believed that she would be delivered near the end of September. To suggest such a miscalculation on the part of her midwives and physicians is reasonable because the nature of the menstrual flow and its association with pregnancy were not then understood, a further complication being that women do some-times menstruate in early pregnancy. Anne's behavior in August indicates that she must have been told that the conception had occurred in late December. Even if she actually believed that she had become pregnant earlier in December, on 25 January when she was married to the king, she, being without access to modern medical knowledge and technology, could only have been hopeful but not absolutely certain that she was an expectant mother.[3]

In anticipation of the child's birth, the king had selected the names of Edward and Henry and had ordered his advisers to prepare the more elaborate protocol customarily used for welcoming a son's safe delivery. A tournament and a pageant were planned in his honor and the French resident envoy was asked to hold him at the font during his christening. Neither of these arrangements was put into effect since the child was a female and undeserving of this extraordinary attention. Henry's expectation that a son would be born may have been bolstered by the reports of astrologers and prophets who predicted the child would be a male. In one of his love letters to Anne in 1528, he had indicated a personal interest in astrology: in attempting to dispel her fears about their forced separation, he had consoled her with the message that the farther off the sun was the greater was the heat that it generated. As Melancthon later said in his dedication to the *Commonplaces*: Henry is "the most learned of kings not only in theology, but also in other philosophy, and especially in the study of the movement of the heavens." Since the king and his learned contemporaries held "a complex view of conception in which both the physical and spiritual" were intertwined, he may have been persuaded of the validity of the prophecies about the child's sex because he had personally done all that was necessary for him to earn and to merit a divine blessing in the form of a son.[4]

Contemporary records abound with references to prophecies and predictions that were normally taken quite seriously. Many of them were similar to the one of the Nun of Kent that had foretold the king's downfall. Anne's skeptical attitude toward the most superstitious of them must have been well known, for John Foxe later claimed that through her "christian and faithful counsel" she had "so armed" Henry against "all infidelity" that he had disregarded an old "blind prophecy" predicting dire consequences for the monarchs of England who hunted in the park at Woodstock or entered into the town of Oxford. That this story is apocryphal there is no doubt, for Henry had hunted at Woodstock long before Anne became his love.[5]

Some of the predictions, such as the one George Cavendish recalled, foretold ruin for the Church when a dun cow, a symbol of the Tudor earldom of Richmond, "rideth" a bull, a symbol of the Boleyn family. From 1535 a similar prophecy, detailing the death of priests, featured a white falcon, which was Anne's device as queen and which had been so prominently displayed during her entry into London. Others spoke vaguely of the burning of a queen and some bishops at Smithfield. As early as 1530 Chapuys had claimed that Anne had vowed to Henry: "it is foretold in ancient prophecies that at this time a Queen shall be burnt; but even if I were to suffer a thousand deaths, my love for you will not abate one jot." Four years late Chapuys had heard that she was quite willing to permit Catherine to suffer this fiery death.[6]

Quoting his relative who had attended Anne, George Wyatt related her reaction to a similar prophecy. The details of his story seem to indicate that despite Anne's awareness of these dire predictions, she remained confident that she was destined to give birth to the long-awaited male heir. When there came into her possession, Wyatt revealed, a book with the letters "H," "A," and "K" in which it was foretold that she would meet destruction if she became Henry's wife, Anne reportedly said: "I think the book a bauble; yet for the hope I have that the realm may be happy by my issue, I am resolved to have him [the king] whatsoever might become of me."[7]

During an audience with the Venetian envoy in June 1533, the queen remarked that God had "inspired his Majesty to marry her." This comment, which may have been a veiled allusion to Henry's reason for divorcing Catherine, seems to corroborate the later stories that Anne believed she had been destined to become queen of England. Her chaplain William Latimer also recalled that she had attributed her royal estate to the "kyndness of almightie God."[8]

Such deep confidence in her fate seems to belie an anecdote related by Chapuys to the emperor on 3 September, only four days before she was delivered of Elizabeth and about a week after she had entered her lying-in chamber. The envoy wrote that recently the royal couple had quarreled because he had given her "legitimate" cause to be jealous. The king had allegedly responded to her protests with the remark that "she must shut her eyes and endure as those who were better than herself had done."

For a few days after the dispute, there had been, the diplomat said, coldness and grumbling between the royal couple.[9]

Although Anne could have had a minor disagreement with Henry during the days just before she took to her chamber, Chapuys' word cannot be trusted, for he was seldom able to confirm the ubiquitous rumors he forwarded to the emperor. Checking on the validity of his stories was an extremely difficult if not impossible task for him since, unlike the envoys of France and Venice, he rarely attended functions at court and never had an audience with Anne, whom he refused to recognize as queen. An indication of how much credence can be given to this and other gossip that was based on his dispatches is that one year earlier rumors abroad had indicated at about the same time that the king was consummating his love for Anne, that he was actually courting another lady.[10]

The birth of a healthy male heir was so important to Henry that it is unreasonable to credit the report that he had used such harsh language to his consort only days or even weeks before she was due to be delivered of his child, especially as there was a widespread belief that the mother's imagination could adversely affect the looks and well being of her unborn infant. To avoid deformities in their children, contemporaries admonished husbands to dote on their pregnant wives. On the same day that Chapuys was writing about this alleged quarrel, the French envoy, who was in Henry's confidence, wrote to his king about the pending birth without mentioning any disagreement between the royal couple.[11]

Given these reservations, it is still reasonable to speculate that in the months after his child was conceived, the king may have engaged in a few extra-marital liaisons. By the standards of the day, a gentleman's honor would be diminished by several actions but a simple adulterous affair with a woman was not one of them. In a discussion of Henry's sexual reputation, it is relevant that long before he gained notoriety as the husband of six women an anonymous author of a manuscript at Rome was willing to predict that Anne's child would be weak, "owing to his father's complexion and habits of life." Contemporaries generally believed that when a man engaged in sexual intercourse too frequently, he would suffer from physical debility. Equally important to the question of the mores of the English aristocracy is that husbands were warned against having conjugal relations with their pregnant wives because a childbearing woman was believed to be in an unclean state; there was an abiding fear of injuring the unborn infant; and the Church condemned sexual acts that could not lead to conception.[12]

After the birth of Elizabeth, Anne was expected to remain in seclusion for between thirty and forty days before emerging to be purified in a churching ceremony. The anniversary of the Virgin Mary's churching, "one of the greatest solemnities celebrated during the year" by Henry, was honored on 2 February, exactly forty days after 25 December. Apparently, Anne was churched in less than forty days after her delivery, for Sir Richard Page wrote on 15 October that the king and queen were merry. Until a childbearing woman had participated in this service that was derived ultimately from the Jewish rite of Purification, she was considered unclean and unfit to resume her normal social relationships. As late as the nineteenth century, a belief in rural Norfolk claimed that it was disgraceful for an unpurified woman to cross the highway or go to a neighbour's home. The medieval service, which was basically the one included in the first Book of Common Prayer, required the new mother to approach the choir door of the Church where she was met by a priest, who conducted the short service that was composed largely of a reading of Psalm 121: "I have lifted mine eyes unto the hills, from whence commeth my help?" Afterwards the woman normally received communion.[13]

That Henry had been disappointed by his child's sex, there is no doubt, but, although the protocol for the birth of boys was more elaborate than that for girls, it is ridiculous to assume that the king felt the same about his daughter as the eighteenth-century earl of Buckingham, who reportedly said when told about his newest female infant: "Then you had better go and drag the baby through the horse-pond." As the king's only legitimate child, Elizabeth was, until the birth of a prince, his heir and was to be treated with all the respect that a female of her rank deserved. Regardless of her child's sex, the queen's safe delivery could still be used to argue that God had blessed the marriage.

Everything that was proper was done to herald the infant's arrival: letters were dispatched announcing her birth; *Te deum* was sung for the queen's safe delivery; prayers were said on behalf of the king, his consort, and heir; and 10 September was set aside for the christening.[14]

Traditionally, scholars have pointed to the king's absence at Elizabeth's christening as one certain sign of his disappointment with her birth, but it would have been astonishing had he been present for the ceremony, for godparents, not parents, were the individuals of rank on such occasions. Because the Church had been careful to preserve a distinction between spiritual and carnal relationships, biological parents, who were prevented from serving as godparents, customarily were not present at the christenings of their children. Had the king's absence from Elizabeth's ceremony appeared unusual, Chapuys would surely have forwarded to the emperor the gossip that Henry had publicly slighted his daughter. Given the circumstances, the most disparaging comment this envoy could make was: "The christening ceremony was as dull and disagreeable as the mother's coronation." As Henry's behavior during Anne's coronation had earlier indicated, a king, for social reasons, also did not participate in most of the ceremonies honoring his relatives because, as he outranked them, his presence would only serve to detract from their glory.[15]

Elizabeth's christening was held at the Friars' Church in Greenwich where her elder half-sister's ceremony had taken place in 1516. As early as July, when the queen's servants were preparing her lying-in chamber, they were also making arrangements for this first Christian ritual for her child. If Chapuys was correct – and it seems likely, as he was in secret communication with Catherine – the king, and perhaps Anne, had hoped to have for Elizabeth the "very rich and gorgeous piece of cloth" that had been used in Mary's service. Since Catherine, who had maintained possession of it, refused their request on the basis that she had brought it with her from Spain especially for her own children, another precious cloth was obtained for Elizabeth. Following ancient custom the Lord Mayor and aldermen of London and many esteemed members of the nobility, including Suffolk, Norfolk, and his daughter, Mary Howard, were invited to salute the new royal heir. Her godfather was the archbishop of Canterbury and her godmothers were Agnes, dowager duchess of Norfolk, who bore the child in a mantle of purple cloth, and Margaret, dowager marchioness of Dorset.[16]

Immediately following her christening, the archbishop confirmed Elizabeth into the Church with Gertrude, marchioness of Exeter, serving as her godmother. After his infant was led in a procession back to Anne, the king, who did not appear, ordered that refreshments be served and commissioned Norfolk and Suffolk to thank the Londoners for honoring his daughter. A few months later when her parents visited her at Eltham, Sir William Kingston wrote "her Grace [Elizabeth] is much in the King's favour as a godely child should be, God save her."[17]

Very little evidence has survived about Anne's duties as a new mother. There are occasional references in the State Papers to her visits to the nursery, as at Eltham during Lent and Easter in 1534 or at Richmond in October 1534 when she was accompanied by Norfolk and Suffolk. Following the custom of the English nobility, Elizabeth was placed in the care of a wetnurse under the general supervision of her governess, Margaret, Lady Bryan. The mother of Sir Francis and a distant cousin of the queen, Lady Bryan had also served as governess for the king's elder daughter. About three months after her birth, Elizabeth and her household were dispatched to Hatfield, a manor near Hertford. Here and at Hunsdon in Hertfordshire the princess spent much of her childhood although, like her parents, she traveled from house to house, staying in such places as Richmond, Eltham, Langley, and the More. In late 1535 following her second birthday, her governess wrote to Cromwell, seeking permission to wean her. After the secretary had forwarded this request on to her parents, Sir William Paulet, the king's comptroller, informed Lady Bryan of their consent that she be weaned.[18]

An account book of William Locke, the king's mercer, which covers the early months of 1536, also has some information about the childhood of Elizabeth. In it are listed numerous items of apparel he obtained for the queen and several for the princess, including an orange satin gown and a russet velvet kirtle. The king's heir, who was not yet three years old, was quite properly to be dressed in fashionable and expensive clothing. William

Latimer also reported that Anne had wanted her child, as her elder half-sister had been, trained in classical languages.[19]

By 1533 Chapuys had for a long time been expressing concern about the well being of both Catherine and her daughter. The envoy had complained to the king's advisers about the treatment of the ex-queen, protesting the confiscation of her barge, her jewels, and other possessions. Believing that Anne was conspiring to effect first the disgrace and then the death of Mary, he blamed her personally for the rustication of the princess. He feared that Mary would be required to attend her new stepmother at court, but from the point of view of this princess an equally dire and perhaps worse fate was in store for her. After the birth of Elizabeth, Henry demanded that his elder daughter relinquish the title of princess of Wales to her younger half-sister. This demotion was the first of many unpleasant occurrences for Mary, soon officially to be pronounced illegitimate. In October she was evicted from Beaulieu, a manor that had been recently granted to Rochford, and in December she was moved into Elizabeth's household under the supervision of Lady Anne Shelton, her new governess and a sister of the queen's father.[20]

As Mary was frequently ill, her unhappy removal to her sister's household became for her an even greater ordeal. It was because of her sickness that some information has survived about the way the household of the new princess was run. Mary had normally skipped breakfast and had eaten dinner earlier than the usual eleven a.m. When she was denied permission to continue this habit, she asked to be permitted to have a larger breakfast containing more meat in exchange for eating "little more meat unto supper."[21]

By his divorce and remarriage Henry had created for himself a domestic tangle that was unusual for his day. Unlike most of his contemporaries, he had two living wives, and when his second consort presented him with a female child, confusion reigned in the minds of many about which daughter had the better claim to the throne. Normally, the battle to inherit the kingdom, as in the early case of Edgar the Peaceable or in the later cases of Henry I and Edward IV, was fought out after the death of the king between the households of his heirs and their relatives. In Henry VIII's reign that struggle began immediately with the birth of

Elizabeth and was not ended, as he had hoped, by the passage in early 1534 of the Succession Statute, designating her as his official heir.[22]

If Chapuys were to be believed, Mary's demotion and her daily trials were solely the new queen's fault. In the early months of 1534 he forwarded tales to the emperor about how Anne was mistreating the young lady, thus casting her in the role of the evil stepmother. In February he claimed that she had ordered her aunt Shelton not to tolerate Mary's use of the title of princess and to "slap her face as the cursed bastard that she was." The next month when Anne visited the nursery, he reported a more believable incident. The king's concubine, he said, had sent word to Mary that if she would only honor Anne as queen, in effect recognizing her own illegitimacy, she would regain her father's favor and would again be received at court. Henry had, after all, treated Richmond, his natural son, quite well.[23]

Even had Anne been content to ignore Mary's uncooperative attitude, the king would still have been determined to enforce his will upon his elder daughter. Because he personally believed that his union with Catherine was invalid, he required Mary to agree to both her parents' divorce and his royal supremacy, which was recognized by statutory law in late 1534. In February of that same year, when Chapuys had protested her demotion, the king had retorted that "he could dispose of his daughter as he pleased without having to render account to anyone," and the next month he informed the French envoy that he was unhappy with her because she would not recognize Anne as queen or Elizabeth as princess. His handling of his elder daughter in June 1536, after Anne's death, is instructive about who the author of her earlier treatment was. Before her father would permit her to join him and his new consort, Jane Seymour, at court, he required her to state in writing that the divorce was valid and that he was the supreme head of the Church. When she submitted, Cromwell wrote triumphantly that she was a "most obedient child."[24]

Even after Elizabeth's birth the king remained confident that his wife would soon have a son. Early in December 1533, apparently in a jovial mood, he introduced Anne to Christopher Mont, a German in the English diplomatic service, who was incorrectly identified by Chapuys as a servant of Cromwell, perhaps in a misguided attempt to indicate to the emperor that the king had meant to insult his consort by bringing someone of low social status into her presence. At Christmas that year, Henry held a great court with Anne and was reportedly "merry and lusty." For his New Year's present, she chose to give him a gift that must be characterized as a fertility symbol. It was a fountain of gold garnished with rubies and diamonds "out thereof issueth water, at the teats of three naked women standing at the foot of the same fountain." A few days later, in the instructions to Mont and Nicholas Heath, who were being sent on an embassy to the German princes, Henry referred to Anne's virtues, among them her chastity, her noble descent and parentage, her education, and her ability to procreate children. At the end of January amidst rumors that she was once again pregnant, a correspondent of Lisle noted that the king and queen were merry.[25]

During the early months of 1534 when Henry was hoping to persuade Mary to renounce her succession rights in favor of Elizabeth, he was looking forward to the birth of a son. In February he confirmed to Chapuys, who had already heard gossip that Anne was pregnant, that he thought he would shortly be a father again. During that spring, a court observer referred to the queen's "goodly" belly, indicating that her condition had become general knowledge, and described the royal couple as merry. As it was not customary in England for public announcements to be made about the pregnancies of the royal family, physical signs and hints in conversations provided courtiers with the only evidence of the queen's secret. The last dated reference to anyone's having actually seen Anne, before rumors spread in September that she was not pregnant, was at Hampton Court on 26 June when she was with the king and said to be merry. At that time Henry was planning an August meeting with Francis at Calais, apparently to take place after her lying-in.[26]

On 2 July Henry summoned Norfolk and Cromwell to meet with him at the More on 5 July. The decision was made at the More, if not earlier, to send the queen's brother on a special embassy to France. His secret instructions, when he departed a few days later, were to request the queen of Navarre, whom Anne "hath ever entierlie loved," to intercede with the king, her brother, to defer the Calais meeting, leaving open the possibility that it might be rescheduled for April. Rochford was to inform them that Henry had agreed to the delay only because of the persistent suit of Anne, who was "so farre gon with childe" that she was unable to accompany her husband and would be unduly anxious about his safety if he were to cross the Channel at this time. The case for the delay, Rochford was also warned, was to be presented so carefully to Francis "as He smell not the kinges highness to be over much desirous of it, but all in the Queenes name." On 7 July, Chapuys informed the emperor that Lord Montague had sent him a message, which the envoy took seriously but which, considering the above details about Rochford's mission, seems rather ridiculous, that Francis had warned Henry that when he came to Calais he was not to speak against the pope. Either Montague was a dupe of Cromwell, who had misled the nobleman into thinking that the meeting would still take place because it was believed he would leak this erroneous information to Chapuys, or else Montague was commissioned to confuse the envoy about the whole Calais business. The second option is the better guess. The cancellation of the trip was not announced until 29 July, after Rochford's return, when it was claimed that the action had been taken at Cromwell's suggestion.[27]

The next dated reference to Anne, after these diplomatic instructions were written, is in a letter of 18 July that seems to indicate that Henry had left her behind when he went to the More on 2 July and that, from the More, he had continued on his already delayed summer progress, arriving by 8 July at Cheneys, Buckinghamshire. According to the letter of the 18th, which was sent from Woking, Surrey, he was planning to visit Elizabeth at Eltham on the 25th and then to join the queen at Guildford Castle, the park of which was under the keepership of Sir William Fitzwilliam. The king did arrive at Guildford on 28 July and remained there until 7 August. Except for the few weeks during the summer of 1533, when the queen had retired to her lying-in chamber, this was their most extended separation since 1528, when she had left court in anticipation of Campeggio's arrival. Whether after Henry met her at Guildford, she continued on the progress with him in 1534 is uncertain. If she did accompany him, she would have been with him at Woodstock when Chapuys made the last extant comment about this pregnancy. Drawing upon rumors circulating at court, he claimed on 23 September that the king had begun to have doubts about it.[28]

Because no contemporary statement referred to a miscarriage or a stillborn child, it is possible that Anne was never pregnant. Henry could only have been uncertain about it, and it is noteworthy that the only testimony for this uncertainty survives in Chapuys' correspondence, if his queen had either failed to be delivered of a child or had a miscarriage. A failure such as this could have been, as Sir John Dewhurst has suggested, the result of her having suffered a false pregnancy, called a pseudocyesis. This disorder is manifested by the visible swelling of the abdomen and occurs in women who are "desperate to prove their fertility." Other women of the English royal family, as for instance Anne's stepdaughter, Mary, and the seventeenth-century monarch Mary II, are thought to have developed this condition. Both of these queens remained childless.[29]

Anne was anxious to have a son, but it seems unreasonable to argue that just six or seven weeks after she had been delivered of a normal child, her body would take on the physical signs of pregnancy in response to deep emotional fears concerning her fertility. Although the sex of Elizabeth was unfortunate for the queen, that she had conceived her child in late 1532 so quickly, after what may have been her first sexual union with the king, would seem to be solid evidence for the argument that this birth had served to raise rather than to lower her confidence in her fertility. As Anne believed she was fated to present Henry with a son and heir, that in late 1533 she still had a positive attitude toward childbearing seems a reasonable conclusion.

A more likely speculation about her condition in 1534 than a false pregnancy is that some time after 26 June but before 2 July she was delivered of a stillborn child. On 2 July Henry decided to go without her on his already delayed summer progress while she ultimately spent some time in a castle, the park's keepership of which was held by Fitzwilliam, one of her husband's most trusted household advisers. The decision of the royal couple to separate at this time can only be viewed as extraordinary, for in 1533 she had traveled with him until less than two weeks before she had taken to her chamber at Greenwich.[30]

On 5 July the king met with Cromwell and her uncle Norfolk at the More, probably for the purpose of discussing the implications of this most recent tragedy in his nursery. As Henry considered a miscarriage or stillbirth an ill omen for his kingdom as well as for his dynasty, he would have preferred for it to be assumed that the pregnancy, which had never been announced officially, had been falsely diagnosed. He surely would have wanted to avoid a discussion that summer about either of these possibilities with Francis who was already the father of three sons. As Henry had been attempting to negotiate the marriage of Elizabeth to one of the French princes, Anne's condition, for the purpose of clarifying the status of her daughter in the succession, would have been an unavoidable topic at Calais. Without having the birth of a son to look forward to, Henry may also have been reluctant to press forward vigorously at this time with these marriage arrangements for Elizabeth, who was still his heir. If this speculation about Anne's pregnancy is correct, then it is ironic that although it had already been terminated, it was still considered the best excuse for canceling the Calais meeting.[31]

That a stillbirth or miscarriage could have been kept a secret was entirely possible. In 1510, for example, Catherine of Aragon's miscarriage was known only to the king, her chancellor, two Spanish women, and a physican. The evidence for this miscarriage survives solely in letters that Catherine and her chancellor wrote to Ferdinand of Spain four months after it had occurred. The only miscarriage (including stillbirths) of Henry's wives to be reported by Edward Hall, the chronicler, was the one of Anne in January 1536. That extraordinary announcement was, as events were to prove, to be an important sign of her downfall.[32]

In the same September letter that he discussed the uncertainty of Anne's pregnancy, Chapuys reported that the king had taken a new mistress. Later the envoy revealed that this lady had sent a message to Mary that she would be her friend and would persuade Henry to be more kind to her. Although these remarks of Chapuys, who believed naively that the treatment of the king's elder daughter had been carried out largely without her father's knowledge, must be read with great caution, it is likely that Mary had actually informed the envoy of oral messages allegedly sent to her by an anonymous lady at court, probably through the agency of Sir Nicholas Carew who had been in communication with the princess that autumn. In December Carew, who was ingratiating himself with both the French and Imperial ambassadors, also revealed to Chapuys the details of an argument between Anne and Henry over this mistress.[33]

Besides informing the emperor about Henry's mistress, Chapuys revealed that the king had been displeased with three of the queen's relatives. He had rusticated Rochford's wife, the envoy claimed, because she had conspired with Anne to get rid of his new lady friend. As very little evidence has survived about the viscountess, it is impossible to discover whether in fact she had left court, or, if so, whether in disgrace or for personal reasons. Chapuys further reported that Rochford had lost a dispute with Sir Francis Bryan, who had been able to draw upon the support of the king in the controversy, and that Mary Rochford, the queen's sister, had been expelled from court for secretly marrying a commoner. Of these allegations, only the one about Mary can be corroborated by independent evidence, but it is clear from a letter that she wrote to Cromwell that it was not the king but her own family who had disowned her. All these events had happened some weeks earlier, and the envoy, who had to admit that he could discern no further sign of the king's ill humor towards his consort's relatives, speculated that the royal couple must merely have been having a lovers' quarrel. The timing of Chapuys' recognition that the favor of the king was being restored toward Anne and her relatives is interesting, as will be discussed below, because it coincided with the departure from England of Philip Chabot, sieur de Brion, admiral of France, and a special envoy of Francis.[34]

The discovery that in September 1534 rumors were claiming that Henry had taken a mistress is not unexpected given the disappointment he must have felt at Anne's failure to give birth to the long-hoped-for heir that summer. He probably did fault his queen for this latest tragedy, since his contemporaries usually blamed women for failures in childbirth and conception. That there might well have been a strained relationship between the royal couple in the autumn of 1534 is a reasonable conclusion even without the use of Chapuys' gossip as supporting evidence. The extent of that estrangement, if it occurred, must not be overstated, for on 2 October John Husee, who seems to have perceived no diminution in Anne's influence, warned Lord Lisle that Robert Wheathill was still hoping to obtain a letter from both the king and queen in support of his appointment to a spear's post at Calais. On 16 October, Cromwell received a complaint from John Hilsey who feared that he might lose his offices in part because of the influence of a member of the queen's household, and on 22 October the king granted a yeoman usher of Anne the office of bailiff on one of the royal manors. Shortly thereafter, Henry presented his consort with a manor in Hertford-shire and at the height of the Christmas season kept a "great house" with her.[35]

As Carew, who had developed a special relationship with the admiral of France, was the courtier that leaked the information to the Imperial envoy and perhaps to Mary about her father's new mistress, these stories were probably fabrications to distract them both from asking embarrassing questions about Anne's recent pregnancy. Since the queen's interests were identified publicly with those of France, the rumors could also be interpreted as signs of unfriendly relations between Henry and Francis. It will be helpful, therefore, to review briefly the diplomatic goals of these two monarchs between 1532 and 1536. At their Calais meeting in 1532, they had agreed to coordinate their efforts in Germany and at Rome. High on Henry's agenda had been the promise of Francis to lobby the pope for a delay in publishing a bull that would validate his union with Catherine. For about a year after their return to their respective kingdoms, communications between the two monarchs had remained cordial. In March 1533, Francis sent Anne a letter written in his own hand and in June, after his envoys had participated in her coronation cele-brations, he authorized the presentation to her of a sedan chair. Caution should be used in treating this friendship as personal, for it serves as a microcosmic view of Anglo-French rapport at this time.[36]

Shortly after Elizabeth's birth, the actions of Francis and Clement at a Marseilles meeting caused Henry to become suspi-cious of the French king's motives. Instead of delaying the previously agreed upon marital union between his second son, Henri, duke of Orléans, and the pope's niece, Catherine de

Medici, in an attempt to pressure Clement to act on behalf of the English king, Francis permitted the two young people to be wed at that time. Although he had also been able to persuade the pope to suspend, albeit only temporarily, the publication of Henry's excommunication, the English king was not mollified. Francis responded to Henry's anger by sending John du Bellay, now bishop of Paris, on a special assignment to London in December 1533. The visit of the bishop, who had been in England to negotiate the Calais meeting in 1532, failed to smooth over the difficulties, for Henry kept him waiting for four days before granting him an audience. The queen, perhaps recalling with pleasure the halcyon days of 1532 when she had hunted with du Bellay, gave him a kiss when he presented a letter to her from Francis.[37]

For a time relations between England and France did not seem to improve. In April 1534, after Henry had been excommunicated, Chapuys noted that the royal couple had failed to dine publicly with the resident French diplomat as was their usual custom during the religious festivals. That Henry's attitude toward the representatives of other kingdoms was viewed as a gauge of his relations with their rulers there is no doubt. Earlier that year Chapuys had claimed that the king's cordial treatment of the Scottish envoys clearly meant that he was interested in establishing peaceful relations with their country. Even though he had not invited the resident French ambassador to his Easter banquet, the king did permit him and two other special envoys, who had just arrived in England, to pay their respects to Elizabeth. Chapuys reported the following about that meeting: "[she] was brought out to them splendidly accoutred and dressed, and in princely state, with all the ceremonial her governess could think of, after which they saw her quite undressed."[38]

Henry's display of his perfectly formed daughter in the nude to the envoys was a signal that Anglo-French relations were on the mend. In May 1534, the queen's brother returned from a conference with Francis in which plans were tentatively made not only for an alliance between them that was to be bolstered by the marriage of Elizabeth and Charles, duke of Angoulême, the third son of Francis, but also for another meeting of the two kings at Calais. Overjoyed at this response, Henry and Anne publicly praised Francis during a special banquet at court. Apparently the two kingdoms had become "entirely reconciled," for Chapuys noted that Henry had "shown more vivacity and content than is his wont." Events seemed to be back on a positive track for the king: he had learned that his wife was pregnant for a second time and that his daughter might marry into the French royal family.[39]

In July, of course, the meeting at Calais was called off, perhaps in an insulting manner from the point of view of Francis, as Chapuys was to spread rumors that Anne had never been pregnant. Relations between the two kingdoms again deteriorated, an estrangement that continued even after the death of Clement in September of that year. In the meantime Henry's ministers were attempting through Chapuys to open up communications with the emperor. Before the arrival on 16 November 1534 of the sieur de Brion, one of Francis' principal ministers, who had been sent to England with a special proposal, Cromwell was assuring Chapuys that Catherine would soon be better treated. It was during this period that Henry's alleged new mistress sent to Mary friendly messages, promising to speak to her father on her behalf. Although Chapuys also claimed that no one at court dared to criticize the king's elder daughter, he did worry, with good reason, that the sudden kindness might have its origins in dissimulation. A few weeks later Norfolk was questioning Mary closely in an attempt to discover which one of her maids had been forwarding messages to the Imperial envoy.[40]

At first the visit of the admiral, who was escorted to London by Norfolk, would seem to have inaugurated friendly relations between England and France once again. He was lodged at Bridewell Palace, entertained with tennis and dancing, and invited frequently to court where he dined publicly with the king. Norfolk threw a grand party for him on 29 November and Suffolk on 30 November. Later, when the admiral and his entourage stopped at Calais on their way home, they were still talking about how well they had been entertained at the English court. In reporting the visit, Chapuys, who must have been envious that the crown was defraying so many of the Frenchmen's expenses, perceived a problem. He observed, "Nor has he, as I am told, made much of the Lady Anne." That there continued to be a coolness in relations between the two kingdoms was further

17   Mary Boleyn, sister of Anne. Hans Holbein the Younger. Gavin Astor, Hever Castle.

18   William Carey, husband to Mary Boleyn. Attributed to Hans Holbein
the Younger. Private Irish Collection.

Henry Carey
Lord Hunsdon
BY MARK GERARDS.

ÆTATIS SVÆ 66
AN° 1591

19   Henry Carey, Lord Hunsdon. Son of Mary and William Carey and
ward of Anne Boleyn. Trustee of the Will of the eighth earl of Berkeley.
Courtauld Institute of Art.

20   Thomas Howard, third duke of Norfolk, uncle to Anne Boleyn. Hans Holbein the Younger. Royal Collection.

21   Henry Howard, earl of Surrey, son of the third duke of Norfolk.
Portrait by Hans Holbein the Younger wrongly inscribed "Thomas, earl of
Surrey". Royal Collection.

The Lady of Richmond.

22   Mary, duchess of Richmond and Somerset, daughter of the third duke of Norfolk. She married Henry, duke of Richmond and Somerset, the illegitimate son of Henry VIII, in 1533. Hans Holbein the Younger. Royal Collection.

The Lady Henegham.

23   Mary Shelton (?), daughter of Anne Boleyn's aunt and her husband, Sir John Shelton the elder. She married Sir Anthony Heveningham in 1546. Hans Holbein the Younger. Royal Collection.

EARL OF ESSEX.

24   Thomas Cromwell. After Hans Holbein the Younger. National
Portrait Gallery.

25   William Fitzwilliam, later earl of Southampton. Hans Holbein the
Younger. Royal Collection.

26 The Chapel of St. Peter ad Vincula at the Tower of London, which
was rebuilt for the third time in 1515. Before the high altar are the tombs of
Anne and Katherine, the second and fifth wives of Henry VIII,
respectively. Ministry of Public Buildings and Works.

27   A Tudor dynastic portrait. Henry VII and Elizabeth of York in the
background with Henry VIII and his third wife, Jane, the mother of his
only legitimate son, Edward, Prince of Wales, who was born in 1537. Copy
made by R. van Leemput in 1667 of a painting by Hans Holbein the
Younger commissioned in 1537 for the Privy Chamber of Whitehall Palace.
The original was destroyed by fire in 1698. Royal Collection.

28   The coronation portrait of Queen Elizabeth I. National Portrait
Gallery.

29   Thomas Cranmer, archbishop of Canterbury. Gerhard Flicke. National
Portrait Gallery.

proved by the admiral's actions at a public reception he held on 5 December only days before his departure for home. When Chapuys arrived at his party, the admiral displayed unexpected affection for his guest and spoke in praise of Mary, to whom he was sorry he had been unable to pay his respects.[41]

The news that Chapuys later learned about the admiral's visit explained his distant treatment of Anne and his warm greeting to the Imperial envoy. The admiral had brought a proposal to England from Francis, who had apparently obtained the idea from the emperor, that Mary not Elizabeth should marry Angoulême. Henry, who at first thought the sieur de Brion was joking, was outraged but conceded the alliance on the condition that the two young people would relinquish all claim to the English throne. Henry's alternative proposal was that if Elizabeth were to marry the duke and the pope were to lift the excommunication, then he would surrender England's territorial claims to France. Clearly, the unexpected expression of sympathy by Henry's alleged mistress for his elder daughter and the admiral's praise of Mary had been signals of the strained Anglo-French relations.[42]

On 14 January 1535, a few weeks after the departure of the admiral, Chapuys forwarded to the emperor the following anecdote. The sieur de Brion reportedly had been seated near Anne who suddenly burst out laughing, and when he asked if she were "mocking" him, she had responded: "I could not help laughing at the King's proposition of introducing your secretary to me, for whilst he was looking out for him he happened to meet a lady, who was the cause of his forgetting everything."[43] The belated date on which this suspect story was sent by Chapuys makes it seem even more suspect, but if the exchange had taken place the point was not that Anne had been ignored by the king but that she had taken care to emphasize to the envoy that for an entirely frivolous reason Henry had forgotten all about the secretary, who happened to be Palamedes Gontier, the treasurer of Brittany and an important member of the French aristocracy![44]

Later that month, when, thanks to Chapuys, this anecdote was circulating in Christendom, Gontier returned to England with messages from the admiral. Upon his arrival, the treasurer wrote home that he had met with the French resident ambassador, who had complained that he dared not ask for an audience with the king, who was unhappy about the delay in the French response to his proposals. Following his subsequent meeting with Henry, Gontier had been escorted by Cromwell to the queen to whom he had delivered the admiral's letters. After complaining that the long delay had caused her husband "many doubts,"

She said the Admiral must think of applying some remedy, and act towards the King so that she may not be ruined and lost, for she sees herself very near that, and in more grief and trouble than before her marriage. She charged him to beg the Admiral to consider her affairs, of which she could not speak as fully as she wished, on account of her fears, and the eyes which were looking at her, her husband's and the lords' present. She said she could not write, nor see him again, nor stay longer.[45]

After the interview, Anne did not join Henry in the dancing and other entertainment, perhaps to emphasize by her actions the validity of the strong words she had spoken to the treasurer. For his part, Gontier later summed up her remarks with the statement that "As far as he can judge, she is not at her ease on account of the doubts and suspicions of the king, which he has mentioned before." Clearly, her concern was that the French had preferred Mary to her daughter as a bride for Angoulême.[46]

It is obvious from her conversation that she believed the French had betrayed her. When her two pregnancies had left England without the expected male heir, Francis had made her insecure position seem even more perilous by rejecting her daughter as a bride for his son. Her comments must ultimately be looked upon as an attempt to persuade Gontier to abandon the proposed union between Mary and Angoulême on the basis that if Anne and her lineage were disgraced in England, the French cause would be lost. Were Henry to return to Catherine, the domestic reconciliation would almost certainly be accompanied by a renewed Anglo-Imperial alliance, which Francis would surely want to prevent, as he was even then preparing to embark upon another offensive war against Charles V. Although she was eager to impress upon the French how their cause in England was tied to hers, it must not be assumed that her life was in great peril or that Catherine was on the verge of being reinstated as queen. One of the Imperial advisers, in a letter dated March 1535, indicated a shrewd understanding of these diplomatic exchanges when he warned Chapuys that the English had treated him better merely "to render the French jealous."[47]

During the next few months, only bits of information about Anne have survived. In February Chapuys reported that the young lady who was lately in the favor of the king had been replaced by a daughter of Lady Shelton, the queen's aunt. She was probably Mary Shelton whom Anne chastised for writing idle poesies in her prayer book. Since on this occasion Chapuys identified the last name of the lady rumored to be the king's mistress, his statement must be taken a little more seriously than his remarks about the anonymous woman the previous autumn. Although a few years later, in fact, rumors reported by an English observer were once again to link the names of Henry and Mary Shelton, it is possible that Chapuys' report in February 1535 was based on gossip about Anne's disapproval of the marked attention some gentlemen of her husband's privy chamber, especially Sir Francis Weston, were paying to her young cousin. The queen was presented with a problem of an entirely different nature in April 1535 when she was forced to remove to Hampton Court after one of her ladies had caught the measles. As he aged, Henry's anxiety about illness seems to have increased rather than lessened. In the spring of 1528, after Catherine's maidens had been stricken with smallpox at Greenwich, for example, although he had isolated himself from them, he had not expelled them from the grounds of the palace altogether. His fears must have been very well known. In 1534 while it was thought he would go to Calais, a top priority on Lisle's list of tasks to accomplish in preparation for the royal visit was to make certain that the town was free from the plague and dirt.[48]

During his audiences with Henry in January 1535, Palamedes Gontier, the treasurer of Brittany, had explored the possibility of another Calais conference between the two kings. According to Gontier, the English monarch asked that Francis, who was still married to the emperor's sister, be accompanied by Margaret of Navarre, a request that indicates Henry's intention to invite Anne to attend the meeting. Although the monarchs did not meet, a conference at Calais was held between high-level diplomats of the two kingdoms. The queen's brother was one of the English envoys, and upon his return home at the end of May 1535, or so

Carew informed Chapuys, Rochford had, before he reported the deliberations to Henry, discussed them with his sister at great length. She was reportedly unhappy about the delay in negotiating the marriage treaty between Elizabeth and Angoulême, which had been a major topic of discussion at Calais. One of the stumbling blocks to this agreement was the necessity for Henry to require, since he had no son of his own, that Angoulême, who was about thirteen years old, be sent to England to complete his education.[49]

By the summer of 1535, Cromwell was increasingly taking on the same role with Chapuys that Norfolk had previously played. To ingratiate himself with the ambassador, the secretary revealed the details of an alleged dispute with Anne in the course of which she had exclaimed angrily that she wished "to see his head off his shoulders." Cromwell joked about the disagreement: "I trust so much on my master, that I fancy she cannot do me any harm." Chapuys had difficulty believing in the veracity of this anecdote, as well he might, for nearly everyone, as he said, considered the secretary to be her right-hand man. And, indeed, during July, she wrote to the secretary twice, seeking and clearly expecting to obtain his assistance with some administrative problems. In another dispatch that summer, Chapuys explained that in an attempt to divert the king from Fisher's creation as Cardinal, Anne had entertained her husband at one of her residences. To her party she had invited many important individuals, but had overlooked the French diplomat, who was reportedly unhappy about the snub. By the end of July, Chapuys had also heard that the king had nearly murdered his fool for speaking well of Catherine and Mary and disparaging Anne as a "ribauld" and Elizabeth as a "bastard." This rumor seems to support the remark of Mary to Chapuys that Henry still loved Anne more than ever and belie the belief of the Venetian ambassador that the king was "tired to satiety" of his new wife, although Henry's anger might have been aroused more by the fool's disparaging comment about his daughter than about his consort. It is noteworthy that the rumors about Anne in the summer of 1535 were inconsistent, indicating both the king's love and his "satiety" of her at a time when Anglo-French relations can at best be described as ambiguous.[50]

The story about the king's fool circulated in July just as Paul III, the new pope, was announcing his intention to deprive Henry of his kingdom, and Queen Eleanor of France was arranging to meet with her sister, Queen Mary of Hungary and the regent of the Low Countries, for the purpose of effecting a Franco-Imperial truce. Because of these events, which greatly displeased the English king, Anthony de Castelnau, bishop of Tarbes, the new French ambassador, was snubbed when he arrived in England at the end of June. The bishop began immediately to complain about his treatment, for he was denied lodgings at Bridewell Palace where his fellow ambassadors had been housed for the past five years. Cromwell at first refused even to see him and then broke two appointments with him. In July the envoy called on the secretary, who sent word that he was not at home, apparently because he was too busy playing at bowls. At the same time that the bishop was being ignored, Chapuys was receiving very favorable treatment and was being invited to hunt in the royal parks.[51]

By October the bishop was completely alienated and a querulous letter written by him at that time must be viewed as an expression of this hostility. It stands as an excellent example of how the relations of two kingdoms affected first the treatment of their ambassadors and then the dispatches written by those envoys. In his letter Castelnau claimed that the English were so disenchanted with Henry that they would join any prince who took up their cause. He identified the reasons for this discontentment as both dislike of the religious changes and ill-feeling toward the new queen. The king's love for Anne, he also asserted, was diminishing daily, for he had taken "amours." The tone of this letter is similar to that of many of the reports of Chapuys with whom, indeed, Castelnau had had several conversations. The Frenchman had most recently taken care to explain to the Imperial agent that he had gone to visit Elizabeth only because of the "importunities" of her mother.[52]

Although events in Christendom seemed to be mounting against the king, he was as usual traveling on his summer progress and was said to be merry. On 15 September, there is evidence that Anne was with him at Winchester, for she sent word from there to the queen of Navarre that her greatest wish next to having a son was to see her again. Whether Anne traveled with Henry on all his short trips in Hampshire is not now known, but she was definitely with him again at Winchester on 2 October, when a correspondent of Lisle wrote that the king and queen were merry and hawking daily. On 6 October, at about the same time as the bishop of Tarbes was referring to Henry's diminishing love for her, John, bishop of Exeter was noting that the king, his consort, and all the other nobles in court were merry and in good health. Three days later another correspondent claimed that the royal couple had been very merry in Hampshire. On 19 October, Sir Francis Bryan indicated that she had been with Henry at the Vine and was going to accompany him to Windsor Castle, where they were scheduled to arrive on 30 October. By that time Cromwell had forwarded to her a book of "Physick" which she had requested when the court was at Waltham in late September. The record does not state for what reason she sought this book.[53]

If the diplomatic dispatches are correct that Henry and Anne had suffered an estrangement during the previous year, the two were completely reconciled in October, for during that month she seems to have once again became pregnant, an achievement that may have elicited a mixed response from Chapuys. In March 1535, he had reported his belief that Anne had bribed a man to say that he had had a revelation to the effect that she would never conceive as long as Catherine and Mary were alive. Anne had sent the man to Cromwell and, Chapuys suspected, to Henry. If she were to have a son, the envoy could at least hope that she might spare the lives of the ex-queen and her daughter.[54]

Even before he could be certain of her pregnancy that autumn, the king gave evidence of his continuing affection for his consort. On 6 November the duke of Richmond informed Cromwell that although he had granted to a servant the keepership of the park in Collyweston, which had formerly belonged to his great-grand-mother Richmond, the king had decided instead to award the appointment to the queen. Forced to look for some other recompense for his dependent, the duke asked Cromwell for assistance in resolving his problem. During that same month Chapuys claimed that Henry did not dare contradict Anne, who ruled over all and governed the kingdom. Almost at the precise moment that the Imperial envoy perceived a recovery of Anne's power at court, he also discovered the renewal of friendly relations between England and France. First, he witnessed a solemn procession held in London to celebrate the convalescence of Francis, who had just recovered from a serious illness, and then he learned that Cromwell was regularly conferring with the French ambassador. The relations of the two kingdoms had become warmer largely because Francis and Charles were known to be on the verge of another war.[55]

There is no reason to believe, as has often been asserted, that by the end of 1535, Anne had lost all political significance; nor is there any validity to the argument that the king had grown tired of her or that he had enjoyed the courtship but not their marriage. All of the troubles that they had encountered had been largely a result of her inability to give birth to a surviving male child. Still caring for her enough to continue in his efforts to have his heir with her, he had apparently had an exceedingly merry time with Anne during the autumn of 1535 when she conceived for the third time in as many years. It is no wonder that Henry was frustrated by his lack of a son, for his great fertility and that of his wives had been demonstrated repeatedly. His first consort, of course, had become pregnant at least six times in a nine-year period.[56]

During the religious festivals of 1535–6 the health of Catherine, who had long been ill, deteriorated, and she died on 7 January. When he learned of her death Chapuys quickly concluded that Anne had succeeded at last in poisoning the ex-queen, although he had no evidence that she had ever conspired to kill anyone. It is easy to fault Anne for failing to lament Catherine's death, but her private feelings were surely no more insensitive than the public stance of her husband and his advisers. Six months earlier Cromwell had enraged Chapuys with his statement that were God to take away both Catherine and her daughter, "all matters would soon be settled," for no one would challenge the king's second marriage or the right of Elizabeth to succeed. In December, the king had speculated about her demise and had predicted that when it occurred, the emperor would refrain from meddling further in England's domestic affairs.[57]

Edward Hall, the chronicler, made the most celebrated comment about Anne's reaction to the ex-queen's death. She had, he reported, worn yellow for the mourning. This intriguing statement may have been a reference to her pregnancy, for the chamber at Eltham, which had been prepared for her confinement in 1534, had been redecorated in yellow ochre. It can also be interpreted to mean that she failed to mourn, as Polydore Vergil claimed, for black was the traditional color worn to honor the dead. Chapuys, interestingly enough, wrote that it was Henry, not Anne, who wore yellow and who celebrated Catherine's death by displaying Elizabeth to his courtiers. Probably the king, as well as Anne, did feel a sense of relief at Catherine's death, for it had opened up the possibility of a rapprochement with the emperor that might be used as a lever against the French to push forward the Angoulême marriage for Elizabeth. Without her mother's support, Mary would also pose a less serious threat to Elizabeth's or her unborn sibling's place in the succession. Indeed, on 21 January, Chapuys reported that Mary had sent him a message that the governess had on behalf of Anne entreated Mary to recognize the queen as her "second mother." If she would "wave her obstinacy," she would be welcome at court and would be exempted from being Anne's train-bearer.[58]

Perhaps equally important to Anne, Catherine's demise might lead to an appreciable lessening of criticism in England concerning her status as Henry's wife. Despite the statute that made it treason to impugn the king's union with Anne, many people continued to view her as the woman who had destroyed Henry's first marriage. There were and are implicit in this attitude two important but erroneous views. The first is that it was possible for Anne to deny the desires of an extremely autocratic man who was accustomed to self-gratification. Even had she wanted to repudiate his love, and surely she did not, both the king and her family, including uncle Norfolk, would have made that action difficult if not impossible. Whether or not he had a strained personal relationship with his niece, as Chapuys asserted, the duke would have wanted Anne, who had generally treated the Howards quite well, to remain the king's consort, for he could not afford to have her replaced at court with someone, like Jane Seymour, for example, whose family was hostile to his.[59]

The second implicit assumption of the argument that Anne should have disappeared from the king's life is that he would then

have been content to resume his former relationship with Catherine. Since Henry's ex-queen died before Anne, it is possible only
to speculate about what his reaction would have been had she
predeceased Catherine. His greatest wish, however, was to beget
a legitimate son, a compelling desire that made him pay special
tribute to 2 February, the anniversary of the Virgin's Purification. From at least 1525 it had become increasingly unlikely that
Catherine would be capable of childbirth, notwithstanding Chapuys' optimistic listing to Cromwell in 1535 of several fifty-one-
year-old Englishwomen who had been delivered of surviving
children.[60]

Although Anne had been crowned queen of England, many of
the king's subjects continued to describe her as an adulteress.
Numerous individuals, especially women, who felt personally
threatened by her marriage to Henry because it was perceived as
an assault on traditional family values, denounced the liaison of
the royal couple. After they were wed, in fact, the protests seemed
to have increased in number, for as long as the ex-queen was still
living at least a part of the populace was more willing to accept
Anne as the king's mistress than as his consort. Henry's ministers
were anxious to punish these critics because implicitly and
sometimes explicitly they also attacked the king and his offspring.
In early 1535 Cromwell investigated a report about a man who
allegedly accused Henry of having lived in adultery with Anne
both before and after he married her. Another individual claimed
that the king was not a Christian since he had two wives and a
concubine. One moralist argued that it would have been better
had Henry had no children to succeed him, while another
insensitive soul asserted that the christening water of Elizabeth
had not been nearly hot enough.[61]

In January 1536, despite this continuing criticism, Anne could
be optimistic about her future. She was pregnant again; the king
had been publicly supportive of her; Catherine was at long last
dead; and Francis and the emperor were going to war against
each other, thus lessening considerably the danger of their
heeding the pleas of Paul III for a crusade against England. Even
so, scholars have often asserted that Anne's subsequent execution,
occurring as it did in May, only four months later, was the result
of her husband's long-term disenchantment. Instead, her fall was

almost certainly triggered by the nature of the miscarriage she was to suffer in late January, for there is no evidence in the months just prior to that tragedy that she had been in any personal or political danger. When her disgrace and downfall occurred, it was to catch Chapuys, that inveterate gossipmonger, with as much surprise and astonishment as it did the rest of Christendom.

8 SEXUAL HERESY

In January 1536, Anne was delivered prematurely of a male child. That it was no ordinary miscarriage is an essential clue to an understanding of the events that culminated in her execution some four months later. The first major sign that this miscarriage was unusual is that it was not kept a secret, for unlike the other fetuses delivered by Henry's consorts, information about its sex, age, and day of birth was made public. The chronicler Edward Hall, who had formerly noted only the arrival of live Tudor infants, dated its birth to early February and Charles Wriothesley, another chronicler, to 30 January.[1]

Since the king's ministers also leaked information about the queen's delivery to the Imperial envoy, his dispatches must be studied to discover what it was the crown wanted this partisan of Catherine to know and when. As Chapuys had heard rumors even before he learned of her miscarriage that Henry had begun to accuse Anne of bewitching him, it will be useful to examine contemporary beliefs about witches and other sexual heresies before turning to a discussion of this fetus, which, it will be argued here, was born deformed, a tragedy constituting the sole reason for the king's setting in motion the process that led to Anne's execution. Attention will then focus on the charges against the five men who were alleged to be her lovers. Evidence from extant documentation supports the speculation that they were all thought to be libertines and that at least two of them were suspected of having violated the statute that made buggery a capital offense. This version of Anne's fall contradicts the prevailing view that Cromwell used her miscarriage as an excuse to persuade the king of the need for her removal and then set out in cold blood to eliminate five of his political enemies in the privy chamber. It also responds to the views of Paul Friedmann and other historians about the evidence which suggests that Anne and some of these men were actually guilty of crimes for which they deserved to be punished.[2]

Virtually all early modern Europeans believed in the existence of evil spirits; Satan was for them an actual demon who worked ceaselessly to lure mortals into becoming his followers. Among his worshippers, witches were considered such a menace that in 1542, less than six years after Anne's death, parliament enacted a statute that, among other prohibitions, specifically forbade the use of witchcraft to incite a person to illicit love. Although evidence from later English trials indicates that witches were commonly accused of *maleficium*, that is injuries, such as an animal's death or a person's illness, the kingdom's legends had references to their fantastic activities: they made pacts with the devil, brewed poisons, flew at night, and changed into werewolves, a feat that caused them to be associated with forests and to be described as hairy.[3]

Universally, witches were decried for their use of aphrodisiacs and for their excessive lust. In medieval England, for example, several noblewomen had been accused of obtaining sortileges to entice men into marriage, one of the most recent incidents involving Elizabeth, wife to Edward IV. Witches also allegedly engaged in illicit sexual intercourse, for they reportedly committed a number of sexual acts that their contemporaries viewed as deviant. Although experts continued to argue about whether the union between witches and the devil, called sodomy, could result in normal childbirth, they agreed that witches gave birth to deformed children, made demonic sacrifices of infants, including their own offspring, and committed incest. Witches were also accused of afflicting men, even their spouses, with impotence, an act that was from the mid-twelfth century recognized by the canon law as a marriage impediment. For the following 300 years, these cases were, according to George L. Kittredge, "so numerous that this species of sorcery became an everyday matter."[4]

A discussion of sodomy and incest, which were closely associated with witchcraft, is relevant to an analysis of Anne's fall, since she was accused of enticing her brother into having relations with her and since, it will be argued here, he had violated the Buggery Statute. This legislation, which was passed in February 1534, declared buggery a felony because there was not then "sufficient and condigne puynshment . . . for [this] abhomynable vice . . . comytted with mankinde or beast." Undoubtedly, bestiality was included because of the belief that demons and witches changed into beasts and of the fear that a union between humans and animals might result in hybrid births.[5]

An anonymous Protestant zealot, perhaps as late as the reign of James I, made the following statement about the statute:

Of Chastity they monks and nuns make great outward shew but very litle was fownd amonge them, for it plainlie appered their filthie lusts were not satisfied with maidens wifes & widows but also they practised one with another that detestable sodomitishe & Romishe unnatural Acte wherof St Paul in the first to the Romans [Romans I, 26–27] writeth which was the Cause that horrible vice was made by parliament felonie without helpe or benefitt of Clergie.[6]

This author raised several interesting issues. As he suggested, people were neither categorized as homosexual nor as heterosexual, for libertines were expected to move in a progression from adultery and fornication to buggery and bestiality. Often referred to under the general term of sodomy, buggery was condemned both as an unnatural act and as a sin against God, views that have long prevailed in western society. The Judaeo-Christian tradition had treated sodomy as idolatry and heresy, the Hebrew God having forbidden this practice principally because of its centrality in the worship of competing gods. In Tudor England sodomites were still regarded as devil worshippers.[7]

Because the Buggery Statute was enacted by the Reformation Parliament, later scholars have echoed the anonymous author's assertion that it was an anti-clerical measure. Although churchmen were accused of committing sodomy, they were also criticized for engaging in what were regarded as natural but illicit heterosexual acts. Had buggery been identified solely with the clergy, parliament, which later condemned clerical concubinage, surely would have said so. The above author may well have been thinking about the government's alleged discovery of numerous sexual violations in the monasteries, but Cromwell's agents did not begin their inquiries until after the Buggery Statute was passed.[8]

This Protestant writer and most of his contemporaries associated acts of sodomy with Rome and the Italian people. Sir Edward Coke, for example, blamed some medieval Lombards for introducing into the realm this "shamefull sin," which was an act "amongst Christians not to be named," or, as William Thomas remarked in the 1540s, a "cruelty not to be spoken with the human tongue."[9]

Before the Reformation, however, accusations of sodomy were often directed at courtiers with French manners. According to Baldassare Castiglione, who had visited England late in the reign of Henry VII, there was at some courts "a most wanton life in every kinde of vice: the women enticefull ... and the men womanish." He maintained that these men "seeing nature ... hath not made them women ought ... to be banished not only out of princes courtes but also out of the company of gentlemen." *The Treatise of the Galaunt*, first published in 1510, associated sodomy with men who aped French fashions. It described the courtiers with "womanlike dress" as transvestites. Proud and drunken, these "progeny of Lucifer" committed lechery, "abusyon," "abhomynable" acts and defied "the noble course of nature."[10]

The charges against two men convicted of buggery in Henry VIII's reign indicate that this legislation was not aimed at a particular group of people. In July 1540, Walter, Lord Hungerford, became the first man executed for violating this statute. He lost his life for having engaged in sexual relations with his male servants and with his daughter and for having procured witches' magic to predict the length of the king's life. It is interesting that Hungerford was charged specifically with consulting with "mother Roche," a professional witch.[11] The second person convicted of buggery was Nicholas Udall, a cleric, who had written verses for Anne's entry into London as queen. By June 1534, within four months of the statute's enactment, he had become headmaster of Eton College. Then in March 1541, less than a year after Hungerford's death, Udall admitted to having committed buggery with two of his male pupils. His sentence was reduced to imprisonment probably because his felonies had not been complicated by acts of treason, but after he was freed, Udall complained that "no man of honor" would "receive" him or "favour" him. The Church Fathers had feared that some male teachers might be tempted to seduce their students, a concern also raised in England where sodomy reportedly flourished at the public schools.[12]

Sodomy and witchcraft, as Hungerford's death indicated, were associated with incest. Although forbidden, this latter act horrified Tudor Christians less than it has modern people, for it did not become a secular crime until the twentieth century. Perhaps this difference is based on the former's ignorance of the rules of heredity and on their awareness that papal dispensations could permit some incestuous unions, although not between full-blooded siblings. Before Henry married Anne, in fact, rumors had circulated that to resolve the succession crisis his daughter Mary might wed Richmond, her illegitimate half-brother. Many canon lawyers maintained that if a woman engaged in the authorized form of intercourse (beneath her partner) with a male relative, even her father, it was less sinful than if she had relations with her husband in any position other than this approved one.[13]

A major reason for these restrictions was that illicit sexual acts were blamed for the birth of deformed children. On all levels of society, midwives inspected babies, even miscarried ones, for these defects. Since fetuses were thought to have been completely formed physically from the eighteenth day after conception, numerous, even minor, irregularities could cause them to be described as monstrous: an extra tuft of hair on the navel, folds of loose skin or "ruffles" on the back, and especially siamese twins; one father reportedly fled in terror when he learned of the birth of his twins whom he viewed as a two-headed monster. Asserting that the visitation of deformities upon their infants was God's way of punishing parents for committing sexual sins, clerics interpreted the appearance of these babies both as bad omens and as "wonderful" examples of divine justice.[14]

Before turning to the activities of Anne, her alleged paramours, and her accusers in 1536, it will be useful to present a summary of the arrests. On 24 April, a secret commission of *oyer et terminer* for Kent and Middlesex, the members of which included Cromwell, the queen's father, and her uncle Norfolk, was named to inquire into unspecified treasonable practices. The same week as this appointment, the privy council met daily at Greenwich, sifting through evidence concerning the sexual life of Anne and her alleged paramours. The first arrest was that of Mark Smeaton at Stepney, the home of Cromwell, on 30 April. After the May Day tournament at which Henry Norris had been principal defendant and Rochford the chief challenger, the king left Greenwich for Westminster in the company of six men, including Norris who was questioned and placed in the Tower where Mark had previously been transferred. On 2 May, the queen was interrogated at Greenwich and then transported by barge to the Tower. Her brother had been arrested earlier that day. Subsequently, Sir Francis Weston, Sir Richard Page, Sir Thomas Wyatt, and William Brereton were imprisoned. These men, except Wyatt and Page who were later released, were accused of having had sexual intercourse with the queen at divers times between October 1533 and December 1535. On 12 May, the four commoners were convicted at Westminster Hall, and on 15 May, Anne and her brother were tried separately in the King's Hall at the White Tower. The five men were executed on 17 May, the same day that Cranmer invalidated the queen's marriage to Henry. Two days later she was beheaded.[15]

Chapuys, who in 1534 had been left to guess about the results of the queen's pregnancy and who had been distracted from asking questions about it by rumors that the king had a new love, discussed this last miscarriage at great length. He noted that: (1) she had been delivered prematurely of a boy on 29 January, the day on which Catherine was buried; (2) she had been three and a half months pregnant; (3) she had blamed the tragedy on Norfolk who had frightened her with news of the king's fall from a horse; (4) she was upset about Henry's love affairs; and (5) attendants of Mary were closely interrogated to learn what she knew about the delivery.[16]

Attention needs to be given to the dates on which this information was forwarded. On 29 January, when, according to his later dispatches, she miscarried, Chapuys revealed to the emperor that some days earlier he had heard that although she had shown great joy at Catherine's death, Anne had begun to fear that she would meet the "same end." And, the envoy continued, he had received an "incredible" report that very morning from an absolutely "authentic" source that the king had determined to find a new wife because, as he had admitted to one of his "principal courtiers," he had begun to realize that he had been "seduced and forced into his second marriage by means of sortileges and charms." The word "incredible" correctly described the diplomat's reaction, for he did not yet know about Anne's miscarriage, and, as he later said, he had thought the royal couple had been looking forward to the birth of a son. He was treating this report seriously, however, for it had been brought to him by a messenger of the marquess and marchioness of Exeter. Although Lady Exeter had earlier been one of his informants, after she had been forced to seek royal forgiveness for her dealings with the Nun of Kent she had communicated only rarely with the envoy. A noteworthy feature of Chapuys' dispatch is that here for the first time her husband was identified as an active conspirator against Anne.[17]

In a letter to another correspondent on 29 January, the envoy referred to Henry's recent accident. On 24 January, the eve of the Conversion of St. Paul and the eve of his third wedding anniversary, the king, mounted on a large horse in preparation for running at the lists, "fell so heavily that every one thought it a miracle he was not killed, but he sustained no injury." Wriothesley, the chronicler, confirms that the king "had no hurt" from this fall. The evidence that this had been a serious accident that had left Henry lying in a coma for two hours can be found only in letters written by foreign agents abroad. By the time this news reached them, the details had been greatly exaggerated, a common occurrence in the dissemination of information across Christendom.[18]

It is possible, but not likely, that when on the 29th Chapuys wrote the above two letters Anne had not yet miscarried, but in fact he failed to report this event until 10 February. This silence was not based on a lack of communication with the king's ministers, for in a dispatch dated 3 February, Chapuys referred to recent messages from Cromwell. That the diplomat had known about an event as momentous as the queen's premature delivery, which could affect the well being of Mary, and had ignored it is not to be credited. These facts seem to indicate that, like Hall the chronicler, Chapuys did not learn about the incident until

February, well after the information had been leaked to him that the king had begun to accuse Anne of witchcraft.[19]

On 10 February, Chapuys wrote that the queen had been prematurely delivered on 29 January of "a child, who had the appearance of a male about three months and a half old, at which miscarriage the King has certainly shown great disappointment and sorrow." She had blamed the mishap on the fright she had taken when Norfolk had told her about Henry's accident, the envoy continued, but the "general opinion" was that she had a "defective constitution" and could not bear male children. He rejected the king's fall as a valid excuse for her tragedy because she had reportedly reacted with indifference when she had learned about it. As contemporaries believed that pregnant women had to be protected from bad news, this story about her fright must have been invented. Surely, her husband, whose presence would have confirmed his well being, would have gone himself, instead of the duke, to tell her about the accident.[20]

In discussing the miscarriage, Chapuys seems not to have challenged the association of the birth with the accident because they took place some six days apart. As the queen surely realized, it would have been easier for her to win credit for the claim that it was her shock at hearing about the king's fall that had triggered the miscarriage had these two important events occurred on contiguous days. If, on the other hand, she was using her fright to explain a deformity, the time lag would pose a less significant problem. Completely independent of this timing difficulty, the argument will be made here that she was delivered of the child earlier than 29 January and, as will be discussed below, probably before 23 January, the day on which in a February letter Chapuys dated the king's accident although he had earlier placed it on 24 January. Henry's ministers, rather than Anne, had apparently used the incident to explain the premature birth, which they privately attributed to the sexual crimes that would lead to her execution. As Catherine was buried on 29 January, Cromwell may have adopted that date for the miscarriage merely to please the envoy.[21]

On 10 February the diplomat also revealed that Henry, who had gone to London for the opening of the final session of the Reformation Parliament, had been sending gifts to Jane Seymour, whose brother, Sir Edward, was shortly to become a member of the privy chamber, and that Mary's attendants had been closely interrogated about Anne's delivery. Despite this harassment of her staff, Chapuys was confident that the princess would soon be better treated. Within the next few days, as a result of an incredible episode, he became even more optimistic about her welfare. Allegedly, Lady Shelton had carelessly dropped a letter written to her by Anne in Mary's oratory. The princess had found it, had made a copy of it, which she had forwarded to Chapuys, and had returned the original to the oratory. On 17 February, the envoy sent to the emperor his copy of the note in which the queen had ordered Lady Shelton to cease her attempts to persuade Mary to obey her father, for the king would himself punish his daughter for her recalcitrance after the birth of his son. This message relieved Chapuys' mind greatly, for he had only recently charged that both the king and queen were planning to poison Mary. That the letter, which was probably not even of Anne's authorship, was mistakenly dropped in Mary's oratory cannot be taken seriously. Undoubtedly, this episode was one of the calculated tactics of the king's ministers to cover up the date and nature of the miscarriage and to discover as quickly as they could if the princess had any information about it, for they would have anticipated that she would discuss the letter and its contents with Chapuys. Surely, the crown's agents perused all of her written messages to the envoy, for they had the resources to curtail communications between the two at any time they chose to use them.[22]

On 24 February, Chapuys commented further about the tragic birth and discussed Cromwell's increasing friendliness. The envoy had heard that after the king had been informed of the miscarriage, he had visited his consort and had exclaimed: "I see that God will not give me male children." He had reportedly concluded the visit with the remark: "When you are up, I will come and speak to you." By this date, Chapuys had been told that Anne was blaming the premature delivery on her husband's love affairs as well as on his accident. Rumors had also surfaced that for three months the king had not spoken ten times to her, gossip accepted by the envoy although it contradicted his belief that the royal couple had been looking forward to the birth of a male heir.

Henry's ministers probably leaked false information about a lengthy estrangement to pave the way for a later denial of his responsibility for Anne's last pregnancy.[23]

Chapuys' dispatch of 24 February is equally interesting because of its information about Cromwell. In response to his urging, Chapuys had met privately with Cromwell on the eve of St. Matthias (23 February) at which time he had approved concessions to the emperor about the royal supremacy and about Mary's rank. A close look at the secretary's subsequent career, his commitment to a national Church and his harassment of Mary until she agreed to submit to the Reformation Statutes, will indicate just how deeply he was deceiving the envoy about his intentions. Besides pretending to agree with Chapuys on these matters, Cromwell also claimed that he was opposed to the kingdom's cordial relations with Francis, a posture that was blamed on the influence of Anne, for Norfolk, Suffolk, Fitzwilliam, and even her father had all, according to him, been futilely pressing the king for friendship with the emperor. A reading of the March 1536 dispatch of Antoine de Castelnau, bishop of Tarbes, to his monarch, about which Chapuys was, of course, to remain ignorant, indicates that Henry was even then taking advantage of Catherine's death to threaten the French with neutrality during their expected war with the emperor. By means of this subterfuge, the secretary had cleverly created a fictitious reason (Anne's support for the French) for asserting with credibility to Chapuys that he had decided he must orchestrate her fall. Indeed, on the day of her execution, the envoy was to note that Cromwell had said that if Chapuys would only recall the secretary's comments to him on the eve of St. Matthias he "should own that [Cromwell] was right in his prediction with regard to her." This strategy was similar to that which the king had previously demanded when changes in his policy had to be effected; in 1534, for example, while rumors were spread at court that the secretary had recommended against the Calais conference, Rochford privately told Francis that it was Anne's fault that it had been called off. The fact remains that in 1536 her fall was not essential to establishing an Anglo-Imperial alliance, for Catherine's survival had been its major impediment, as Cromwell had admitted shortly after her death.[24]

From late January, the councillors moved to protect the king's honor by leaking erroneous information about his consort before the unprecedented public admission of her miscarriage. They claimed that she had bewitched him and was unable to bear male children. During the subsequent weeks by feeding diplomats and courtiers lies about the reason for her disgrace, Cromwell concealed the true cause, as is being argued here, namely her deformed fetus. While he let Chapuys believe that it was Anne's support for the French that had led to her downfall, he let reformers, as Alexander Alesius later revealed, believe that it was partly her friendship for the Germans. Alesius also speculated that she had been executed because her son had been born dead. In this environment of deception and cover-up about Anne's downfall, that attempts were made to discover what Mary actually knew about her stepmother's delivery makes good sense.[25]

Scattered bits of otherwise incomprehensible evidence take on meaning when viewed from this perspective. After Anne's arrest, Sir Edward Baynton wrote a letter to Fitzwilliam in which he claimed that besides the statement extracted from Mark, the sole prisoner to confess to adultery with Anne, the king's honor required admissions of guilt from two other unnamed men, probably Norris and Rochford. His exact words were:

this shalbe to advertyse yow that here is myche communycacion that noman will confesse any thyng agaynst her, but allonly Marke of any actuell thynge. Wherefore(in my folishe conceyte) it shulde myche toche the Kings honor if it shulde no farther appeere. And I cannot beleve but that the other two bee as ... culpapull as ever was hee.

Baynton also asked for a meeting with Fitzwilliam and Cromwell so that he could "more plainly" speak. His statements are puzzling in light of the events later culminating in Queen Katherine Howard's execution, for at that time no one expressed fear that the king's reputation would suffer greatly if only two men admitted to indiscreet relations with her. In Anne's case, it would seem more reasonable for Baynton to have argued that Henry's honor would have been less disparaged if Mark alone had confessed. It is relevant to this discussion about honor that Brantôme, that great gossipmonger, claimed that a man should defend himself against charges of cowardice, sodomy, or being a cuckold but should refrain from revealing to the world details of the slanders involved. Given the widely accepted link between the honor of a man and public awareness of his and his wife's sexual habits, the comments of Baynton make sense only if Anne had been delivered of a defective fetus. The ministers had the task of identifying several men among her acquaintances who could plausibly be accused of fathering her child, in order to establish that her gross sexual behavior had caused its deformity.[26]

As a prisoner the queen seemed to be hinting to Kingston, the constable of the Tower, that her miscarriage had been unusual. In his reports about her comments, Kingston revealed to Cromwell her claim that she was "clere from the company of men" and the "king's trew wedded wife." Then amazingly, since he had charge of three men accused of sexual crimes with her, when she asked, "do you know wher for I am here?" he replied that he did not. After first changing the subject, she then volunteered that Elizabeth, countess of Worcester, was unable to feel her unborn baby move because of "the sorow" she had "toke" for her. Anne's arrest was surely not the occasion for this sorrow, for rumors identified the countess as a government witness. The queen must have been referring to the lady's reaction to her own recent miscarriage. As she had used the word "sorow" to describe physical pain or mischief rather than outward show of grief, she seems to have been suggesting that there was something especially tragic about her delivery that had adversely affected the unborn child of the countess.[27]

An incident Alesius later revealed can be interpreted to support this speculation about the queen's miscarriage. Shortly before her arrest he had seen Anne, holding her daughter in her arms and pleading with her husband, who was very angry. If one of her problems was that she could not bear sons, as Alesius had heard, then displaying Elizabeth to Henry would have served no purpose. But if she had been delivered of a deformed fetus, her action could be interpreted as a last-minute effort to demonstrate her innocence with a reminder of her previous success in giving birth to a child so perfectly formed that the king had proudly displayed her in the nude to the French ambassadors.[28]

If the fetus was defective, the nature of its condition must remain unknown, for reports referred only to its sex and age. Although accounts differed as to whether it was three and a half months or fifteen weeks, all agreed that it was a boy, a determination the midwife could have made had she inspected it very closely. According to a modern obstetrician, the sex of a fetus at the end of sixteen weeks, which today on the average weighs 110 grams and has a rump-crown length of about 12 centimeters, can with "careful examination" be determined. Experts have identified several congenital defects that can cause the female genitalia to look somewhat male. A fetus with this problem or with any kind of abnormality would have led an early modern midwife to describe it as monstrous. Approximately one third of all conceptions are spontaneously terminated because of problems in the natural development of the fetus. Among the crown's alleged witnesses was a woman familiarly described as Nan Cobham, who has never been identified. The use of the diminutive makes it unlikely that she was of high aristocratic birth, and it can be speculated that she had served as Anne's midwife.[29]

Information from the indictments can also be used to argue that the queen had been delivered of a deformed child. She was charged with inciting, in witchlike fashion, five men to have sexual relations with her by the use of touches and kisses that involved thrusting her tongue into their mouths and theirs in hers (called pigeon kisses by Brantôme). The kisses, touches, and caresses were minutely described probably because by reason of their motive they could be viewed as mortally sinful. That Anne was identified as the initiator of these contacts was consistent both with the need to prove that she was a witch and not a passive victim and with the contemporary belief that "demonic" women were thought to be able to entice men into unnatural carnal acts by first causing them to have sexual fantasies. The illicit encounters occurred on divers days with ten specified, one for each man at Greenwich or Eltham and one for each man at Hampton Court or Westminster. The first dated rendezvous was with Norris at Greenwich in October 1533, when she was still considered unclean because she had not yet been churched after Elizabeth's birth; this charge led to the rumor that he had fathered her daughter. The last date was with Rochford at Eltham in December 1535, only a few weeks before her miscarriage. Crucial to Henry's case was the unstated assumption that if she were convicted of having committed adultery with five men between these two dates, and if the rumor were credited that he had spoken to her less than ten times in the three months before the January delivery, his paternity of her fetus would have been substantially disproved. That his ministers chose these specific dates supports the suggestion that their goal was more to deny his fatherhood than to prove Anne's adultery, although the latter was essential to their strategy. If the fetus had been normal, there would have been no reason to go to such lengths to deny his paternity or to place her last sexual crime in 1535 rather than in 1536.[30]

She was also accused of presenting the men with gifts, of creating competition and jealousy among them, (thus causing disorder in the royal household), of afflicting the king with bodily harm (surely an allusion to his alleged impotence), and of conspiring to effect his death. Although most of these acts did not fall under the Treason Statute, conspiring to bring about his demise clearly did.[31]

To enforce secrecy about the miscarried fetus, which was the reason for her downfall, Cromwell not only spread the word abroad that the king was merry and in good health but also took unprecedented measures at home. Besides deceiving the resident diplomats, he later prevented the archbishop of Canterbury from having access to the king and Sir Richard Bulkeley, an associate and deputy of Norris, as chamberlain of North Wales, from returning to court. To threaten into silence the few who knew about the incident, the secretary could also rely on recent legislation that made it a treasonable offence to disparage the king's heirs. After May 1536, he continued to monitor statements about the executions of Anne and her alleged accomplices, as the arrest of George Constantine, a servant of Norris' who had related details about their deaths to John Barlow, the Boleyns' former chaplain, demonstrates.[32]

Cromwell likewise controlled access to Mary's household. Although she continued to send enough notes to Chapuys to support the conclusion that her messenger was a double agent, perhaps Carew, she was prevented in late January from talking privately with her visitors. By the 20th her governess in obedience to court orders had forbidden her to speak with Chapuys' servant, although, in exchange for a few gifts, he was permitted a quick look to confirm that she was alive and well. A few days later, Lady Shelton permitted Catherine's apothecary and physician, who had earlier secured royal permission to meet with Mary, only extremely limited access to the princess. The ex-queen's almoner was also prohibited from leaving the kingdom. Chapuys believed that the king was trying to prevent news from spreading that Catherine had been poisoned, but as the first evidence of these measures did not surface until 20 January, almost two weeks after her death from natural causes, it is more likely that Cromwell was seeking to control the dissemination of news about Anne's miscarriage. If this speculation is correct, the tragic birth occurred shortly before 20 January. This date is reasonable since it would have given the ministers time to leak the news indirectly to Chapuys on 29 January about Henry's claim that she had bewitched him into marrying her. Only later would they inform the envoy about the miscarriage.[33]

While Cromwell, Baynton, and Fitzwilliam were building a case against Anne, little evidence has survived about her activities. For about a month after the birth, she remained in retirement, awaiting her churching, perhaps for a few days seriously ill. George Wyatt later repeated the tradition that she had been "brought abed before her time with much peril of her life." After she emerged from seclusion, possibly in late February just before the onset of Lent when conjugal relations were forbidden, life at court seemed to have continued as usual. Plans were finalized for a May visit to Dover; the king, who was in London during most of this final session of the Reformation Parliament, confirmed the grant to her of two manors, and Cambridge University sent her a letter thanking her for promoting their petition to the king for a remission of their payment of first fruits and tenths. Henry approved two separate grants that altered favorably the terms of her father's lease of the crown honor of Rayleigh in Essex; her brother, who was confirmed as a joint holder of this property, played a prominent role in this parliament, holding two proxies and supporting the statute that dissolved the monasteries. William Locke continued to purchase material to clothe her and her daughter, and on the continent William Latimer was completing his assignment to obtain books in French for her. Until parliament was dissolved and the council could direct its attention to Anne's miscarriage, public life could not reflect the details of the king's domestic crisis. Similar tactics had been employed in 1527 when negotiations for Mary's bethrothal to the dauphin had been conducted although Wolsey was secretly planning to obtain her parents' divorce, an act that would result in her being declared illegitimate and thus make her an unsuitable bride for the Frenchman.[34]

In the spring of 1536 suitors, unaware of her mounting troubles, still sought Anne's assistance. On 27 and 28 April, just before her arrest, Henry, Lord Stafford, wrote separately to Ralph, earl of Westmorland, his brother-in-law, and to Cromwell seeking support for his suit to the queen about the priory of Ranton. He had heard that both Anne and Henry, who were aware of the numerous children (at least ten and perhaps twelve) that had created his financial need, favored his request. Given the modern theory that for selfish political reasons the secretary and his allies joined with an Aragonese faction to effect the death of Anne, it is noteworthy that one of her suitors was Stafford, who was willing to discuss his petition to her with both Cromwell and Westmorland. If the children of Margaret Pole, countess of Salisbury, had been involved in a long-term, active conspiracy against Anne, then Lord Stafford, who was married to her daughter, Ursula Pole, seems to have been unaware of it. The heir of the deceased duke of Buckingham, this nobleman was also the brother of Lady Norfolk, the queen's aunt by marriage, who was then living apart from the duke. Westmorland had married another sister of Stafford and the duchess. There is no indication in Stafford's letters that he feared these family connections might in any way hinder his suit to the queen;[35] he undoubtedly believed that they had already helped his cause.

Although it is true that some, perhaps all, members of the Pole family were privately sympathetic to Mary, they had previously been powerless to help her. Of the three sons of Lady Salisbury, Reginald was in exile and Geoffrey was unwelcome at court. Only the eldest, Lord Montague, belonged to the king's household, although he may have remained under some suspicion, not so much because of his friendship for Catherine as because he was a Yorkist claimant. Montague had communicated only rarely

with Chapuys before March 1536, when he joined Sir Thomas
Elyot, a friend of Cromwell's, Elizabeth, dowager countess of
Kildare, whose husband the Boleyns had supported in Ireland,
and the marquess of Exeter to dine at the envoy's home. At that
meal, Montague, whom Chapuys trusted because he was a son of
Lady Salisbury, assured the diplomat that the king was looking
for a new wife and that Cromwell and the queen were on bad
terms, thus corroborating news the secretary had already
imparted to him.[36]

The evidence in Chapuys' dispatches, particularly details
about this dinner, is the primary support for the argument that an
Aragonese faction composed, among others, of Montague and
Exeter, joined with Cromwell to bring about the queen's downfall. The significance of their lordships' presence at the envoy's
lodgings is diminished greatly when the incident is viewed in
association with other political events. In fact, a wide range of
people, who were reputed to be allies of neither Cromwell nor
Mary, were at least as active as the secretary and much more
active than these Yorkist claimants in the effort to prove that
Anne had committed sexual crimes with a number of men. These
individuals included Fitzwilliam, Baynton, and some of the
queen's ladies. Among others known to have turned against her
was her cousin, Sir Francis Bryan, whom Cromwell later referred
to as a "vicar of hell." It was Bryan who carried to yet another
cousin, Jane Seymour, then in residence at Carew's home at
Beddington, the news of Anne's conviction and sentence of death.
From late January when the royal ministers began to make it
clear to observers that the queen was losing Henry's favor, no one
at court with the exception of a few close friends would remain
loyal to her. It was not a coalition of factions that brought down
Anne but Henry's disaffection caused by her miscarriage of a
defective child, the one act, besides adultery, that would certainly
destroy his trust in her. Someone was to blame for God's visitation
of that tragedy upon his nursery, and Henry would never admit
to any personal culpability.[37]

Privately, because of the appearance of her fetus, Anne must
have worried about the future of her marriage. When she
emerged from her childbearing seclusion, the king was at Westminster, where parliament was in session, celebrating the last

days of festival before the Lenten season. With his deep fear of illness and deformities, Henry would have seized any excuse to distance himself from her, for John Russell, who later characterized Anne as accursed, recalled that the king had acted that spring as though he were living in hell. She must also have been amazed to discover that Henry had strayed from his usual practice of secrecy and had permitted news of her miscarriage to be spread abroad.[38]

The extant information about Henry's affair with Jane Seymour can be understood only in association with his relationship to his consort, for once the king had thought Anne might be pregnant, if not before, he must have been looking for a new lady friend. Surely, he had already begun a flirtation with Jane before the premature birth of his child that January. Since he was in London during most of this spring parliamentary session while Jane, a member of the queen's household, remained at Greenwich, he would otherwise have had little time to court her before their marriage, which took place in May only a few days after Anne's execution. Even so, the rumors claiming that the queen had suffered a miscarriage because she had stumbled upon information about Henry's extra-marital affairs cannot be credited. Needing and wanting a perfectly formed male heir, the king would have taken great precautions to prevent the queen from suffering a shock that might have impaired the physical well being of her infant. By March at the latest, he had agreed, as part of the strategy to confirm rumors about his estrangement from Anne, to publicize his commitment to Jane. At that time word was leaked to Chapuys that after Jane had refused gifts from a messenger who had brought them to her from the king, in what can only have been a staged performance, if it occurred at all, she had been moved into Cromwell's apartments at Greenwich Palace. If this gossip was true, it would have caused Anne great anger and fear, for Henry had not provided her with chambers separate from Catherine's until early in December 1528, after Campeggio's arrival in England to convene the divorce hearings.[39]

Amidst rumors that the king was either going to marry Jane or a French princess, Chapuys was invited to court on Easter Tuesday, 18 April, where, among other councillors, he was greeted by Rochford. Because of Anne's required seclusion after childbirth, the somber Lenten season that followed, and Henry's prolonged absence at Westminster, the Easter celebrations offered her the first opportunity since early January to appear publicly with the king. According to Chapuys' account of this visit, Cromwell, at the behest of Henry, had invited the envoy, but only if he so chose, to go to Anne's apartments and to pay his respects to her as queen. Since, as Chapuys later admitted, he had heard she was not in favor with the king, he had been emboldened to refuse this invitation that normally would have been extended and would have been interpreted as a royal command. A short while later, in response to the envoy's refusal to perform this minimal courtesy to his consort, Henry paid marked attention to him and had Rochford escort him to the royal chapel for mass. This was an extraordinary occurrence, for diplomats did not routinely attend mass with the royal family. During the service, Anne, who had obviously not been informed of Chapuys' previous snub, accompanied the king from the royal pew to make her offering and graciously turned to face the envoy, who was partially hidden behind the chapel door. He bowed, as protocol absolutely required, and she returned his reverence. The envoy was aware that it was a momentous occasion, for he noted that the people present crowded around to watch his interaction with her. Afterwards, the king dined in Anne's apartments where reportedly she had expected Chapuys to attend and recognize her formally as queen. Since, unlike other diplomats on their visits to court, he had refused the invitation to dine with her and had eaten separately with Rochford in the presence chamber, Anne was made to understand that despite Catherine's death he still regarded her as the royal concubine.[40]

Unhappy when they learned of the envoy's salute to Anne, Mary and her friends were concerned that it might be interpreted as Imperial recognition of her as queen, for courtiers and diplomats alike monitored gestures such as this for hidden meanings. In March, for example, Chapuys had reported to Charles V a conversation with Cromwell in which the secretary had placed his hand reverently on his hat at the mention of both Mary's and the emperor's names. The princess failed to view, as most scholars have failed to view, the incident on Easter Tuesday from the perspective of Anne and her family. Instead of snubbing Chapuys, who had refused to pay his respects to her as his consort, Henry had invited him to attend mass in the royal chapel where he would, for the first time since his arrival in England some six years earlier, find himself in her immediate presence. Unaware that he had previously refused to attend her in her apartments, the queen had chosen to honor Chapuys with a personal salute rather than to ignore him, as she would have done had she known he still viewed her as a concubine. Under normal circumstances individuals with the potential for insulting her were not permitted to confront her. Access to her was limited; some years earlier, Chapuys himself had sneered when the king had introduced to her a gentleman whom the diplomat described as a mere clerk of Cromwell. As a Tower prisoner, Anne was said to have spoken of the events of Easter Tuesday as ill omens. One of her hostile attendants sent word to Chapuys that the queen recalled his visit to court as an ominous sign, for the king "no longer looked upon her with the same eyes as before." It was the first occasion on which Henry had used protocol to snub her, thus alerting courtiers to the seriousness of their estrangement. Since on that day, Anne's brother had been required to greet and to entertain the envoy, the king had also used protocol to signal to observers that he, too, was out of favor.[41]

After dinner on this Easter Tuesday, Cromwell and Henry staged an argument for the benefit of Chapuys, but out of his hearing. The king allegedly refused to approve the concessions to the emperor that since St. Matthias' Day the secretary had been deceiving the envoy into believing that he had been pressing Henry to accept. Before and during the dispute between Cromwell and the king, Chapuys conversed with Sir Edward Seymour, who, the envoy realized, was the brother of the new royal mistress. On the basis of this April confrontation, Cromwell could with credibility inform Chapuys in June that the king's continuing friendship for France, which he claimed was solely the fault of Anne's influence, had forced him to arrange her execution. It is interesting that Chapuys was persuaded, as many scholars have since become persuaded, that in the period of about one month Cromwell actually could unleash a conspiracy that would successfully unseat a queen consort, whose overwhelming influence with the king about diplomatic measures the secretary had previously been unable to overcome. Neither Chapuys nor modern historians have explained why if the secretary could manipulate Henry into agreeing to the execution of Anne, he could not simply persuade the king to ignore her advice on foreign policy. This claim in June about the importance of the Easter dispute is also interesting because it contradicted Cromwell's earlier statement in May that he remembered having predicted her ruin in his meeting with the envoy on St. Matthias' Day; undoubtedly by June the secretary wished to direct the attention of Chapuys away from their February meeting because it had occurred only weeks after the January miscarriage.[42]

On 23 April, a few days after the first public humiliation of Anne and her brother, Sir Nicholas Carew, identified by Chapuys as an ally of Seymour, was elected to the Garter instead of Rochford, who had been one of the gentlemen considered for this honor. Although he was aware that the French ambassador had recommended Carew for this position, Chapuys still maintained that this Englishman actually favored the Imperialist cause. The envoy also believed that Carew's election instead of Rochford's was a certain sign of Anne's disgrace. Rumors about her fall were likewise fueled by reports that the bishop of London had given a non-commital answer to an inquiry about whether the king could abandon his second marriage. Despite the expectation that great changes were about to occur, the appointment on 24 April of the commission of *oyer et terminer* was momentarily kept a secret. Three days later writs were issued for a new parliament, the legislation of which was to confirm Anne's fall.[43]

The queen's Tower revelations, carefully reported to Cromwell by the constable, about Norris and Weston, two of her alleged paramours, have sometimes been cited as proof that her life resumed its usual carefree, flirtatious manner that spring. This is an unrealistic interpretation, for she was certainly aware of the king's hostility. Not only had he publicly insulted her on Easter Tuesday, he had earlier given her maid of honor, Jane Seymour, separate quarters in the palace. During the week of the 24th, furthermore, his council was meeting daily at Greenwich amidst rumors that he wanted to end his second marriage. Although only a few people, probably Baynton, Fitzwilliam, Cromwell, and surely some of the ladies whose testimony was used against her, could have known about the specific reason the king was acting as though he were living in hell and Anne were accursed, most of the courtiers (at least from Easter Tuesday) would have been as aware as Russell was of their estrangement. Since the queen's relations with Norris and Weston were totally innocent, the most reasonable speculation is that she gave details about her discussions with them because word had been leaked to her that their names, or at least that of Norris, were being linked with hers.[44]

Anne revealed her conversation with Norris in response to a question posed by one of her Tower attendants about why he had sworn, as he had done on 30 April to her almoner, John Skip, that she was a virtuous woman. Her answer was that she had asked Norris to do so during a discussion in which she had tried to discover why he had not married her cousin Mary Shelton. When he had responded only that he still wished to "tarry" awhile, she had probed for some deeper meaning to his comments, predicting that if something were to happen to the king, Norris "would loke to have" her. He had strongly denied this claim, and their ensuing argument had ended with his agreeing to go to her almoner and swear to her honor. Surely, she would not have insisted upon this desparate favor unless she had heard that Norris was thought to have been her lover. Their disagreement was probably over what, if anything, could be done to disprove this dangerous assumption. When Cromwell learned about their conversation, he was able to add to the indictment, if he had not done so already, the claim that she had conspired to effect the king's death.[45]

The queen also admitted in the course of the above discussion that Weston had told her on Whit Tuesday in 1535 that Norris had been visiting her maidens more to see her than his betrothed. As a kind of postscript to the letter, which contains these remarks, Kingston added that after he had written his report, Anne had revealed that the purpose of that earlier conversation with Weston, who was a married man, had been to admonish him for flirting with Mary Shelton. The queen recalled that she had "defyed" the young man when he had explained that he actually loved her more than either her maiden or his own wife. Weston's reaction can be viewed more as a feeble, but clever, attempt to distract attention from his questionable behavior with Mary and perhaps to protect the girl's honor than as true evidence of a courtly exchange with the queen. His defense was that his intention was not to flirt with Mary but to reverence her mistress, and, in any case, he was not intruding on Norris' romantic territory because he too cared for the queen more than her maiden. Anne's ability to recall the exact date on which the conversation with Weston had occurred and her defiant response to his protest of loyalty seem to indicate that it was not her normal practice to encourage her husband's attendants to approach her with indiscreet and familiar comments. Although the behavior and well being of her young kinswoman, especially as she was a member of her household, had been an entirely appropriate matter for Anne to raise with Weston in 1535, the unsolicited declarations of devotion remained troublesome, for, if they were true, they might well be used to corroborate the more serious innuendos in 1536 that linked her name to Norris. By revealing this incident to her jailers, Anne removed any chance, however slim, that Weston might have had to be spared a trial and conviction when he was later arrested. At the time of this confession, she may well have assumed that he was already in custody, for she had been led to believe that she was being accused of adultery with three men, of whom only Norris and Mark were explicitly named. Out of kindness to her on this, her first day of imprisonment, Kingston had purposely refrained from telling her that the third incarcerated man was her brother. Ironically, despite her attempt to be honest about her relationship to Norris and Weston, the charges against them alleged events that had occurred in 1533 and 1534.[46]

Most of the evidence used against Anne and her accused lovers came from members of her privy chamber. In a report to English diplomats in France, Cromwell asserted that her crimes were so abominable that her own ladies could not conceal them. The three women witnesses, identified by rumor, had probably been with her during the delivery. Childbirth at this time was an all-female affair, for besides the midwife, who had to swear that she would not use sorcery or incantations, several other women were expected to be present in an official capacity. If the infant died, for example, they had the duty of testifying to the mother's culpability in its death and of preventing the midwife from replacing it with another child.[47]

Besides Nan Cobham, possibly the queen's midwife, a second witness was Elizabeth, countess of Worcester, a half-sister of Fitzwilliam who was one of the leading ministers in the investigation into Anne's sexual habits. As a Tower prisoner, the queen seemed to indicate that she blamed Fitzwilliam more than Cromwell for accusing her of these crimes. She told Kingston that "master treasurer" was in Windsor Forest (he was a joint keeper of its great park), probably a reference to his attempts to uncover information proving her to be a witch. In reporting this comment to Cromwell, the constable wrote, "and you know what she meynes by that." Another witness was an unnamed maid, undoubtedly Mrs. Margery Horsman of the queen's wardrobe, who was usually addressed by her first name and title even in official records. In the letter to Fitzwilliam cited above, Baynton mentioned a Mrs. Margery, who had at first assisted him, probably in response to the promise of rewards, but who had more recently been somewhat less than cooperative.[48]

After they were questioned about the delivery, the women were surely also asked to identify men with whom Anne had been in some contact between October 1533 and December 1535 and with whom she might plausibly be charged with having carnal relations. Henry's ministers could not forward evidence to the courts about a deformed fetus both for fear of opening up questions about the king's responsibility for this disaster and out of an unwillingness to reveal its existence to the public. Cromwell later admitted that a great part of the information that had been gathered was not used in court.[49]

It is extremely likely that the men identified as Anne's lovers were known for their licentious behavior and that some of them were also suspected of having violated the Buggery Statute. One clue to these speculations is the widespread acceptance of their guilt. Chapuys, who had been misled so often by the royal advisers, most recently Cromwell, was one of the few observers who expressed doubts about the verdicts. Two other clues to these speculations about the reputation of her alleged lovers can be found in the dates used for their arrests and in those cited for the sexual liaisons. All of the accused, including Anne, were arrested on the last day of April and during the first week of May, a time associated with eroticism and transvestism. The first two prisoners were taken on 30 April and 1 May, the eve of and the actual day of one of the most enduring of pagan holidays. It is also intriguing that in the indictments little care was taken to ensure that the men were actually with the queen in the place and at the time stipulated; Rochford, for example, was charged with having relations with her at Westminster on 5 November 1535, when she was with the king at Windsor. In legends, at least, witches had the ability to fly to their rendezvous. Equally significant is that many of the days on which the crimes reportedly occurred, as her second encounter with her brother on 29 December, fell during seasons traditionally associated with eroticism and transvestism.[50]

The most important of the accused lovers was Rochford, who was to be given primary responsibility for her last pregnancy. This fact is evident from the dates in late 1535 on which the incestuous relations reportedly occurred. In 1559 Alesius was to recall that one significant piece of evidence against Anne was her correspondence with her brother in which she announced her conception, thus seeming to imply that he had fathered her child. Constantine, an eyewitness to the executions, had also heard that a letter had figured prominently in his conviction.[51]

Even sympathetic statements after his death referred to the viscount's pride, but they also praised his poetic talents and his good looks. Anthony Wood, the Oxford historian, who believed incorrectly that Rochford had been educated at Oxford, reported that women had admired him, perhaps because his wife Jane was thought to have resented his attention to other ladies. Wood's claim could also have been a polite summary of George Cavendish's verses about Rochford's licentiousness, for generally the Oxford biographies contain positive information. Wood, for example, omitted references to Udall's buggery conviction.[52]

Since Cavendish was no friend of the Boleyns, his hostility is not surprising. He had Rochford say in his execution speech:

> My lyfe not chast, my lyvyng bestyall
> I fforced wydowes, maydens I did deflower
> All was oon to me, I spared non at all
> My appetit was all women to devoure
> My study was bothe day and hower.

My onleafull lecherey. howe I myght it fulfill
Sparyng no woman to have on hyr my wyll.

Cavendish went on to repeat the viscount's actual statement that he had declined to describe his deeds for fear of tempting his listeners to imitate him. As he had Rochford admit to lusting after "all women" and to living bestially, there was hardly any other sexual act to which he could confess except sodomy. It is noteworthy that in descriptions of two lovers of the same sex traditionally one has been referred to as a woman and one as a man.[53]

The evidence about Rochford's trial is sketchy. Writers have claimed that his wife accused him of incest, but the only extant specific contemporary reference to her is about another matter. Chapuys reported that Cromwell had supposedly passed a note to Rochford to which he was to respond without revealing its contents. His lordship defiantly read aloud the inquiry about his wife's admission that he had discussed the king's impotence with the queen. The defiance rings true and, if the analysis here is correct, Henry would have wanted this evidence entered into the record so that it could be cited as proof that he was not responsible for Anne's last pregnancy. The alleged incident also implicitly supports the charge that she had engaged in illicit sexual acts with five men, for rumors at court claimed that she had taken these lovers because of her husband's impotence, a disability that she, as a witch, would have been expected to have imposed upon him. Rochford was also said to have refused to answer the charge that he had expressed doubts that the king was Elizabeth's father.[54]

The prevailing assumption that Lady Rochford informed against her husband to get even with him for his attention to other women needs to be reassessed. At the time of his arrest, she may not have believed the charges against him, for word was sent to him in the Tower that she would make suit to the king. Equally noteworthy are the facts that her evidence seems to have played a minor role in his trial and that her status as his wife did not exempt her from revealing information about his treasonable activities. A failure to do so could result in her own imprisonment. Since after his death, she had to plead for his effects and wait three years to secure her jointure, she seems not to have made any deal with the crown in exchange for her testimony. In a letter to Cromwell seeking financial support "as a power desolat wydow," she actually beseeched God to pardon her late husband.[55]

Surely Lady Rochford's plea to God on behalf of her late husband reflected her own belief in his guilt. Why she had become persuaded that he had committed incest with his sister must be considered. Had Rochford's attentions to other women been the cause, her contemporaries would have viewed her behaviour as a grave over-reaction because of the prevailing double standard that condoned a husband's extra-marital liaisons. Given this custom, she must have been greatly provoked to condemn him. If in May 1536 she were told that he had committed buggery with a male friend, she could have felt dishonored enough by the perceived insult to her womanhood to be receptive to the charge that he had engaged in other illicit sexual acts. Recent studies of married homosexuals have indicated that even if the husband can be described as bi-sexual, his same-sex inclinations are disrupting to the marriage. Admittedly, modern women are socialized to expect romantic liaisons, but, even considering this difference, a husband's need to commit sodomy at a time when it was equated with heresy held the potential for creating significant marital strain.[56]

Whether or not his wife confessed to the investigators that he had discussed the king's impotency with Anne, Rochford's alleged defiance at his trial can be confirmed by his last speech. Customarily, the condemned made statements to onlookers that demonstrated in the tradition of the *ars moriendi* that they had prepared properly for a Christian death. So crucial was the ritual of a witnessed death to a confirmation of the dying's membership in the human family that even criminals were permitted to die in the presence of observers and not alone like a "beast." Klaus Jankofsky has also pointed out that a public execution "could provide a very subtle interplay of learning and teaching how to die on the part of the executed and the spectators alike." An integral part of the condemned men's atonement was their admission of their offenses against the king and their request for his pardon. Besides the verses of Cavendish, which were not intended as an exact account of Rochford's final words, some fairly complete eyewitness accounts do exist. These reporters revealed that even though the viscount was convicted of crimes against the king in a personal as well as a public sense, he broke tradition and admitted to no fault against his brother-in-law. He was, they had him say, to "die under the law" because it had condemned him, not because he had violated it; he could hardly give a clearer statement of his innocence without denying the charges, an action that could have led to the imposition of a worse execution than the one already planned for him.[57]

According to these writers, he went on to confess that he deserved to die "for more and worse shame and dishonor than hath ever been heard of before" but refused to detail his sins out of fear that his listeners might imitate him. Contemporaries, even priests in the confessional, were admonished to be vague in describing illicit sexual acts, for it was believed that too graphic a discussion would not only teach their listeners how to perform them but also encourage them to do so. The reporters further revealed that after Rochford had warned against "the vanities of the world" and the "flatteries of the court," he admitted to having committed terrible sins against God, words that were interpreted by some observers as a confession that he was guilty of engaging in incestuous relations with his sister. That Rochford refrained from specifying his crimes is consistent with the suggestion that he was guilty of sexual acts, including buggery, which were considered unnatural. When looking for evidence that can be associated with homosexuality, as it is now understood, researchers have had difficulty finding explicit information about it. This historical wall of silence descended early and has continued well into modern times. George L. Kittredge said in his work on witchcraft, first published in 1929, that Lord Hungerford (who had been executed for committing buggery) "was somehow involved in a horrible scandal, into which we need not enquire," an attitude that recalls the words of William Thomas in 1540, "a cruelty not to be spoken with the human tongue."[58]

Of the other four men arrested, Mark, who was almost always addressed by his first name (often spelled Markes by those who knew him) was the one most likely to have been Rochford's intimate friend. This young man, who was at least ten years the viscount's junior, was of lower-class birth, his mother a seamstress and his father a carpenter. He had joined the boys' choir in the Chapel Royal after the disgrace of Wolsey, whom he had served in that capacity; this was an esteemed position, for noblemen competed with each other to obtain young male singers for their choirs. Upon reaching adulthood, some time after 1532 he became a groom of the privy chamber. Although the beginning of his friendship with Rochford cannot be dated, the two of them had a common interest in music, since his lordship wrote poetry which was often sung to old refrains.[59]

There is extant evidence of this friendship, for they both owned a manuscript now at the British Library. It contains a French version of a Latin work that is entitled "Les Lamentations de Matheolus," which is a satirical poem on women and the miseries of marriage. In it the author lamented the great sadness of his soul and dated the beginning of all his torments from the day he was wed. It is interesting that on fo. 2b, Rochford, probably its original owner, wrote, "Thys boke ys myn, George Boleyn. 1526," since the first evidence of his marriage to Jane is from that year. Near the end of the volume is Mark's statement in the language of courtly love, "A moy m marc S," indicating that it belonged to him. That he should refrain from signing his last name is not surprising, for Cavendish, who identified him as "Marke alias Smeton" recalled he had "dysdayned" his father and refused to see him. It is extraordinary that a manuscript, attacking the institution of marriage, should belong within the period of one decade to two of the five men executed for illicit sexual relations with the queen. Such volumes were expensive and normally changed hands only in the form of gifts.[60]

Probably aware of their friendship, Cromwell may have decided to begin the interrogation with Mark because he thought his youth, his lower-class origins, and his musical talents would make him especially vulnerable to questioning. Contemporaries generally believed that a "propensity" towards music, such as Mark's, was "of the devil's party," indicating in the person, as John Stevens has pointed out, a "weakness, an irresolution of character, which could lead its possessor into concupiscence and abomination." Cromwell's role in Mark's arrest, for he was first questioned at Stepney, becomes even more interesting when the details of a story reported by John Foxe are revealed. According to the martyrologist, Cromwell had kept imprisoned at the Marshalsea a man with long locks, who was "ashamed to be seen like a man would rather go like a woman," until he had agreed to cut his hair.[61]

On 30 April, after Smeaton had confessed to having sexual relations with the queen on three different occasions, he was taken to the Tower. When pressured by Cromwell and Fitzwilliam, Mark may have belatedly considered his family's honor. As J. A. Sharpe has recently pointed out, this concept, particularly concerning sexual matters was of great concern to the lower classes, for "eagerness to defend [one's] reputation ... was something which ran from the top to very near the bottom of English society." By Tudor values, being executed for adultery with the queen was more honorable than suffering death for an act that, as Coke later confirmed, ought not to be named among Christians. Experts have also determined that homosexuals have psychological problems induced not just by society's reaction to their sexuality but also by their dread of what they anticipate society's reaction will be if they are discovered. This fear creates in them an intense vulnerability to psychological blackmail. If Mark had wished to keep secret the nature of his sexual acts, there would have been no need to rack him, as some have suspected, to extract the confession that he had been Anne's lover.[62]

No evidence of his friendship for the queen exists except for this admission, which most modern scholars discredit completely. In the Tower, Anne could remember him in her apartments on only two occasions. The first was when she, along with the king, had been at Winchester in the autumn of 1535, and she had sent for him to play on the virginals for her. The second time was on 29 April, the day before his arrest, when she found him in her presence chamber with a sad demeanor on his face and rebuked him, as an "inferior person," for attempting to speak with her. He undoubtedly had already been ordered to appear before Cromwell and may have been seeking a sign of support from her or looking for Rochford. Ironically, she focused on the wrong periods, for the charges specified that their adulterous relations had taken place in the spring of 1535. At his execution he asked his listeners to pray for him and admitted that he deserved to die.[63]

The second prisoner taken was Norris, who, as Constantine, his servant, later recalled, had accompanied the king to Westminster at the end of the May Day jousting. During the trip the king allegedly promised him a pardon if he would "utter the trewth" about his relations with Anne, but Norris refused to make any confession to Henry and was committed to the Tower the next morning. It can be speculated that if the king did give Norris this extraordinary, personal attention it was because he had sworn to Anne's almoner that she was a good woman, an act that would naturally have caused attention to focus on him. Constantine also remembered: "And . . . as his chapleyn tolde me he confessed, but he sayed at his arrayning, when his owne confession was layed afore hym, that he was deceaved to do the same by the Erle of [South] Hampton that now ys [Sir William Fitzwilliam]." In discussing their executions with John Barlow, Constantine remembered that Norris alone "sayed allmost nothinge at all."[64]

Weston was one of four men arrested after Anne. Although her remarks in the Tower may have been the sole evidence for his conviction, there are valid objections to this assumption. The plans for the indictments and the paperwork must have already been in place when she made her admissions to the constable, for the council, which was informed of them on 3 May, would surely have needed more than one day of investigation before arresting a gentleman of the privy chamber. As Sir Richard Page, also taken to the Tower after the queen's incarceration, had left for home at the end of April, the delay in Weston's arrest may have resulted from nothing more complicated than his similar absence from court. In his execution speech, according to Constantine, the young man admitted that he was guilty of "abominations" for which he had expected to have twenty or thirty years to make "amends" and that he had asked everyone to take "example at hym," remarks that were interpreted by some onlookers as a confession of guilt. Since the word "abominations" can encompass a number of illicit sexual acts and since he admitted in a farewell letter to his family that he had been "a great offender to God," it is possible that Weston had committed buggery, although the evidence remains inconclusive.[65]

Brereton, also imprisoned after Anne, was a friend of Constantine, who later recounted a conversation he had held with him on the morning of the day he was arrested. He reported about his execution:

What was layed against hym I know not nor never hearde. But at his deeth these were his wordes: I have deserved to dye if it were a thousande deethes, But the cause wherfore I dye judge not: But yf ye judge, judge the best. This he spake iii or foure tymes. If he were gyltie, I saye therfor that he dyed worst of them all.

Brereton's comments can be interpreted to mean that although he was not guilty of the crimes for which he was to die he had committed offenses for which he did deserve death. His admissions were somewhat more severe than those a penitent Christian might ordinarily make in his last confession. The factional theory has blamed his death on the machinations of Cromwell whose attempts to reorganize the government of Wales, it is supposed, Brereton must have been resisting. Although as chamberlain of Chester and steward of Holt Castle he may have opposed these plans of the secretary, this explanation for his death seems contrived since he was not the only powerful courtier in that region.[66]

This interpretation rests in part on the assumption that Brereton, who was married to the sister of the earl of Worcester, was not an intimate friend of the other prisoners. It is interesting, however, that in 1533 Rochford had been involved with him in some matter about which Baynton, one of the officials who questioned Anne's ladies in 1536, wrote to her brother.[67] Thus Rochford can be linked to two of the other reputed lovers of his sister in matters unrelated to their membership of the king's privy chamber. It is, furthermore, a reasonable speculation that Anne revealed her discussions with Mark, Weston, and Norris only because she thought that they were the three men already in custody. If on 2 May she had believed that Brereton was a Tower prisoner, she might very well have reported a recent conversation with him. If her Tower comments are not viewed as foolish babblings about indiscreet flirtations but rather as evidence of her attempts, however misguided, to defend herself against unmerited charges and gossip, then only Rochford of the men arrested can be said, as her brother, to have indisputably belonged to a Boleyn faction. This conclusion seems to take on even greater merit when it is recalled that Norris had been reluctant to marry a cousin of the Boleyns, perhaps out of concern about allying himself with their family.

The mystery of why these five men were arrested cannot be adequately resolved by the claim that it was because they were members of the powerful Boleyn faction which Cromwell had deserted and had decided to destroy. If his initial intentions had been to purge the court of the queen's friends, he might better have directed his attentions toward her kinsman, Sir Thomas Cheyney, with whom she had been associated on more than one occasion and who was also of the privy chamber, or even toward Sir James Boleyn and others of her council, since there is no evidence that after she became queen the men with whom she most frequently conversed were actually the attendants of her husband. In the final analysis, the answer to the question of why these men were selected must take into account two practical needs. First, with the exception of Mark's confession and perhaps Anne's revelations, the principal evidence against them was that offered by three female witnesses, who had undoubtedly been asked to identify all suspicious individuals with whom the queen had been personally in contact between 1533 and 1535. Secondly, Cromwell had to make their affairs with Anne seem plausible to a wide range of people: to sympathetic, neutral, and even hostile observers, to the royal councillors, to members of the commission of *oyer et terminer*, and to those on the special commission summoned to try her and her brother. Surely, a conspiracy for the purpose of furthering Cromwell's own political standing at court that involved such a diverse and huge number of individuals, many of them well above him in social rank, was beyond even his abilities to pull off, especially as it required the participation of the powerful Fitzwilliam family, the members of which have never been linked either to him or to a so-called Aragonese faction. A reputation for lecherous habits, known either publicly among courtiers or privately among kinsfolk who would be willing to testify about that promiscuity would seem to offer the best answer.

In Brereton's case, since he was married to her husband's sister, it must have been Lady Worcester, the principal witness against Anne, who possessed the inside information about his character.

Besides the belief of the countess that his sexual appetites were excessive (since he was executed for adultery after claiming he deserved death) she would have been the most likely one of the ladies to have recalled any meetings he had had with Anne. It is also possible, although on the surface the nature of the incidents seem to be different, that he had earned such an infamous reputation, because of the death in 1534 of John ap Gryffith Eyton, a Flintshire gentleman, that the ladies and others were willing to believe him capable of any heinous crime. Indeed, George Cavendish revealed that because of Brereton's "old Rankor" toward Eyton, which arose from an incident left unexplained, he had had him arrested in London and returned to Wales to be hanged. An anonymous poet, often identified as Wyatt, also had heard that Brereton had had many loves.[68]

At the latest by 24 April, when the council began its inquiries into the activities of the queen and her alleged lovers, Anne had to have become aware that the king no longer favored her. Her clues would have been his insulting use of court etiquette on 18 April followed by his complete avoidance of her company. Perhaps her father, a member of the council, would have seen that she was warned about the investigation. It was surely during the week of the 24th, when rumors were spreading about the intentions of the councillors who were meeting daily at Greenwich, and about the king's desire to obtain a divorce, that she held the conversation with Norris. Whatever occurred in that interchange, the version reported by Kingston was probably accurate, for in it Anne maintained her innocence. Matthew Parker, as archbishop of Canterbury, later corroborated the suggestion that during this last week of April she was aware that her position as queen was in some jeopardy. "Not six days before her apprehension," he recalled, she asked him to have a special regard for her daughter. It may have been Mark's appearance in her presence chamber on 29 April that alerted Anne to the immediacy of the danger. He surely made the unscheduled visit to her rooms to inform her of his orders to attend Cromwell at Stepney the next day. While Mark was being questioned on 30 April, Anne put her own futile plans into operation. Norris was dispatched to her almoner to swear to her innocence and, with her daughter in her arms, she confronted Henry, hoping by her personal intervention to change his mind about her destiny. She knew, as Katherine Parr, his sixth consort, was to know when, according to John Foxe, she was to make a similar albeit successful plea to the king for mercy, that Henry was master in his own house. By 30 April the die had been cast. That same day, on the eve of May Day, their trip to Dover was cancelled.[69]

After failing to change her husband's mind, Anne had only two more days of freedom remaining. On Monday the royal couple attended the festivities planned for May Day, a pagan holiday customarily celebrated with erotic symbols, such as the may pole. Although Anne and Henry sat in their usual places, they had probably arrived separately at the tournament where two of her alleged lovers, Rochford and Norris, were to compete with each other, a public enactment of the charge that she had caused dissension and jealousy among them. Then, when following the jousting, Henry abruptly left for Westminster with only six gentlemen, many individuals, according to Hall, the chronicler, "mused but moste chiefely the quene" who had been so conspicuously deserted. If she were unaware of the reason for his hasty departure, she was not left to wonder long. On the morning of 2 May, a day on which some of her contemporaries gathered mountain ash branches to protect themselves from witches, Norfolk, Sir William Paulet, and Fitzwilliam accused her of having engaged in carnal relations with three men, only two of whom, Norris and Mark, were identified. Later, she was to claim that her uncle had said, "Tut, tut, tut!" that Fitzwilliam had been looking for something in Windsor Forest, and that only Paulet, the controller, had been kind to her. She thought "to be a Quene, and creuely handled was never sene" and speculated that the king was doing it "to prove" her.[70]

At two o'clock that afternoon, she was taken by barge to the Tower where she arrived some three hours later. When she asked Kingston, who reported her comments in the first of his six extant letters to Cromwell, if she would be locked up in the dungeon, he assured her that she would be placed in the lodgings (Beauchamp or Cobham Tower) where she had stayed before her coronation. Her response was to fall on her knees and to say "Jesu have mercy on me." Although she was not to be meanly housed, she was carefully watched. Her unsympathetic aunt, Anne Boleyn, the widow of Sir Edward and a former attendant of Catherine, and Mrs. Coffin, probably Margaret, the wife of Anne's master of the horse, lay in her chamber. Mary Kingston, the constable's wife, who had also attended Catherine, and two others, Mrs. Stoner, perhaps the wife of John, the king's sergeant at arms, along with an unnamed gentlewoman, slept nearby. Mrs. Coffin, Kingston assured Cromwell, told him everything that was said in Anne's presence. It was during her first few hours of imprisonment that the queen made her comments about Weston and Norris and about the child of Lady Worcester. On a later day she would complain that she had been denied the company of her favorite attendants.[71]

As she had been under extreme physical and emotional strain since her January miscarriage, her arrest for sexual crimes that she had not committed understandably made her extremely emotional. Kingston informed Cromwell that for at least one full day after she arrived at the Tower she alternated between "great" laughing and weeping. These outbursts must have been fueled in part by her fear for her family, for she inquired about the whereabouts of both her father and of her "sweet broder." She also lamented that her mother would die of "sorow" for her.[72]

From the first moment of her imprisonment, she turned to her religion for comfort. She asked Kingston that the sacrament be placed in the closet by her chamber so that she could pray for mercy and that she might be attended by her almoner. After a day or so in the Tower, when her emotional state improved, she began to hope that she might have justice. In his second letter to Cromwell, Kingston reported that she had longed for her bishops who would appeal to the king for her, a remark that surely indicated she thought they would give him some theological advice about the meaning of her miscarriage, which was the reason, she must have suspected, for the charges that she was guilty of witchlike conduct. Still she did not deny that death might come, predicting that as most of England were praying for her, God would punish the kingdom if something happened to her. On another day, when she said more specifically that it would rain until she was released, Kingston responded that there was yet fair weather. Unfortunately for her, the constable may have interpreted these comments in a sinister way, since witches were thought to be able to control the wind and the weather. She also asserted that because of her many good deeds she would go to heaven.[73]

In the third extant letter of Kingston to Cromwell, he revealed her comments about Mark and told of her calm reaction to the arrests of Wyatt, Brereton, and Page. She discussed the two occasions on which Mark had been in her apartments and informed Mrs. Stoner that he had been placed in irons because he was no gentleman. This letter is so mutilated that her remarks about Page and Wyatt have largely been lost. Near the end of the document Kingston reported her assertion that no one could write better ballads than Rochford. When Lady Kingston responded that Wyatt could, Anne agreed with her assessment. It is possible that she was as yet unaware of Cromwell's major role in her arrest, for she asked Kingston if he would send a note to the secretary for her. The constable refused but offered to give him an oral message instead.[74]

The last letters of Kingston to Cromwell were written following her trial, which took place on Monday, 15 May, two days after the confident Fitzwilliam and Paulet had broken up her household and had discharged her servants. Her uncle Norfolk, the Lord High Steward, sat under the cloth of estate in the King's Hall at the Tower with his heir, the earl of Surrey, at his feet. On the scaffolding around them, which had been constructed for the trial, were the twenty-six noble judges, who had been chosen by a system that was essentially impartial. After their commission was read, Anne and her two attendants, Lady Kingston and Lady Boleyn, were led into the room by Kingston and the lieutenant, Sir Edmund Walsingham. She was seated when the indictments charging her with enticing five men to have illicit relations with her were read aloud. The crown was represented by Cromwell and Sir Christopher Hales at whose house Henry and she had stayed en route to Calais in 1532.[75]

One compelling and unexpected witness was Bridget Wingfield, who testified from the grave. Shortly before her death, perhaps as early as 1533, she had conveyed to a confidant some information about Anne's sexual habits that may have taken place before she was officially recognized as the king's wife. Anne had become his mistress by the late autumn of 1532, a fact that may have greatly upset Lady Wingfield, whose house the royal couple also visited en route to Calais that year. How the statement was discovered is unknown, but it can be speculated that it was revealed by Thomas Harvey, a son of Lady Wingfield's second husband by his first wife, who was a sister to Fitzwilliam. After the succession of Anne's daughter, Elizabeth, Harvey went into exile, remaining abroad until his death. The significance of his stepmother's testimony lies more in its existence than in its details, which are now lost, for her contemporaries, including Sir John Spelman, one of the judges present in an official capacity at Anne's trial, attached special meaning to deathbed statements. By confirming that the queen had been a libertine prior to 1533, it made the otherwise incredible charge that she had subsequently engaged in carnal relations with five men seem plausible.[76]

Unrattled by these lurid details, Anne, whom the law did not permit to employ counsel, kept her composure and, as Wriothesley stated, excused "herselfe with her wordes so clearlie, as thoughe she had never bene faultie to the same." After the noblemen had been individually polled, all twenty-six declaring her guilty, Norfolk, with tears in his eyes, gave the sentence that she deserved death but that the king would decide whether she would be burned or beheaded. There is no reason to doubt that his emotion was genuine, if not because the duke personally had any affection for his niece at least because his status as the king's relative had been diminished and his honor as her uncle had been disparaged. In response to the verdict, Anne reportedly said she regretted that innocent men were to die because of her and asked for time to prepare her soul for death. By the standards of the day, the queen had received a fair trial, for, as G. R. Elton has pointed out, it was not true that once charges were made against political prisoners, the crown manipulated the courts to obtain their condemnation. Only two years earlier, for example, a similar panel had acquitted Lord Dacre. Had the king and Cromwell not believed that they had enough evidence to prove her guilty, a bill of attainder could have been used against her at this stage. Probably this public trial with the embarrassing claims that five men had cuckolded the king had been considered necessary as a precautionary measure in case word leaked out about the fetus.[77]

In two letters written after her trial, Kingston discussed with Cromwell the preparations for her execution and those of her convicted lovers. In these messages the constable revealed that the archbishop of Canterbury, who was by the king's command, her confessor, had been with her. Cranmer may have succeeded in comforting her, for at dinner, perhaps on the 16th, she told Kingston that she thought she might be sent to a nunnery. She may have clung to this hope because to resolve the domestic crisis in 1528 Campeggio had suggested that Catherine retire to a monastery.[78]

What Anne thought about the divorce hearing presided over by Cranmer on 17 May was not recorded. This must have been a difficult time for the archbishop, for earlier, when Cromwell had denied him access to the king until he had spoken with the council, Cranmer had written to Henry from Lambeth. In his letter he had at first assured the king that if what he had heard openly about the queen were true then her honor only and not his would be "disparaged." And then he continued:

for I never had better opinion in woman, than I had in her; which maketh me to think, that she should not be culpable. And again, I think your Highness would not have gone so far, except she had surely been culpable. Now I think that your Grace best knoweth, that next unto your Grace, I was most bound unto her of all creatures living.[79]

After Thomas Audley and some other councillors had persuaded the archbishop of her guilt, he agreed to convene a session on 17 May to have her union with the king declared invalid, although in her confession to him she had admitted to no wrong doing. Anne, who was not present at the inquiry, was represented by Nicholas Wotton and John Barbour, and the king by Richard Sampson. The only extant record of this hearing is the bare statement of the invalidation, for the deliberations, which contained the specific reasons for the decision, have disappeared. A widely accepted assumption is that Cranmer based his decree on the supposition that she must have entered into a *de praesenti* vow with Northumberland, for individuals were often not fully aware of the difference in the wording of this oath and in that of the more temporary *de futuro* version. A major problem with this assumption is that the earl himself swore that no such pre-contract had ever existed. Any attempt to interpret this strong negative response and his illness on the day of her treason trial as the result of deep feelings he still held for her will be misguided. He had sat through her entire trial, and it was not until the beginning of Rochford's that the chronic sickness of Northumberland, which was to take his life in 1537, forced his departure from the King's Hall. The other most widely accepted speculation about Cranmer's decision is that it was based on the illicit liaison between Henry and Anne's sister, but this impediment had been dispensed with by a bull of Clement VII, a copy of which was at Lambeth Palace. Chapuys had heard that it as well as the Percy episode was used.[80]

Although Wyatt had been married, if he had been the queen's "acknowledged suitor" in 1527, he, like Northumberland, would surely have been questioned about a pre-contract with her. It is noteworthy that in 1542 one of the alleged lovers of Katherine Howard was executed for his dealings with Henry's fifth consort before she became queen. Since there is no contemporary evidence that prior to his imprisonment Wyatt had ever been viewed as a special friend of Anne, he, along with Page, was surely arrested on the basis of his reputation as a libertine. Indeed, there is extant corrobative evidence, which dates from the lifetime of Wyatt, of his reputation for sexual excesses. In two letters to Cromwell, dated in May and June 1536, even his own father, when referring to the reasons for his imprisonment, alluded to his vice and the "displeasure he hath done to God." Perhaps the poet did guess correctly when he blamed Suffolk, who may have known about his promiscuity, for this crisis in his life. Both Page and Wyatt surely gained their freedom because Anne's ladies could not remember any close or intimate encounters between her and them from October 1533 through December 1535.[81]

Clearly, neither the alleged pre-contract of Anne and Northumberland nor the sexual relationship of her sister with the king had formed a legal impediment to this royal marriage. No evidence has survived of the grounds Sampson, who had been closeted with Cromwell for four days at the end of April, used to obtain the royal divorce, but almost certainly, given the circumstances, Henry would have wanted information cited that was unquestionable and uncontrived. Since the indictments had failed to accuse Anne of sexual misconduct before Elizabeth was conceived, it seems unlikely that the king would have sought the divorce solely for the purpose of having his child declared illegitimate. The licentious charges against the queen, even if the rumors of her attempted poisonings and of her causing her husband's impotence were never introduced into any of the trials, indicate that Henry believed that she was a witch. That he would want it to be a part of the official record that she had caused his impotence, making it seem impossible for him to have fathered the fetus delivered to her in January, is a reasonable conclusion. Since it was widely believed that witches did afflict men with impotence, this claim would have come readily to the minds of both the king and his advisers. Indeed, the thought of the dead child born to Anne in January might very well have caused Henry to feel sexually diminished in her presence. That Sampson must have cited the king's alleged incapacity in the divorce case is an obvious speculation and actually makes more sense than Cromwell's charge that Anne had committed incest with her brother at Westminster in November 1535, when she was in residence with her husband at Windsor. If Cranmer, whom Alesius saw crying on the day of her execution, did not destroy the records of this hearing, then it is a safe assumption that Parker did so when he became archbishop, for he recalled with nostalgia that he had been her "countryman."[82]

On Thursday, 18 May, the day after the invalidation of her marriage, Kingston had a conversation with Anne about which he wrote to Cromwell. Upon his arrival in her chamber, Anne, who had been saying devotions with her almoner since two o'clock, had told the constable that she regretted that she would not die before noon because she had hoped by then that the deed would be done and she would be past all pain. When he assured her that there would be no pain for the deed would be so sudden, she said: "I heard say the executor was very gud, and I have a ly[tel neck and put h]er hand abowt it, lawynge hartely." He was astounded at this "joy and pleasure in dethe," but surely her reaction was not from "joy" but from pent-up shock and disbelief. A few months earlier she had miscarried a second child; since then she had lost the affection of her husband and had been convicted of sexual crimes with five innocent men, including her brother, all of whom had been executed the previous day. Surrounded by hostile attendants, she must have doubted that she had any friends left in the kingdom, for there is no evidence that her mother, her father, or even her sister ever tried to communicate with her in the Tower. Anne's almoner was continually with her on the 18th, and Kingston predicted that in her last speech she would deny her guilt. For that reason he recommended that the number admitted into the Tower be limited. The Imperial envoy, he noted, had sent a servant to witness the execution, but he and other foreigners had been expelled from the premises.[83]

Despite her hopes of dying on that Thursday, it was not until about eight in the morning of 19 May, probably the fourth months' anniversary of her miscarriage, that her execution took place on a low platform of only four or five steps that had been newly constructed on Tower Green. Near it Audley, Norfolk, Suffolk, Richmond, Cromwell, and others of the council had gathered to witness the first public execution of an English queen. The Mayor of London, some aldermen, and a few citizens were also present. Dressed in a robe of black damask covered by an ermine mantle of white, Anne entered the courtyard in the company of four ladies and Kingston. The constable handed her over to the sheriff, who escorted her to the platform. Although she had been given only a few days to prepare for death, she had come to prove her innocence by dying "boldly."[84] Edward Hall quoted her as follows:

Good Christen people, I am come hether to dye, for according to the lawe, and by the lawe I am judged to dye, and therefore I wyll speake nothynge agaynst it. I am come hether to accuse no man, nor to speake any thyng of that, whereof I am accused and condempned to dye, but I pray God save the king and send him long to reygne over you, for a gentler nor a more mercifull prince was there never: and to me he was ever a good, a gentle and soveraygne lorde. And if anye persone wyll medle of my cause, I require them to judge the best. And thus I take my leve of the worlde and of you all, and I hertely desyre you all to praye for me. O Lorde have mercy on me, to God I commende my soule.[85]

She dispensed alms of £20 as customary, exchanged her headdress for a little cap of linen, thanked her ladies for their diligence in her service, and exhorted them not to forget her and to be faithful to the king. Having asked for prayers to be said for her soul, she knelt down, was blindfolded by one of her attendants, and repeated, "To Jesus Christ I commend my soule; Lord Jesu receive my soule" several times until with a "stroake of [his] sword" the hangman from Calais had "sealed the debt that she owed unto death."[86]

9 ROYAL LEGACY

Mercifully, after only one blow of the "very sharp basterd sword," Anne's head "fell to the ground with her lips moving and her eyes moving." As the executioner left the scaffold to collect his fee of almost £24 for completing his morning's task efficiently and quickly, the late queen's weeping ladies prepared her remains for burial, covering the head and body with a sheet and placing them in a chest of elm for removal to their final resting place in St. Peter's ad Vincula, the chapel at the north end of Tower Green.[1]

As proof that she had prepared well for her death, Anne had quite properly directed a few kind words to these women in her execution speech. Because they had subsequently reacted to the sword's work with great sadness and grief, Agnes Strickland and other historians have speculated (or out of pity hoped) that in her last hours the king and his advisers had permitted his ex-consort to be served by attendants of her own choosing. Regardless of how unsympathetically the four women had acted during the first days of Anne's imprisonment, that they should display shock and horror when viewing the decapitation of an ex-queen of England at such close range would seem to have been a perfectly normal reaction. As her attendants it would also have been their responsibility to see that the remains of this noblewoman were properly cared for in the customary mourning tradition.[2]

The story surfaced in the eighteenth century that just before her execution, Anne had given a book of devotions to a member of the Wyatt family, perhaps Margaret Lee, the married sister of the poet. That Margaret, presumably a friend of Anne, might actually have been a witness to the queen's death was part of the evidence Stickland used to argue that substitutions must have been made in her attendants. There are two insurmountable

234

problems with this legend: first, it was unknown to the poet's grandson George Wyatt in the 1590s when he wrote his "Reminiscences," and secondly, the volume in question has never been indisputably identified. Although Margaret Lee might well have been the fourth Tower attendant, who has remained anonymous, the story that Anne presented her with one of the disputed books of devotions is surely as apocryphal as the misguided hope that, near the end of his ex-wife's life, Henry was actually moved by pity for her.[3]

Because of their need to have Anne surrounded by trustworthy women who had been sworn to secrecy, neither the king nor his principal secretary was likely to relent on this issue. Since she had continued to proclaim her innocence, even Kingston had believed it was necessary to restrict the number of individuals permitted to observe her execution. Far from acting in a remorseful way at his consort's plight, Henry, himself, if Chapuys can be believed, was displaying a mixture of relief and euphoria. The king reportedly confided to Richmond that Anne had planned to poison both Mary and him (the duke) and displayed to the bishop of Carlisle a tragedy about her death that he had allegedly written prior to her arrest. All of his actions, including the marriage to Jane Seymour on 30 May 1536, indicate that Henry genuinely believed that Anne was guilty of the crimes for which she had died. The shock of discovering a deformed fetus in his nursery would surely have been sufficient to cause the king some momentary impotence, at least toward Anne. He soon regained his sexual powers, for in the summer of 1537 his new consort lost her life presenting him with his heart's desire, a son who was named Edward. When the king died in 1547, he chose to be interred at Windsor by the side of the mother of that child.[4]

While Henry was preparing to remarry, Anne's remains were being buried at St. Peter's. In 1876–7 the chapel, which had become "mean and unsightly, the result of successive alterations and additions," was thoroughly remodeled and restored under the direction of two architects, Anthony Salvin and John Taylor. In November 1876, the workman discovered a skeleton under a paving stone near the choir of the chapel. A medical man assisting at the renovation said that the bones belonged to a woman between the ages of twenty-five and thirty who had a delicate frame with a very small neck. The remains were not positively identified as Anne's but the supposition was strong that they were.[5]

Despite her burial at St. Peter's, rumors have persisted that her body was secretly conveyed elsewhere. Just as residents of the small village of Salle, Norfolk, near which Blickling is located, claim that she was born and married at this manor, so they believe that her final resting place is under a small flat black slab in their parish church. This belief is supported by the legend that on its journey to Salle, the body rested at Thorndon on the Hill, Essex, the church of which commemorates her passage through their parish with a black slab. Another Essex tradition maintains that her heart was actually buried in the nave of the church of East Horndon. When Norah Lofts, a recent biographer of Anne, visited Salle, she learned from the sexton that he had dutifully watched for the queen's ghost throughout one 19 May night but had seen only a hare that had escaped in the darkness. Perhaps unintentionally confirming the folklore that Anne was a witch, Lofts reminded him that these individuals sometimes took the form of a hare. A legend also persists at Hever Castle that on the anniversary of her death Anne wanders around the countryside as a "white, almost transparent phantom."[6]

In 1536 as her execution drew near, her anticipated death was also accompanied by strange visions and happenings. On the morning of 19 May, as Alesius later recalled, he awoke about two in the morning, troubled by a vision in which the queen's neck had been revealed to him in some detail. Unable to sleep, he went abroad for the first time since her arrest (he thought she had been imprisoned on 30 April). When he asked the archbishop of Canterbury, whom he later found at Lambeth, why he was crying, Cranmer had responded that on that day the queen was to die. This news caused Alesius to wonder and to muse about the meaning of his vision, for he had not known about her trial and conviction. Word also spread that the day before Anne's death the wax tapers about the tomb of Catherine at Peterborough Abbey took fire of themselves and after matins were quenched of themselves. The king was said to have sent thirty men to the abbey to see if the story were true.[7]

The members of Anne's immediate family did not long survive

her execution, for most, except those of the younger generation, died during the reign of Henry. The life of Lady Wiltshire ended on 3 April 1538 at the abbot of Reading's place beside Baynard's Castle in London; she was subsequently buried in the aisle of Lambeth parish church. Her husband, deprived of the earldom of Ormond and of the office of Lord Privy Seal, continued to serve, in the short time remaining to him, on the royal council. A few months after his wife's demise, gossip, surely untrue, circulated that he might marry Margaret Douglas, the king's niece. To commemorate his death on 12 March 1539, the crown had "oraisons, suffrages, and masses" said for him, and his heirs had him interred in St. Peter's at Hever where a large tomb surrounded by a brass indicates his final resting place. Even though his remains are not at Salle church, by the nineteenth century folklore had begun to claim that his specter resided at Blickling manor. Another Norfolk legend insists that for 1,000 years he must drive a coach of four headless horses over twelve bridges and carry his head under his arm, flames coming from its mouth.[8]

Although technically the earl had owned Blickling, after his marriage in 1501 he never actually resided at the manor. In 1505 when his father died, it became a part of the jointure of his mother, Margaret, daughter to the earl of Ormond. A long-lived woman, she survived her son by a few weeks; following her death, Blickling was transferred to her grandchild by marriage, the widowed Jane, Lady Rochford, as part of her jointure. After Lady Rochford's execution in 1542, as an accomplice in the alleged adulterous affairs of the king's fifth consort, Katherine Howard, Blickling passed to Sir James Boleyn. It was surely Lady Rochford's association with Queen Katherine that persuaded later writers that she must have been a major factor in the earlier trials of Anne and her five accused lovers.[9]

On 19 July 1543, about a year after Jane's execution, her sister-in-law, Lady Mary Rochford, died. The widow of William Carey, Mary had taken as her second husband William, the second son of Humphrey Stafford of Blatherwick, Northampton, and seems to have resided principally at Rochford, Essex. Before her death, her daughter, Catherine, about fifteen years old, won appointment as a maid of honor to Anne of Cleves, the fourth consort of Henry VIII. Sometime in 1540, Catherine married Sir

Francis Knollys, a member of the royal household and gave birth to Lettice, the future countess of Essex and of Leicester and the first of the numerous Knollys children. Until her death early in 1569, Catherine was one of her cousin Elizabeth's closest friends. Her husband, Francis, served this relative, after her succession as queen, in a number of positions, as did his brother-in-law, Henry Carey, the son of Mary and the former ward of Anne Boleyn. Elizabeth ennobled Carey as Lord Hunsdon but refused to bestow upon him their grandfather's earldom of Wiltshire.[10]

In May 1536, after her household was discharged, Anne's servants were left free to be employed by other masters. Some, like George Taylor, who reportedly was "merry," joined the king's household; others, like Baynton, Coffin, Mrs. Horsman, and Mrs. Stoner served the new queen. Lady Bryan, who continued in her post as governess of Elizabeth, wrote to Cromwell for instructions about the ambiguous position of the king's child, who had recently been declared illegitimate: "Elizabethe is put from that degre she was afore And what degre she is at now, I know not bot be heryng say; therfor I know not how to order her nor myself, nor non of hars." After complaining about the lack of clothing for her, a problem that seems to have arisen for the first time, and challenging the rule of Sir John Shelton, steward of the household, Lady Bryan ended with the comment: "For she is toward a child, & as gentle of conditions, as ever I knew one in my leyf."[11]

Following Henry's death, many individuals, among them certainly Matthew Parker, who was later to write that he had no doubt that Anne's soul was in "blessed felicity with God," must have assured her daughter of their belief in her innocence. Within two years of the execution, verses by two French poets, Nicholas Bourbon and Etienne Dolet, had been printed in praise of Anne, and shortly after Elizabeth's accession the comments of various other individuals, among them William Latimer and Alesius, anticipated the published statements of John Foxe and André Thevet that celebrated and defended her mother's tenure as queen consort. The marriage of Henry to Jane so quickly after the execution even gave rise to the erroneous claim that he had put Anne to death out of lust for his third wife.[12]

That Elizabeth wished to establish the validity of her parents' union, if not to refute the charges against her mother, there is no doubt, for she asked Parker, as her archbishop of Canterbury, to look for a papal bull, which he found in 1572, that had permitted their marriage. From the beginning of her reign Elizabeth's actions occasionally indicated a personal belief in her mother's innocence; a representation of Anne was included, for example, in one of the pageants commemorating Elizabeth's entry into London in 1559. Despite this positive attitude and the complimentary statements of Protestants, the old rumors about Anne's gross sexual habits persisted, partly because Europe was increasingly divided into two camps, one favoring Spain, a leader of the Catholic Reformation, and one supporting England, a defender, however reluctantly, of Protestantism abroad. In Spain the name, Anna Boleyn, became a term of opprobrium, a development anticipated by the remark in 1536 of Mary, regent of the Netherlands and Anne's old playmate, that the English queen had been a French woman and thus an enemy of the Imperial cause that was so closely identified with Spain.[13]

How much the knowledge that her mother had been executed for activities associated with witchcraft affected Elizabeth's psychological outlook and her self-confidence as a woman can only be guessed at. She must surely have believed in the existence of witches, for in 1563 she approved a statute making witchcraft a capital offense, although not on the first conviction. Even before the publication of Sander's work describing Anne as a monstrous creature, Elizabeth's ministers had sought to refute other scurrilous statements of his and his Catholic fellow polemicists. Their efforts at censorship are interesting in light of Elizabeth's unwillingness to marry, for her decision was both remarkable and extraordinary since it was a challenge to at least four strong impulses: the sex drive to perpetuate the human species; the social desire to advance one's lineage; the political ambition to continue the Tudor dynasty; and the reformed belief that the vocation of womankind was marriage.[14]

From both a modern and a contemporary viewpoint her momentous decision can be justified in a rational manner. It could be argued that she did not wish to accept any man as the head of her household, which was in some sense a microcosm of the kingdom, although in her sister's reign a statute had indisputably placed the governance of England in the hands of the queen regnant. From a practical point of view, it must be noted that some queens regnant have been able to influence, even control, the actions of their husbands, either because the men were endowed with weak personalities, as was the spouse of Anne Stuart of England, or because the wives have had the perseverance and the nerve to overcome their husband's challenge to their political rule, as did Mary Stuart of Scotland. The union of Mary Tudor of England and Philip of Spain need not be viewed as a model for all married female monarchs. Even Margaret, countess of Richmond, for example, proved in her third marriage to be a far more independent noblewoman than her great-granddaughter, Mary Tudor, is thought to have been as queen. Another argument that surely has special meaning for modern women, if not for Renaissance women, is that Elizabeth may have wished to retain her single status out of fear that she would not survive childbirth. That fear cannot be entirely discounted in her specific case, especially as she approached her fortieth birthday, although in general the views of early modern Europeans about conception and pregnancy intermingled magical or spiritual causes with biological and human ones. Death from childbirth was thought to be as much God's will as a natural phenomenon.[15]

Beyond the above reasons, the decision of the queen of England or of any sixteenth-century woman not to marry, in the absence of financial or social impediments, would be a complex one involving psychological impulses that are impossible to penetrate some 400 years later. Even so, one approach, which has been somewhat neglected, might be fruitful. It involves looking at Elizabeth's decision in association with her mother's trial, for the taint of witchcraft, so contemporaries believed, could be passed on to one's children. When Anne miscarried her fetus in 1536, the rumors circulated at home and abroad that it was her "defective constitution" that had prevented her from delivering live male sons. From early in Elizabeth's reign, far too early for it to have arisen as part of the speculation about why she had chosen never to marry, gossip maintained that there was something wrong with her anatomy, that in fact she was unable to conceive and bear children. Throughout her life she seems to have harbored a personal fear about her fertility that led her to submit to medical examinations, all of which indicated that she was physically normal, at least to the human eye.[16]

On a rational level surely she did not believe that her mother had been a witch. But the psychological impact of knowing that her father had approved Anne's execution for activities associated with witchcraft could have created an uncertainty and even an apprehension in Elizabeth. This uncertainty, together with a possible fear of childbirth and the anticipated problems with spousal relationships, could have effectively offset all the positive reasons she might have had for taking a husband. It is interesting that her last flirtation with marriage ended in 1582 just three years before the scurrilous Latin work of Sander in which her mother was described as a monster who had given birth to a shapeless mass. Many individuals in England, such as George Wyatt, who were not renowned intellectuals, read this extremely popular work. Whether Elizabeth, a classical scholar, knew about its existence is unknown. It is to be hoped that her councillors were able to shield her from its devastating remarks.[17]

Regardless of the reason or reasons, since she chose not to marry, she doomed her mother's efforts to raise the Boleyn lineage permanently into the royal family. Anne's greatest legacy to sixteenth-century England and to subsequent generations lay in providing the kingdom with her daughter, but her drive to continue the Tudor dynasty with either her son or a grandson of that child failed. This failure together with the violence of her death has lent credence to the persistent claims that she was actually a witch. In modern schoolbooks and historical novels she is still depicted as a modified version of Sander's monstrous woman. For many she remains the queen with a malformed finger whose social conduct was too unrestrained for her own well being and whose carefree sexual behavior irresponsibly courted death.[18]

In the late nineteenth century this view of her character was given renewed impetus by the discovery of the letters of Chapuys. In Paul Friedmann's monumental work on Anne, the dispatches of this hostile and prejudiced ambassador formed the principal source of evidence about or rather against her. For Chapuys, as well as for Friedmann, she became the symbol of the corruption and evil at the English court that had first given rise to and then had nourished the divorce crisis and the accompanying religious schism. Other scholars, following the guidelines set down by Friedmann, have also credited, in eclectic and modified form, Chapuys' many contradictory statements about the queen's sexual and political nature. In his writings, Professor E. W. Ives, one of Anne's recent biographers, has advanced scholars to a better understanding of the possibilities of factional maneuvers at court, but, as his evidence relies heavily upon the untrustworthy comments of Chapuys, his assertions that for mere political reasons Cromwell joined with an Aragonese faction to cause Anne's death are doubtful.[19]

Since Professor Ives' first work on court faction was published in 1972, most Tudor scholars have accepted his version of her spectacular rise and tragic fall.[20] It is now time for this view to be amended, for the real story is somewhat more mundane: she was a victim of her society's mores and of human ignorance about conception and pregnancy. Cranmer's words to Henry VIII in May 1536, already quoted in Chapter 8, deserve to be repeated here, for they are a reminder of how inadequate the scholarly treatment of her has been:

for I never had better opinion in woman, than I had in her; which maketh me to think, that she should not be culpable. And again, I think your Highness would not have gone so far, except she had surely been culpable. Now I think that your Grace best knoweth, that next unto your Grace, I was most bound unto her of all creatures living.

Since by the standards and values of her day, she must be judged both guilty and innocent, the insightful and troubled testimony of Cranmer, who was to be her last confessor, serves Anne the Queen well as her final epitaph.

APPENDIX A THE LEGACY OF NICHOLAS SANDER

During the centuries since her death, the work that has had the greatest influence on interpretations of Anne Boleyn is that of Nicholas Sander. Born about 1530 at Charlwood Place, Surrey, he probably never saw the queen, but if he did, it would have been only from a distance, leaving him with vague childhood recollections of her. In 1540 he went to Wykeham's School near Winchester College and afterward to New College, Oxford, where he surely became acquainted with Nicholas Harpsfield, another Catholic historian of the English Reformation. Early in the reign of Elizabeth, Sander left England to be ordained as a priest at Rome. In about 1564 he traveled to Louvain, the home of many English Catholic refugees, and at their request settled at Madrid in 1573 as their spokesman and lobbyist. After several years at Madrid, he decided that more aggressive action against the Protestant regime of England was needed. In 1579 he traveled to Ireland to promote resistance against Elizabeth and died there early in 1581.[1]

Sander seems to have written his *De origine et progressu schismatis Anglicani* before he joined the Irish rebellion. Using his incomplete notes, Edward Rishton published the work posthumously at Cologne in 1585. While he made only minor changes in the sections on the reigns of Henry, Edward, and Mary, he completely rewrote the section on that of Elizabeth. Sander did not have to create the portrait he painted of Anne as an extraordinarily libidinous woman, for there existed a wealth of material in print, in manuscript, and in rumors upon which he could draw. Her execution for having engaged in illicit sexual acts with five men was an indisputable fact. Paolo Giovio, the Italian author, had referred to her lovers and her gross lust in his history, which

243

appeared a few years after her death. It cannot be established that Sander knew about an anonymous Spanish chronicle, probably written in the 1550s but unpublished until the nineteenth century. In this chronicle, with its many glaring inaccuracies and omissions, is the first written assertion that Sir Thomas Wyatt had been Anne's lover.[2]

Because, after he was released from prison, Wyatt went on to serve the crown as ambassador to the emperor, his arrest in 1536 proved to be of special interest to the Spanish chronicler and to other Catholic writers, among them Nicholas Harpsfield. A contemporary of the Spanish author, Harpsfield, who also asserted that Wyatt and Anne had been lovers, indicated he had obtained his information from Antonio Bonvisi, a moneylender who had dealings with Wyatt but who was not in England at the time of the arrests and executions in 1536. Surely Harpsfield's evidence was simply that Bonvisi had informed him about the arrest of Wyatt, whose incarceration would have been sufficient to convince him, as well as the anonymous chronicler, that the poet had been Anne's lover. Acquainted with Harpsfield, Sander may have learned the story of Wyatt's arrest from him. In their studies none of the Catholic writers mentioned Sir Richard Page, who was also imprisoned and released in 1536.[3]

Sander was the first author to give information (that is extant and can be dated) about Anne's sexual habits as a child. According to him, Sir Thomas Boleyn had sent her to France to complete her education because she had engaged in sexual relations with his butler and with his chaplain. Earlier, while Sir Thomas, himself, had been absent in France, Sander also claimed, Lady Elizabeth had conceived her daughter during an affair with Henry. Thus when Anne became the king's wife, she actually married her father. This assertion was undoubtedly an enlargement of rumors current during Anne's lifetime that her mother had been the king's mistress.[4]

One of the first to respond to Sander's charges was George Wyatt, a grandson of the Tudor poet. The somewhat naive approach of Wyatt, who was not a great scholar, was to assume that the gross statements of the priest were merely exaggerations of small defects or innocent events. As part of his effort to refute the claims that Anne and the poet had been lovers, George Wyatt asserted that his grandfather had only been a suitor of Anne and that she had merely favored him. To better explain their relationship, the grandson created a courtly episode in which she was given the opportunity to deny to Henry that she had ever taken Thomas' suit seriously. Probably, the poet had never even courted her, for his first datable association with Anne was his arrest in 1536. The mere fact of his imprisonment cannot be used as evidence of his involvement with the queen, especially since Page has not been credited with having had a similar relationship with her.[5]

While it was more probably the story that his grandfather had engaged in illicit relations with Anne than the description of her as a disfigured woman that moved George to write in refutation of Sander, still he would surely have been outraged at the suggestion that Anne had looked like a monster. Apparently adopting both a medieval custom and the Neo-Platonic tradition that evil and wicked beings ought to be clothed in outward ugly features, Sander painted a monstrous portrait of Anne, whose bewitching ways, as he believed, had first destroyed a marriage and then created a schism in the Church. She was, he said, very tall (tall women were thought to be excessively lusty), sallow in complexion (perhaps a reference to their perceived habit of living in forests), with a wen under her chin (possibly an early reference to the witches' teat which could be found in various places including the pudenda); with a projecting tooth under the upper lip (gobber teeth were associated with witches) and six fingers on her right hand (fingers and fingernails played a prominent role in witchcraft).[6]

George's method in denying Sander's description was to reduce some of these features to proportions as normal as he could make them. The sallow skin became clear; the tooth and her height were ignored; the wen became moles; the sixth finger became a fingernail. As the claim that she possessed a deformed hand especially troubled him, he created a card game between Catherine and Anne in which the young lady displayed her extra digit that was usually kept hidden for Henry to see. The problems with this anecdote are that Catherine never played cards and that Anne could never have kept even a small fingernail hidden; even had she been able to accomplish this impossible feat, once Henry had seen it, he would have rejected her for his bride as he rejected Madame Renée, for even a discolored spot on a fingernail was viewed as a bad omen. In short, the eyewitness account of the Venetian ambassador in 1532 must be accepted as a more valid description of her than that of George, who was born after her death. Had Anne possessed an extra fingernail the envoy would have noticed and would have said so, for his description was already as unattractive a portrait as he could paint.[7]

For his depiction of Anne, Sander may have been inspired by accounts of her coronation. Extracts from an anonymous French statement now lost and undated, for example, not only said that on her day of triumph she had warts and a swelling in her neck but also that she wore a dress decorated with tongues pierced with nails. As contemporaries believed that a swelling of the veins in the neck was a sign of pregnancy, this account may have been a reference to her very obvious condition on 1 June 1533.[8]

A final assertion of Sander, that she had miscarried of a "shapeless mass" related to one tragedy associated with witchcraft that Wyatt entirely ignored. Witches were thought to give birth not only to deformed creatures and monsters but also to stillborn children, which reportedly had been bewitched to death by their devil-worshipping mothers.[9]

Besides describing her with monstrous features and with gross sexual habits, even as a teenager, Sander stated that her father had sent her to France to live at the home of a nobleman, not far from "Brie." Two years after the publication of Sander's book, Adam Blackwood, writing about the death of Mary, Queen of Scots, also referred to Anne's residence at "Brie" and her six fingers, closely repeating Sander's remarks. This is the origin of a legend, still extant, that Anne's childhood education had occurred in France at the home of a nobleman rather than in the royal nursery. In 1654 Julien Brodeau's posthumous work, quoting both Sander and Blackwood as his authorities, identified the nobleman as Philippe de Moulin de Brie to whom, he thought incorrectly, the Boleyns were related. It was his statements that gave rise to the erroneous claims that the ancestors of the Boleyns were French aristocrats. In subsequent decades, it became customary for a Tower at the little village, Briis-sous-Forges, on the road from Limours to Arpajon, to be recognized as the actual place where Anne was educated. It is close to Rambouillet, a hunting lodge of Francis I's. As Anne was reared with Madame Renée and as no extant evidence suggests that a royal nursery was ever established in this little village, the whole legend is undoubtedly a fabrication based on Sander's incorrect claim that her sexual misconduct as a child caused Sir Thomas Boleyn to send her to France to be educated.[10]

That a legend such as this could develop from erroneous claims and not from actual facts is entirely possible. There is a tradition, for example, that Henry VIII had a tower built for Anne on Green Street in East Ham, Essex, but there is no extant evidence that he did so or even that she ever visited that village.[11]

Sander's scandalous work was extremely popular. Not only was it quoted by Blackwood but also many editions of it were published. After its first appearance at Cologne in 1585, it was printed at Rome in 1586 and 1588; a French version surfaced in 1587 and a German one in 1594; in 1610 and 1628 the Latin version was re-issued at Cologne. Ultimately, it was rendered into six different languages. It was the new French translation in 1676 (re-issued in 1678 and 1715) that moved Gilbert Burnet to make his now famous attack on Sander. Others before him had refuted it: Edward, Lord Herbert, and William Lloyd, for example. Burnet's denials were in turn refuted by Joachim Le Grande and other Catholic polemicists. The result was that 100 years after its first appearance in print it remained the "foremost Catholic indictment of the English Reformation." An integral part of that indictment was the depiction of Anne as a witch. The details were so compelling and so fascinating that, even though they were entirely fictitious, they have survived through the ages and still form the basis for references to her in modern textbooks.[12]

APPENDIX B THE CHOIRBOOK OF ANNE BOLEYN

Edward E. Lowinsky may well have been correct in believing that Choirbook 1070, a manuscript at the Royal College of Music in London, belonged to Anne Boleyn but his speculations about its illumination and its authorship are problematic. Assuming that a reference to Mrs. Anne Boleyn and the words, "nowe thus," the motto of her father, meant that the manuscript was in her possession, Lowinsky went on to identify two of its figures as Anne and Catherine of Aragon, two drawings of a bird and a pomegranate as their devices, and its handwriting as that of Mark Smeaton. Since many of the composers in the manuscript were Flemish and all of the music was of Franco-Flemish origin, Lowinsky believed that Smeaton, whom he identified as its scribe, must have emigrated to England from Flanders. As he also pointed out, the compositions were all written by 1515 but could have been copied down years later.[1]

That Anne was referred to as Mrs. surely misled Lowinsky, for modern historians have often been unaware that this abbreviation for mistress in early modern England, unlike its usage today, denotes social rather than married status. A young gentlewoman, even of some five or six years of age, was quite properly referred to as Mrs. Interpreting the abbreviation by modern usage, Lowinksy dated the manuscript in the mid-1530s, after Anne's marriage. He then looked with some interest at the drawings on two facing pages. At the top of one page was a figure with a full face and a turban headdress and further down the page was a bird. The page facing it had a pomegranate at the top and further down a figure with a long face and long hair. Lowinsky concluded that these must have been intended as representations of Anne and her falcon and Catherine and her pomegranate.[2]

Besides the extremely relevant fact that the figures do not actually resemble extant portraits of Anne and Catherine, there are other problems with this interpretation. In December 1529, when her father became an earl, Anne gained the right to be addressed as Lady Anne Rochford rather than Mrs. Anne Boleyn. For the choirbook to have been intended especially for her use when she was still being addressed as Mrs., it would have had to have been composed before the end of 1529 and would have necessarily had a bull for her device rather than a falcon, for the latter only became her device in 1533. Furthermore, although the drawing in the choirbook can be said to represent a falcon, it is certainly not the magnificent white crowned bird that was so celebrated at her coronation. It should also be noted that besides serving as Catherine's personal device, the pomegranate was also used as the symbol of Spain and of Granada, as the rose was that of England, the lily of France, the olive of the pope, and the pineapple of the Empire.[3]

The figures themselves can only with difficulty be identified as women, for the gem in the middle of the turban is the only jewelry either one of them wears. The individual with long hair and no headdress has a squared neckline but not the fashionable square of Anne's dresses. Although her hair was worn long at her elevation to the peerage and at her coronation, it was also adorned with a circlet of jewels. It is relevant to this discussion that there were contemporary references, one as late as 1520, to Catherine with her hair falling on her shoulders. The individual with a turban, identified as Henry's first consort, interestingly enough, can also be found on an earlier page in the choirbook. This drawing was smudged, either by mistake because the figure was incompletely and crudely done or because the intention of the artist was to give it dark skin like that of a moor. The turban, which does not at all resemble the gable headdress usually associated with Catherine, became popular for women in western Europe after the fall of Constaninople in 1453. It remained popular until the end of the fifteenth century, but it was certainly not fashionable in England between 1521 and 1536.[4]

Although the handwriting in the choirbook is consistent with Smeaton's signature in Royal 20 B XXI, a manuscript at the British Library, it cannot with certainty be identified as his composition. It is highly unlikely that he was this scribe, for he was not from Flanders, as George Cavendish, who knew him, pointed out, but the son of poor English parents. After serving in Cardinal Wolsey's chapel, Smeaton seems to have joined the king's chapel where he remained as a boy singer at least to the end of 1532. When he subsequently became a groom in the king's privy chamber, he ceased to be employed primarily as a professional musician, although he could, of course, still be called upon to entertain members of the court with his musical talents. During the time that Anne was addressed as Mrs., he was a child singer, first working for Wolsey and then for Henry. There is no reason to believe that he was ever a music scribe; indeed, many of the songs popular at court were simply sung to old refrains.[5]

The actual owner or owners of the choirbook may never be known, but it will be assumed here that it did belong to Anne Boleyn. That it is crudely and incompletely illuminated could mean that she took it with her, away from the scribe, when she moved suddenly from one court to the other. Two occasions are possible: either it was written by mid-1514 when she left Malines or by 1521 when she returned to England from France. Its incomplete state might also mean it was a failure, a reject, saved for the use of a child in which case she could have obtained it at either royal nursery.[6]

The best clue to its origins lies with the figure wearing a turban. The headdress of the individual resembles somewhat those of a few ladies portrayed in Simon Bening's *Genealogical Tree of the Kings of Aragon*. Bening, the finest Bruges illuminator of the sixteenth century, worked on this particular illumination in the 1520s and 1530s, too late for it to have influenced the scribe of Anne's choirbook. Even so, the turbaned figure in her manuscript could have represented either a moor from Grenada or one of the ancestors of the Spanish royal family. While it is possible that the Franco-Flemish artists could have composed the choirbook in either France or England, it is highly likely that these drawings, which celebrated Iberian culture in a manuscript that belonged to Anne Boleyn, were sketched when she was in Malines, living at the headquarters of Charles, prince of Castile, the future Holy Roman Emperor. For these reasons, the best speculation seems to be that Anne carried the choirbook with her when she left Malines for Paris and from there to England.[7]

APPENDIX C TWO POEMS OF SIR THOMAS WYATT

Two other poems of Sir Thomas Wyatt besides "Who so list to hounte I know where is an hynde," which was discussed in Chapter 3, have been incorrectly associated with Anne Boleyn. The first is:

> Some tyme I fled the fyre that me brent
> By see, by land, by water and by wynd;
> And now I folow the coles that be quent
> From Dovor to Calais against my mynde.
> Lo! how desire is boeth sprong and spent!
> And he may se that whilome was so blynde;
> And all his labor now he laugh to scorne.
> Mashed in the breers that erst was all to torne.[1]

There is no internal evidence in this verse indicating that it was written in 1532. Wyatt crossed the Channel from Dover to Calais (the usual route to the continent) many times. Before 1532 he had traveled to Italy and had served as marshal of Calais. After 1536 he went abroad on diplomatic assignments. Even had he been Anne's lover, and had this verse applied to her, it could have been written any time after 1527 not just the year she, herself, journeyed to Calais.[2]

The second Wyatt verse incorrectly associated with her is:

> If waker care is sodayne pale Coulour
>   If many sighes with litle speche to playne
>   Now ioy, now woo, if they my chere distayne,
>   For hope of smalle, if muche to fere therfore,
> To hast, to slak my pase lesse or more,
>   Be signe of love then do I love agayne.
>   If thow aske whome, sure sins I did refrayne
>   Brunet that set my welth in such a rore,

Th'unfayned chere of Phillis hath the place
  That Brunet had: she hath and ever shal.
  She from my self now me in her grace:
She hath in mind my witt, my will, and all
  My hert alone wel worthie she doth staye,
  Without whose helpe skant do I live a daye.[3]

Because in the Egerton Manuscript Wyatt changed in his own hand the eighth line of this verse from "our country in a rore" to the above "welth in suche a rore," it has been assumed that he must have been trying to obscure his reference to Anne, as only she could have caused a sensation in the kingdom. It is more likely that by country Wyatt meant the county of Kent than the kingdom of England, for country was often used synonymously with county. In that case the brunette could have been his wife or anyone else from Kent.[4]

No one has yet ventured to speculate about the identity of Phillis. In fact, this name was not often given to Englishwomen. It is interesting that the most popular comic example of female rule and domination in Christendom from the thirteenth to the seventeenth centuries was the figure of Phyllis riding upon the back of Aristotle. After he had admonished his pupil, Alexander, about his excessive attention to a woman by this name, she revenged herself upon him by persuading Aristotle to crawl on all fours, saddled and bridled, with her riding on top.[5]

It is not being argued here that Wyatt was actually referring to the comic Phylllis, but this example serves as a warning that caution must be used in reading historical facts into his poetry. From Anne's lifetime, there is no surviving evidence except for his arrest in 1536 that his name was ever linked to hers.[6]

NOTES

The following abbreviations are used in the notes.

BIHR	*Bulletin of the Institute of Historical Research*
BL	British Library
Burnet	Gilbert Burnet, *The History of the Reformation of the Church of England*, new edition (3 vols. in 6 pts., Oxford, 1816).
DNB	*Dictionary of National Biography*
Cal.SP Ireland	*Calendar of the State Papers Relating to Ireland of the Reigns of Henry VIII, Mary and Elizabeth, 1509–1573*, ed. H. C. Hamilton, E. G. Atkinson, and R. P. Mahaffy (11 vols., London, 1860–1912)
Cal.SP Span.	*Calendar of Letters, Despatches, and State Papers, Relating to the Negotiations between England and Spain*, ed. G. A. Bergenroth, P. de Gayangos, G. Mattingly, M. A. S. Hume, and R. Taylor (13 vols., 2 supplements, London, 1862–1954)
Cal.SP Ven.	*Calendar of State Papers and Manuscripts Relating to English Affairs, Existing in the Archives and Collections of Venice and in Other Libraries of Northern Italy*, ed. R. Brown, G. Cavendish-Bentinck, H. F. Brown, and A. B. Hinds (38 vols., London, 1864–1947)
Cavendish, "Wolsey,".	George Cavendish, "The Life and Death of Cardinal Wolsey," in *Two Early Tudor Lives*, ed. R. Sylvester and D. Harding (New Haven, Ct., 1962)
Ellis	Henry Ellis, ed., *Original Letters Illustrative of English History* (11 vols. in 3 series, London, 1824–46)
Elton, *Reform*	G. R. Elton, *Reform and Reformation: England, 1509–1558* (Cambridge, Ma., 1977)
Elton, *Studies*	G. R. Elton, *Studies in Tudor and Stuart Politics and Government* (3 vols., Cambridge, 1974, 1983)

Forrest	William Forrest, *The History of Grisild the Second: A Narrative in Verse of the Divorce of Queen Katherine of Aragon*, ed. M. D. Macray (London, 1875)
Foxe	*The Acts and Monuments of John Foxe*, ed. G. Townsend (8 vols., New York, reprint, 1965)
Friedmann	Paul Friedmann, *Anne Boleyn: A Chapter of English History, 1527–1536* (2 vols., London, 1884)
George Wyatt	George Wyatt, "The Life of Queen Anne Boleigne," in *The Life of Cardinal Wolsey by George Cavendish*, ed S. W. Singer, 2nd edition (London, 1827)
Hall	Edward Hall, *Henry VIII*, ed. C. Whibley (2 vols., London, 1904)
HMC	Historical Manuscripts Commission
HPT	The History of Parliament Trust: *The House of Commons, 1509–1558*, ed. S. T. Bindoff (3 vols., London, 1982)
Ives, *Anne*	E. W. Ives, *Anne Boleyn* (Oxford, 1986)
Knecht	R. J. Knecht, *Francis I* (Cambridge, 1982)
Latimer	William Latimer, "A brief treatise or cronikelle of the most vertuous Ladye Anne Bulleyne, late Queen of England," Bodleian MS C. Don 42
Lisle Letters	*The Lisle Letters*, ed. M. St. Clare Byrne (6 vols., Chicago, 1981)
LP	*Letters and Papers, Foreign and Domestic of the Reign of Henry VIII*, ed. J. S. Brewer, J. Gairdner, and R. H. Brodie (21 vols., London, 1862–1932)
Metrical	George Cavendish, *Metrical Visions*, ed. A. S. G. Edwards (Columbia, S.C., 1980)
Peerage	G. E. Cockayne, *The Complete Peerage*, ed. V. Gibbs, H. A. Doubleday, D. Warrand, Thomas Lord Howard de Walden, and G. White (13 vols., London, 1910–59)
Reassessing	A. Fox and J. Guy, eds., *Reassessing the Henrician Age* (Oxford, 1986)
Richardson	W. C. Richardson, *Mary Tudor: The White Queen* (London, 1970)
RO	Public Record Office
Sander	Nicholas Sander, *The Rise and Growth of the Anglican Schism*, ed. D. Lewis (London, 1877)
Scarisbrick	J. J. Scarisbrick, *Henry VIII* (Los Angeles, 1968)

StPap   *State Papers of King Henry VIII* (11 vols., London,
               1830–52)
Wood   M. A. E. Wood (Green), *Letters of Royal and
               Illustrious Ladies* (3 vols., London, 1846)

References to *LP*, all *Cals.*, Ellis and *Lisle Letters* are to numbers of
documents unless otherwise specified.

INTRODUCTION: QUEEN ANNE

1 Foxe, V, 136.
2 For recent studies of Foxe, see G. R. Elton, "Persecution and Toleration
   in the English Reformation," *Studies in Church History*, vol. XXI
   (Oxford, 1984); W. W. Wooden, *John Foxe* (Boston, 1983), 30–76; J. N.
   King, *English Reformation Literature: The Tudor Origins of the Protestant
   Tradition* (Princeton, 1982), 438–9.
3 *Cal.SP Span.*, V-ii, 54 (p. 120); Friedmann; see also G. Mattingly, "A
   Humanist Ambassador," *Journal of Modern History*, 4 (1932), 175–85.
4 *Cal.SP Span.*, V-i, 146; one of many examples of this eclectic approach
   can be found in Ives, *Anne*, 355, 358. Although Cromwell reminded
   Chapuys on 19 May (*Cal. SP Span.*, V-ii, 55, p. 123) that he had
   predicted Anne's downfall to him in February, it fitted Ives' chronology
   better to accept Cromwell's claim to the ambassador on 6 June (ibid.,
   V-ii, 61, p. 137) that he had not decided to bring about her fall until
   Easter week. See also Chapter 8.
5 Sander, 24–5; see also Chapter 3 and Appendix A; G. Duby, *Medieval
   Marriage: Two Models from Twelfth-Century France*, ed. E. Forster (Balti-
   more, 1987), 40, indicates that for political reasons similar charges were
   made after Philip I, king of France, divorced his first wife and married
   Bertrade, whom he believed was fertile: "Bertrade was seen as the
   corruptress ... Philip as a prisoner of his lust, much more the victim
   than a seducer, another Adam, another Samson, but definitely not
   another David."
6 Burnet, I-i, 75, I-ii, 419; Edward, Lord Herbert, *The Life and raigne of
   King Henry the Eighth* (London, 1649), 230, 257–8; in a modification of
   the Sander tradition, Ives, *Anne*, 51, conceded a "malformation of one
   finger-tip" and a mole or two. D. Starkey, *The Reign of Henry VIII:
   Personalities and Politics* (London, 1985), 90, believed she had a thick
   neck. See Chapter 1, n. 59, and Appendix A.
7 See Chapter 8.
8 See Chapter 8.

I BOLEYN ORIGINS

1 *LP*, I, 1196; C. A. J. Armstrong, *England, France and Burgundy in the Fifteenth Century* (London, 1983), 201–9; *Correspondance de L'Empereur Maximilien Ier et de Marguerite D'Autriche*, ed. A. J. G. Le Glay (reprint, 2 vols., New York, 1965), II, 461 n. 2; see also Ives, *Anne*, and C. Erickson, *Anne Boleyn* (New York, 1984).

2 *LP*, I, 1322, 1338.

3 Ibid., 1306, 1338, 1370, 1394, 1430, 1871; in 1535 (VIII, 189) Wiltshire reportedly spoke French best of the councillors.

4 J. de Iongh, *Margaret of Austria: Regent of the Netherlands*, tr. M. D. H. Norton (New York, 1953), 94–5, 180.

5 Ibid., 17–42; M. J. Tucker, *The Life of Thomas Howard, Earl of Surrey and Second Duke of Norfolk, 1443–1524* (London, 1964), 89; D. Head, "The Life and Career of Thomas Howard, Third Duke of Norfolk: The Anatomy of Tudor Politics," Ph.D. dissertation, Florida State University, 1978, 25–39; the first duke had escorted Margaret to Burgundy to become its duke's bride. See A. Crawford, "The Career of John Howard, Duke of Norfolk, 1420–1485," M. Phil. thesis, University of London, 1975, 161–80.

6 C. Franklyn, *The Genealogy of Anne the Quene* (Brighton, Sussex, 1977); W. Parsons, "Some Notes on the Boleyn Family," *Norfolk Archaeology*, 25 (1935), 386–407; E. Reilly, *Historical Anecdotes of the Families of the Boleyns, Careys, Mordaunts, Hamiltons, and Jocelyns Arranged as an Elucidation of the Genealogical Chart at Tollymore Park* (London, 1839); W. Cooper, "The Family of Lord Hoo and Hastings," *Sussex Archaeological Collections* (London, 1856), 27–8; R. Clutterbuck, *The History and Antiquities of the County of Hertford* (3 vols., London, 1827), III, 93–6; F. Blomefield, *An Essay Towards a Topographical History of the County of Norfolk*, 2nd edition (11 vols., London, 1805–62), VI, 386–9; see A. Strickland, *Lives of the Queens of England* (11 vols., London, 1842), IV, 167, for their alleged French royal descent and Appendix A.

7 See n. 6 for William; see also *Calendar of the Patent Rolls, 1494–1509* (reprint, 2 vols., Nendeln, Lichtenstein, 1970), II, 269.

8 T. Carte, *The Life of James, Duke of Ormond*, new edition (3 vols., Oxford, 1851), I, lxv–lxviii, lxxxiii–lxxxiv; *LP*, II, 1269; for disputes over the title of Ormond, see Chapter 2.

9 Because James Boleyn held Blickling, he has been incorrectly identified as the elder son, but he obtained it after the death of his niece, Lady Rochford. See J. H. Round, *Early Life of Anne Boleyn: A Critical Essay* (London, 1886), 9; *Calendar of the Fine Rolls*, XXII (London, 1962), pp. 63–4, has a 1501 record of grants in Sussex, Norfolk, and

Kent for the use of Elizabeth during her lifetime, probably the establishment of her jointure; *Metrical*, line 290, may be interpreted to mean that at the age of twenty-seven George became a member of the privy council; *LP*, IV, 546 (2), for his owning a manor in his own right in 1524, XI, 17, for his mother's lyings-in. One of the sons was buried at Hever and another at Penshurst. See M. Stephenson, *A List of Monumental Brasses in the British Isles* (London, 1926), 236, 251; J. Gairdner, "Mary and Anne Boleyn," *English Historical Review*, 8 (1893), 53–60, and "The Age of Anne Boleyn," *English Historical Review*, 10 (1895), 104; H. Paget, "The Youth of Anne Boleyn," *BIHR*, 54 (1981), 163, 166; on the basis of Paget's findings, Ives, *Anne*, 17–19, depicts Anne as a mature woman when she arrived at the English court in 1527. For more about her age, see later in this chapter and R. M. Warnicke, "Anne Boleyn's Childhood and Adolescence," *Historical Journal*, 28 (1985), 939–52.

10 R. M. Warnicke, "Childhood," 942–3, discusses the draft petition of George, Lord Hunsdon, who failed in his attempt to obtain the title of Ormond by proving that his grandmother Mary had been the elder Boleyn daughter. Hunsdon's daughter later confirmed his error by having it engraved on her tombstone that Mary was younger than Anne; for why Mary was wed before her older sister, see Chapter 2; C. Franklyn, *Genealogy*, 9, says that both girls were born at Hever Castle. H. Spelman, *Icenia: Sive Norfolciae*, in *Reliquiae Spelmannianae* (London, 1723), 151, reported that Anne was born at Blickling. T. Fuller, *The History of the Worthies of England* (reprint, 3 vols., New York, 1965), II, 351, revealed that some of her still living relatives thought she had been born in London. E. Benger, *Memoirs of the Life of Anne Boleyn*, 3rd edition (Philadelphia, 1850), 49, said that Anne was born at Rochford Hall, a manor her father did not own in 1507 (P. Morant, *The History and Antiquities of the County of Essex* [2 vols., London, 1768], II, 12), for in 1510 (*LP*, I-i, 438 [3], m. 7) he owned Blickling, Hever, New Inn without Temple Bar in London, and Hoo in Bedfordshire. Ives, *Anne*, 3, believed she was born at Blickling because Matthew Parker, who became her chaplain in 1535, later referred to himself as her "countryman," but regardless of her birthplace, she would have been viewed as hailing from Norfolk, since the family's chief holdings were in that country; *Correspondence of Matthew Parker, D. D.*, ed. J. Bruce and T. Perowne (Cambridge, 1853), 400. In 1506, in the *Calendar of the Close Rolls: Henry VII* (2 vols., London, 1953–63), I, p. 233, her father was described as "late" of Blickling, the residence of his widowed mother, and in 1538 (*LP*, XIII-i, 937) he confirmed that he had lived at Hever for thirty-three years. Even if Anne had been born in Norfolk, the Howards could have provided her

mother with a lying-in chamber as easily as her mother-in-law. Thus, Parker's statement is not evidence of her specific birthplace.

11 C. Franklyn, *Genealogy*, 7; M. J. Tucker, *The Life of Thomas Howard*, 72; J. Nichols, "Female Biographies of English History: Anne, Lady Howard," *Gentleman's Magazine*, N.S. 23 (1845), 147–52; J. Gairdner, ed., "'The Spousells' of the Princess Mary, 1508," *Camden Miscellany*, IX (reprint, New York, 1965); A. R. Myers, "The Book of Disguisings for the Coming of the Ambassadors of Flanders, December, 1508," *BIHR*, 54 (1981), 120–9.

12 R. Virgoe, "The Recovery of the Howards in East Anglia, 1485–1529," in *Wealth and Power in Tudor England*, ed. E. W. Ives, R. J. Knecht, and J. J. Scarisbrick (London, 1978), 5–16; D. Head, "Norfolk," 28–40.

13 *Calendar of the Patent Rolls*, II, 479, 484; *LP*, I, 20 (p. 13), 81–2, 257 (40), 698, 707, and for his lands in Essex, Hertfordshire, and London, forfeited by viscount Lovel, 833 (14), 1415 (3); Oxford's death also resulted in his obtaining lands in Essex. See P. Morant, *The History and Antiquities*, II, 12–13; in 1511/12 (*LP*, I, 833 [60], 1221 [27], 1415 [4]) he obtained other manors, including Wykmer, Norfolk, and the custody of the lands and the wardship of John Hastings.

14 For envoys on the council see Elton, *Studies*, I, 130; *LP*, I, 132 (92), 257 (49), 632 (26), 709 (19), 1083 (26), 1732 (12), pp. 1541, 1544.

15 *Correspondance de L'Empereur*, I, 92, 461 n. 2, II, 159; *LP*, I, 2564 for Bouton, 1777 for Mary's letter to the regent on 13 April 1513, II, p. 1460 for the Burgundian servant; Bouton wrote *Miroir des Dames*. See K. Brandi, *The Emperor Charles V*, tr. C. V. Wedgwood (London, 1939), 27–37.

16 *Correspondance de L'Empereur*, I, 461 n. 2; *LP*, I, 1841, 2480 (49); M. Bruchet and E. Lancien, *L'Itineraire de Marguerite d'Autriche, Gouvernante des Pays-Bas* (Lille, 1934), 134–40; J. de Iongh, *Margaret*, 182–3.

17 *Peerage*, VI, 142–3, XII, 458; Richardson, 149–85. Margaret also invited to her court his adopted child, Magdalen Rochester, who was eight years old. Although Lady Anne could have been born as early as 1503, she still would have been no more than ten when she went to Malines; for Sidney, *LP*, I, 2488, 2924; for her recall, BL Add. MS 14,840, 30 May 1515, in *LP*, II, 529.

18 R. M. Warnicke, "Childhood," 943–4; R. A. Houlbrooke, *The English Family, 1450–1700* (New York, 1984), 65–8; L. Stone, *The Family, Sex and Marriage, 1500–1800* (New York, 1977), 46–54; those who wed at twelve did not usually live together for several years; for Anne's youth, see William Camden, *Annales rerum Anglicarum et Hibernicarum regnante Elizabetha* (London, 1615), 2; Cavendish, "Wolsey," 31, said she was young and in the Wyatt papers she was referred to as a "yonge

Gentlewoeman" during the year 1528. See D. M. Loades, ed., *The Papers of George Wyatt, Esquire, of Boxley Abbey in the County of Kent*, Camden Society, 4th series, vol. V (London, 1968), 143; Forrest, 53, referred to her as "a fresche younge damoysell" in 1527; *Correspondance de L'Empereur*, II, 461 n. 2; HMC, *The Manuscripts of Eliot Hodgkins, esq. F.S.A. of Richmond, Surrey*, vol. XVI-2 (London, 1897), 30.

19 G. Toudouze, *Anne de Bretagne, Duchesse et Reine* (Paris, 1938), 190; V. Wilson, *Queen Elizabeth's Maids of Honour* (New York, 1922), 10; *Lisle Letters*, III, pp. 142-8, 163-4, 172-3; for the quotation, R. Strong and J. Oman, *Eliz R* (London, 1971), 6; for royal children, K. Brandi, *The Emperor*, 48, and W. K. Jordan, *The Chronicle and Political Papers of King Edward VI* (Ithaca, N.Y., 1966), xi-xii.

20 J. de Iongh, *Margaret*, 10, 138-68; C. Moeller, *Eleonore d'Autriche* (Paris, 1895), 39-41, for Mary as *petite* and the vacations.

21 J. de Iongh, *Margaret*, 13-20, 167-8; and *Mary of Hungary*, tr. M. D. H. Norton (New York, 1958), 21-31; C. Moeller, *Eleonore*, 12-42; Anne called her French tutor Semmonet (*LP*, IV, 1; and Ellis, 2nd series, II, 97). A Symonnet was in Charles' household in 1510, but there is no evidence that he was the same person. See *Correspondance de l'Empereur*, I, 273; for the music book see Appendix B.

22 For the quotation see H. Trevor Roper, *Princes and Artists, Patronage and Ideology at Four Habsburg Courts, 1517-1633* (New York, 1976), 14-18; A. Durer, "Diary of a Journey in the Netherlands, 1520-21," in *Records of Journeys to Venice and the Low Countries*, ed. R. Fry, tr. R. Tombo (Boston, 1913), 11-95; M. Picker, ed., *The Chanson Albums of Marguerite of Austria* (Berkeley, Ca., 1965); H. Paget, "The Youth of Anne," 169-70.

23 HMC, *The Manuscripts of Eliot Hodgkins*, 30; J. de Iongh, *Margaret*, 195; many scholars have thought that Mary Boleyn went to France in 1514, but her father's letter indicates it was Anne. See also n. 32 below and R. M. Warnicke, "Childhood," 951-2; for foreign policy, see Scarisbrick, 41-55.

24 *LP*, IV, 1; and Ellis, 2nd series, II, 97.

25 HMC, *The Manuscripts of Eliot Hodgkins*, 30.

26 For another stilted letter, see N. Williams, *Thomas Howard, Fourth Duke of Norfolk* (New York, 1964), 12.

27 *Correspondance de l'Empereur*, II, 190, 254-6; M. Bruchet and E. Lancien, *L'Itineraire*, 149-53; HMC, *The Manuscripts of Eliot Hodgkins*, 30; if Boleyn's man, who left Greenwich on or after 14 August, was delayed, he might not have found the regent at Brussels. On 19 August she allegedly did not believe the rumors about the French alliance (*LP*, I, 3174). Between 21 and 31 August, she was on progress, probably without the children, but was back in Brussels by 2 September.

28 H. Paget, "The Youth of Anne," 163–7 n. 26, claimed an earlier date for her letter because he thought she meant to return home. Part of his argument was based on her verb choice. In the letter to her father, who, Paget assumed, would stay at Greenwich, if she had meant that she was to accompany Mary to France, she would have said go, rather than "come," but "come" was the proper verb since both her father and Mary would be in France. A misprint in *LP*, I, 3348 (3) where he is listed as T. Botrym, has left some scholars unaware that he was in Mary's train. See Hall, I, 123.

29 For Thomas in 1514, see n. 28; Richardson, 89–91, and H. Chapman, *The Thistle and the Rose* (New York, 1969), 171, claimed that the crossing took several days, but she landed on 3 October (*LP* I, 3331), after having left on 2 October; J. Bridge, *A History of France From the Death of Louis XI* (reprint, 5 vols., New York, 1978), IV, 252–3.

30 P. Jourda, *Marguerite d'Angoulême, Duchesse d'Alençon, Reine de Navarre* (2 vols., Paris, 1930), I, 44, called Renée *petite*; Richardson, 94–6.

31 H. Cocheris, *Entrées de Marie D'Angleterre, Femme de Louis XII à Abbeville et à Paris* (Paris, 1859); see also F. Wormald, "The Solemn Entry of Mary Tudor to Montreuil-sur-Mer in 1514," in *Studies Presented to Sir Hilary Jenkinson*, ed. J. Conway Davies (London, 1957), 471–9.

32 Richardson, 108; *LP*, IV, 1 for Anne's letter, I, 3411 for Renée; relying on extracts from an original now lost, Ives, *Anne*, 19, 33 n., argues that both Mary and Anne went to France. This invitation was too great an honor to be extended to two daughters of a knight. Although the extracts do have the name of Mary Boleyn, Ives admitted they are not perfect, for they omit Mary Fiennes. It is possible that the scribe wrote Mary and then his eye jumped to Boleyn, which has no first name in the BL Cotton MS Vitell. C XI, fo. 155 (*LP*, I, 3357). Except for the continuing debate about who this M. Boleyn was, there is no other evidence for Mary's unlikely visit to France. An interesting observation about the above manuscript is that M. Boleyn was the only commoner. All of the other ladies (except for the chamberers) were members of the nobility. In the document, which is signed by Louis XII, the noble ladies, whose relatives were identified, were lumped together under "Mesdemoiselles" and then follows "Madamoyselle Boleyne" all by herself without any other identification. This silence is consistent with the suggestion that Anne was already with Renée.

33 Richardson, 108–9; *LP*, I, 3416 for the envoy's comment, 3308 for Francis, 3411 for Claude and Renée.

34 Richardson, 97–115; a chronicler wrote Anne had been "brought up in France with Madame —, a very noble lady & one that was desirous to understande the worde of God." As the daughters of French kings were

called Madame, and as Renée later flirted with Protestantism, it was quite likely her name the writer did not know. See D. M. Loades, *The Papers of George Wyatt*, 143.

35 R. Strong, *Art and Power: Renaissance Festivals, 1450–1650* (Woodbridge, Suffolk, 1984), 6–16; for the quotation, R. Strong, *Splendor at Court: Renaissance Spectacle and the Theatre of Power* (Boston, 1973), 22; see also S. Anglo, *Spectacle, Pageantry and Early Tudor Policy* (London, 1969).

36 Richardson, 116; *LP*, I, 3417; R. Withington, *English Pageantry: A Historical Outline* (reprint, 2 vols., New York, 1963), I, 171–2.

37 Richardson, 118–21; J. Bridge, *A History*, 262.

38 Richardson, 123–6; S. Putnam, *Marguerite of Navarre* (New York, 1935), 26.

39 C. Jackson, *The Court of France in the Sixteenth Century* (2 vols., Boston, n.d.), I, 45; Richardson, 132; P. Jourda, *Marguerite d'Angoulême*, I, 44; Knecht, 13–16.

40 Richardson, 143–85.

41 D. M. Mayer, *The Great Regent: Louise of Savoy. 1476–1531* (New York, 1966); Knecht, 33–42.

42 Knecht, 88, L. de Carles, *Epistre Contenant le Procès Criminel Faict à Len Cointre de la Royne Anne Boullant D'Angleterre* (Lyons, 1545), lines 37–80, also in G. Ascoli, *La Grande-Bretagne devant l'opinion française* (Paris, 1927), and G. A. Crapelet, ed., *Lettres de Henri VIII à Anne Boleyn avec la traduction* (Paris, 1826), 168–214. De Carles, who first arrived in England in the summer of 1535, was incorrect about later public occurrences (lines 183–5). For a long time one copy of his work was thought erroneously to have been written by Anthonine Crispin. See G. Colletet, *Vies des poètes Bordelais* (2 vols., Paris, 1873), I, 33–4 n.; C. J. Blaisdell, "Renée de France between Reform and Counter Reform," *Archiv für Reformationsgeschichte*, 63 (1972), 196–225; J. Bonnet, "La Jeunesse de Renée de France," *Bulletin de la Société d'Histoire de Protestantisme Français*, 15 (1866), 65–77, 175–96; George Wyatt, 442–3; W. Thomas, *The Pilgrim: A Dialogue on the Life and Actions of King Henry the Eighth*, ed. J. A. Froude (London, 1861), 49.

43 RO, SP 70/22, fo. 552, 10 January 1561, State Papers, Foreign, General Series, Elizabeth I, in *Calendar of State Papers Foreign, Elizabeth, 1560–61* (London, 1865), 870 (pp. 489–90); Ives, *Anne*, 22–46, does not refer to Renée.

44 C. J. Blaisdell, "Renée de France," 198–201.

45 So important was physical regularity that in *LP*, I, 1241, Robert Wingfield made a point of indicating that the prince of Castile and his sisters "go right upon their joints and limbs"; for Wolsey and Henry, *StPap*, I-i, p. 203; K. Park and L. Daston, "Unnatural Conceptions:

The Study of Monsters in Sixteenth- and Seventeenth-Century France and England," *Past and Present*, 92 (1981), 20–54.

46 Knecht, 84–90, 103; C. Marchand, *Charles Ier De Cosse, Comte De Brissac et Marechal de France, 1507–1563* (Paris, 1889), 8–9.

47 S. Melchior-Bonnet, *Châteaux of the Loire*, tr. A. Armstrong (Paris, 1984), 36–47; C. Marchand, *Charles*, 8–9; J. Bonnet, "La Jeunesse," 177.

48 Knecht, 99, 103; D. Seward, *Prince of the Renaissance: The Golden Life of François I* (New York, 1973), 94; S. Melchior-Bonnet, *Châteaux*, 82–91; *LP*, III, 468.

49 *LP*, II, 4655, III, 9, 69, 126, 289, 306, 446, 468, 661.

50 J. Pardoe, *The Court and Reign of Francis the First, King of France* (3 vols., New York, 1887), I, 277; Richardson, 133; *LP*, III, 663 for Claude's references to Boleyn, 111, 122, 416, 684, 726, 1161 for her illnesses; Ives, *Anne*, 40, doubted that Anne resided in Margaret's household, but among the early authors with whom he disagreed, he failed to include William Camden, *Annales rerum Anglicarum et Hibernicarum regnante Elizabetha*, 2, who said Anne did reside in Margaret's household. This is a crucial omission, as Camden also revealed that Anne was born in 1507, a date Ives rejects.

51 P. Jourda, *Repertoire analytique et chronologique de la correspondance de Marguerite d'Angoulême, Duchesse d'Alençon, reine de Navarre (1492–1549)* (Paris, 1930), pp. 7–15, No. 605; for the Field of Cloth of Gold, *LP*, III, 673, 702, 704 (pp. 243, 245), 869–71; J. G. Russell, *The Field of Cloth of Gold* (New York, 1969); for the tradition that Anne lived at Briis-Sous-Forges, see Appendix A.

52 Richardson, 133; Knecht, 86–98; P. de Bourdeille, Seigneur de Brantôme, *The Lives of Gallant Ladies* (London, 1961), 386.

53 Knecht, 44–6, 83–110.

54 I. D. McFarlane, *A Literary History of France: Renaissance France, 1470–1589* (New York, 1974), 73–84, 103; P. M. Smith, *Clément Marot: Poet of the French Renaissance* (London, 1970), 6–35; Sir Arthur Tilley, *The Literature of the French Renaissance* (reprint, 2 vols., New York, 1959), I, 57–61; A. L. Prescott, *French Poets and the English Renaissance* (New Haven, Ct., 1978), 1–36.

55 I. D. McFarlane, *A Literary History*, 84–5, 117–26; Sir Arthur Tilley, *Literature*, I, 97–137; M. Tetel, *Marguerite de Navarre's Heptameron: Themes, Language and Structure* (Durham, N.C., 1973), 6–14.

56 I. D. McFarlane, *A Literary History*, 84–5; J. Huizinga, *Erasmus of Rotterdam* (New York, 1952), 2–6.

57 I. D. McFarlane, *A Literary History*, 84–5; Sir Arthur Tilley, *Literature*, I, 10–28, 41; P. E. Hughes, *Lefèvre: Pioneer of Ecclesiastical Renewal in France* (Grand Rapids, Mi., 1985); Ives, *Anne*, 42, questions the extent to

which Anne was religiously influenced in France and does not refer to
Clément Marot as Margaret's protégé.

58 For the Butler marriage and the argument of Ives, *Anne*, 43–4, that her
father was not pressing for this match, see Chapter 2; a later tradition,
History of the Life of Henry VIII (London, 1632), 72, has her returning
from France with Sir Thomas; *LP*, III, 1994 for Francis, 1004, 1011,
1762 (*StPap*, I, p. 91, II, pp. 50–7) for Ormond's heir and Anne, 1705,
1778 for Boleyn at the Imperial court; whatever Boleyn's goals had been
for the future of Anne when she went abroad, Suffolk indicated that he
had originally planned for his daughter to remain at Malines. See BL
Add MS, 14,840, 30 May 1515 (*LP*, II, 529).

59 For an excellent discussion of her portraits, see Ives, *Anne*, 52–8 and
between 206–7; D. Starkey, *The Reign of Henry VIII*, 90, claimed one
Holbein portrait was of the queen, although the model had a thick neck,
and although, just before her execution, Anne described her neck as
little (see Chapter 8 and Appendix A).

2 FAMILY ALLIANCES

1 C. Rawcliffe, *The Staffords, Earls of Stafford and Dukes of Buckingham,
1394–1521* (Cambridge, 1978), 43; B. J. Harris, *Edward Stafford, Third
Duke of Buckingham, 1478–1521* (Stanford, Ca., 1986); H. Miller, *Henry
VIII and the English Nobility* (Oxford, 1986), 47.

2 H. Miller, *Henry VIII*, 47–8; *Statutes of the Realm*, ed. A. Luders, *et al.* (9 in
10 vols., London, 1810–28), III, 249–57; *LP*, III, 1284.

3 *Peerage*, IX, 219–22, XII, 738; F. Blomefield, *An Essay*, II, 441.

4 Lambeth MS (Lambeth Palace) 602, fos. 71–8 for Henry's letter,
printed in *StPap*, II, 51–7 (*LP*, III, 1004); for Surrey's letter, *StPap*, II,
pp. 50–1 (*LP*, III, 1011); for his arrival in Ireland, *LP*, III, 669–70;
Cal.SP Ireland, I, 19; S. G. Ellis, *Tudor Ireland: Crown, Community and the
Conflict of Cultures, 1470–1603* (New York, 1985), 116–18.

5 D. Head, "Norfolk," 88–95.

6 S. G. Ellis, *Tudor Ireland*, 12–115, and for the quotation, 108; S. G. Ellis,
"Parliament and Community in Yorkist and Tudor Ireland," in
Parliament and Community, ed. A. Cosgrove and J. McGuire (Belfast,
1983), 55.

7 *LP*, III, 972, 1004, 1011; his complaints must have been exaggerated for
Henry did write him a letter in July. See *StPap*, II, pp. 31–5.

8 Lambeth MS 602, fos. 71–8 (*LP*, III, 1004), in which Henry referred to
dispatches of Surrey he had received in late September; T. Carte, *Duke
of Ormond*, I, lxxxiv–lxxxv; *Cal.SP Ireland*, I, 7–8.

9 See Chapter 6 for Boleyn's loss of the earldom; *StPap*, II, p. 50; Ives,

Anne, 44–6, indicates that Boleyn took no initiative in the negotiations for the marriage and hinted that he might not have been eager for it. In fact, in late 1521 her father made arrangements for Anne to return home with that marriage in mind. Surrey was not insulting Sir Thomas by assisting Anne to become a countess.

10 *StPap*, I, pp. 91–2 (*LP*, III, 1762); Ives, *Anne*, 45 n. 73, says that Piers pressed for the marriage but there is no mention of the match in the references cited.

11 *LP*, III, 1762, 1778, 1817; Ives, *Anne*, 45–6.

12 *LP*, III, p. 1539; *StPap*, II, p. 50; for Suffolk's letter, BL Add.MS 14,840, 15 May 1515 (*LP*, II, 529).

13 H. Clifford, *The Life of Jane Dormer, Duchess of Feria*, tr. E. Estcourt, ed. J. Stevenson (London, 1887), 81, said that Anne was not quite twenty-nine on 19 May 1536. Allowing an eleven-month period between the births of the two, Mary could not have been born before 20 April. See also R. M. Warnicke, "Childhood," 939–52. In 1523, Lady Parr was planning the marriage of her daughter before she was twelve years old. See *LP*, III, 3178, and for the Carey marriage, III, p. 1539; Mary's daughter Catherine was surely born before 1526 the year of her son Henry's birth. The *DNB* says that in January 1569, when she died, Catherine was thirty-nine, an age that would have required a posthumous birth as her father died in March 1528. Other evidence suggests that she married in 1540 and had her first child by 1541. It was not likely that in 1528 or 1529 a godparent would name her Catherine. See also *Pedigree of the Family of Knollys and Title to the Manor of Rotherfield Greys* ... (London, 1809).

14 J. Fletcher, "A Portrait of William Carey and Lord Hunsdon's Long Gallery," *Burlington Magazine*, 123 (1981), 304–5; for the purge see Elton, *Reform*, 78–9, D. Starkey, "The King's Privy Chamber, 1485–1547," Ph.D. dissertation, University of Cambridge, 1973, and "Representation through Intimacy," in *Symbols and Sentiments*, ed. I. Lewis (London, 1977), 201–92; *LP*, IV, 1939(4); for the Field of Cloth of Gold, see Chapter 1, n. 51.

15 E. Reilly, *Historical*, 11–12; J. G. Nichols, "Cary Family: Arms in East Croker Church," in *Herald and Genealogist* (8 vols., London, 1865), II; T. Percy, *The Regulations and Establishment of the Household of Henry Algernon Percy, the Fifth Earl of Northumberland, at His Castles of Wressle and Leckonfield in Yorkshire, Begun Anno Domini MDXII* (London, 1770), intro.

16 *LP*, III, 317, 664, 2074 (5), 2297 (12), 2993, 2994 (26), p. 1539, IV, 464 (15, 18), 1264, 2002 (20), 2218 (12), 3087 (und.)

17 Ibid., II, 1573, 3489, III, 447, 2481; Lambeth MS 602, fos. 71–8 (*StPap*, II, p. 57) is a rough draft of a letter in which Boleyn was called

comptroller. Both H. Miller, *Henry VIII*, 174, and Ives, *Anne*, 17, thought he held this post.

18 *LP*, III, 306, 2567. See also *DNB; Cal.Sp Span.*, III-i, 315.

19 *LP*, III, 1778, 1994, 1705, and 1778; *Life of Henry VIII*, 72; Hall, I, 239–41; Ives, *Anne*, 47.

20 Cavendish, "Wolsey," 31–6; for Percy's betrothal, see *LP*, III, 3322; Cavendish, "Wolsey," 95, also thought Queen Catherine had been rusticated earlier than 1531. Even so the story about Percy and Anne was basically true for it has corroboration. The Imperial envoy, *Cal.SP Span.*, V-i, 10 (p. 33), V-ii, 48, referred to the "credit" Northumberland enjoyed with Anne and to their betrothal, and Forrest, 58, mentioned her and a "certain young lord"; Ives, *Anne*, 43–5.

21 *LP*, II, 3489, III, 491, p. 1559; Richardson, 204, 240; Anne's letter to Lady Wingfield, now BL Cotton MS Vesp. F XIII, fo. 109, in *LP*, V, 12; the Boleyns also had diplomatic connections with Richard, who died at Toledo on 22 July 1525. He had served in Flanders and in France when Anne was there and had been with her father in Spain in 1521. See *LP*, III, 1768; for the Wingfields and Suffolk, see HPT, III, 640; for Richard, see also Ellis, 3rd series, II, 134; M. C. Brown, *Mary Tudor, Queen of France* (London, 1911), 244.

22 Cavendish, "Wolsey," 31–6; in 1536 the Imperial envoy referred to the liaison of Anne and Percy that had occurred more than nine years previously, but he probably meant prior to the marriage of Henry and Anne since Percy was Mary Talbot's husband by 1524 (*Cal.SP Span.*, V-ii, 48).

23 Scarisbrick, 125; Elton, *Reform*, 85–6.

24 S. J. Gunn, "The Duke of Suffolk's March on Paris in 1523," *English Historical Review*, 101 (1986), 596–634; G. W. Bernard, *War Taxation and Rebellion in Early Tudor England* (New York, 1986), 11–13.

25 *LP*, III, 3153; Elton, *Reform*, 89–91.

26 Cavendish, "Wolsey," 31–6; W. Peeris, *The Chronicle of the Family of Percy* (Newcastle, 1845); R. A. Houlbrooke, *The English Family*, 39, 86.

27 Cavendish, "Wolsey," 31–6.

28 C. Richmond, "The Pastons Revisited: Marriage and the Family in Fifteenth-Century England," *BIHR*, 58 (1985), 25–36; G. W. Bernard, *The Power of the Early Tudor Nobility: A Study of the Fourth and Fifth Earls of Shrewsbury* (Totowa, N.Y., 1985), 11–16; E. B. De Fonblanque, *Annals of the House of Percy* (2 vols., London, 1887), I, 345–7.

29 Cavendish, "Wolsey," 31–6; M. E. James, *English Politics and the Concept of Honour, 1485–1642*, Past and Present Society, Supplement 3 (Oxford, 1978), 28.

30 E. B. De Fonblanque, *Annals*, I, 354.

31 Ibid., I, 374, and *LP*, III, 3322; Cavendish, "Wolsey," 31–6; G. W. Bernard, *Power of the Early Tudor Nobility*, 11–16.

32 T. Percy, *Regulations*, intro.; E. B. De Fonblanque, *Annals*, I, 377–85; J. M. W. Bean, *The Estates of the Percy Family, 1416–1537* (Oxford, 1958), 157.

33 Cavendish, "Wolsey," 31–6; *LP*, III, 3006, 3008, 3322; D. Head, "Norfolk," 145.

34 Richardson, 204; *LP*, II, 3018.

35 C. Richmond, "The Pastons," 25–36; G. W. Bernard, *Power of the Early Tudor Nobility*, 11–16; *LP*, III, 3322.

36 D. Head, "Norfolk," 167.

37 Scarisbrick, 125–9.

38 E. Armstrong, *The Emperor Charles V* (2 vols., London, 1910), I, 14; J. R. Hale, *War and Society in Renaissance Europe, 1450–1620* (Leicester, 1985), 22, for the quotation.

39 *LP*, IV, 1431, 1500, 1510; R. Wernham, *Before the Armada: The Growth of English Foreign Policy, 1485–1558* (New York, 1966), 111; W. Childe-Pemberton, *Elizabeth Blount and Henry the Eighth* (London, 1913), 24–5; *LP*, III, 2982, indicated that Boleyn was to be called as baron to parliament in 1523 but he was in Spain and was not elevated to the peerage. In 1525 he was first to be made Lord Bollayne but it was decided to give him a viscountcy instead (*LP*, Add. I, 458); the title of Nottingham was held by Richard, the younger son of Edward IV, but only because he had married the Mowbray heiress. See J. G. Nichols, ed., *Inventories of the Wardrobes, Plate, Chapel Stuff, etc., of Henry Fitzroy, Duke of Richmond and of the Wardrobe Stuff at Baynard's Castle of Katharine, Princess Dowager*, Camden Society, vol. LXI (London, 1855), xv; M. J. Lechnar, "Henry VIII's Bastard: Henry Fitzroy, Duke of Richmond," Ph.D. dissertation, West Virginia University, 1977.

40 *Cal. SP Span.*, III-ii, 37 (p. 110), 39 (p. 123); for Mary's title, see R. M. Warnicke, *Women of the English Renaissance and Reformation* (Westport, Ct., 1983), 49–50; J. M. Stone, *The History of Mary I, Queen of England* (London, 1901), 23, quoted Henry from BL Harl. MS 6807, fo. 3, as follows: "dearest, best beloved, and only daughter, the Princess . . . to reside and remain in the Marche of Wales."

41 Elton, *Studies*, III, 48; *LP*, X, 450; Scarisbrick, 160–2.

42 Ives, *Anne*, 20, thought the liaison had occurred by 1523 because of the name given to the king's ship, *Mary Boleyn*. Surely Henry would not have announced his affairs in such a manner. *LP*, IV, 2751 also refers to a ship, *Anne Boleyn*. Since the king's treasurer paid Rochford money for it, it may have been either the viscount's ship that was damaged or one that he sold to the crown, as privately owned vessels were employed on

royal business. See N. H. Nicolas, *The Privy Purse Expenses of King Henry the Eighth, November 1529–December, 1532* (London, 1827), 351, and D. Head, "Norfolk," 206. It is likely that the *Mary Boleyn* had once also belonged to Sir Thomas. For an allegation that Carey resembled the king, see J. Fletcher, "A Portrait," 304 n. 5; *LP*, VIII, 567 for the vicar, IV, 464 (18); 2002 (20) for Carey's manors; *Peerage*, VI, 627.

43 *LP*, II, p. 1501, refers to a Mr. Boleyn, possibly one of the brothers of Thomas; *LP*, III, 2214 (29), IV, 546 (2) for the grants. For his age, see also Chapter 1, n. 9; C. Rawcliffe, *The Staffords*, 182, for his share of Buckingham's possessions; F. Blomefield, *An Essay*, II, 441–2, V, 267 for the Parkers and the Sheltons; *Peerage*, IX, 219–22.

3 HENRY'S CHALLENGE

1 One of the sons lived for a few hours. G. Mattingly, *Catherine of Aragon* (Boston, 1941), 169; S. Giustinian, *Four Years at the Court of Henry VIII*, tr. R. Brown (2 vols., London, 1854), I, 181–2.

2 S. Giustinian, *Four Years*, I, 237, 240; *StPap*, I, p. 1.

3 For childbirth, witchcraft, and monsters see Chapter 8; see also R. M. Warnicke, "The Physical Deformities of Anne Boleyn and Richard III; Myth and Reality," *Parergon: Bulletin of the Australian and New Zealand Association for Medieval and Renaissance Studies*, N.S. 4 (1986), 135–53, and "Sexual Heresy at the Court of Henry VIII," *Historical Journal*, 30–2 (1987), 247–68; for witchcraft, see, for example, K. Thomas, *Religion and the Decline of Magic: Studies in Popular Belief in Sixteenth and Seventeenth Century England* (London, 1971).

4 S. Giustinian, *Four Years*, I, 312.

5 Scarisbrick, 105–6. Much of the discussion about the king's religion comes from Scarisbrick, although the view that his theology and scholarship were related to the succession crisis is my own; for the anecdote, see P. S. Crowson, *Tudor Foreign Policy* (New York, 1973), 83.

6 Scarisbrick, 248–9.

7 P. Gwyn, "Wolsey's Foreign Policy: The Conferences at Calais and Bruges Reconsidered," *Historical Journal*, 23 (1980), 755–72, has pointed out that Wolsey's aims in 1521–3 were somewhat different from those of Henry, who was more interested in the dynastic issue and who warned that if Mary were to wed the dauphin, the Channel might be shut to the emperor. It is also interesting that in 1532 Clement, upon learning that Francis was encouraging Henry to marry Anne in the hope that the English king would thereafter be subservient to him, could only scoff that as soon as the wedding was over Henry would immediately negotiate an Imperial alliance (see *LP*, V, 746).

8 *Cal.SP Ven.*, III, 167.

9 Scarisbrick, 110–13.

10 Ibid., 110–15.

11 Ibid., 111–17.

12 For the archduchess, see Chapter 1; P. S. Crowson, *Tudor Foreign Policy*, 84.

13 Scarisbrick, 99–105; *Cal.SP Span.*, IV-ii-i, 590 (p. 13); Catherine had served as Henry's regent, an office that was less powerful than the one in the Netherlands; in *A glasse of truthe* was discussed the problem of finding a proper husband for Mary. See N. Pocock, ed., *Records of the Reformation* (2 vols., Oxford, 1870), II, 386–415. See also G. R. Elton, *Policy and Police: The Enforcement of the Reformation in the Age of Thomas Cromwell* (Cambridge, 1972), 176–80.

14 Scarisbrick, 79, for the quotation; P. S. Crowson, *Tudor Foreign Policy*, 89.

15 Scarisbrick, 138–40; G. W. Bernard, *War, Taxation and Rebellion*, 43–5.

16 Scarisbrick, 139–42; P. S. Crowson, *Tudor Foreign Policy*, 84.

17 *LP*, IV, 1785, 2407, 2420, 2452, 2475; *Cal.SP Ven.*, IV, 105.

18 *LP*, V, 1114; Scarisbrick, 150-2.

19 *LP*, IV, 2712; Scarisbrick, 163–97.

20 Cavendish, "Wolsey," 77; Scarisbrick, 163–97; see also H. A. Kelly, *The Matrimonial Trials of Henry VIII* (Stanford, Ca., 1976); F. V. Cespedes, "The Final Book of Polydore Vergil's 'Anglica Historia:' Persecution and the Art of Writing," *Viator*, 10 (1979), 391, points out that because Vergil wished to leave Mary's parents "spotless" about the divorce, he chose to blame Wolsey.

21 Foxe, V, 229–34; Scarisbrick, 384–423.

22 *LP*, IV, 2742 for the announcement, 3105 for the envoys, and 2968 in Ellis, 3rd series, II, 167, for the duke; see also *LP*, IV, 1868.

23 Ibid., IV, 2791–2, 2974, 3080, 3105; in 1530 Chapuys thought the French envoys had questioned the validity of the marriage (*Cal.Sp Span.*, IV-i, 373 [p. 630]) but their MS journals indicate that no such question was raised. See H. Herbert, *Memoirs of Henry the Eighth of England* (New York, 1860), 148, and J. Gairdner, "New Lights on the Divorce of Henry VIII," *English Historical Review*, 11 (1896), 675; see Chapter 7 for another attempt of Henry to blame a change in policy on someone else; Ives, *Anne*, 101 n. 56, suggests that the French first raised doubts about her legitimacy.

24 *LP*, IV, App. 99 (1–3) for Rochford's expenditure on her in December, 1939 for her relatives, 3105 for Rochford in May 1527; for the ship, *Anne Boleyne*, see Chapter 2, n. 42; a letter from Anne to Henry discussing her appointment as maid of honor is surely fictitious. See Wood, II, 7; that

she did not become a maid of honor until 1527 is also a clue to her age, as she would have been too old, if born in 1501, for an initial appointment to this position.

25 Journal, 5 de May, MS de Brienne, quoted by J. Lingard, *The History of England* (6 vols., Dublin, 1878), IV, 237.

26 Forrest, 52–3; in his different, more hostile, version of her arrival at court, Ives, *Anne*, 101–10, failed to cite the evidence of Forrest, a chaplain of Catherine, who had no reason to give a false version of these events.

27 *LP*, XV, 179, for his delight in French styles.

28 Foxe, V, 52–3, 60; for the Catholics, see nn. 29 and 31; for this attitude, see S. Turner, *The History of the Reign of Henry the Eighth* (2 vols., London, 1826), I, 436–7; Ives, *Anne*, 105, said she refused to become his mistress and encouraged him to get a divorce. Ives did not speculate about what she might otherwise have done.

29 *Cal.SP Ven.*, IV, 824; for the portraits of her, see Chapter 1, n. 59; it was the fashion to flatten the bosom. See A. Hollander, *Seeing Through Clothes* (New York, 1978), 99.

30 Sander, 24; N. Rhodes, *The Elizabethan Grotesque* (London, 1980), 118 for the quotation, and I. Maclean, *The Renaissance Notion of Women* (Cambridge, 1980), 24, for Neo-Platonism.

31 Sander, 24, and Appendix A.

32 *Cal.Sp Ven.*, IV, 236; for Barlow, see BL Add.MS 28,585, fo. 45, which was translated by Ives, *Anne*, 51, correcting *LP*, V, 1114; see also L. de Carles, *Epistre*, lines 37–68; verses she was reputed to have written are in H. Walpole, *A Catalogue of the Royal and Noble Authors of England, Scotland and Ireland*, ed. T. Park (5 vols., London, 1806), I, 42–4, and A. Strickland, *Lives*, IV, 281–2.

33 *Cal.SP Ven.*, IV, 386; S. Giustinian, *Four Years*, I, 312.

34 *Cal.Sp Ven.*, IV, 105, for the slipper; *LP*, IV, 3098, 3105; S. Anglo, "La Salle de Banquet et le Théâtre," *Le Lieu Théâtral à la Renaissance*, ed. J. Jacquot (Paris, 1964), 273–88.

35 *LP*, IV, 3140; Scarisbrick, 155–6 for the cardinals.

36 G. Mattingly, *Catherine*, 241, 250; *LP*, IV, 3174 for the king at Windsor, 3148 for Fisher; Scarisbrick, 194–5.

37 *LP*, IV, 3302, printed in N. Pocock, *Records*, I, 11.

38 Henry had found a husband for the mother of his illegitimate son, Henry Fitzroy; Knecht, 192–3.

39 *StPap*, I, p. 203; Vergil and Hall mentioned only Francis' sister as a bride but as she was almost as old as Henry, he surely would not have considered her as a bride, given that he wished most of all to have a male child. She had also married the king of Navarre early in 1527. It

can be speculated that because of her handicap he did not wish it known that he had considered marrying Renée. Denys Hay, ed., *The Anglica Historia of Polydore Vergil, 1485–1537*, Camden Society, vol. LXXIV (London, 1950), 327; Hall, II, 96; in 1528 the French envoy (*LP*, IV, 4649) referred only to Renée as the bride.

40 *LP*, IV, 3246, 3265 for the envoy, 6307 for Richmond; *Cal.SP Ven.*, IV, 694; M. E. James, *English Politics*, 18, 63, 74; for Anne's ancestry, see Chapter 1.

41 *LP*, IV, 3124, 3318, 3354, 3360; for the return of the other envoys, see *Cal.SP Ven.*, IV, 212–13; *Cal.SP Span.*, III-ii, 152 (p. 327); N. H. Nicolas, *Privy Purse*, 300; for the ring, Ives, *Anne*, 109.

42 R. M. Warnicke, "The Eternal Triangle and Court Politics: Henry VIII, Anne Boleyn, and Thomas Wyatt," *Albion*, 18/4 (1986), 565–79. See also Appendix C; H. Richmond, *Puritans and Libertines: Anglo-French Literary Relations in the Reformation* (Berkeley, Ca., 1981), 9–10, doubted that Anne had an affair with Wyatt because he viewed her as an "autonomous" woman, an anachronistic concept; Ives, *Anne*, 178, similarly called her a "self-made woman," an inexplicable comment since her parents had provided her with a noble lineage and a superb education. Ives (107–10) also believed that Wyatt courted her in December 1526 before he left for Italy, but George Wyatt, 426–7, described a courtship (the king's playing of bowls) that took place out of doors and was not likely to have occurred in December. Ives also believed that the extant love letters were penned in 1527, but they were almost certainly all composed in 1528. See Chapter 4 for them.

43 For Sander, see Appendix A; Forrest, 58, who was a chaplain to Catherine, discussed the Percy episode, as did Cavendish, "Wolsey," 31–7, but neither mentioned Wyatt; Sergio Baldi, *Sir Thomas Wyatt*, tr. T. Prince (London, 1961), 12, believed Wyatt would have been executed had he confessed to such an affair. The king certainly had the man reputed to be Katherine Howard's first husband executed; see also W. H. Dixon, "Anne Boleyn," *Gentleman's Magazine*, N.S. 16 (1876), 291–2.

44 H. Richmond, *Puritans*, 156; C. Erickson, *Anne*, 55–7, said that "more likely than not" they had an affair; Ives, *Anne*, 93 and 97, thought Wyatt was one of "Anne's acknowledged suitors"; *Cal.SP Span.*, IV-i, 302 (p. 535); R. M. Warnicke, "The Eternal Triangle," 565–79; Appendix C.

45 For death rumors, *Cal.Sp Span.*, III-i, 571, 575; *LP*, IV, 6016 for Henry's remark, 5255 for more death rumors, 6452 for Surrey.

46 M. Levine, *Tudor Dynastic Problems, 1460–1571* (New York, 1973), 55–66, for example.

47 J. Stevens, *Music and Poetry in the Early Tudor Court* (London, 1961), 151;

Appendix C; E. Bapst, *Deux gentilshommes-poètes de la cour de Henry VIII* (Paris, 1891); Ives, *Anne*, 83–99; for a discussion of social relationships at court and how kings manipulated the competition for office and prestige, see N. Elias, *The Court Society*, tr. E. Jephcott (London, 1983), especially 88–99.

48 K. Muir and P. Thomson, eds., *Collected Poems of Sir Thomas Wyatt* (Liverpool, 1969), 5; R. Harrier, *The Canon of Sir Thomas Wyatt's Poetry* (Cambridge, Ma., 1975), 104, 151, 204; see also Appendix C; R. A. Rebholz, *Sir Thomas Wyatt: The Complete Poems* (New Haven, 1981), presents the poems in modern English.

49 *LP*, IV, 3420, 3422 (*StPap*, VII, p. 3) for Knight, 3354 for the king's whereabouts; Scarisbrick 158–62; see also J. Gairdner, "New Lights on the Divorce," 685–6, for Henry's letter to Knight.

50 *LP*, IV, 3686, 3749, 3756, 6626, 6627; for the quotation, see Scarisbrick, 158–62, 203–4; E. G. Rupp, *Studies in the Making of the English Protestant Tradition* (Cambridge, 1966), 70–1 n. 1, believes that this Barlow was William, not John, as he has usually been identified; N. Pocock, *Records*, I, 428.

51 *Cal.SP Span.*, III-ii, 224 (p. 432); Freidmann, I, 58, accepted the ambassador's version; for etiquette, see N. Elias, *Court*, 8, 89.

52 *LP*, IV, 3217; Cavendish, "Wolsey," 183.

53 *Cal.SP Span.*, III-ii, 224 (p. 432).

54 *LP*, IV, 4251 for Fox, 5393, 5519 for the letters to her from Bryan and Gardiner.

55 *LP*, IV, 3548 for Renée, 3564 for the revels; *Cal.SP Ven.*, IV, 201, 208 for the treaty and orders; Hall, II, 107–10.

56 *LP*, IV, 3748, 3757, 3765.

4 PAPAL RESPONSE

1 A. F. Pollard, *Wolsey*, illus. edition (London, 1953), 165–85; Elton, *Reform*, 47–9; Cavendish, "Wolsey," 119; *Cal.SP Ven.*, III, 210.

2 Elton, *Reform*, 47–9.

3 Scarisbrick, 205–10; *LP*, IV, 4251.

4 Scarisbrick, 205–14.

5 Ellis, 3rd series, II, 166 (*LP*, IV, 4005).

6 *LP*, IV, 4081; see n. 53.

7 Ibid., IV, 4335; for Anne's letter, BL Cotton MS Vitell. B XII, fo. 4, which is mutilated; see also *Harleian Miscellany*, ed. W. Oldys and T. Park (reprint, 7 vols., New York, 1965), III, 60; Burnet, I-i, 99–100; *LP*, IV, 4360.

8 *Cal.SP Ven.*, IV, 569; *StPap*, I, pp. 312–13; *LP*, IV, 4440, 4486, 4542.

9 *LP*, IV, 4356 for Waltham, 4391 for Anne's lady. This was translated inaccurately in *LP*. It was not Anne but her lady who became ill. See Friedmann, I, 72; G. A. Crapelet, *Lettres*, 160.

10 For the letters, I shall give my number, then the *LP* and *Harleian* numbers. All quotations are from *Harleian*, III; see H. Savage, ed., *The Love Letters of Henry VIII*, 3rd edition (London, 1945); V. Trovillion and H. Trovillion, eds., *Love Letters of Henry VIII* (Herrin, Ill., 1945); G. A. Crapelet, *Lettres*, 101–43; *The Private Lives of the Tudor Monarchs*, ed. C. Falkus (London, 1974); J. Halliwell-Phillips, ed., *The Love Letters of Henry VIII to Anne Boleyn* (London, 1907); for Henry and writing, see *LP*, IV, 4538.

11 My 17, *LP*, IV, 4539, *Harleian*, XV; for the interception, *LP*, IV, 4649.

12 *LP*, IV, 3913, 4251.

13 *LP*, IV, 5154, 5255, 5283, 5425, 5470; Scarisbrick, 218–23.

14 The six are: my 1, *LP*, IV, 3326, *Harleian*, II; my 2, *LP*, IV, 3220, *Harleian*, X; my 3, *LP*, IV, 3218, *Harleian*, IV; my 4, *LP*, IV, 3219, *Harleian*, VIII; my 5, *LP*, IV, 3325, *Harleian*, V; my 6, *LP*, IV, 3221, *Harleian*, I.

15 *LP*, IV, 4404.

16 My 1, *LP*, IV, 3326, *Harleian*, II; my 2, *LP*, IV, 3220, *Harleian*, X; Ives, *Anne*, 104, actually thought Henry was offering her a *maitresse en titre* by mail.

17 My 3, *LP*, IV, 3218, *Harleian*, IV.

18 My 4, *LP*, IV, 3219, *Harleian*, VIII; my 5, *LP*, IV, 3325, *Harleian*, V; my 6, *LP*, IV, 3221, *Harleian*, I.

19 My 7, *LP*, IV, 4403, *Harleian*, III; my 8, *LP*, IV, 4383, *Harleian*, XII; my 9, *LP*, IV, 4477, *Harleian*, XIII; my 10, *LP*, IV, 4410, *Harleian*, IX; my 11, *LP*, IV, 4537, *Harleian*, XI.

20 My 8, *LP*, IV, 4383, *Harleian*, XII; see also *LP*, IV, 4408–9, 4277; *StPap*, I, pp. 296–301.

21 *LP*, IV, 4710, in Wood, II, 13.

22 BL Cotton MS Otho C X, fo. 218 in *LP*, IV, 4480; Burnet, I-i, 100–1; R. Fiddes, *The Life of Cardinal Wolsey*, 2nd edition (London, 1726), App. 204; *Harleian*, 61; Ellis, 1st series, I, 100.

23 BL Cotton MS Vesp. F XIII, fo. 141, in R. Fiddes, *Wolsey*, App. 205; Wood, II, 17–18; H. Walpole, *Catalogue*, I, 42.

24 *LP*, IV, 4197, 4408; D. Knowles, "'The Matter of Wilton' in 1528," *BIHR*, 31 (1958), 92–6.

25 *StPap*, I, pp. 314–15; my 9, *LP*, IV, 4477, *Harleian*, XIII.

26 *LP*, IV, 4488, 4507.

27 For the wardship, *LP*, V, 11, the annuity, p. 306; my 10, LP, IV, 4410, *Harleian*, IX.

28 My 11, *LP*, IV, 4537, *Harleian*, XI; *LP*, IV, 4538, 4542 for her return to court, 4647 for her father's request; for Anne's letter, BL Cotton MS Vesp. F III, fo. 34, in R. Fiddes, *Wolsey*, App. 204, *LP*, IV, App. 197; for Barlow, see E. G. Rupp, *Studies*, 70–1. See Chapters 5 and 6 for Anne's religious beliefs.

29 *Cal.SP Span.*, III-ii, 541, 550 (p. 789).

30 *LP*, IV, 4857; *Cal.SP Span.*, III-ii, 586 (pp. 840–3); Scarisbrick, 212–14.

31 *LP*, IV, 5681; F. Powicke and R. Cheney, *Councils and Synods with Other Documents Relating to the English Church* (2 vols., Oxford, 1964), II-i, 198.

32 Despite the number of nobility who were divorced, only a small number of marriages was broken up. See R. A. Houlbrooke, *The English Family*, 115; N. Harpsfield, *A Treatise on the Pretended Divorce Between Henry VIII and Catherine of Aragon*, Camden Society, N.S., vol. XXI (reprint, New York, 1965), 177; see also A. Crawford, "The King's Burden? The Consequences of Royal Marriage in Fifteenth-Century England," in *Patronage, The Crown and the Provinces in Later Medieval England*, ed. R. A. Griffiths (Atlantic Highlands, N.J., 1981), 34; for the second quotation, Hall, II, 145; for the women, *LP*, IV, 5702.

33 The letters are: my 12, *LP*, IV, 4742, *Harleian*, VI; my 13, *LP*, IV, 4597, *Harleian*, XVI; my 14, *LP*, IV, 4894, *Harleian*, XVII; my 15, *LP*, IV, 4648, *Harleian*, VII; my 16, *LP*, IV, 3990, *Harleian*, XIV; my 17, *LP*, IV, 4539, *Harleian*, XV; see also *LP*, IV, 4766, App. 206.

34 My 15, *LP*, IV, 4648, *Harleian*, VII; for Durham House, see A. Strickland, *Lives*, IV, 220; N. H. Nicolas, *Privy Purse*, 217; *Cal.SP Span.*, III-ii, 586 (p. 846), 600 (p. 861); *LP*, IV, 5016, 5063, 5679; *Cal.SP Ven.*, IV, 385.

35 *LP*, IV, 5152, 5393, 5519, 5422; for Anne's letter, see also Burnet, II-ii, 406; *StPap*, VII, pp. 166–70.

36 Scarisbrick, 222–8; *LP*, IV, 5685; for a study of the treatises prepared to argue Henry's case for the divorce, see V. Murphy, "The Debate Over Henry VIII's First Divorce: An Analysis of the Contemporary Treatises," Ph.D. dissertation, University of Cambridge, 1984.

37 *LP*, IV, 3901, 5707, 5966.

38 *Cal.SP Span.*, IV-i, 83; *LP*, IV, 5885, 5983.

39 *LP*, IV, 6019, 6738; *Cal.SP Span.*, III-ii, 621 (p. 886) for factions, IV-i, 354 for the need to keep Anne from court, 302 (p. 535), 373 for the dukes in 1530, IV-ii-ii, 1061 (p. 643) for the first quotation; Cavendish, "Wolsey," 36–7; the French envoys were hostile because the king's love for Anne had deprived Renée of a husband and was making it difficult for Orléans to wed Mary. By late 1530, when Francis had decided to support the divorce, his envoys had become friendlier to Anne. See

Knecht, 225–7; for the second quotation, see Elton, *Studies*, III, 48–55; George Wyatt, 444; N. Elias, *Court*, 88–9.

40 For an annuity out of Wolsey's lands, see *LP*, IV, 6115; *Cal.SP Ven.*, IV, 632; a letter from Anne to Wolsey printed by Wood, II, 19, complaining about his betrayal is surely apocryphal.

41 *Cal.SP Span.*, III-ii, 550 (p. 790), IV-i, 249 (p. 416), 257 (p. 449), IV-ii-i, 993 (p. 509), for Cranmer, V-i, 207; for Norfolk's retirement before 1527, see D. Head, "Norfolk," 200; for the wardship see later in this chapter; S. J. Gunn, *Charles Brandon, Duke of Suffolk c. 1484–1545* (New York, 1988), 228, concluded that Suffolk "did not work consistently with others in a 'faction'."

42 Hall, I, 168, II, 153; Cavendish, "Wolsey," 117–20; S. Giustinian, *Four Years*, II, 225–6.

43 *Cal.SP Ven.*, IV, 761; R. Virgoe, "The Recovery of the Howards," 17–18; D. Head, "Norfolk," 263 4, also 231 2 for the claim that Norfolk blocked Suffolk's nomination as Lord Chancellor; S. J. Gunn, *Charles Brandon*, 228.

44 Cavendish, "Wolsey," 95–100.

45 *LP*, IV, 5936; *Cal.SP Span.*, IV-i, 160 (p. 222).

46 *Cal.SP Span.*, IV-i, 160 (p. 235); *LP*, IV, 5953 in Ellis, 1st series, I, 101, where Greenwich is mistaken for Grafton; Ives, *Anne*, 149.

47 Cavendish, "Wolsey," 95–100; W. W. Wooden, "The Art of Partisan Biography: George Cavendish's *Life of Wolsey*," *Renaissance and Reformation*, 12 (1977), 24–5; *Cal.SP Span.*, IV-i, 160 (p. 234); *LP*, IV, 6011; N. Elias, *Court*, 8, 84–9; Hall, II, 154–5.

48 Cavendish, "Wolsey," 101–36; *LP*, IV, 6026; *Cal.SP Ven.*, IV, 563–4, 652; Elton, *Reform*, 111–14.

49 Scarisbrick, 232; *LP*, IV, 5581.

50 *Cal.SP Span.*, IV-i, 257 (p. 450); Edward, Lord Herbert, *The Life and raigne*, 275, said Anne sent Wolsey a ruby with an image of the king on it.

51 *LP*, IV, 6067, 6076, 6114; for Winter, see VII, 964; *StPap*, I, p. 353, also in Ellis, 2nd series, II, 101, and R. Merriman, ed., *Life and Letters of Thomas Cromwell* (reprint, 2 vols., Oxford, 1968), I, 13; for the Germans, see *Cal.SP Span.*, IV-i, 255 (p. 444), 257 (p. 450).

52 *Peerage*, X, 132–6; T. Carte, *Duke of Ormond*, I, lxxxii; *LP*, IV, 3728, 3937, 3973 for Ormond, 5983, 5996 for Rochford to France, 6083, 6085, 6163 (1), 6355 for Wiltshire; S. G. Ellis, *Tudor Ireland*, 118; Ives, *Anne*, 279.

53 For her religion, see Chapters 5 and 6; for the wardship, D. Willen, *John Russell, First Earl of Bedford: One of the King's Men* (London, 1981), 16 n., and *LP*, IV, 4081, 4436, 4456, 4584, 4710, 5210, 6072 (21); for Barlow,

see E. G. Rupp, *Studies*, 70–1 n. 1; Lord William Howard married the daughter whose wardship was granted to his mother. For the kinship of Cheyney and the Boleyns, see HPT, I, 634–5; C. Franklyn, *Genealogy*, 7.

54 *LP*, IV, 5210, V, 283.

55 Ibid., 5965, 6149, Foxe, VIII, 6–9; Scarisbrick, 255–8; *Cal.SP Span.*, IV-i, 252 (p. 436), 429.

56 *Cal.SP Span.*, IV-i, 224 (p. 352) for Anne, 232 (p. 366) for the fete, 509 (p. 818) for another reference to the younger duchess of Norfolk, who became estranged from her husband in 1530 (see also D. Head, "Norfolk," 240–2), *Cal.SP Span.*, IV-ii-i, 814 (p. 272) for the seating at an informal fete in 1531; the only evidence of the former French queen's hostility is in diplomatic reports, although she apparently was unwilling to visit the court in April 1528 (*LP*, IV, 4183); Richardson, 245, 253; N. Elias, *Court*, 8, 62, 84–9; for the dowager duchess, see N. Pocock, *Records*, II, 473.

57 *Cal.SP Span.*, IV-i, 241 (p. 385), 249 (p. 417), 257, 270 (p. 476), 345 (p. 586) for the whereabouts of Anne and the queen, 252 (p. 436) for the French envoy; N. H. Nicolas, *Privy Purse*, 4, 10, 13; for the treatise, BL Royal MS 20 B XVII, fo. 51; there were many Flemish individuals in England. See *LP*, IV, 5018, *Cal.SP Span.*, IV-i, 302; for the ridiculous allegation of Chapuys that Anne, who had lived in Burgundy and France, did not recognize a Burgundian motto expressed in the French language, see IV-i, 547. For the motto, see Friedmann, I, 128, n. 3, and Ives, *Anne*, 175.

58 N. H. Nicolas, *Privy Purse*, 47, 50; *LP*, IV, App. 256; *Cal.SP Span.*, IV-i, 302 (pp. 535–6), V-i, 10 (p. 33).

59 *Cal.SP Span.*, IV-i, 354 (p. 600) for the shirt episode and for her dismissal of friends of Catherine from court, 152 for Catherine's contacts with Chapuys, 224 (p. 351) for a statement by Henry that Catherine was mistress of her household, 422 (p. 710) for spies in Catherine's household. See Scarisbrick, 151, for Wolsey placing spies there.

60 *Cal.SP Span.*, IV-l, 492 (p. 803).

61 Ibid., 152, 290 (p. 508) for Wolsey's and Catherine's contact with Chapuys; *LP*, V, 1187 for Du Bellay; *StPap*, VII, pp. 148–51, 234–8 for Bryan and Wiltshire; N. Elias, *Court*, 62, 104–15, 144.

62 *Cal.SP Span.*, IV-i, 555 for the ambassadors, IV-ii-i, 598 (p. 28), 646 (p. 78) for Anne and Henry; *LP*, V, 276; N. H. Nicolas, *Privy Purse*, 72, 74, 88, 97–8, 101; *Cal.SP Ven.*, IV, 642.

5 ANNE'S TURN

1 *Cal.SP Span.*, IV-ii-i, 590 (p. 12), 720 (p. 153), 753 (p. 198), 765 (p. 212), 775, 778, IV-ii-ii, 1061 (p. 643); *Cal.SP Ven.*, IV, 682; Ives,

Anne, 181, accepted the claim of John Stowe, *Survey of London*, ed. C. L. Kingsford (2 vols., Oxford, 1908), II, 36, that Catherine was at Ely House on 10 November 1531, but the antiquary must have mistaken the year. G. Mattingly, *Catherine*, 334–5, and Hall, II, 197, said Henry never saw her again after July. She was at the More on 6 November. See *LP*, V, 513, 531.

2 J. Guy, "Henry VIII and the *Praemunire* Manoeuvres of 1530–1531," *English Historical Review*, 384 (July 1982), 481–503; the king's unexpected decision to make this demand of the convocations may have been related to a message from Clement. See, for example, *LP*, V, 27.

3 Elton, *Reform*, 142–5.

4 For Warham's death, see later in this chapter; Forrest, 59, referred to Cromwell but not by name.

5 J. Guy, "Thomas Cromwell and the Intellectual Origins of the Henrician Revolution," in *Reassessing*, 157–61, utilizes the work of G. D. Nicholson, "The Nature and Function of Historical Argument in the Henrician Reformation," Ph.D. dissertation, University of Cambridge, 1977; Ives, *Anne*, 161, 165–8, argues that the radical ideas in *Collectanea* were fostered by Anne who was a close ally of Fox, identified by Ives as the leading compiler.

6 J. Guy, *The Public Career of Sir Thomas More* (New Haven, 1980), 131; J. Guy, "Manoeuvres," 487–9, 498; for the argument that the convocation was called for an attack on the pope, see G. W. Bernard, "The Pardon of the Clergy Reconsidered," *Journal of Ecclesiastical History*, 37–2 (April 1986), 258–82, which is followed by a comment of J. Guy and a response of G. W. Bernard; see also G. R. Elton, *Reform and Renewal, Thomas Cromwell and the Common Weal* (Cambridge, 1973), 129–34.

7 J. Guy, "Manoeuvres," 490, 503; *LP*, V, 225, 283; Elton, *Reform*, 142–8; Ives, *Anne*, 169, supports this view of Henry.

8 *LP*, 27, 30–1, 75, 216; *Cal.SP Span.*, IV-ii-i, 659, 664 (p. 96); J. Guy, "Manoeuvres," 500–1; for Cromwell in 1531, see G. R. Elton, *Reform and Renewal*, 92–3, and Elton, *Reform*, 133, 142 6; J. Guy, "Thomas More and Christopher St German: The Battle of the Books," in *Reassessing*, 100–4.

9 *Cal.SP Span.*, IV-ii-i, 635 (p. 63), 641 (p. 71).

10 Ives, *Anne*, 154, 175, 181, for the scolding.

11 Elton, *Studies*, I, 107; Elton, *Reform*, 151–5, 181–2; *LP*, V, 610, 691, 721, 750, 831, 852, 1016, 1018, 1023.

12 Friedmann, I, 135–6, was one of the first to insist on an alliance between Cromwell and Anne, but he offered no evidence to support his speculation; Ives, *Anne*, 186; for Anne and Wolsey, see Chapter 4.

13 *LP*, IV, 5366 for the credence, V, 367 for Wharton, V, 80 (29), VI, 245,

VII, 1671, for Appleyard (Cromwell later purchased the lands of Appleyard's); for Wolsey, see Chapter 4; the competition did not mean hostility between Cromwell and the Boleyns, for in 1527 he had written to Anne's father about a family matter. See R. Merriman, *Cromwell*, I, 5.

14 *LP*, V, 723, 1299.

15 Ibid., 1274, 1285 (ix), 1398, 1408, 1430, 1434, 1499 (23), 1548, VI, 299 (iii, iv).

16 Ibid., V, 1142, 1525, VI, 115, 116, 168, 334, 512, 1264, VII, 302; Ellis, 3rd series, II, 209 for Lyst's letter to Anne, p. 246 n. for Lyst; a recent statement of their cooperation, with Cromwell given a subordinate position is in M. Dowling, "Anne Boleyn and Reform," *Journal of Ecclesiastical History*, 35 (1984), 31; J. Venn and J. A. Venn, *Alumni Cantabrigienses* (5 vols., Cambridge, 1924), III.

17 *Cal.SP Span.*, IV-ii-i, 926 (p. 417).

18 Foxe, V, 53, 58, 135, 137.

19 *Cal.SP Span.*, IV-ii-i, 664 (p. 96); B. Hall, "The Early Rise and Gradual Decline of Lutheranism in England (1520–1600)," in *Reform and Reformation: England and the Continent, c. 1500–c. 1700*, ed. D. Baker (Oxford, 1979), 108–10; see also J. F. Davis, "The Trials of Thomas Bylney and the English Reformation," *Historical Journal*, 24 (1981), especially 777–8.

20 B. Hall, "The Early Rise," 108–10; *LP*, X, 797; for her imprisonment, see Chapter 8.

21 H. Bornkamm, "Faith and Reason in the Thought of Erasmus and Luther," in *Religion and Culture: Essays in Honor of Paul Tillich*, ed. W. Leibrecht (New York, 1959), 133–9; for the medieval version, D. Wallace, Jr., *Puritans and Predestination: Grace in English Protestant Theology, 1525–1695* (Chapel Hill, N.C., 1982), 14; *LP*, X, 797; for the epistles, see BL Harl. MS 6561; D. Carnicelli, *Lord Morley's "Tryumphes of Fraunces Petrarcke"* (Cambridge Ma., 1971), 15, does not believe that Morley translated Harley MS 6561 for Anne. See also R. M. Warnicke, "Lord Morley's Statements about Richard III," *Albion*, 15 (1983), 173–8.

22 *LP*, IV, 4409, 5422; Latimer, fo. 26; for the book of hours, BL Kings MS 9; for another book of hours, see Ives, *Anne*, 293.

23 D. Wallace, Jr., *Puritans*, 7–8; Scarisbrick, 243–4.

24 For her education, see Chapter 1; P. E. Hughes, *Lefèvre*, xiii, 35–40; for Loys de Brun, see BL MS Royal 20 B XVII; for manuscripts from abroad, see BL Add. MS 43,827, fo. 2, and M. Dowling and J. Shakespeare, "Religion and Politics in Mid-Tudor England through the Eyes of an English Protestant Woman: The Recollections of Rose Hickman," *BIHR*, 55 (1982), 95; Ives, *Anne*, 293.

25 See, for example, H. White, *Tudor Books of Private Devotion* (Madison, Wi., 1951).

26 For these incidents, see Chapter 1.

27 For Wyatt, see Chapter 3; for Hawkins, *LP*, V, 1564 (*StPap*, VII, pp. 386–91), 1660; Latimer, fos. 31–2.

28 *LP*, IV, 40, 4317, 6487.

29 Ibid., 6401 for Henry and heretical books, 3962–3 n., 4004, 4017, 4030, 4073, 4175, App. 197 (Anne's letter to Wolsey), V, 1432 n. for the death of Forman on 31 October 1528. The parson to whom Anne referred was almost certainly Forman and not Thomas Garrett, who became rector in 1537. In contemporary documents Forman was called the parson (IV, 3963, 4073, for example); Foxe, V, App. 802–9, 829–33; J. Strype, *Ecclesiastical Memorials* (Oxford, 1822), I-i, 124.

30 BL Sloane MS 1207; M. Dowling, "Anne Boleyn," 30–1; Foxe, V, 35; *LP*, IV, 5925, V, 982, VI, 299 (ix, G), 573, VII, 923 (ii, xii, xx, xxvi), VIII, 169, 1063; G. Mattingly, *Catherine*, 181.

31 N. H. Nicolas, *Privy Purse*, 112, 116, 137, 190; *LP*, IV, 6385, V, 248, 952; for Fish, see Foxe, IV, 657–8. Foxe also printed a different story about how Henry obtained a copy of Fish's book.

32 Foxe, V, 53, IV, 657–8; *LP*, IV, 2607 for prohibited books; Simon Fish, *A Supplication for the Beggars*, ed. E. Arber (London, 1880), 3–7; Scarisbrick, 247–9; Chapuys claimed she was more Lutheran than her father. See *Cal.SP Span.*, IV-ii-i, 972, V-i, 179.

33 Scarisbrick, 247–9; J. Strype, *Ecclesiastical*, I-i, 171–2; J. G. Nichols, *Narratives of the Days of the Reformation*, Camden Society, vol. LXXVII (London, 1859), 52–3.

34 J. Strype, *Ecclesiastical*, I-i, 171–2; J. G. Nichols, *Narratives*, 52–3; Sampson represented the king in Anne's divorce trial; in George Wyatt's account, 422, 429, 438–40, Anne marks passages in the book with her fingernail.

35 C. Cross, "Churchmen and the Royal Supremacy," in *Church and Society in England: Henry VIII to James I*, ed. F. Heal and R. O'Day (Hamden, Ct., 1977), 16; for the quotation, see Scarisbrick, 397; Ives, *Anne*, 161, 167–8, claimed a more radical stance for Tyndale than this; *Cal.SP Span.*, IV-i, 539.

36 M. Dowling, "Anne Boleyn," 31–2, 35–6, 44–6, has her using her religious posture for political reasons.

37 *Cal.SP Span.*, IV-ii-i, 646, 802; *LP*, V, 276, 364 (9, 28), 457 (6), 506 (16), pp. 305–6; N. H. Nicolas, *Privy Purse*, 113, 123, 128, 131, 133.

38 *Cal.SP Span.*, IV-ii-i, 584 (p. 3), 739 (p. 177), 853 (p. 323); *LP*, V, 61, 64, 686, 759, 1063–4, 1069, 1532; Friedmann, I, 145; Elton, *Reform*, 203, n. 7 for Griffith; for Daubeney, see Chapter 6, *LP*, V, 563, 724, IX, 577.

39 *LP*, V, 628, 907; Hall, II, 202, 209; *Cal.SP Span.*, IV-ii-i, 838, 880
 (p. 354).

40 *Cal.SP Span.*, IV-ii-i, 802 (p. 254), 814 (p. 272); *LP*, V, 1117, 1187.

41 P. Jourda, *Marguerite d'Angoulême*, No. 569; *LP*, V, 1187, VI, 692; *Cal.SP
 Span.*, IV-ii-i, 1044; S. Putnam, *Marguerite*, 268, says there is no record of
 her reaction to the marriage; for the picture, see N. H. Nicolas, *Privy
 Purse*, 221.

42 The king visited his sister in July 1532, and the Venetian envoy stated
 that she refused to go to Calais. She was not well and died less than
 a year later. This same foreign expert on the royal family speculated
 that in Calais the king would marry either Anne or a daughter of
 Francis (*Cal.SP Ven.*, IV, 792, 802). The Imperial envoy had heard
 the same rumors about the French queen. Richardson, 245, 253–5,
 cited only the evidence of Chapuys as proof that she refused to go to
 Calais (*Cal.SP Span.*, IV-ii-i, 739 [p. 177], 993). It was also rumored
 that Anne had been the cause of the duchess of Norfolk's dismissal
 but she had been estranged from the duke since 1530. See D. Head,
 "Norfolk," 242; *LP*, IV, 6738, V, 1247 n.; H. Miller, *Henry VIII*, 12, for
 the heralds.

43 *LP*, V, 1139 (32), 1274, 1285 (ix), 1370 (1–3), 1499 (23); T. Milles,
 Catalogue of Honor (London, 1610), 41–2. See also BL Harley MS 303;
 Cal.SP Ven., IV, 802; HMC, *Calendar of the Manuscripts of the Most Hon.
 the Marquess of Salisbury Preserved at Hatfield House, Hertfordshire* (24 vols.,
 London, 1883), I, 10; the first names of the countesses are as given by H.
 Miller, *Henry VIII*, 24; Ives, *Anne*, 208–9, noted that the word "legitimate" was left out of the Latin charter, but this was probably not
 significant as the rules of the common law would still determine how the
 title and lands would descend.

44 *Cal.SP Span.*, IV-ii-i, 1003 (p. 525); see 986 where Chapuys discusses a
 letter Anne sent to a friend about the trip. If she actually sent such a
 letter, it would have been helpful had he identified the recipient, for
 little is known about her friendships; see also 993 (p. 509) where he
 asserts that Suffolk was against the French trip. Obviously, the envoy
 did not know of the honor in store for the duke there; *Cal.SP Ven.*, IV,
 808, 824; *LP*, V, 1354, 1373–4, 1398, 1411, 1484–5, 1616; P. A. Hamy,
 Entrevue de François Premier avec Henry VIII à Boulogne sur Mer en 1532
 (Paris, 1898); Knecht, 226–8; *The Chronicle of Calais*, ed. J. G. Nichols,
 Camden Society, vol. XXXV (London, 1846), 116–18; *English Garner*,
 ed. E. Arber (8 vols., London, 1877), II, 35–40; for the quotation, see
 Hall, II, 220–1.

45 Ives, *Anne*, 201–2.

46 *LP*, V, 1268, 1273, 1315, 1326, 1352, 1380, 1545, 1564, 1620, Add. I,

799; *Cal.SP Span.*, IV-ii-i, 990–1, 993 (p. 507); J. Guy, "Thomas Cromwell and the Henrician Revolution," in *Reassessing*, 172–3.

47 *LP*, V, 1495, 1502, 1510, 1522, 1529, 1537, 1571, for Calais; 1231, 1377, 1429, 1484, 1548, 1579, 1598, for the journey and Dover; *Cal.SP Span.*, IV-ii-i, 1008.

48 N. H. Nicolas, *Privy Purse*, 216, 222–3, 272–6; *LP*, V, 1548, 1685; *Cal.SP Span.*, IV-ii-i, 995, 1033 (p. 566).

49 HPT, II, 310, III, 501; N. H. Nicolas, *Privy Purse*, 197; *Cal.SP Span.*, IV-i, 345 (p. 586); *LP*, IV, 6511, V, 686, 1711, pp. 599 n., 761; Anne's letter is in BL Cotton MS Vesp. F XIII, fo. 198, in *LP*, V, 12, Wood, II, 74; see also E. Hasted, *The History and Topographical Survey of the County of Kent* (reprint, 12 vols., Menston, Yorkshire, 1972), II, 393–6.

50 BL MS Cotton Vesp. F XIII, fo. 198; *LP*, VI, 32, VII, 1672; HPT, III, 501.

51 A. Strickland, *Lives*, IV, 230; Friedmann, I, 183, speculated that the archbishop of Dublin married them; whether Anne knew for certain from physical signs or merely just hoped that she was pregnant is open to question. Rachel Fuchs of the History Department at Arizona State University has studied statements made by nineteenth-century French lower-class women about when they first realized they were pregnant. She has pointed out that many did not know until about the fifth month when they felt their babies stir. Unlike Anne Boleyn, they would almost certainly have been suffering from malnutrition because of the scarcity of food. See Chapter 7.

52 *Cal.SP Span.*, IV-ii-i, 1047 (p. 600), 1048 (p. 602), 1055.

53 Ibid., IV-ii-i, 1056, IV-ii-ii, 1061 (p. 644); *Cal.SP Ven.*, IV, 867, 893.

54 Elton, *Reform*, 177–9; *Cal.SP Span.*, IV-ii-ii, 1061 (p. 643), 1062, 1077 (p. 699); *Cal.SP Ven.*, IV, 870, 873.

55 For pregnancy rumors, *LP*, IV, 5679, V, 594; *Cal.SP Span.*, IV-ii-i, 872, IV-ii-ii, 1077 (p. 699); *Cal.SP Ven.*, IV, 768; see Friedmann, I, 190, for the apple story, which he credited; A. R. Wright, *British Calendar Customs*, ed. T. E. Lones (reprint, 3 vols., Nendeln, Lichtenstein, 1968), II, 99; Chapuys may have found the rumor interesting because this fruit was used in divination. See K. M. Briggs, *The Fairies in English Tradition and Literature* (Chicago, 1967), 84–5.

56 *Cal.SP Span.*, IV-ii-ii, 1061 (p. 638).

57 N. Pocock, *Records*, II, 497–501, 677; *StPap*, I, pp. 408–9; *LP*, VI, 759, 760, 765, 807; Elton, *Reform*, 179. The announcement that the marriage was invalid was suspended until September.

58 The description is from Hall, II, 229–42. See also *LP*, VI, 396, 561–4, 583–5, 601–2, 395 for the summons to Lady Cobham in Ellis, 1st series, II, 113; for the Tower's repair, see *Cal.SP Span.*, IV-ii-i, 993 (p. 509),

1033 (p. 566); H. Colvin, *The History of the King's Works* (6 vols., London, 1975), III, 267; R. Withington, *English Pageantry*, 180–4; W. Jones, *Crowns and Coronations: A History of Regalia* (London, 1898), 149–55; *English Garner*, II, 43–60.

59 Hall, II, 231–2; *Cal.SP Ven.*, IV, 912; the crown monitored the preparations for her entry into London. See *LP*, VII, 923 (xxxviii), p. 353.

60 *Cal.SP Span.*, IV-ii-ii, 1073 (p. 678), 1077 (p. 693); *LP*, V, p. 306.

61 Hall, II, 232.

62 S. Anglo, *Spectacle*, 98; the order for the festivities went out during the second half of April. See *Cal.SP Ven.*, IV, 878.

63 Hall, II, 232–3; *Cal.SP Span.*, IV-ii-ii, 1077 (p. 700).

64 Hall, II, 233.

65 Ibid., 233–4.

66 Ibid., 234–5; for the Holbein sketch, R. Strong, *Splendor*, 17.

67 F. J. Furnivall, ed., *Ballads from Manuscripts: Ballads on the Condition of England in Henry VIII's and Edward VI's Reign* (2 vols., London, 1868–72), I, 374.

68 *Cal.SP Span.*, IV-ii-ii, 1100 (p. 740), 1107 (p. 755), 1117 (p. 776); R. Strong, *Splendor*, 17; for the ampulla, L. Tanner, *The History of the Coronation* (London, 1952), 89.

69 F. J. Furnivall, *Ballads*, I, 376.

70 Hall, II, 236–7.

71 See also V. Turner, ed., *Ceremonial Masks* (Washington, D.C., 1982), 21; Cromwell kept a record of the charges for the coronation (*LP*, VII, 923 [xix]).

72 Hall, II, 237–8.

73 Ibid., 238–9.

74 Ibid., 239–41.

75 Ibid., 241–2; *Cal.SP Ven.*, IV, 912; for the canopy, see L. Tanner, *Coronation*, 44.

76 BL Royal MS 16 E XIII; *LP*, VI, 661, in Ellis, 1st series, II, 114.

77 *Cal.SP Span.*, IV-ii-ii, 1077 (p. 699); as it was thought that a swelling of the neck was a sign of pregnancy, her condition may have given rise to reports about a wen on her neck. See *LP*, VI, 585; Appendix A.

6 QUEEN'S PATRONAGE

1 H. Colvin, *King's Works*, III, IV; N. Williams, *The Royal Residences of Great Britain* (London, 1960), 5, 19–20, 42.

2 H. Colvin, *King's Works*, III, 317, IV, 104–5; for her lying-in chambers, see Chapter 7.

3 H. Johnstone, "The Queen's Household," in *The English Government at Work, 1327–1336*, ed. J. Willard and W. Morris (3 vols., Cambridge, Ma., 1940), I, 251; *LP*, VI, 1188 for the farmers, VII, 1204 for the vellum, 1498 (1) for the manor, IX, 477 for her rents; B. P. Wolffe, *The Crown Lands, 1461–1536* (New York, 1970), 45–6; *Statutes of the Realm*, III, 479–81.

4 H. Johnstone, "The Queen's Household," 250–99; Latimer, fo. 24; *LP*, VI, 1176 for Uvedale, VII, 352, X, 252 for her lands, IX, 45 for Smith, Add., I, 991, X, 147 for her council; Coffin was not officially knighted until 1537. See HPT, I, 666.

5 *LP*, IV, 4449 for Compton, VI, 1189, VII, 352, IX, 179 (3, ix) for the receivers; H. Johnstone, "The Queen's Household," 252.

6 *LP*, VII, 419 (26) for felons, 1672 for silver; W. Prynne, *Aurum Reginae* (London, 1668), 4–7, 120–2; D. H. Jones, "A Household Account of Queen Elizabeth Woodville," M.A. thesis, Liverpool University, 1949, 12; A. R. Myers, "The Household of Queen Elizabeth Woodville, 1466–7," in *Crown, Household and Parliament in Fifteenth Century England*, ed. C. H. Clough (London, 1985), 251–318.

7 *LP*, VI, 6, 1364, 1382, 1591, VII, 137, VIII, 209 (ii), 937; for Holbein, Ives, *Anne*, 287.

8 *LP*, VII, 922 (9), 1352 (12), VIII, 149 (30), 1007, IX, 729 (2).

9 R. Strong and J. Oman, *Eliz R*, 1–6; A. Somerset, *Ladies in Waiting: From the Tudors to the Present Day* (London, 1984), 9–33; *LP*, VII, 9 for Marshall, 1529, App. 13, IX, 184, 218 for the Scots; D. H. Jones, "A Household Account," 33; F. Blomefield, *An Essay*, V, 266; see Chapter 8 for the countess.

10 *Lisle Letters*, I, pp. 518–19, *LP*, IV, App. 99 for Taylor, 2599 (12), 4476, 4488 for Baynton, 1939 (8) for Coffin, 3448, 6748 (8) for Smith, 2436, 5430, XI, 164 for Uvedale, IV, 4520, V, p. 755, IX, 729 (2) for Bartlett, V, pp. 747, 753, 757–8 for Scott.

11 *LP*, VI, 6, 1194, VIII, 358 for Cromwell, VII, 1352 (8) for King, VIII, 801 (p. 302) for Baynton; H. Johnstone, "The Queen's Household," 252; see also D. M. Loades, *The Tudor Court* (London, 1986).

12 *LP*, VII, 122, 923 (vi, xxxii) for Brabazon, V, 363, IX, 85, E. Reilly, *Historical*, 11–12, for Denny.

13 *Cal.SP Span.*, IV-ii-ii, 1165 (p. 902) for factions, V-i, 58 (p. 164), 170 for Cromwell; N. Elias, *Court*, 88–94; M. E. James, *English Politics*, 15; for Fisher and More see later in this chapter; for the act of succession, see Elton, *Reform*, 182–6; D. Cressy, "Kinship and Kin: Interaction in Early Modern England," *Past and Present*, 113 (1986), 38–69.

14 *LP*, VI, 559, in Ellis, 3rd series, II, 201; *LP*, VII, 1623, X, 914.

15 *LP*, VI, 222, 225–6, 456, 670 for Casale, V, 1453, VII, 112, 964 for

Winter, VIII, 1031 for Wiltshire, IX, 450 for Audley; BL Add. MS 19,398, fo. 49 for Anne in *LP*, VIII, 1057; for Mary see later in this chapter.

16 *LP*, VI, 1642; for Jane, see Friedmann, II, 200; for her kinship with Bryan, *LP*, V, 202; H. Clifford, *Jane Dormer*, 40–1, said he was her uncle. Early modern Europeans were sometimes vague about relationships. See D. Cressy, "Kinship," 38–69; Ives, *Anne*, 372 n. 43, denied that they were related; for more about Bryan, see Chapter 8.

17 M. L. Bush, "The Lisle-Seymour Land Disputes: A Study of Power and Influence in the 1530s," *Historical Journal*, 9 (1966), 255–74, details Cromwell's attempt to assist Lisle; *Lisle Letters*, I, pp. 27, 100, 333–4; for ease in finding these letters, the *LP* number will be given except when there is a quotation or a dispute about the information and then the Lisle reference will also be given. The peewit letter is dated earlier in the *Lisle Letters*, I, xxxii, than in *LP*, IX, 402.

18 *LP*, VII, 92, IX, 991 for Purkoy, whose death *Lisle Letters*, II, 299a dates one year earlier; *LP*, VII, 613, 654, 795, 824, VIII, 1084 (*Lisle Letters*, II, 421); for the greyhound, see N. H. Nicolas, *Privy Purse*, 74.

19 *LP*, VIII, 977, 1103; *Lisle Letters*, II, pp. 528–31.

20 *Lisle Letters*, III, p. 417; *LP*, VII, 386, 533, 1128, 1165, 1167, 1182, 1224, 1288, 1543, 1581, VIII, 45.

21 *LP*, VII, 734; *Lisle Letters*, II, p. 164.

22 *LP*, VII, 25, 349, 989, 1338, 1440, 1461, VIII, 939, 1028; for Wilkinson, see *Lisle Letters*, IV, 859; M. Dowling, "Anne Boleyn," 43.

23 *LP*, VII, 1581, VIII, 15, 123, 184, 232, 371, 378, 860, IX, 991; *Lisle Letters*, I, pp. 586, 687–8.

24 *LP*, VII, 415, 594, IX, 577.

25 Ibid., VII, 125; see also IX, 463 (2) which lists the queen's secretary along with Cromwell and the king as whom to petition for redress.

26 Ibid., IX, 850, 892; on different issues, a suitor might seek different patrons. Sir Richard Grenville, a nephew of Lord Lisle, seems to have been a client of Sir Francis Bryan in 1532 and a client of Cromwell in 1534. See *LP*, V, 1553, VII, 1475.

27 Ibid., VI, 1604.

28 N. Elias, *Court*, 90–1; in 1534 Chapuys had heard a rumor that the king was warning his "vassals of the crown" to be loyal. *Cal.SP Span.*, V-i, 4 (p. 13).

29 For factional politics see E. W. Ives, *Faction in Tudor England* (London, 1979), 178–86 and *Anne*, 335–82; M. Dowling, "Anne Boleyn," 30–46; Friedmann, I, 157–8; for whether an Aragonese faction effected her execution, see Chapter 8; it is interesting that in January 1536, one of this alleged group, John, Lord Hussey, wrote to Cromwell a

friendly letter (*LP*, X, 206) seeking a place in his household for a relative.

30 Ibid., VI, 1642; N. H. Nicolas, *Privy Purse*, 245; for the wardship controversy, see Chapter 4.

31 *DNB*; see n. 29 above for factions.

32 For Anne's lands, see *LP*, VII, 352; H. Miller, *Henry VIII*, 57 n. 84, reveals that because Chapuys called the marquess young, for a long time it was assumed he meant Dorset. That Chapuys was often confused is nowhere made clearer than in these references, for he seems not to have realized that there were two marquesses: Dorset was young but Exeter had been born in the 1490s. Chapuys also referred to the old marquess when he meant Dorset's paternal uncle (*LP*, IX, 429 [p. 168] corrects the document as printed in *Cal.SP Span.*, V-i, 142 [p. 432]); W. R. Harwood, "The Courtenay Family in the Politics of Region and Nation in the Later Fifteenth and Early Sixteenth Centuries," Ph.D. dissertation, University of Cambridge, 1978, 100, 118–19; the Pole statement quoted by Harwood (118) from *Cal.SP Ven., 1553–1554*, 423; H. Miller, *Henry VIII*, 65, claims the earliest evidence that Exeter was against the king dates from July 1536; in October 1534 Chapuys quoted Norfolk and him as saying that the king might return to the papacy, but there is no way of determining the source of these alleged remarks. *Cal.SP Span.*, V-i, 97.

33 W. R. Harwood, "Courtenay Family," 100–12, 124–9; *Cal.SP Span.*, IV-ii-i, 1024 (p. 550), IV-ii-ii, 1124, 1127 (p. 800), V-i, 105; *LP*, VI, 1464; Scarisbrick, 351–3, took seriously Chapuys' claims that the life of the princess was in danger.

34 *Cal.SP Span.*, IV-i, 182 (p. 279), 265 (p. 471), 290 (p. 514), 411 (p. 692), V-i, 118 (p. 344), 170; *LP*, VII, 1172 for Carew and Mary, VIII, 174 for the French envoy, 596 for the letter to Cromwell, 962 (1) for Neville; for the mistress, see Chapter 7.

35 *LP*, VII, 1040 for the king's suspicions, VIII, 573, 1074, 1084 for Lisle, 263 for Francis, 960 for Cromwell; *Cal.SP Span.*, V–i, 70.

36 *Cal.SP Span.*, V-i, 75; Elton, *Reform*, 98, 265–6; *Peerage*, IV, 21–2; H. Miller, *Henry VIII*, 51–7; *Lisle Letters*, II, pp. 205–6; Foxe, V, 60.

37 *Cal.SP Span.*, IV-ii-ii, 1077 (p. 699), V-i, 17 (p. 57), 111 (p. 329) for inconsistent remarks about who it was that favored Catherine and Mary. See also IV-ii-ii, 1058 (p. 631), 1127 (p. 794), 1164 (pp. 892–4); D. Head, "Norfolk," 276–94, doubted that the duke was involved in an Aragonese party; Friedmann, I, 157–8, believed Chapuys implicitly. In 1531 Augustine de Augustinis wrote to Norfolk from Ghent about rumors that Anne had forced the duke to be rusticated. Augustinis had denied them for he knew that Norfolk had been planning to go home to

attend to some personal matters. See *LP*, V, 283 for this letter, 6 (9) for Norfolk's testimony, VI, 1404 for his comment to the French envoy, VII, 1629, VIII, 342 for Fitzwilliam.

38 Norfolk may have deliberately misled Chapuys into believing that in reaction to Anne's fear his heir would marry the princess, the duke was forced to betroth him to an undesirable bride, thus creating a personal reason, believable to the envoy, to be angry with his niece. See *Cal.SP Span.*, IV-ii-i, 934 (p. 428); for rewards, see Chapter 5; see also *LP*, IX, 308.

39 *LP*, VI, 351, 1111, 1460, XII, 976 in Wood, II, 148; *Cal.SP Span.*, IV-i, 460 (p. 762) for his version of Anne's opinion about Norfolk's daughter and Richmond, 182, IV-ii-i, 934 (p. 428) for Chapuys' change of mind about whether Anne wanted Surrey to wed Mary Tudor; see also W. Childe-Pemberton, *Elizabeth Blount*, 212–13.

40 *LP*, VI, 1572 for Henry on Norfolk's status in 1533, IX, 398 for Norfolk's displeasure, Add. I, 746 for Anne's support in 1531 of a Howard; for the role of the nobility, see B. Coward, *The Stanleys, Lords Stanley and Earls of Derby, 1385–1672: The Origins, Wealth and Power of a Landowning Family* (Manchester, 1983), 149; B. Harris, "Marriage Sixteenth-Century Style: Elizabeth Stafford and the Third Duke of Norfolk," *Journal of Social History*, 15 (1982), 371–82; *Cal.SP Span.*, IV-ii-i, 619 (p. 44), 720, IV-ii-ii, 1130 (p. 814); D. Head, "Beyng Ledde and Seduced by the Devyll: The Attainder of Lord Thomas Howard and the Tudor Law of Treason," *Sixteenth Century Journal*, 13 (1982), 5, for the quotation.

41 *LP*, IV, 6437 for the Roman agent, IX, 358 for the Irish lands; *Cal.SP Span.*, IV-ii-ii, 1072 (p. 670), 1077 (p. 699); Elton, *Reform*, 250–72; *StPap*, II, pp. 434–7; E. Curtis, *Calendar of Ormond Deeds* (6 vols., Dublin, 1935), IV, 307.

42 *StPap*, I, pp. 439–48 for Wiltshire, II, p. 272 for Cromwell and Ossory; *LP*, VIII, 723, IX, 358, Add., I, 926, 982, 1016 for Wiltshire, IX, 700 for Anne and Grey; *DNB* for Grey and Skeffington; for Lady Skeffington's letter, *LP*, X, 185; Elton, *Reform*, 207–10; S. G. Ellis, *Tudor Ireland*, 119–27; see also S. G. Ellis, "Henry VIII, Rebellion and the Rule of Law," *Historical Journal*, 24 (1981), 513–32.

43 *LP*, VII, 922 (16), VIII, 632 (13), H. Miller, *Henry VIII*, 25 for Rochford; Mary's letter to Cromwell is *LP*, VII, 1655, also in Wood, II, 80; for Stafford see C. Garrett, *The Marian Exiles* (Cambridge, 1938), 295–7, C. Robinson, "Carey, Barons Hunsdon, Etc.," in *Herald and Genealogist* (8 vols., London, 1867), IV, 33–48, 129–44, 389–98. Relatives of the queen were expected to obtain permission to marry. See, for example, *LP*, VI, 837.

44 Because Latimer, fo. 28, indicated that Butts had obtained Anne's patronage for Bourbon and because of his own connections with Gonville College, M. Dowling, "Anne Boleyn," 39, argued that he influenced Anne's patronage. There is no other evidence of his association with her on religious matters but there is for Cranmer. See later in this chapter. The wife of Butts was until the end of 1533 a member of Mary's household (*LP*, VI, 1199); Nicolas Bourbon, *Nugarum Libri Octo* (Lyons, 1538); J. Jaquot, *Notice sur Nicolas Bourbon de Vandoeuvre* (Paris, 1857), 14; HPT, II, 311, identifies Thomas Harvey as the third pupil and not Thomas Howard, as alleged by M. Dowling, "Anne Boleyn," 42. This Thomas Harvey was too old to be a student of Bourbon in 1534, but as an Edmund Harvey owed Anne 100 marks at her death (*LP*, XI, 117), it is possible that there was a misprint in Harvey's first name in the verses of Bourbon. In 1538 an abbot recalled that a Mr. Norris, Mr. Cary, and Mr. Harvey had been tutored by a Mr. James. See *LP*, XIII (1), 981 (2); N. Roelker, *Queen of Navarre: Jeanne d'Albret, 1528–1572* (Cambridge, 1968), 31.

45 *LP*, IV, 3731–2.

46 Foxe, V, 60–1; Latimer, fos. 23–4.

47 *LP*, VIII, 435; Catherine probably did not keep the Maundy, since she could do so only as the princess dowager. *Cal.SP Span.*, V-i, 40 (p. 118); Latimer, fo. 26; R. M. Warnicke, "The Lady Margaret, Countess of Richmond," *Fifteenth Century Studies*, 9 (1984), 215–48; Forrest, 27–8, 46.

48 Foxe, V, 60.

49 Latimer, fos. 23–7; *LP*, IX, 186.

50 Marshall's work has been reprinted in F. R. Salter, *Some Early Tracts on Poor Relief* (London, 1926), 32–47; Elton, *Studies*, II, 137–55.

51 M. Underwood, "The Lady Margaret and her Cambridge Connections," *Sixteenth Century Journal*, 13 (1982), 67–82; Forrest, 48; Latimer, fo. 28b; Foxe, V, 60; for a letter to her from Cambridge, BL Cotton MS Faust C III, fo 456, in *LP*, VIII, 1067; W. Bercher (Barker), *The Nobility of Women*, ed. R. Bond (London, 1904), 7; for Becansaw, see *Lisle Letters*, III, pp. 112–13, *LP*, XI, 63, 337, 344; for Bill see *DNB*; for the monk, *LP*, VIII, 710 in Wood, II, 79.

52 F. Blomefield, *An Essay*, V, 267; Latimer, fos. 31–2. It is possible that the prayer book she gave to the nuns at Syon was similar to or even the same as those she presented to her household, although Latimer did not specify that; for the devotions and Margaret Lee, see Chapter 9.

53 R. Southall, *The Courtly Maker: An Essay on the Poetry of Wyatt and his Contemporaries* (Oxford, 1964), especially 160–75, for the Devonshire Manuscript; see also R. M. Warnicke, *Women*, 39 n. 25, and "The Eternal Triangle," 571–9; R. Harrier, *The Canon*, 29–32,

141–2, established that Anne did not write poems in the Devonshire Manuscript.

54 Friedmann, I, 55; M. Bruce, *Anne Boleyn* (New York, 1972), 24, stressed the sexual habits she learned in France; A. Strickland, *Lives*, IV, 207–52.

55 *LP*, VI, 613, 1194.

56 C. Russell, "Arguments for Religious Unity in England, 1530–1650," *Journal of Ecclesiastical History*, 18 (1967), 201–6; *LP*, IX, 386.

57 BL Add. MS 43,827B, fo. 2; M. Dowling and J. Shakespeare, "Religion and Politics," 95; for Marot, see Chapter 1; M. Dowling, "Anne Boleyn," 44.

58 Latimer, fos. 31–2; *LP*, V, 153, 201 for Tyndale; F. F. Bruce, *History of the Bible in English*, 3rd edition (New York, 1978), 36–59; E. G. Rupp, *Six Makers of English Religion, 1500–1700* (New York, 1957), 13–26; Elton, *Reform*, 275, for prefaces; in the king's collection in 1535 were two great books of the Old Testament and other scriptures (*LP*, VIII, 44), but the language in which they were printed was not mentioned.

59 *Memoirs of Peregrine Bertie, Eleventh Lord Willoughby de Eresby* (London, 1838), 12–27; Foxe, V, 52–60; E. G. Rupp, *Studies*, 128–31; F. Lambert, *The Summe of Christianitie*, tr. T. Revell (London, 1536); *LP*, X, 371.

60 R. W. Dunning, "Patronage and Promotion in the Late-Medieval Church," in *Patronage, the Crown, and the Provinces: In Later Medieval England*, ed. R. A. Griffiths (Atlantic Highlands, N.J., 1981), 177; P. W. Fleming, "Charity, Faith, and the Gentry of Kent, 1422–1529," in *Property and Politics: Essays in Later Medieval English History*, ed. A. J. Pollard (New York, 1984), 52–3; L. B. Smith, *Tudor Prelates and Politics, 1536–1558* (Princeton, 1953), 133–44; for Cromwell and kin, see *LP*, VII, 403, VIII, 301.

61 BL Cleop. MS E V, fo. 330b, in *LP*, VII, 664 and Ellis, 2nd series, I, 45; see also *LP*, IX, 746.

62 P. N. Brooks, "The Principle and Practice of Primitive Protestantism in Tudor England: Cranmer, Parker and Grindal," in *Reformation Principle and Practice: Essays in Honour of Arthur Geoffrey Dickens*, ed. P. N. Brooks (London, 1980), 122–32; for Betts, see A. B. Emden, *A Biographical Register of the University of Oxford, A. D. 1501–1540* (Oxford, 1974), 47, who says that he was by 1535 in the king's household; see also Chapter 4.

63 *LP*, V, 1366, VIII, 412, IX, 1091; E. G. Rupp, *Studies*, 62–72, for the Barlows.

64 Foxe, V, 60; Latimer, fo. 30. All of the bishops Latimer named were elected during Henry's reign although some of them after Anne's death; Chapuys also reported that she favored Fox, the king's almoner, who

became bishop of Hereford. See *Cal.SP Span.*, IV-ii-i, 796; for the quotations about Barlow, see *DNB*.

65 See Chapters 4 and 5.

66 *LP*, IV, 6247 (ii) for the committee; M. Dowling, "Anne Boleyn," 38–9, suggests that the key to Anne's patronage lay in Gonville College. If so, it was an indirect one. There was a reformed religious atmosphere at Gonville that seems to have encouraged its scholars to become members of the 1530 committee. See *LP*, IV, 6385 (I wish to thank John Guy for this reference). In his list of the Protestant martyrs of Cambridge, E. G. Rupp, *Studies*, 197, included none from Gonville.

67 W. Gilpin, *The Life of Hugh Latimer, Bishop of Worcester* (London, 1755), 57–8; *LP*, VII, 29, 30, 32 for Latimer's preaching.

68 *LP*, VII, 29, 30, 32; see also IV, 6176, 6325, VI, 412, VIII, 1063, IX, 203, 272; Latimer, fo. 31; A. G. Chester, *Hugh Latimer: Apostle to the English* (Philadelphia, 1954), 100; for whether he was a Protestant, see P. Cricco, "Hugh Latimer and Witness," *Sixteenth Century Journal*, 10 (1979), 21–34.

69 *DNB*; *LP*, IV, p. 2699, VII, 171.

70 *The Court of Venus*, ed. R. Fraser (Durham, 1955), vii, 3–33; A. B. Emden, *Biographical Register*, 517; see also M. Dowling, "Anne Boleyn," 40; the letter about Power is in BL Add. MS 19,398, fo. 48, in *LP*, VIII, 1056, Wood, II, 78; for Thetford, *LP*, VIII, 834.

71 M. Dowling, "Anne Boleyn," 32; J. Block, "Thomas Cromwell's Patronage of Preaching," *Sixteenth Century Journal*, 8 (1977), 37–50; *LP*, VI, 433 (iii), 1229, VII, 1265; there were other anomalies: J. K. Yost, "German Protestant Humanism and the Early English Reformation: Richard Taverner and Official Translation," *Bibliothèque d'Humanisme et Renaissance*, 32 (1970), 613–14, reports that in 1532 Norfolk had promised an annuity to Taverner, who later became a client of Cromwell.

72 *LP*, VIII, 7, 722; J. Le Neve, *Fasti Ecclesiae Anglicanae* (12 vols., London, 1963), V, 7, 39, 68.

73 Scarisbrick, 401–4; Elton, *Reform*, 129, 184; *LP*, V, 153, IX, 113, X, 265; see also H. Jacobs, *The Lutheran Movement in England during the Reigns of Henry VIII and Edward VI and its Literary Monuments* (Philadelphia, 1890), 3–61; J. Pragman, "The Augsburg Confession in the English Reformation: Richard Taverner's Contribution,"*Sixteenth Century Journal*, 9 (1980), 75–83; E. G. Rupp, *Studies*, 89–127.

74 Latimer, fos. 24, 28b–31; *LP*, IX, 52 for Winchcombe; for Catesby, X, 383 in Ellis, 3rd series, III, 273; Elton, *Reform*, 232–8; Ives, *Anne*, 308.

75 *LP*, VII, 685, VIII, 85, 172, 176, IX, 561.

76 BL Lansdowne MS 1045, fo. 62, in Wood II, 76, a copy of the manuscript in *LP*, VII, 89; see also VI, 1570, IX, 741.

77 BL Lansdowne MS 1045, fo. 64, in Wood, II, 77, a copy of the manuscript in *LP*, VII, 693; see also *DNB*.

78 J. Venn and J. A. Venn, *Alumni*, I-i, 421; *LP*, VI, 1468, VII, 522, 923 (xl).

79 Elton, *Reform*, 180–5, 193; *LP*, V, 472, VII, 498–500; T. Fuller, *The Church History of Britain; From the Birth of Jesus Christ Until the Year MDCXLVII* (London, 1655), 205, told the legend of Anne's demanding to see Fisher's head and being bitten by his tooth; *Cal.SP Span.*, IV-ii-i, 646 (p. 79), 805 (p. 261), V-i, 174, 208, the latter containing the rumor circulating abroad that the son of More had killed the king in revenge for the martyrdom; see also G. R. Elton, *Policy*, 403; N. Harpsfield, *A Treatise*, 254, blamed Anne for More's death.

7 HAREM POLITICS

1 *LP*, VI, 879, 948, the latter in *Lisle Letters*, I, 34.

2 For the lying-in chamber, J. Leland, *Rebus Britannicis Collectanea* (6 vols., London, 1770), IV, 179, and *Lisle Letters*, I, p. 517; *LP*, VI, 890, VII, 923 (xxxvi); see also R. M. Warnicke, "The Lady Margaret," 223 n. 11.

3 *LP*, VI, 891, 948, 1004; *Cal.SP Ven.*, IV, 971; *Cal.SP Span.*, IV-ii-ii, 1124; A. Eccles, *Obstetrics and Gynaecology in Tudor and Stuart England* (Kent, Ohio, 1982), 44–60; Ives, *Anne*, 229, cited L. de Carles, *Epistre*, lines 148–64, that Anne was ill in this pregnancy, but de Carles is not a good source and he had other facts wrong about Elizabeth's birth. He could have been giving credence to the belief that sickly pregnancies usually produced a female.

4 *Cal.SP Span.*, IV-ii-ii, 1123 (p. 788) for the preparations; *LP*, IV, 3221 for the love letter, VI, 1070 for the names and the French envoy, 1599 for the prediction of a daughter, IX, 223 for Melanchthon; *Cal.SP Ven.*, IV, 971 for the entertainment; see also D. Starkey, "Representation through Intimacy," 187; A. McLaren, *Reproductive Rituals: The Perception of Fertility in England From the Sixteenth Century to the Nineteenth Century* (New York, 1984), 5.

5 Foxe, V, 136; *LP*, IV, 1151, 2407; A. Fox, "Prophecies and Politics in the Reign of Henry VIII," in *Reassessing*, 77–94.

6 Cavendish, "Wolsey," 131; *LP*, VIII, 736 for the falcon; see also VI, 733, App. 10; *Cal.SP Span.*, IV-i, 373 (p. 634), V-i, 60 (p. 172).

7 George Wyatt, 422, 429.

8 *Cal.SP Ven.*, IV, 873, 923; Latimer, fo. 22.

9 *Cal.SP Span.*, IV-ii-ii, 1123 (p. 788).

10 Ibid., IV-i, 224 (p. 348), 249 (p. 416), IV-ii-ii, 1186; Chapuys did dine at court but after 1529 usually only with a few royal ministers.

11 A. McLaren, *Reproductive Rituals*, 50; *LP*, VI, 1070; a child's timidity, it was thought, could be caused by its mother's distress during pregnancy. See P. Crawford, "'The Sucking Child': Adult Attitudes to Childcare in the First Year of Life in Seventeenth-Century England," *Continuity and Change*, 1 (1986), 27.

12 *LP*, VI, App. 7 for the quotation; A. McLaren, *Reproductive Rituals*, 45–7; T. N. Tentler, *Sin and Confession on the Eve of the Reformation* (Princeton, 1977), 211.

13 For the quotation, *LP*, VIII, 174; F. E. Brightman, intro., *The English Rite* (2 vols., London, 1915), I, 879–85; F. Procter and W. Frere, *A New History of the Book of Common Prayer* (New York, 1901), 638–41. The length of time varied. In 1489 Elizabeth of York was churched on 27 December after the birth of her daughter on 29 November (*Privy Purse Expenses of Elizabeth of York*, ed. N. H. Nicolas [London, 1830], lxxxiii). In 1555 the Spanish envoy indicated that it was an ancient English custom for women to remain in retirement for forty days before and after their confinement (*Cal.SP Span.*, XIII, p. 166). Anne of Denmark was not churched until 3 August 1606 after her 22 June delivery (G. B. Harrison, *Jacobean Journal* [New York, 1941], 314). For purification, see A. Van Gennep, *The Rites of Passage*, tr. M. Vizedom and G. Caffe (Chicago, 1960), 12, 20, 34, 41–5; *The Norfolk Garland*, ed. J. Glyde (London, 1872), 3.

14 *Leaves from the Notebooks of Lady Dorothy Nevill*, ed. R. Neville (London, 1907), 49; *LP*, VI, 1089, 1190, VII, 1.

15 Scarisbrick, 324; P. Johnson, *Elizabeth I* (London, 1974), 10; D. S. Bailey, *Sponsors at Baptism and Confirmation* (London, 1952), 54, 84, 102; *A Collection of Ordinances and Regulations for the Government of the Royal Household Made in Divers Reigns from King Edward III to King William and Queen Mary* (London, 1790), 125–6; *Cal.SP Span.*, IV-ii-ii, 1127 (p. 795); for Mary's christening, see *LP*, II, 1573, and Hall, I, 150, also II, 279 for Edward.

16 *Cal.SP Span.*, IV-ii-ii, 1107 (p. 756), 1123 (p. 788); *LP*, VI, 1111; Hall, II, 242.

17 Hall, II, 242; *LP*, VI, 1111, VII, 509 (*Lisle Letters*, II, 169); Foxe, V, 62.

18 *Cal.SP Span.*, V-i, 10 (p. 34), 22, 45 (p. 129), 102 (p. 299); *LP*, II, 3802, VII, 509, 1297, IX, 568. See also N. Williams, *The Royal Residences*, 162–4; for M. Bryan, *Lisle Letters*, V, 89 n.; for Francis, the *DNB*.

19 W. Loke, *An Account of Materials Furnished for the Use of Queen Anne Boleyn and the Princess Elizabeth*, ed. J. B. Heath (London, 1862–3); see also *LP*, VIII, 197, 1071.

20 For complaints about her possessions, see Chapter 5; *Cal.SP Span.*, IV-ii-i, 802 (p. 254), 818 (p. 278), 1003 (pp. 524, 527), IV-ii-ii, 1058 (p. 630),

1133 (p. 821), 1137, 1158 (p. 877), 1161, 1165 (p. 898), V-i, 8 (p. 27), 102; *LP*, VI, 1207, 1486, VII, 9 (ii), 38, 1129, 1172; for Beaulieu, "George Boleyn," in *DNB*.

21 *LP*, VIII, 440.

22 P. Stafford, "Sons and Mothers: Family Politics in the Early Middle Ages," in *Medieval Women*, ed. D. Baker (Oxford, 1978), 80–3.

23 Ibid., 100; *Cal.SP Span.*, V-i, 10 (p. 34), 22.

24 *Cal.SP Span.*, V-i, 19 (p. 68); *LP*, VII, App. XIII, XI, 29 for Cromwell; H. Prescott, *Mary Tudor* (New York, 1953), 80–2.

25 *LP*, VII, 9 for the gift, 21, 24, 126, VIII, 1062; *Cal.SP Span.*, IV-ii-ii, 1158 (p. 878), V-i, 7 (p. 21).

26 *LP*, VII, 556 (*Lisle Letters*, II, 175), 682, 784–5, 888, 926, 930; *Cal.SP Span.*, V-i, 19 (p. 67), 90 (p. 264).

27 *LP*, VII, 937, 949, 958, the latter in *StPap*, VII, pp. 565–9; Friedmann, II, 10, and other scholars who have accepted Chapuys' claim that Anne threatened to kill Mary (*Cal.SP Span.*, V-i, 68 [p. 198]), have argued that Henry canceled the trip because he was unwilling to allow Anne to act as regent. In fact, Chapuys could only guess about why Rochford went to France in July (*Cal.SP Span.*, V-i, 70–1); for the announcement, *LP*, VII, 1014.

28 *LP*, VII, 965, 989, 1144, 1180; *Cal.SP Span.*, V-i, 75 (p. 224), 90 (p. 264).

29 Sir John Dewhurst, "The Alleged Miscarriages of Catherine of Aragon and Anne Boleyn," *Medical History*, 28 (1984), 49–56.

30 HPT, I, 195; Anne could have given birth and been churched during this time. It is possible that there was a shorter period of seclusion after a miscarriage or a stillbirth.

31 On 9 July (*LP*, VII, 964) Thomas Winter wrote to Cromwell that he had talked with the king and queen. Winter revealed that he was sending a note to Cromwell, who was so busy, rather than seeking an interview. Unfortunately, Winter did not state the precise date when he saw Anne. Although it was a recent audience, it could have been in late June or at least before 2 July when the king left for the More. Winter was not the only individual who had trouble finding Cromwell. Chapuys complained that he was unavailable (*Cal.SP Span.*, V-i, 75) and Lisle's agent was amazed that although the secretary had appointed 3 July for a hearing in London, he had not appeared (*LP*, VII, 959). The trip to the More (or the planning for it) had interferred with this business. As the Dacre trial began on 9 July (*LP*, VII, 979), it is possible that it was this issue troubling Henry, but the extraordinary instructions for Rochford's embassy and the royal couple's unusual separation give greater weight to the conclusion that Anne

had given birth to a stillborn child; for the marriage see later in this chapter.

32 *Cal.SP Span.*, II, 113; Sir John Dewhurst, "Miscarriages," 50; Hall, II, 266.

33 *Cal.SP Span.*, V-i, 90 (264), 97, 118, 155; *LP*, VII, 1172; for Carew and the envoys, see Chapter 6.

34 *Cal.SP Span.*, V-i, 97, 118 (p. 344); for Mary, see also Chapter 6.

35 A. McLaren, *Reproductive Rituals*, 38–40; *LP*, VII, 1224, 1265, 1352 (12), 1498 (1), 1581 (*Lisle Letters*, II, 298).

36 *LP*, VI, 242, 584–5, 720, VIII, 174; Knecht, 224–8; *Cal.SP Ven.*, IV, 923.

37 Knecht, 229–31; Scarisbrick, 309–34; *LP*, V, 1187, VI, 1404, 1435, 1479; *Cal.SP Span.*, IV-ii-ii, 1161 (p. 885), 1165 (pp. 899–901).

38 *Cal.SP Span.*, IV-ii-i, 1043 (p. 584), 1055, V-i, 17 (p. 56), 40 for the quotation; *LP*, VII, 434, 469, 476.

39 *Cal.SP Span.*, IV-ii-ii 1127 (p. 794), V-i, 57 (p. 155) for the quotation; *LP*, X, 410.

40 *Cal.SP Span.*, V-i, 102 (pp. 294, 300).

41 *LP*, VII, 1427, 1466, 1522; *Cal.SP Span.*, V-i, 112, 114.

42 There was some confusion, even at the time, as to whether Mary was to wed the Dauphin or Angoulême. See *LP*, VII, 1483; Knecht, 234–5; *Cal.SP Span.*, V-i, 123 (p. 359), 127 (p. 376), 131 (p. 398), 136 (p. 404), 205 (p. 543), 213 (p. 555).

43 *Cal.SP Span.*, V-i, 127 (p. 376).

44 For Gontier, see below.

45 *LP*, VIII, 111, 174, 327, 355.

46 Ibid., 174.

47 *Cal.SP Span.*, V-i, 147 (p. 435); Knecht, 274–80.

48 *LP*, VII, 780, 823, 965 for Calais, VII, 365, VIII, 516 for the measles, 263 for the mistress, XIII-i, 24 for Mary Shelton in 1538; Friedmann, II, 57, 62, 249–50, changed the name "Mage" in Kingston's mutilated letter (*LP*, X, 793), as read by J. Strype, *Ecclesiastical*, I-i, 433, and printed by George Singer, ed., *Life of Cardinal Wolsey* 2nd edition (London, 1827), App. 451–2, to "Madge" and identified her as Margaret Shelton. Other evidence (Latimer, fos. 31–2; R. Southall, *The Courtly Maker*, 17–26, 172–3, indicates that the troublesome maiden was Mary Shelton, not Margaret Parker, who was the wife of Mary's brother, Sir John Shelton the younger, and the daughter of Lord Morley.

49 *Cal.SP Span.*, V-i, 170, 182 (p. 514); *StPap*, VII, pp. 608–15.

50 *Cal.SP Span.*, V-i, 156 (p. 454), 170 (p. 484 for Cromwell's comment), 174 (p. 493), 184 for the fool; *LP*, VIII, 1056–7 for Anne's letters; *Cal.SP Ven.*, V, 54.

51 *LP*, VIII, 1095, 1116, IX, 39; *Cal.SP Span.*, V-i, 178 (pp. 502, 505), 181 (p. 511), 183 (p. 519), 221.

52 *Cal.SP Span.*, IV-ii-ii, 1072 (p. 675) for the invasion, V-i, 213 (p. 551) for the "importunities", 193 (p. 529) for the Welsh story; *LP*, IX, 566.

53 As in some of the smaller manor houses the king visited, the quarters were very tight, it is possible that the queen did not accompany him to all of them. See D. Starkey, "The Age of the Household: Politics, Society and the Arts, c. 1350–c. 1550," in S. Medcalf, ed., *The Later Middle Ages* (New York, 1981), 277; *LP*, IX, 378, 525, 555, 571, 619, 639, 663, 723.

54 *Cal. SP Span.*, V-i, 144.

55 *LP*, IX, 779; *Cal.SP Span.*, V-i, 229 (pp. 569, 571), 244; Knecht, 274–80; Elton, *Reform*, 251.

56 Friedmann, II, 137–8 for the king weary of her; Sir John Dewhurst, "Miscarriages," 49–53; this number of spousal pregnancies belies Ives' claim (*Anne*, 20) of Henry's "known low fertility."

57 *Cal.SP Span.*, V-i, 10 (p. 33), 178 (p. 500), 183 (p. 518), 246 (p. 600).

58 Hall, II, 266, commented about her yellow clothes immediately before referring to her miscarriage. For mourning clothes, see *LP*, X, 65; in *The Anglica Historia*, 336–7, Vergil said she "rejoiced at Catherine's death"; for the decorations, H. Colvin, *King's Works*, IV, 82; many historians, following Hall and Vergil, said Anne but not Henry rejoiced. Burnet, I-i, 351, even claimed Henry received the news with regret; *Cal.SP Span.*, V-ii, 3 (p. 5), 4, 9 (pp. 11–12, 19).

59 Friedmann, I, 198, 212, 217, had difficulties in keeping the factions straight. In 1533 he could not decide to which one Norfolk belonged; *Cal.SP Span.*, V-i, 122 (p. 355), 170 (p. 484); see also *LP*, VIII, 909.

60 *Cal.SP Span.*, V-i, 165 (p. 468).

61 *LP*, V, 907, VI, 923, 964, 1122, 1254, VII, 61 (the Treason Statute), 454, 497, 559, 678, 840 (2), 939, 1510, 1609, 1624, VIII, 196, 324, 480, 727, 737, 838, 844, 862 (2), IX, 52 (2), 136, 691, 1123; see also G. R. Elton, *Policy*, 277–300.

8 SEXUAL HERESY

1 For secrecy, see Chapter 7; C. Wriothesley, *A Chronicle of England during the Reigns of the Tudors from A.D. 1485 to 1559*, ed. W. Hamilton, Camden Society, vol. I (London, 1874), 33; Hall, II, 266. Tradition accepted 29 January. See J. Stowe, *The Annales of England* (London, 1592), 966.

2 Parts of this follow closely R. M. Warnicke, "Sexual Heresy," 247–68; for bewitching Henry, see *Cal.SP Span.*, IV-ii-ii, 1161 (p. 884), *LP*, V,

1114; Ives, *Anne*, 355–60; M. Levine, "The Place of Women in Tudor Government," in *Tudor Rule and Revolution: Essays for G. R. Elton from his American Friends*, ed. D. Guth and J. McKenna (Cambridge, 1982), 122–3; Friedmann, II, 265.

3 The statute is 33 Henry VIII, c. 8. For a distinction between village and clerical witchcraft, see C. Larner, *Witchcraft and Religion: The Politics of Popular Belief*, ed. A. Macfarlane (London, 1984), 3–5, 69–78; J. B. Russell, *Witchcraft in the Middle Ages* (Ithaca, 1972), 53–8; G. L. Kittredge, *Witchcraft in Old and New England* (reprint, New York, 1972), 25, 30, 41, 52, 62, 72, points out that all the charges against the witches, except the elaborate sabbath, were a part of England's medieval heritage. In art the appearance of lower-class women as witches dates from about 1530–40, at the earliest. See Dale Hoak, "Art, Culture, and Mentality in Renaissance Society: The Meaning of Hans Baldung Grien's Bewitched Groom (1544)," *Renaissance Quarterly*, 28–3 (1985), 506; see also K. Thomas, *Religion*; A. Macfarlane, *Witchcraft in Tudor and Stuart England: A Regional and Comparative Study* (New York, 1970).

4 G. L. Kittredge, *Witchcraft*, 33–4, 51, 56–7, 104–5, 113, 117–23. He points out (53, 123) that since the prosecutor of the case of the Irishwoman, Dame Alice Kyteler, was from London, her trial belongs to the history of English rather than Irish witchcraft. See *A Contemporary Narrative of the Proceedings against Dame Alice Kyteler*, ed. T. Wright, Camden Society, vol. XXIV (London, 1843), iii–xii. In its foreword (iii–iv) T. Wright referred to the allusion of John of Salisbury (*Johan. Salisb. Policraticus*, lib. i. c. 17) to the meetings of witches; E. Fenton, *Certaine secrete wonders of nature* (London, 1569), 17–18; L. M. Sinistrari, *Demoniality*, tr. M. Summers (London, 1927), 25–90; *The Malleus Maleficarum of Heinrich Kramer and James Sprenger*, ed. M. Summers (New York, 1971), 25–55; H. A. Kelly, "English Kings and the Fear of Sorcery," *Mediaeval Studies*, 39 (1977), 235, and *The Matrimonial Trials*, 249.

5 For witchcraft and sodomy, see E. W. Monter, *Witchcraft in France and Switzerland* (Ithaca, 1976), and G. Ruggiero, *The Boundaries of Eros: Sex Crime and Sexuality in Renaissance Venice* (New York, 1985), 118–45; K. Thomas, *Man and the Natural World, Changing Attitudes in England, 1500–1800* (London, 1983), 39, 94, 134–5; S. Lehmberg, *The Reformation Parliament, 1529–1536* (Cambridge, 1970), 185; *Statutes of the Realm*, III, 441.

6 D. M. Loades, *The Papers of George Wyatt*, 156.

7 M. Foucault, *The History of Sexuality*, tr. R. Hurley (3 vols., London, 1980), I, 38–43; A. Bray, *Homosexuality in Renaissance England* (London, 1982), 14–31; A. Karlen, "Homosexuality in History," in *Homosexual*

Behavior, ed. J. Marmor (New York, 1980), 88; for sodomites as devil worshippers, see *Purchas His Pilgrimes* (4 vols., London, 1625), I, 67 and W. Thomas, *Pilgrim*, 44–9; the claim of J. Boswell, *Christianity, Social Tolerance, and Homosexuality: Gay People in Western Europe from the Beginning of the Western Era to the Fourteenth Century* (Chicago, 1980), that homosexuality was tolerated in the medieval period has been challenged by, among others, P. J. Payer, *Sex and the Penitentials, the Development of a Sexual Code, 550–1150* (Toronto, 1984), 135–9.

8 *Statutes of the Realm*, III, 754; *LP*, X, 364; R. M. Wunderli, *London Church Courts and Society on the Eve of the Reformation* (Cambridge, Ma., 1981), 83–4.

9 E. Coke, *The Third Part of the Institutes of the Laws of England*, 4th edition (London, 1669), 58–9, and *The Twelfth Part of the Reports of Sir Edward Coke*, 2nd edition (London, 1677), 36; M. Goodich, *The Unmentionable Vice: Homosexuality in the Later Medieval Period* (Santa Barbara, Ca., 1979), 9–15; J. Harris, *The Destruction of Sodome* (London, 1628), 9; W. Thomas, *Pilgrim*, 48–9.

10 B. Castiglione, *The Book of the Courtier*, tr. T. Hoby, ed. D. Henderson (New York, 1946), 39, 89; *The Treatise of the Galaunt*, in F. J. Furnivall, *Ballads*, 438–51; T. Moffet, *Nobilis: Or, A View of the Life and Death of A Sidney and Lessus Lugubris*, ed. V. Heltzel and H. Hudson (San Marino, Ca., 1940), 78.

11 *LP*, XV, 498 (i, 59, ii, c. 49), 926; for Mother Roche, see G. L. Kittredge, *Witchcraft*, 65; M. Goodich, *Unmentionable Vice*, 86; E. Coke, *The Twelfth Part*, 36; see also J. Van Patten, "Magic, Prophecy, and the Law of Treason in Reformation England," *American Journal of Legal History*, 16 (1983), 1–32.

12 *Proceedings and Ordinances of the Privy Council of England*, ed. H. Nicolas (7 vols., London, 1837), VII, p. 153; G. Scheurweghs, ed., *Nicholas Udall's Roister Doister* (Louvain, 1939), xvi–xviii; V. L. Bullock, *Homosexuality: A History* (New York, 1979), 106; W. D. Cooper, ed., *Ralph Roister Doister* (London, 1847), xix, for the quotation.

13 A. McLaren, *Reproductive Rituals*, 81, points out that pregnant women could use other positions but that intercourse was not recommended; for incest, see J. T. Noonan, Jr., *Contraception: A History of its Treatment by the Catholic Theologians and Canonists* (Cambridge, Ma., 1965), 260–1, and K. Thomas, *Man and the Natural World*, 39.

14 K. Park and L. Daston, "Unnatural Conceptions," 20–54; E. Fenton, *Certaine secrete*, 12–13; J. Barker, *The true Description of a monsterous chylde* (London, 1564); Anonymous, *A most straunge and true discourse of the wonderful judgement of God. Of a Monstrous, Deformed Infant, begotten by incestuous copulation ...* (London, 1600); and for the terrified father, W.

Elderton, *The true fourme and shape of a monsterous chylde borne in Stony Stratforde* (London, 1565); P. Crawford, "Attitudes toward Menstruation in Seventeenth-Century England," *Past and Present*, 91 (1981), 62–3, points out that conception during menstruation was thought to result in the births of monsters; the suggestion here that Anne had a deformed child was made independently of Sander's statement (132–3) that she had given birth to a "shapeless mass of flesh," a claim that formed part of his description of her as a witch. See R. M. Warnicke, "The Physical Deformities," 135–54, and Appendix A. For witchcraft and deformed infants, see also N. Remy, *Demonolatry*, tr. E. A. Ashwin (London, 1930), 92–9.

15 Elton, *Reform*, 250–6; relying on manuscript jottings on the 1679 edition of Edward, Lord Herbert's biography of Henry VIII, Ives, *Anne*, 368 n., 370 n., 373 n., 374 n., has pointed out that Wyatt and Page were taken to the Tower on 8 May and Weston and Brereton on 5 May, but as Ives also notes, George Constantine said Brereton was arrested on 4 May. Perhaps he was arrested then but not taken to the Tower until the 5th. Ives noted the claim that Smeaton was arrested at six p.m. on 30 April, but Constantine had said May Day morning. Alesius (RO, SP 70/7, fos. 5–6, printed in *Calendar of State Papers Foreign, 1558–59*, 1303) stated that he believed on account of a shot he heard from its cannon that an important prisoner (he thought Anne) was taken to the Tower late on 30 April. In one of Kingston's letters (*LP*, X, 797) it states that it was ten p.m. before Smeaton was well lodged. Perhaps Smeaton arrived about six o'clock, was well lodged by ten p.m. when the cannon went off, but word of his arrival was not leaked out until the next morning.

16 For Anne's earlier pregnancy, see Chapter 7.

17 *Cal.SP Span.*, V-ii, 13 (p. 28); see Chapter 6 and below for Exeter.

18 *LP*, X, 200 for Chapuys, 294 for the February report of an Italian envoy abroad that Henry was thought to have been dead for two hours; *Cal.SP Span.*, V-ii, 35 for the March report of an Imperial agent abroad that the king had been unconscious for two hours. In the same letter this agent said that the king wore mauve for Catherine's death; see also *LP*, X, 838; *Cal.SP Span.*, V-ii, 58; C. Wriothesley, *Chronicle*, I, 33.

19 *Cal.SP Span.*, V-ii, 17, 21.

20 Ibid., 21; the 10 February dispatch is incorrectly dated here. See *LP*, X, 282.

21 *Cal.SP Span.*, V-ii, 21; see n. 18 for the accident; for frights, see P. Crawford, "'The Sucking Child'," 23–51; *LP*, X, 283 for the rumor that she had not been pregnant, 352 for Chapuys' rumor that Anne was glad about the abortion because the son might have been considered illegitimate since he was conceived during the lifetime of Catherine.

22 S. Lehmberg, *The Reformation Parliament*, 221, 227; *Cal.SP Span.*, V-ii, 9, 21; *LP*, X, 307; Friedmann, II, 198.

23 *Cal.SP Span.*, V-ii, 29 (p. 59).

24 Ibid., 9 (p. 11), 29 (pp. 54–9), 55; *LP*, X, 410; for the Calais meeting, see Chapter 7; for more about the timing of the plot, see later in this text and n. 42.

25 RO, SP 70/7, fos. 1–7b, and Foxe, V, 137, reported her friendship with the Germans.

26 BL Cotton MS Otho C X, fo. 209, printed in Ellis, 1st series, II, 121, and in *LP*, X, 799; for Mark's confession, see Burnet, I-i, 368–9; Brantôme, *Lives*, 385; Scarisbrick, 429–33.

27 Of Kingston's six letters to Cromwell those in the Cotton (Otho) collection at the BL have the most relevant information, but they are in decayed condition and must be read in association with a printed version. Another is in the Harleian collection and still one more is at the RO. They can be found in George Cavendish, *Life of Cardinal Wolsey*, ed. George Singer, 2nd edition (London, 1827), App. 451–60, and in Ellis, 1st series, II, 118–23. Extracts are in J. Strype, *Ecclesiastical*, I-i, 431–4, who read them before they were so terribly mutilated. References here, unless otherwise noted, are to the *LP*. The first letter of Kingston is X, 793; for sorrow, see *Oxford English Dictionary* and T. Tentler, *Sin and Confession*, 288.

28 RO, SP 70/7, fos. 5–6.

29 C. Wriothesley, *Chronicle*, I, 33; *Cal.SP Span.*, V-ii, 21; A. Eccles, *Obstetrics and Gynaecology*, 47; K. L. Moore, *The Developing Human: Clinically Oriented Embryology*, revised edition (Philadelphia, 1974), 5, 71, 220–35; *Williams Obstetrics*, ed. P. Pritchard and P. MacDonald, 16th edition (New York, 1980), 169–73; P. Crawford, "'The Sucking Child'," 28, 47; A. McLaren, *Reproductive Rituals*, 47; *LP*, X, 953 for the witnesses, VII, 9 (ii) for a Mrs. Cobham who received a New Year's gift in 1534. This woman may have been Anne Cobham, widow, who was granted a manor in May 1540 (*LP*, XV, 733 [55]).

30 For the indictments, see *LP*, X, 876, C. Wriothesley, *Chronicle*, I, 189–226; A. Amos, *Observations on the Statutes of the Reformation Parliament* (London, 1859), 324–31; for touches as mortal sin, see D. S. Bailey, *The Man–Woman Relation in Christian Thought* (London, 1959), 160–1; for the rumor about Norris, see *Cal.SP Span.*, V-ii, 54; Brantôme, *Lives*, 129; for betwitching men into unnatural thoughts before entrancing them to perform them, see Dale Hoak, "Art, Culture, and Mentality in Renaissance Society," 505; T. Wright, *Dame Alice Kyteler*, iii, pointed out that in Anglo-Saxon law "notorious adulteresses" were associated with witches.

31 *LP*, X, 876; S. Clark, "Inversion, Misrule, and the Meaning of Witchcraft," *Past and Present*, 87 (1980), 100–1, 112–27; J. H. Baker, ed., *The Reports of John Spelman*, Selden Society, vol. XCIII (London, 1977), 71. The justices were concerned about whether she had actually violated the Treason Statute. E. Coke, *The Third Part*, 9, later cited Spelman's reports as evidence that if a king's wife consents to one who commits treason, "it is treason in her"; Chapuys had heard that she had laughed at the king's dress (*Cal.SP Span.*, V-ii, 55 [p. 126]).

32 *LP*, X, 255 for Cromwell's letter, 785, 820 for Bulkeley (VIII, 925 for his friendship with Cromwell and Norris); J. H. Baker, *Reports*, 71, for the legislation. See also Ives, *Anne*, 394 n. 24, 399; T. Amyot, "Memorial from George Constantyne to Thomas Lord Cromwell," *Archaeologia*, 13 (1831), 56–78; Cranmer's letter is in *LP*, X, 792, and Burnet, I-i, 364–7.

33 *LP*, X, 410; *Cal.SP Span.*, V-ii, 9 (pp. 14, 16–18), 13 (p. 28), 17; Friedmann, II, 173–8, believed Catherine had been poisoned.

34 George Wyatt, 443; for Lenten continence, see G. May, *Social Control of Sex Expression* (London, 1930), 56–8; *LP*, X, 243, 345, 597 (3, 4), 827, and for the trip to Dover, 669, 738, 747–8; Latimer, fo. 28b, said she obtained a pardon for the university tenths; Ives, *Anne*, 364, believed they were planning a trip to Calais; S. Lehmberg, *The Reformation Parliament*, 218–27; H. Miller, "Attendance in the House of Lords during the Reign of Henry VIII," *Historical Journal*, 10/3 (1967), 345; W. Loke, *An Account of Materials*; for Mary's marriage, see Chapter 3.

35 *LP*, X, 741; *Peerage*, XII, 182–4; *DNB*.

36 *LP*, VII, 1040 for the suspicion, VIII, 263 for complaints in front of Montague about Francis in February 1535; 1074, 1084 for Lisle; *Cal.SP Span.*, V-i, 70, V-ii, 43 (p. 81); for earlier contacts, see Chapter 7.

37 For factions and her fall, see Ives, *Anne*, 335–82; for Bryan, *DNB, LP*, V, 202, XI, 29 for part of an annuity that Bryan obtained from the spoils of Norris' estate, X, 1134 (4), XIII (1), 981 (2) for his interrogation in June about his support for Mary and an abbot's comment about it. Ives argues that Bryan was also a member of the Boleyn faction and was summoned to court to be questioned about his relationship to Anne (for his role, see R. M. Warnicke, "The Fall of Anne Boleyn: A Reassessment," *History*, 70 [February, 1985], 4–5, 14 n. 30). The only evidence that the questioning, which did not take place until 14 June, was associated specifically with Anne is the later testimony of the abbot of Woburn. He recalled that at the fall of the queen, Bryan, then at Woburn, was commanded to appear at court. It seems clear that the questions asked of Bryan, as well as of Sir Anthony Browne, a brother of Lady Worcester and never associated with the queen, were about the succession, specifically Mary's place in it, and not about Anne's

adultery. In his responses Browne connected these two events. It is natural that Bryan's recall would be associated with Anne, both in his and the abbot's memory, for her death caused the succession to be the subject of new legislation. By the word, "fall," the abbot might well have meant her execution, and he might not even have learned about her arrest or imprisonment until well after her trial and perhaps her death. There was confusion even in London. On 2 May at least one letter writer thought Wiltshire had been arrested, and on 19 May Alesius did not know that she had been tried and scheduled for execution. See RO, SP 70/7, fo. 6; *LP*, X, 815, 1133–4, 1136–7, 1150; Cromwell gave a horse to Chapuys presented to him by the earl of Sussex. See *Cal.SP Span.*, V-ii, 43 (p. 82), for Sussex, 55 (p. 129); N. Elias, *Court*, 8, 84–94.

38 For secrecy see Chapter 7; *Cal.SP Span.*, II, 43, V-ii, 29 (p. 59); *LP*, X, 1047.

39 For Henry at her home in late 1535, see *LP*, VIII, 989, IX, 504 (2, 3); H. Clifford, *Jane Dormer*, 79, said Anne miscarried after she found Jane with Henry; T. Tentler, *Sin and Confession*, 211; P. Crawford, "'The Sucking Child'," 11; *Cal.SP Span.*, V-ii, 29 (p. 59), 43 (p. 84); for Anne's housing, see Chapter 5.

40 *Cal.SP Span.*, V-ii, 43A (pp. 91–3), 55 (p. 123), 61 (p. 156); for Anne out of favor, see *LP*, X, 720; A. Montagu, *Sexual Symbolism: A History of Phallic Worship*, 2nd part (New York, 1957), 90, says licentious sexual activity and reversal of sex roles were associated with Easter Monday and Tuesday.

41 This incident may have given rise to the legend in H. Clifford, *Jane Dormer*, 81, that in Anne's presence, Mary curtsied during mass at Eltham. Anne reportedly sent word to her that she would have responded had she known Mary was going to curtsy, but Mary retorted that she was reverencing the altar only. The two probably never met face to face after Anne moved into separate housing in 1528; *Cal.SP Span.*, IV-ii-ii, 1158 (p. 878), V-ii, 43A (pp. 91–3), 54. Chapuys wrote "from the very moment of my arrival at this court," a statement that could have meant when he first came to England in 1529. It is more likely that he meant the first time he had participated in a function at court in Anne's presence; *LP*, X, 429 for Cromwell's hat, 720 for Mary's concern; N. Elias, *Court*, 8, 84–94.

42 Elton, *Reform*, 251, and *Studies*, III, 48–9; *Cal.SP Span.*, V–ii, 43A (pp. 86–95), 55 (p. 123), 61; Ives, *Anne*, 358–60, says, "there is no good reason not to [believe]" Cromwell's statement to Chapuys that it was the king's behavior on Easter Tuesday, making it obvious that Anne controlled him, that caused Cromwell to set the plot in motion against

her life. In that same conversation with Chapuys, Cromwell also claimed that Mary was going to become the king's heir. Earlier, Chapuys, (V-ii, 43 [p. 83]) had heard that Cromwell was against the dissolution. He was obviously being fed lies to make him trust the secretary. Indeed, four years later Cromwell's agent, Stephen Vaughan bragged to him (*StPap*, VIII, p. 197) that he had just met with Chapuys in Brussels and had been "wyly ynowgh for hym, he can get no thyng at my hande."

43 *Cal.SP Span.*, V-ii, 47; *LP*, X, 715; Ives, *Anne*, 362–4, discusses why this parliament was called and doubts Henry was capable of so much deception.

44 *LP*, X, 793; H. Clifford, *Jane Dormer*, 76–8.

45 *LP*, X, 793, 876; N. Elias, *Court*, 8, 88–94; Friedmann, II, 249, dated this conversation after 23 April.

46 *LP*, X, 793, with extracts in J. Strype, *Ecclesiastical*, I-i, 433.

47 *LP*, X, 873, 953, 1044; J. Donnison, *Midwives and Medical Men: A History of Inter-Professional Rivalries and Women's Rights* (New York, 1977), 1–9.

48 *LP*, IV, 5243 (29), X, 499, 793, 797, 799, 953, XI, 117; for bribes, see RO, SP 70/7, fos. 4–5; W. R. B. Robinson, "Patronage and Hospitality in Tudor Wales: The Role of Henry, Earl of Worcester," *BIHR*, 51 (1978), 20–36; for a sister informing, see L. de Carles, *Epistre*, lines 339–448; N. Pocock, *Records*, II, 359.

49 *LP*, XI, 29.

50 Ibid., IX, 639, 820. Two of the dates fell in May and June 1534 when she was thought to have been pregnant. The days were 26 April (associated with Pagan eroticism), 19 and 20 May (Francismass), 20 June (eve of old St. John the Baptist), 12 October (St. Wilfrid's), 5 November (Turning the Devil's Boulder), 19 and 27 November, 8 and 29 December (St. Thomas of Canterbury and middle of Saturnalia). Pagan festivals often were transformed into Christian holidays that did not fall on exactly the same day. Because ancient people did not know about the solstices, some of them celebrated the change of seasons (associated with fertility and eroticism) in May and November instead of June and December. Only two of the above dates do not fall into those four months. See also A. R. Wright, *British Calendar*; J. Frazer, *The Golden Bough*, 3rd edition (12 vols., London, 1935), I, 14–16, II, 96; V. Alford, *The Hobby Horse and Other Animal Masks* (London, 1978), xviii, 4; D. G. Spicer, *Yearbook of English Festivals* (New York, 1954), 64–90; M. Cosman, *Medieval Holidays and Festivals: A Calendar of Celebrations* (New York, 1981), 59–68; C. Hole, *British Folk Customs* (London, 1976), 194; P. Burke, *Popular Culture in Early Modern Europe* (New York, 1978), 192–3; for Henry and St. John's Eve, see *Cal.SP Span.*, V-i, 179; Ives, *Anne*,

398, treated Chapuys' disbelief in Anne's guilt as though the envoy had some kind of special insight into the workings at court, but, in fact, Cromwell had been feeding him stories since February about her impending ruin.

51 For a medieval divorce involving incest, see P. Stafford, "Sons and Mothers," 90; for the letter to Rochford, see RO, SP 70/7, fos. 6–6b; T. Amyot, "Memorial," 66; *LP*, X, 1107.

52 *Metrical*, lines 274–343; A. Wood, *Athenae Oxonienses* (4 vols., London, 1813), I, 50, 98–9; see also K. Muir and P. Thomson, *Collected Poems*, 146, line 21.

53 *Metrical*, lines 301–7; H. M. Hyde, *The Trials of Oscar Wilde* (London, 1948), 199; J. C. Brown, *Immodest Acts: The Life of a Lesbian Nun in Renaissance Italy* (New York, 1986), 3–20.

54 *Cal.SP Span.*, V-ii, 54, 55 (pp. 125–7).

55 Her allowance was increased by 50 marks but she did not obtain her jointure until after the death of Wiltshire, and the king assumed the money owed her husband. Some of her possessions were seized and inventoried. For the king forgiving the archbishop of Dublin his debt to Rochford, see *StPap*, III, pp. 394–7. See also *LP*, X, 502, 1011, 1257, XI, 17, XIV, 867 (c. 20), 1171. Brereton's wife was awarded all his debts, deeds, and obligations; X, 1256 (52); Jane's letter is in BL Cotton MS Vesp. F XIII, fo. 199, in *LP*, X, 1010, and Ellis, 1st series, II, 124; for Jane's jealousy of Rochford, see P. Heylyn, *Ecclesia Restaurata* (London, 1661), 91. *Metrical*, lines 971–1024, associated her only with Katherine Howard; Alesius, RO, SP 70/7, fos. 1–7, did not mention her. Ives, *Anne*, 376, speculates about what "probably" was included in extracts from a lost journal and argues for her testimony against her husband. On the margin of a letter (*LP*, IX, 566) dated October 1535, in which the French diplomat mentioned women cheering for Mary, he added the names of "millor de Rochesfort et millord de Guillaume." Since he had only arrived that summer, his information was at best second hand. Friedmann, II, 128–9, who assumed he meant Lady William Howard and Lady Rochford, dated their cheering for Mary in April 1535, when she went from Greenwich to a house 12 miles distant (*LP*, VIII, 501), but she was ill and in a litter and there is no record of any cheering. In late April 1535, in fact, Lady William Howard died and surely could not have been present (*Peerage*, V, 9–10). Chapuys noted that peasants shouted for Mary in 1534 (*Cal.SP Span.*, V-i, 17 [p. 57]) but did not mention any high-born ladies. Had they been in the crowd, he would have said so. Probably the marginal notation was a reference to a different matter, for both Rochford and Howard were diplomats. See Chapter 7 for this diplomat.

56 K. Thomas, "The Double Standard," *Journal of the History of Ideas*, 20 (1959), 195–216; M. Ross, *The Married Homosexual Man* (London, 1983), xi, 1, 31–6.

57 K. Jankofsky, "Public Executions in England in the Late Middle Ages: The Indignity and Dignity of Death," *Omega: Journal of Death and Dying*, 10 (1979), 43–4; for "beast," *Cal.SP Span.*, V-ii, 3; L. B. Smith, "English Treason Trials and Confessions in the Sixteenth Century," *Journal of the History of Ideas*, 15/4 (1954), 482, notes that they normally admitted to offending against the king's laws; for Rochford, see especially *Chronicle of Calais*, 46; S. Bentley, ed., *Excerpta Historica* (London, 1831), 262–4; a manuscript at Brussels, an incomplete version, did have him ask forgiveness of God and the king at the end of his speech. See W. Thomas, *Pilgrim*, 116; *LP*, X, 911; C. Wriothesley, *Chronicle*, I, 39–40, had him say "God save the king."

58 *Chronicle of Calais*, 46–7; S. Bentley, *Excerpta*, 262–4; T. Tentler, *Sin and Confession*, 89–93, for the priests; T. Amyot, "Memorial," 65; see also J. Stevens, *Music and Poetry*, 307; G. L. Kittredge, *Witchcraft*, 65; W. Thomas, *Pilgrim*, 48–9.

59 For the spelling, "Markes," see *LP*, X, 797, 837, 855, 919; for a poem in which the name is spelled Mark, see K. Muir and P. Thomson, *Collected Poems*, 146, line 49; A. Wood, *Athenae*, 98–9; *Metrical*, lines 483–511; for the allegations that he was from Flanders, see n. 60; *LP*, IV, 2696 for a singer, X, 848 for the commoners' trial; J. H. Baker, *Reports*, 70–1; N. H. Nicolas, *Privy Purse*, 237, lists him among the young men supplied with shoes in 1532.

60 BL Royal MS 20 B XXI, fos. 2, 98, summarized in *LP*, X, 877, and printed in A. G. Van Hamel, ed., *Les Lamentations de Matheolus et le Livre de Leesce de Jehan Fevre, de Resson* (Paris, 1892). The second piece is also known as *Le Resolu en Mariage*; The name Wyott was written on the manuscript but does not appear to be his signature. E. E. Lowinsky, "A Music Book for Anne Boleyn," in *Florilegium Historiale: Essays Presented to Wallace K. Ferguson*, ed. J. Rowe and W. Stockdale (Toronto, 1971), 169–97, used Mark's signature from the Royal manuscript as evidence for his being Flemish and the author of an extant choirbook. See Appendix B. Although Ives, *Anne*, 56, 367, believed Lowinsky's arguments were plausible, he did not specifically refer to "Les Lamentations." For references to the spelling of Mark's name, see n. 59; *Metrical*, lines 490–502.

61 Foxe, V, 396; E. Armstrong, *The Emperor*, 9, said Charles intervened in a discussion about whether music made men effeminate; J. Stevens, *Music and Poetry*, 253–6; B. Castiglione, *Courtier*, 98–101; T. Amyot, "Memorial," 64; A. Strickland, *Lives*, IV, 296.

62 J. A. Sharpe, *Defamation and Sexual Slander in Early Modern England: The Church Court at York*, Borthwick Papers, No. 58 (York, 1980), 3; R. von Kraft-Ebing, *Psychopathia Sexualis*, tr. F. Klaf (London, 1967), 198; M. Ross, *The Married Homosexual Man*, 98–100; for Coke, see n. 9; T. Amyot, "Memorial," 64, for the rack; J. H. Baker, *Reports*, 71.

63 J. H. Baker, *Reports*, 65; *LP*, X, 798, 876.

64 T. Amyot, "Memorial," 64–5; *Metrical*, lines 372–5.

65 T. Amyot, "Memorial," 65; *LP*, X, 738, 793, 869; F. J. Furnivall, *Ballads*, I, 83–4, for abominable.

66. T. Amyot, "Memorial," 65; E. W. Ives, *Letters and Accounts of William Brereton*, Record Society of Lancashire and Cheshire, 116 (1976), 2, 36–40; Ives, *Anne*, 395. In May 1531 Brereton delivered jewels to Anne (*LP*, V, 276).

67 *LP*, VI, 613, X, 898 (iii), the latter refers to his holding a receivership of lands belonging to Sir Anthony Browne, a brother of Lady Worcester; for Brereton's wife, see n. 55.

68 Ives, *Anne*, 394–6, without documentation and citing only his article, "Court and County Palatine in the Reign of Henry VIII," *Transactions of the Historic Society of Lancashire and Cheshire*, 123 (1972), 28–30, claims Anne helped Brereton obtain Eyton's arrest. The evidence for Anne's involvement is provided only by the chronicle of Elis Gruffith: E. W. Ives, *Letters and Accounts of William Brereton*, 37. This arrest was raised by Cavendish in *Metrical*, lines 463–9, but he did not indicate that Anne had assisted in it; K. Muir and P. Thomson, *Collected Poems*, 148, lines 41–3, include "Great was thy love with dyvers as I here," without specifying persons.

69 Ives, *Anne*, 361, believes that Henry's letters referring to Anne as "our most dear and most entirely beloved wife, the queen," prove he was ignorant about the commission. Officially, he could have addressed her in no other way until after her arrest. For Anne and her husband on 30 April, see RO, SP 70/7, fos. 5–6. Alesius (n. 15 above) incorrectly thought she was imprisoned that day; *LP*, X, 789, 793, 797; *Cal.SP Span.*, V-ii, 47; *Correspondence of Matthew Parker*, 59, 70, 391, 400; for Parr, see Foxe, V, 553–8.

70 Hall, II, 268; D. G. Spicer, *Yearbook*, 64; *LP*, X, 797.

71 *LP*, X, 793, 797; H. B. Wheatley, *London, Past and Present: A Dictionary of its History, Associations and Traditions* (3 vols., London, 1891), III, 395; C. Wriothesley, *Chronicle*, I, 36; *Cal.SP Span.*, V-ii, 48; for Kingston and Coffin, see *Lisle Letters*, II, p. 56, IV, p. 130; Coffin was not officially knighted until 1537 (HPT, I, 666); for Lady Boleyn, *The Visitations of Norfolk*, ed. W. Rye, Harleian Society, vol. XXXII (London, 1891), 217; W. Parsons, "Some Notes on the Boleyn Family," 400–4, and *LP*, XIII-i, 1309 (32); Mrs. Stoner went on to serve Queen Jane (*LP*, XI, 253).

72 H. Richmond, *Puritans*, 16, for a different version of her laughter; *LP*, X, 793.

73 *LP*, X, 797, 798; G. L. Kittredge, *Witchcraft*, 152–62.

74 Ibid., 798; Edward, Lord Herbert, *The Life and raigne*, 382–4, printed a letter she sent to the king on 6 May, but it was surely not composed by her. It is also in *LP*, X, 808, *Harleian Miscellany*, III, 61–2, Burnet, I-ii, 237–9; for a possible ballad of Rochford's, see H. Walpole, *Catalogue*, I, 246.

75 *LP*, X, 890, 902, 908, 910; see n. 30; BL Harl. MS 2914, in F. J. Furnivall, *Ballads*, I, 406; C. Wriothesley, *Chronicle*, I, 36–7, 189–226; Friedmann, II, 274–6; Alesius mentioned only Richard Pollard as the king's proctor. See Ives, *Anne*, 386 n. 7, for this identification.

76 HPT, II, 142–4, 310–11; Burnet, I-i, 359–60; see also Chapter 5; J. H. Baker, *Reports*, 71.

77 B. Castiglione, *Courtier*, 177, 190, 220, believed an adultress deserved death; *LP*, X, 888 for Charles V's comment that if she were convicted of adultery, she would be executed, 866 for an impartial observer who believed her guilty; G. R. Elton, *Policy*, 275–7, 285–6, 308, 325; see also M. S. Schauer and F. Schauer, "Law as the Engine of State: The Trial of Anne Boleyn," *William and Mary Law Review* 22 (1980), 49–84; R. M. Warnicke, "The Fall of Anne," 1–15; T. Amyot, "Memorial," 66, for Norfolk's tears; L. de Carles, *Epistre*, lines 1002–12, alleged that she mentioned her jealousy of the king, but this is unlikely, for it would have meant publicly accusing him of sexual misconduct. This account must be held suspect, for the poet reversed the order of Rochford's and Anne's trials; see also n. 83 and *Cal.SP Span.*, V-ii, 54.

78 *LP*, X, 890, 902.

79 Ibid., 792; the quotation from Burnet, I-i, 364–7.

80 *Cal.SP Span.*, V-ii, 48, 54; *LP*, VIII, 266 and X, 715 for earlier references to the earl's illness; see also *LP*, X, 864, 876; R. A. Houlbrooke, *Church Courts and the People during the English Reformation, 1520–1570* (Oxford, 1979), 57–8; C. Wriothesley, *Chronicle*, I, 41; Friedmann, II, 286–9; H. A. Kelly, *The Matrimonial Trials*, 249–59; *Correspondence of Matthew Parker*, 414, 420, indicates Parker found the bull.

81 Ives, *Anne*, 93, 97; *LP*, X, 819, 840, 1131 for Wyatt, XI, 107 for Page. See also J. Bruce, "Recovery of the Lost Accusation of Sir Thomas Wyatt the Poet, by Bishop Bonner," *Gentleman's Magazine*, 33 (1850), 563–70; if (see n. 15) Wyatt and Page were taken on 8 May, then surely their arrests were not part of the original plan, for the justices' precepts to the sheriff of Middlesex for the return of the grand jury were dated 9 May (*LP*, X, 848); K. Muir, *The Life and Letters of Sir Thomas Wyatt*

(Liverpool, 1963), 22, for Suffolk; R. M. Warnicke, "The Eternal Triangle," 565–79.

82 H. A. Kelly, *The Matrimonial Trials*, 249; RO, SP 70/7, fo. 6 for Alesius and Cranmer; *Correspondence of Matthew Parker*, 400, 414, 420, 431; Ives, *Anne*, 406, believed the divorce trial was held primarily to declare Elizabeth illegitimate; *LP*, X, 753, for Cromwell and Sampson.

83 *LP*, X, 910.

84 Chapuys, *Cal.SP Span.*, V-ii, 55 (p. 130), said nine o'clock, but C. Wriothesley, *Chronicle*, I, 41, said eight a.m.; *LP*, X, 919 for "boldly." There are several versions of her execution. Friedmann, II, 294–6, cited a manuscript at Paris that said she wore a gray damask gown with a low round neck, but the color of gray was associated with witchcraft (G. L. Kittredge, *Witchcraft*, 12); I have followed S. Bentley, *Excerpta*, 261–5, which is from a Portuguese letter that appears to be a translation of an Italian version printed by P. A. Hamy, *Entreuve de Francis Premier Avec Henry VIII a Boulogne* (Paris, 1898), ccccxxxi-ccccxxxvi. See Ives, *Anne*, 391 n. 20, for this and the following: (2) William Thomas, *Pilgrim*, 116–17, for an Imperial account which is also in a Spanish version calendared in *LP*, X, 911; (3) a French account is printed partially in G. Ascoli, *La Grande-Bretagne*, 273, and P. A. Hamy, *Entreuve*, ccccxxxvii-ccccxxxviii; (4) L. de Carles, *Epistre*, also in G. Ascoli, *La Grande-Bretagne*; (5) *Les regretz de Millort de Rocheffort*, in G. Ascoli, *Le Grande-Bretagne*, 274–8; (6) T. Aymot, "Memorial," 64–6; (7) C. Wriothesley, *Chronicle*, I, 37–42; (8) *Chronicle of Calais*, 46–7.

85 Hall, II, 268–9; see also BL Harl. MS 2194, in F. J. Furnivall, *Ballads*, I, 407; T. Amyot, "Memorial," 65; Foxe, V, 135; S. Bentley, *Excerpta*, 264–5.

86 S. Bentley, *Excerpta*, 264–5; for the quotation, F. J. Furnivall, *Ballads*, I, 407; *Chronicle of Calais*, 47; D. C. Bell, *Notices of the Historic Persons Buried in the Chapel of St. Peter ad Vincula in the Tower of London* (London, 1877), 107, has the legend that she would not wear the bandage; *LP*, XI, 381 for the alms.

9 ROYAL LEGACY

1 J. H. Baker, *Reports*, 59 for the quotation; Friedmann, II, 291; A. Strickland, *Lives*, IV, 291–3.

2 A. Strickland, *Lives*, IV, 291–3; S. Bentley, *Excerpta*, 264–5.

3 A. Strickland, *Lives*, IV, 291–3; one disputed volume is BL Stowe MS 956, which was written by John Croke, one of the six clerks in Chancery, who dedicated it to his wife, and which is printed in *Early English Poetry, Ballads, and Popular Literature of the Middle Ages*, ed. P. Bliss,

Percy Society, vol. XI (London, 1844), 1–79; another is referred to by H. Walpole, *Miscellaneous Antiquities or, a Collection of Curious Papers* (Strawberry Hill, 1772), No. II, 12, and described by R. Marsham in "On a Manuscript Book of Prayers in a Binding of Gold Enamelled, Said to Have Been Given by Queen Anne Boleyn to a Lady of the Wyatt Family," *Archaeologia*, 44 (1873), 259–72; the *Annotationes Upon the Ecclesiastes* referred to in *Third Report of the Royal Commission on Historical Manuscripts* (London, 1872), 113, seems to be a different volume than the above two.

4 *LP*, X, 993, 1000; *Cal.SP Span.*, V-ii, 54, 55 (p. 127).

5 H. B. Wheatley, *London, Past and Present*, III, 75–6 n.; D. C. Bell, *Notices*, 20–8; J. Bayley, *The History and Antiquities of the Tower of London, with Memoirs of Royal and Distinguished Persons* (2 vols., London, 1821), I, 119.

6 N. Lofts, *Anne Boleyn* (New York, 1979), 181–5; H. Herbert, *Memoirs*, 365; H. Cutts, "On an Incised Sepulchral Slab in East Horndon Church," *Transactions of the Essex Archaeological Society*, N.S. 5 (1873), 294–6; for her birth and marriage, see Chapters 1 and 5.

7 RO, SP 70/7, fos. 5b–6; *LP*, X, 1023, also in Ellis, 1st series, II, 125.

8 M. Stephenson, *A List of Monumental Brasses*, 236, 363; *LP*, XI, 41, 320 for the privy seal and his estates, XIII-i, 717 for Lady Wiltshire, 937 for Wiltshire's living at Hever thirty-three years, 1419 for Margaret, XIV-i, 5, 511, 950 for the earl's subsequent activities; *Cal.SP Span.*, VI-i, p. 19; the *DNB* erroneously said 13 March; see also C. Franklyn, *Genealogy*; J. Glyde, *Norfolk*, 66; for his Inquisitions Post Mortem, see RO, E 150/639 and E 150/493. I wish to thank Eric Poole for his assistance in transcribing these.

9 *LP*, XIV-i, 609, 854 for her grandmother and F. J. Furnivall, *Ballads*, I, 478, for her as a lunatic; for Lady Rochford see Chapter 8, and *Metrical*, lines 965–1027; Scarisbrick, 431, 433.

10 See n. 44 in Chapter 6; Inquisitions Post Mortem, RO, C 142/70/107, C 142/68/26, C 142/70/70, and C 142/70/ 64; see also *LP*, XIV-ii, 572, XV, 498 (iii C. 67), 611 (22), XVI, 779 (22), 1308 (7), XVII, p. 696 (119); see also Chapter 2, n. 13.

11 *LP*, X, 920, XIII-ii, 249 (14) for Taylor; X, 1165 for Horsman, XI, 29, 203 for Elizabeth, the latter in Ellis, 2nd series, II, 119; for Coffin and Stoner, see Chapter 8, n. 71; for Baynton, HPT, I, 401–3.

12 *Correspondence of Matthew Parker*, 70; Latimer, fo. 33; for Dolet's verses, scc G. A. Crapelet, *Lettres*, xiv; R. Christie, *Etienne Dolet, the Martyr of the Renaissance: A Biography* (London, 1880); see also Friedmann, II, 300; A. Thevet, *La Cosmographie Universelle* (2 vols., Paris, 1575), II, 657b; for Foxe, see Chapter 6; for Henry, see *LP*, X, 1205.

13 For Anne's name, P. Sergeant, *The Life of Anne Boleyn* (New York,

1924), vi; *Correspondence of Matthew Parker*, 409, 410–14, 430, 440 n.; J. E. Neale, *Queen Elizabeth I* (Garden City, N.Y., 1957), 61, 310; for Mary's letter, *LP*, X, 965, in W. Thomas, *The Pilgrim*, 117.

14 For works Burghley attempted to censor or had in his possession, see, for example, *Calendar of State Papers Foreign, 1558–59*, 1300, and N. Pocock, *Records*, II, 573; G. L. Kittredge, *Witchcraft*, 255–65.

15 P. Johnson, *Elizabeth I*, 109–12; see Chapter 8 for childbirth beliefs; for a discussion of queens regnant, see R. M. Warnicke, *Women*, 47–66.

16 P. Johnson, *Elizabeth I*, 109–14; C. Erickson, *The First Elizabeth* (New York, 1983), 205, 252, 263, 297, 307; J. E. Neale, *Queen Elizabeth*, 225, 246, 251; Brantôme, *Lives*, 344, reported the gossip that she had no genitalia; N. Remy, *Demonolatry*, xli, 92–9, for example.

17 See Appendix A and n. 14.

18 This view is found in almost all modern works. The most recent biographer, Ives, *Anne*, 50–1, 398, says she had a "minor malformation of one finger-tip" and an "inability to keep a safe distance" from courtiers. An early apologist, T. Fuller, *Church History*, 205, also asserted it; for Chapuys, see the Introduction.

19 Ives, *Anne*, 50–1, 398.

20 In my first article on court politics, "The Fall of Anne Boleyn: A Reassessment," I assumed, as earlier scholars had assumed, that Chapuys was a more trustworthy source than he really is. Even in that article, however, I indicated that factions were at least partially built on family alliances and argued that Cromwell was the king's man, not Anne's ally. It was only after I had turned to other research on the queen and especially to this full-length study that I read in entirety, straight through, all of the dispatches of Chapuys from 1529 when he arrived in England until after Anne's death in 1536. That endeavor, which made me realize just how fallible an observer he was, led to this revisionist work on court politics in the 1530s.

APPENDIX A THE LEGACY OF NICHOLAS SANDER

1 T. M. Veech, *Nicholas Sander and the English Reformation: 1530–1581* (Louvain, 1935), 1–229; see also J. H. Pollen, "Dr. Nicholas Sander," *English Historical Review*, 6 (1891), 36–46.

2 *Le Second Tome Des Histoires de Paolo Giovio . . .*, tr. Seigneur du Parq-Champenois (Lyons, 1555); J. H. Pollen, "Dr. Nicholas Sander," 41; *Chronicle of King Henry VIII of England*, tr. M. Hume (London, 1899), 63; W. H. Dixon, "Anne Boleyn," 291; for another statement see N. Pocock, *Records*, II, 359; for Anne and Wyatt, see R. M. Warnicke, "The Eternal Triangle", 565–79, and Chapter 3.

3 N. Harpsfield, *A Treatise*, 253, 332; R. M. Warnicke, "The Eternal Triangle," 574–6.

4 R. M. Warnicke, "The Eternal Triangle," 574–6; Sander, 24–5.

5 Sander, 27–8; George Wyatt, 424–34.

6 Sander, 25; T. M. Veech, *Nicholas Sander*, 250, placed the description in a footnote; R. M. Warnicke, "The Physical Deformities," 135–44; for tallness see Brantôme, *Lives*, 19; M. Summers, *The History of Witchcraft and Demonology* (Seacaucus, N.J., 1956), 70–1, explains the witches' teat and the devil's mark; for Jews as yellow-skinned, see D. Kunzle, *The Early Comic Strip* (Berkeley, Ca., 1973), 24; for wicked beings in monstrous forms, see Chapter 3.

7 George Wyatt, 424–8; Forrest, 28; J. Brand, *Observations on the Popular Antiquities of Great Britain*, rev. edition, H. Ellis (3 vols., London, 1900), II, 177–8; for the Venetian description, see Chapter 3.

8 Extracts from the French statement are in *LP*, VI, 585; S. Anglo, *Spectacle*, 259, referred to the manuscript in which the extracts exist as "modern." Even so, largely on the basis of this manuscript, D. Starkey, *The Reign of Henry VIII*, 90–1, identified a portrait by Holbein of a woman with a fat neck as Anne. See Chapter 1, n. 59; A. Eccles, *Obstetrics and Gynaecology*, 58–9.

9 Sander, 132; R. M. Warnicke, "Sexual Heresy," 247–68, and Chapter 8.

10 Sander, 15; A. Blackwood, *Martyre de la Royne D'Escosse Dowarere de France* (Edinburgh, 1587), 7–8; J. Brodeau, *La Vie de Maistre du Moulin advocat au Parlement de Paris* (Paris, 1654), 5–7; A. Filon, "Anne Boleyn in France," *Athenaeum* (28 May 1887), 704; M. Bruce, *Anne*, 19–20; see W. Stephens, *Margaret of France, Duchess of Savoy, 1523–1574* (New York, 1911), 16, 46, for a discussion of where the royal children were educated.

11 *A History of the County of Essex*, ed. W. R. Powell, The Victoria History of the Counties of England (London, 1973), VI, 12; "The Early History of Stratford and the Surrounding Villages," *Transactions of the Essex Archaeological Society*, O.S. 2 (1863), 99.

12 J. H. Pollen, "Dr. Nicholas Sander", 36–46; Joachim Le Grande, *Histoire du Divorce de Henri VIII* (2 vols, Paris, 1688); *The Works of Henry Howard, Earl of Surrey and of Sir Thomas Wyatt the Elder*, ed. G. Nott (2 vols., London, 1815), II, xviii; Edward, Lord Herbert, *The Life and raigne*, 257–8; W. Lloyd, *Considerations Touching the True Way to Suppress Popery in this Kingdom* (London, 1677), 91; for the quotation, J. E. Drabble, "Gilbert Burnet and the History of the English Reformation: The Historian and his Milieu," *Journal of Religious History*, 121/4 (1983), 351–63.

APPENDIX B THE CHOIRBOOK OF ANNE BOLEYN

1 E. E. Lowinsky, "A Music Book," 160–235; see also J. R. Braithwaite, "The Introduction of Franco-Netherlandish Manuscripts to Early Tudor England," Ph.D. dissertation, Brown University, 1967, I, 46–9; Anne's name is on fo. 157 of the manuscript and a photograph of this is between 194–5 of Lowinsky, "A Music Book."

2 Lowinsky, "A Music Book," 182, and pictured between 194–5; fos. 28–9 of the manuscript.

3 For her falcon, see Chapter 5 and W. Camden, *Remains Concerning Britain* (London, 1870), 373; for her maiden arms, see C. Franklyn, *Genealogy*, 10; for arms of Spain, Hall, I, 171; J. G. Russell, *The Field of Cloth of Gold*, 57.

4 MS 1070, fos. 28–9 for the figures Lowinsky discussed, and fo. 12 for the second turbaned figure; H. Norris, *Costume and Fashion* (reprint, 6 vols., New York, 1931), II, 444 for the fashion, III, 98–9 for a description of Catherine in 1514 with a Venetian cap; H. Amphlett, *Hats: A History of Fashion in Headwear* (Chalfont St. Giles, Bucks., 1974), 81, showed a Portuguese woman in 1516 with a turban; M. G. Houston, *Medieval Costume in England and France* (London, 1939), 163, pointed out that both men and women wore turbans; for Catherine with her hair down, see J. G. Russell, *The Field of Cloth of Gold*, 132, and G. Mattingly, *Catherine*, 181.

5 For Smeaton, see Chapter 8 and R. M. Warnicke, "Sexual Heresy," 247–68; E. E. Lowinsky, "A Music Book," 197; *Metrical*, lines 483–511; for Mark as groom, J. H. Baker, *Reports*, 70; Lady Mary Trefuses, *Songs, Ballads, and Instrumental Pieces Composed by King Henry the Eighth* (Oxford, 1912), did not list him among the king's musicians; see also B. Pattison, *Music and Poetry of the English Renaissance*, 2nd edition (London, 1970), 32–3.

6 E. E. Lowinsky, "A Music Book," 165; R. M. Warnicke, "Childhood," 939–52, and Chapter 1.

7 *Renaissance Painting in Manuscripts: Treasures from the British Library*, ed. T. Kren (New York, 1983), 69–78; E. E. Lowinsky, "A Music Book," 161–2, for the composers, 192, where he admitted that the manuscript might well have been written twenty-five years earlier than he dated it; for composers at Malines, see M. Picker, *The Chanson Albums*; for Flemish workers in England, G. Kipling, *The Triumph of Honour: Burgundian Origins of the Elizabethan Renaissance* (Leiden, 1977), 42–9; for Alamire, see A. Durer, "Diary of a Journey," 27; H. Paget, "The Youth of Anne," 169, pointed out that the songs in the manuscript are consistent with her taste in music having been formed in Malines; the figure of a

moor can be found on some English coats of arms, but it does not resemble the figure in the choirbook. See, for example, A. C. Fox-Davies, *A Complete Guide to Heraldry* (reprint, New York, 1978), 168.

APPENDIX C TWO POEMS OF SIR THOMAS WYATT

1 K. Muir and P. Thomson, *Collected Poems*, 44; the most recent edition is R. A. Rebholz, *Sir Thomas Wyatt*, 85, 96.
2 R. Harrier, *The Canon*, 4, 151, linked this to Anne, although earlier in "Note on Wyatt and Anne Boleyn," *Journal of English and Germanic Philology*, 53 (1954), 581–4, he doubted that it should be associated with her; see also R. M. Warnicke, "The Eternal Triangle", 565–79, and Chapter 3.
3 K. Muir and P. Thomson, *Collected Poems*, 78.
4 R. Harrier, *The Canon*, 204; see also R. M. Warnicke, "The Eternal Triangle," 572 n. 21.
5 W. Camden, *Remains*, 106, does list Phillis among women's names; N. Davis, *Society and Culture in Early Modern France* (Stanford, Ca., 1975), 134–5.
6 See chapters 3 and 8.

INDEX